*The Power of Everyday Politics*

# The Power of Everyday Politics

*How Vietnamese Peasants*
*Transformed National Policy*

Benedict J. Tria Kerkvliet

*Cornell University Press* ITHACA AND LONDON

First published 2005 by Cornell University Press

Library of Congress Cataloging-in-Publication Data

Kerkvliet, Benedict J.
  The power of everyday politics : how Vietnamese peasants transformed national policy /
Benedict J. Kerkvliet.
    p.   cm.
  Includes bibliographical references and index.
  ISBN 0-8014-4301-6 (cloth : alk. paper)
    1. Collectivization of agriculture—Vietnam.   2. Agriculture and state—Vietnam.
3. Peasantry—Vietnam.   I. Title.
  HD1492.V5K47   2005
  338.1'8597—dc22

                                                                    2004019430


Printed in the United States of America

Cornell University Press strives to use
environmentally responsible suppliers and materials to the
fullest extent possible in the publishing of its books. Such
materials include vegetable-based, low-VOC inks and acid-free
papers that are recycled, totally chlorine-free, or partly
composed of nonwood fibers. For further information, visit our
website at www.cornellpress.cornell.edu.

Cloth printing      10  9  8  7  6  5  4  3  2  1

To all my teachers in public schools (Great Falls, Montana), college (Whitman), graduate school (University of Wisconsin, Madison), and later years (University of Hawai'i, Manoa), especially (in chronological order)

*Margaret M. Walsh*  
*Inez Anderson*  
*Urban F. Isaacs*  
*Svein Oksenholt*  
*John J. Stefanoff*  
*Robert Fluno*  
*Robert Whitner*  

*Henry Hart*  
*Fred R. Von der Mehden*  
*Hanna Fenichel Pitken*  
*John R. W. Smail*  
*James C. Scott*  
*Manfred Henningsen*  
*Nguyen Kim Thu*

# Contents

# Tables and Illustrations

viii

Maps

# Acknowledgments

My journey to complete this book benefited from timely directions, assistance, and encouragement. It would be impossible to thank all who helped. Here I name only some of them.

In Vietnam, my greatest debts are to the Trung Tam Nghien Cuu Viet Nam va Giao Luu Van Hoa (Center for Vietnamese and Intercultural Studies) of the Hanoi National University, especially its director, Phan Huy Le, and deputy director, Doan Thien Thuat. Le Van Sinh and Nguyen Quang Ngoc, two faculty members associated with the center, worked assiduously with me during numerous interviews with villagers and other informants. Through their support and companionship, these gentlemen enhanced my work immeasurably. Others with the center helped me on many occasions, especially Nguyen Van Chinh, Phan Dai Doan, Vo Minh Giang, Dang Xuan Khang, Nguyen Dinh Le, Nguyen Van Phong, Phan Phuong Thao, and Dinh Trung Kien. I also thank Phung Huu Phu, rector of the university's College of Social Sciences and Humanities during the 1990s, and Bui Phung, Nguyen Anh Que, and Nguyen Thi Thuan at the university's Vietnamese Language Faculty, where I continued my study of the nation's beautiful language.

I am grateful to the director of Vietnam's National Archives Number 3, Nguyen Thi Man, and to its staff for allowing me to begin reading records in late 1995 just after the archives were moved to a new location. I am also thankful to Vietnam's National Library in Hanoi for its rewarding, invaluable collection.

At various times, Vietnamese researchers who have published on agricultural collectivization kindly explained aspects of their work. I am particularly grateful to Chu Huu Quy, Chu Van Lam, Dang Phong, Dao The Tuan, Nguyen Huu Tien, Phi Van Ba, and Tran Duc. Others in and around Hanoi who aided my work are Duc Thong, Nguyen Thi Minh Hien, Nguyen Thi Tuyet, Pham Thu Lan, Pham Van Hoc, Phan Van Hung, and Tuong Lai.

Among the most memorable times in my research were conversations with villagers in the Red River delta, especially in subdistricts where I spent the most time: Da Ton, Dao Duc, Nghiem Xuyen, Quat Luu, Tam Canh, and Tien Thang. I am also grateful to the people of Binh Minh, Dung Tien, Dai Kim, Kim Lan, Tam Hung, Thanh Liet, Van Hoang, and Van Nhan for sharing their knowledge and experiences.

I am profoundly thankful to Nguyen Kim Thu at the University of Hawai'i, where in 1989–1991 I began to get serious about studying Vietnam. She made it her project to teach me more Vietnamese. Others at the university who were especially encouraging and helpful include Bui Phung, Steve O'Harrow, Kristin Pelzer, and Truong Buu Lam.

The Australian National University's Research School of Pacific and Asian Studies, which I joined in 1992, provided an enormous boost. Thanks to the school's resources and research environment, I made several trips to Vietnam, devoted two or three days a week largely to my own work, and drew heavily on the university's fine library and the nearby National Library of Australia. Librarians Yen Musgrove and Dorothea Polonyi have been especially kind. I am also grateful to members of the Department of Political and Social Change, especially X. L. Ding, Bev Fraser, John Gillespie, Russell Heng, Natalie Hicks, David Koh, Allison Ley, Claire Smith, Drew Smith, Carl Thayer, and Thaveeporn Vasavakul. Others at the ANU who have helped me include Anita Chan, Oanh Collins, Jim Fox, Andrew Hardy, Nguyen Nghia Bien, Merle Ricklefs, Philip Taylor, Ton That Quynh Du, and Jon Unger. My thanks also to Jenny Sheehan for preparing the maps and graph. Adam Fforde shared with me his library and insights on Vietnam while also sharply criticizing my analysis. Shortly after moving to Canberra, my wife and I were lucky to meet Le Thi Ngan, Phan Dinh The, and Phan Dinh Thay. Initially as students, then as colleagues and dear friends, they greatly enhanced my study of Vietnam.

The individuals at the ANU to whom I have the largest debt of gratitude are David Marr and Pham Thu Thuy. David, an eminent historian of Vietnam, has been a mentor, colleague, friend, verbal jousting partner, and critical reader of my manuscripts, including one for this book. Working with him has been an unforgettable experience. Pham Thu Thuy has helped me plow through Vietnamese newspapers and articles. In addition to benefiting from her research assistance, I have learned much from Thuy and her husband, Ngo Van Khoa, about Vietnamese language and culture. Thuy is a shining star of enlightenment about her native land.

As always, Jim Scott has been a constant source of encouragement. He and Thomas Sikor made insightful comments on the book manuscript, some of which I have been able to incorporate. One of the anonymous readers for Cornell University Press gave particularly helpful suggestions for sharpening the analysis. I subsequently learned that reader was David Elliott and I can now thank him in print for his perceptive remarks.

I also thank Cornell University Press, especially Roger Haydon, for taking an interest in the manuscript and efficiently seeing it through to publication, and Karen Laun and Jane Marie Todd for their copyediting.

Many others have given me leads, shared their materials, or commented on draft chapters. Foremost among them is Melinda Tria Kerkvliet, my partner in research and other aspects of life and my best friend. Others include David Boselie, Alasdair Bowie, David Elliott, Mai Elliott, Brian Fegan, Martin Grossheim, Bertrand de Hartingh, John Kleinen, Erik Kuhonta, Jonathan London, Ardeth Maung Thawnghmung, Ngo Vinh Long, Shaun Malarney, Kim Ninh, Steve Sénèque, John Sidel, Benoit de Treglode, and Jayne Werner.

There's a saying in Vietnam: "As you eat the fruit, remember who planted the tree" (an qua nho ke trong cay). Since I have long been eating the fruit of knowledge and learning, I would like to remember my teachers. With deep respect and gratitude, I dedicate this book to them.

BEN KERKVLIET

Canberra, A.C.T.

*The Power of Everyday Politics*

# CHAPTER I

# Introduction

Between 1958 and 1961, the Communist Party government of Vietnam collectivized land in the northern half of the then divided country. It insisted that in this primarily agrarian society, collective farming was central to creating socialism. In 1975, after the epic war against the United States and for reunification had finally ended, the government started to collectivize agriculture in the southern half of the country as well. What is startling, however, is that in the late 1980s the government reversed course. It authorized the redistribution of agricultural land to village households and the end to the centrally planned economy. Collective farming was no longer policy.

In this book I analyze the two processes in northern Vietnam—building collective farming and dismantling it. I show that the first occurred rapidly but the second evolved after the end of the war. Central to that evolution was villagers' widespread behavior that was at odds with how authorities wanted collective farming done. A major reason why the government did a 180-degree policy turn was the weakening and eventual collapse from within of the collective farming cooperatives into which people had been organized. The policy change was less about dissolving collective farming and more about approving what was well under way in many places and had already occurred in some. Put simply, decollectivization started locally, in the villages, and was largely initiated by villagers; national policy followed.

## Themes of the Book

From the early 1960s, the communist government, local leaders, and villagers were absorbed in struggles over the shape and content of the collective farming cooperatives.[1] Those struggles intensified in the second half of the 1970s. National government and party officials struggled to get villagers to farm collectively with diligence and enthusiasm. They also strove to turn local officials into dedicated cooperative leaders. Villagers struggled to make a living while dealing with the reality of collective farming. Most had been wary about collective farming from the beginning and became more skeptical as the promised better life failed to come. They tried to minimize the cooperative's claim on their labor and to maximize their household-based production. Some local officials worked hard to implement central authorities' directives; some accommodated villagers' concerns; many did both. Some used their positions for their own gain, paying little attention to national directives and villagers' objections.

The lack of economic incentives for members is a common reason why agricultural collectives have not functioned well elsewhere. It certainly was a problem in Vietnam. In addition, however, serious political shortcomings plagued Vietnam's collective farming. The collective cooperatives were primarily creations of the central government. They did not grow out of villagers' initiatives to address shared adversities, hence they began without much commitment on the part of their members. Insufficient trust among peasants also undermined collective farming, particularly after the cooperatives were enlarged to incorporate several villages. Poor governance was another significant shortcoming. Local officials were supposed to run the cooperatives in a transparent manner. Many did not. Corruption was often intractable. Consequently, cooperative members frequently had little confidence that leaders were trustworthy, honest, or fair.

The war against the United States and for reunification of the country (early 1960s–1975) affected the rise and fall of collective farming. National defense was one of the communist government's justifications for collective cooperatives in the late 1950s. Initially that rationale meant little to northern villagers because their region was still relatively peaceful. But when the war escalated in the mid-1960s, it became a major factor. Many villagers who were bombed by U.S. planes and had relatives and friends in the armed

1. The term "collective farming cooperative" reflects the fact that the organization was not a simple cooperative. It featured collective ownership of land and other vital resources, collective production, and collective distribution of what members produced. I usually shorten the expression to "collective cooperative" or just "cooperative," however.

forces were motivated to make the collective cooperatives work as well as possible in hopes their efforts would help save them, their loved ones, and their country. War also stymied criticism of the cooperatives. Because of the war, allies of the Democratic Republic of Vietnam sent mountains of grain and other food to the north. In addition to assisting the Vietnamese people, that aid obscured the production deficiencies of collective farming. The war's end had the opposite effect. Food aid quickly dwindled, exposing production deficits. No more war also meant much less reason for villagers frustrated with collective cooperatives to care about them.

Persistent struggles over labor, land, harvests, draft animals, fertilizer, and other resources contributed significantly to the collapse of collective farming. Even more striking, the struggles were rarely open and organized. They manifested themselves instead in the way people lived, worked, and went about doing—or not doing—the things they were supposed to do as collective members. I call this "everyday politics." Some of that behavior was indirect resistance to authorities whom villagers could not confront directly. Much of everyday politics, however, expressed a preference for family-based farming over collective farming and conflicts among villagers over vital resources. Also part of everyday politics were individual households who used their relations with local officials to skirt collective farming regulations.

Scholars have shown that slaves, peasants, and other subordinates who dare not openly object to their situation often express their concerns and anger in surreptitious, unorganized ways. Yet little research has been done on how this resistance and other forms of everyday politics might contribute to significant political change. We know that under certain circumstances widespread discontent below the surface of public life can feed into organized social movements and rebellions. But if no large organized efforts emerge, are the undercurrents of discontent and alternative aspirations of no consequence for the political system? In many cases, they are not significant. In Vietnam, however, everyday behavior—some of it resistance, some of it not—at odds with how collectives were supposed to function contributed to the demise of collectivization. This book explains how.

This analysis also contributes to an understanding of Vietnam's political system. Interpretations that emphasize the top-down, authoritarian, Communist Party–dominated features of the country explain how collectivization started. They cannot, however, account for why and how collectivization ended. The analysis presented here bolsters the relevance of another interpretation, which I call dialogical, for a fuller understanding of the country's political system.

*Approach and Methods*

Within northern Vietnam, I focus on Red River delta provinces and Vinh Phuc, a province slightly above the delta. Unable to research all parts of the north, I chose this area for two reasons. First, it has nearly half the north's rural population and staple food production.[2] Agriculturally speaking, this area is reasonably uniform because the main crop is rice. Second, the Communist Party government concentrated more effort to create and reinforce collective cooperatives in this area than in some others, especially the mountainous regions, which were more remote and harder to monitor.

While writing this book, I had three sets of questions in mind. First, what did collective farming mean to villagers? What did they like and dislike about it and why? How did they provide for their families; handle obligations to fellow villagers, local officials, and government requirements; and deal with collectivization, war, and other major conditions affecting them? Second, what were authorities doing and why? Why did the national government want collective farming? How did officials at various levels try to implement it and related policies and deal with difficulties and obstacles? Why did national policy shift from requiring collective farming to allowing and then encouraging family-based farming? Third, how did interactions among ordinary villagers and between them and local and higher officials affect collective farming and the cooperatives? Did these dynamics affect the collectivization process and authorities' decisions?

Most of my research was done during four stays in Vietnam between 1992 and 2000. The shortest was two months; the longest, in 1995–1996, was eleven. During those stays, I sought out material that had not previously been available. Supplemental library research was done in Australia and Hawai'i.

One main source of information is interviews. In 1992, I visited ten subdistricts (*xa*) of rural Hanoi and Ha Tay province.[3] Because I did not have permission to stay overnight in rural communities, I picked places within a thirty-kilometer radius of my quarters in Hanoi so that I could return

2. In 1961, the area had 8.4 million people (of the 16.7 million in northern Vietnam); 80 percent were farmers. In 1990, the area had 14.0 million people (of 33.1 million in the north); 83 percent were rural. TCTK, "Nhung Chi Tieu, NN, 1955–1967" [GSO, "Agriculture, 1955–1967"], 1968, table 20 (P TCTK, hs 760, vv); and TCTK, *Nien Giam Thong Ke 1990*, 7–8. For a list of Red River delta provinces, see the glossary of selected places and terms.

3. The usual translation of *xa* is "commune." To readers of French, this poses no problem. In English, however, "commune" often suggests a communal society or communal living rather than "the basic administrative unit in rural areas, encompassing a few villages," which is how Vietnamese dictionaries define *xa* (*Tu Dien Tieng Viet*, 1176). Often each *xa* has two to five

there by motorcycle each evening. I also chose them because written accounts indicated that their collective cooperatives had ranged from strong to weak. Most of the people I met at that time were local officials. In subsequent years I returned several times to interview ordinary villagers in two of these subdistricts, one that had had a robust collective cooperative and the other that had had an unstable one. In 2000, I stayed with my wife and a Vietnamese colleague for a month in Vinh Phuc province. Guided by accounts from newspapers and documents, I chose to talk to people in four subdistricts. All together, I had informative interviews with eighty-one villagers distributed mainly among six subdistricts in Hanoi, Ha Tay, and Vinh Phuc provinces. Nearly all these informants were at least fifty-five years old, about a third were women, and all had had lengthy experience farming in collective cooperatives that primarily produced paddy. For all interviews with villagers, a local official arranged the meetings and usually stayed for a while before drifting away. I also talked with about three dozen other people who were knowledgeable about collectivization, policy shifts, and related matters during the 1960s to 1990s. Twenty had been involved in national policy-making circles and research centers in Hanoi; the others were district and subdistrict officials and cooperative leaders. The interviews were open-ended, with one exception: one interviewee in Hanoi requested I submit a list of questions beforehand. The interviews were in Vietnamese, usually lasted two or three hours, and took place in the informant's house (or office in the case of some in Hanoi). I met a few individuals more than once. A Vietnamese researcher usually accompanied me during interviews, took extensive notes while the informant and I talked, and participated in the discussion. I generally use pseudonyms when referring to informants. Some said they would not mind being identified, others that they would, and several I never asked.

Documents are another primary source. A few are published; some unpublished ones came to me from acquaintances. Most of the documents I use are in Vietnam's National Archives Number 3, where records from 1945 to the present are kept. The archive documents are primarily from government agencies; some are from the Communist Party. They include reports, usually from national and provincial offices and infrequently from district ones; qualitative and quantitative surveys; and official correspondence. When using

---

villages (*lang, thon,* or other terms). The *xa* is a unit within a district (*huyen*), which in turn is a subdivision of a province (*tinh*). In using "subdistrict" I do risk overemphasizing the administrative function of *xa,* which may have a different significance for residents. But for an English readership, "subdistrict" is preferable to "commune" or some other translation.

these archives in 1995–1996, I was allowed to see material through the early 1980s. By the time I returned in 2000, new rules put anything after 1970 off limits.[4] Listed in the bibliography are the nine record groups I used.

Also useful are publications from the party and government regarding agrarian conditions and policies, histories of specific subdistricts, and other topics pertinent to my research. Newspapers, especially provincial ones, turned out to be valuable sources. Given that all are official publications, I had expected them to carry bland and self-congratulatory accounts. Such articles do appear. But so do detailed stories, some of them rather forthright. To benefit from the newspapers required reading articles spanning several years. I concentrated on newspapers from four Red River delta provinces, especially many years for the 1970s and 1980s, and on the party's national daily newspaper *Nhan Dan* (The people). Also useful for the 1980s and 1990s were *Dai Doan Ket* (Great unity, published by the Fatherland Front) and newspapers of the official association for peasants.

Additional research could and should be done by others. More documents lie in Vietnam's national archives and in provincial and district archives, which I did not attempt to use. The Communist Party's archives, which are not yet open to scholars, also have pertinent materials. Much more could be learned from villagers, not only in places where I interviewed but also elsewhere. I regret I never obtained permission to stay for weeks or months at a time in villages so that I could soak up stories about collective farming and related activities. As a result, this book lacks the details of village life I had wanted to include. Collectivization in southern Vietnam, a topic I only touch on, merits close investigation. Also not examined in this book are marketing, credit, and nonfarming cooperatives in northern Vietnam.

## Organization

Chapter 2 draws on literature about peasant societies, agrarian organizations, politics, and Vietnam to elaborate the main themes in my argument. It outlines conditions for establishing and perpetuating collective farming. It also offers a theory on how noncollective action among relatively powerless people can have a powerful impact on national policies. The rest of the book analyzes four phases of collective farming in northern Vietnam

4. Some other foreign researchers in Vietnam in 2000 were able to see documents through 1975.

in terms of these conditions and theory. Chapter 3 studies the preparation stage for building collective cooperatives and the period 1958–1961, during which the organizations were hastily constructed throughout northern Vietnam. In 1961–1974, examined in chapter 4, national authorities strove to strengthen the collective cooperatives while villagers and local officials contended with numerous internal problems and with the war engulfing the nation. Following a national assessment that found most collective cooperatives weak, national leaders in 1974 launched a concerted drive to revamp and enlarge the organizations. This campaign and how it backfired by the late 1970s is analyzed in chapter 5. Chapter 6 examines the final period, 1981–1990, during which family farming spread beyond what national policy had endorsed at the beginning of the decade but which the Communist Party government embraced at the end. Chapter 7 synthesizes the importance of everyday politics.

# CHAPTER 2

# Theorizing Everyday Politics in Collective Farming

For collective farming to succeed, certain conditions must be met. Otherwise, the collective organizations become enmeshed in endless struggles over key resources, as they did in Vietnam. Vietnamese villagers' struggles for the most part were indirect, involved little or no organization, and were entwined with their daily practices. Yet their everyday behavior had political meaning and consequences. Understanding how everyday politics significantly affected the course of collectivization in Vietnam will illuminate features of that country's political system and may offer insight into other cases as well.

## Peasants and the Communist Party

From the outset, collectivization exposed tensions between what Vietnam's national leaders wanted and what a large proportion of villagers in the Red River delta preferred. To Vietnam's Communist Party leadership, the war against France (1945–1954) was not only for national independence but for a socialist revolution in "production, technology, and ideology." After setting up its government headquarters in Hanoi following the 1954 Geneva accords, which ended the war and temporarily divided the country, the party hastened efforts to carry out this multifaceted revolution in the north. A key component in rural areas, where more than 80 percent of northern Vietnamese lived, was to replace the land regime left by the French with one compatible with the party's socialist ideals.[1] Two major projects were required, one after the other. The first was to redistribute land, especially arable land, equally, without any compensation to the Catholic Church, large owners, or others. The second was to organize all landholders in a certain locality (a village or, more often, a cluster of villages) into a cooperative and combine their fields and other resources in order to farm collectively. Land redistribution, which started in the early 1950s and was completed in the north by late 1956, was both a "top-down" and a "bottom-up" project. Both the national leadership and a large proportion of the peasantry wanted land reform. Collective farming, by contrast, was "top-down." It was primarily the party leadership's idea. Even within the party there was dissent. Because of land reform and the flight of many landlords to southern provinces, no large landed interests remained to oppose it. The Communist Party government still had to contend with peasants, however, most of whom had received fields from the land redistribution and few of whom clamored for collective farming.

National leaders' justifications for collective farming and cooperatives were similar to those in other countries with Communist Party governments.[2] In the first place, they said, collective farming would significantly increase agricultural production. If Vietnamese households continued to farm their small plots of land separately, authorities argued, they were unlikely to produce much beyond their own needs. Indeed, many would fail to achieve even that, resulting in continued cycles of hunger and famine. By farming collectively, however, peasants would produce efficiently. Yields would climb and total production would exceed what villagers could consume. Working together, villagers could also reclaim unused areas, construct more extensive irrigation systems, diversify their farming, raise more livestock, and develop nonagricultural economic activities.

Second, they argued, collectivization would improve living conditions. In 1955, a party central office made the point succinctly. Which road, it asked, should the party choose: "Let peasants continue to produce individually or encourage them to enter collective production"? If the party were to follow the first, the office predicted, "production will diminish, some

---

1. Note that from 1951 until late 1976 Vietnam's Communist Party was called the Workers' Party (Dang Lao Dong Viet Nam).

2. Justifications for agricultural collectivization in China and the Soviet Union, for example, are synthesized in Nolan, *Political Economy*, chap. 2. For elaborations on the reasons in Vietnam, see Quang Truong, *Agricultural Collectivization*, 49–55; Tran Nhu Trang, "Transformation," 317–25; and Vickerman, *Fate*, 118–19, 124–25. For a justification by one of the party leaders directly involved in implementing the collectivization program, see Nguyen Chi Thanh, "May Kinh Nghiem."

peasants will become rich, and the majority will gradually become wretchedly poor again." The road of collectivization, on the other hand, "will carry [the peasants] to happy and comfortable lives."[3]

Third, they argued, without collectivization a few successful farming households would end up owning much of the land, thus undermining the ideal of social and economic equality. The majority of rural households would become tenants, low-paid laborers, and servants of the wealthy. Collectivization would keep land in the hands of those farming it, not individually but as a community. Farm products would be distributed according to the work each person had done and according to need. No one would starve. Moreover, some of the surplus would fund health, education, and other social services for the benefit of all residents.

Fourth, collective farming would change peasants' thinking. Villagers, many party leaders said, tended to focus on their own families. Sharing and working together, they argued, would enhance villagers' "collective spirit," which is necessary for creating a socialist society.

Fifth, collectivization was crucial for other aspects of the socialist political economy. One was state industries, which needed food for workers, raw materials such as sugar cane and tobacco, and capital earned from selling agricultural commodities. For these necessities the government would take part of what the collective farms produced. Collective production also would make it easier to extract that share. Collective cooperative leaders would know how much was produced and would distribute a portion to members, retain another portion for local needs, and give a third portion to the government. Collective farming cooperatives, consequently, were significant components of the centrally planned economic system, which the party moved rapidly to create.

Finally, and perhaps peculiar to Vietnam, collectivization was part of national defense. "Having peasants in cooperatives," a 1958 national party pronouncement stressed, "will be highly favorable for strengthening the home front, increasing national defense capabilities, and preserving peace and order." Given that "the home country is temporarily divided in two," according to another statement, peasants organized into collective cooperatives could readily "form local militia, guerrilla groups, and reserve forces as well as contribute to bolstering defense in the north and nationwide." The improved life that would result from collective farming would also

3. Instruction 31, June 30, 1955, from a central office of the party, cited in Bui Cong Trung and Luu Quang Hoa, *Hop Tac Hoa*, 10. The office is not specified; but it is probably the party's Secretariat.

"strongly encourage our peasant compatriots in the south to exert every effort in the struggle against the United States and Diem in order to push ahead for reunification of our homeland."[4]

As authorities began to publicize plans for collective farming in the mid-1950s, villagers were busy farming their own fields. Like poor peasants elsewhere, the primary concern of most villagers in northern Vietnam was securing enough food and other essentials for their families.[5] Their next ambition was to climb out of poverty. They believed that having their own land would help immensely on both counts. For that they were grateful to the communist government's land reform, despite the turmoil accompanying it.[6] Also boosting their prospects for a better life were the government's vigorous programs for adult literacy, rural schools and libraries, and village health clinics.

The family, particularly the household, was the main unit of production in the Red River delta and most other parts of northern Vietnam. Household members typically worked together and shared what they earned from farming, handicrafts, petty trade, and wage labor. Daily routines, annual celebrations, and major rituals in life also revolved principally around the immediate and extended family.

Villagers emphasized their own households and relatives, but not in an "amoral familist" manner that excluded larger associations and obligations to other entities.[7] Red River delta villagers exchanged labor with neighbors, established rotating credit associations, and had organizations built around religious beliefs, lineage, and other interests. People also shared a village identity, marked by ceremonies, festivals, deities, shrines, and temples.[8] Many villages had previously had some communal land that was supposed to be used to aid elderly residents and others in desperate straits. Retrieving such land from local elites who had usurped it was one of the aims of peasant protests and revolts earlier in the twentieth century. Other objectives included reviving redistributive norms and practices that had

4. BCHTU, DLDVN, "NQ, Hoi Nghi Trung Uong, lan thu 14," 21; and BCHTU, DLDVN, "NQ, Hoi Nghi Trung Uong, lan thu 16," 12.

5. Scott, *Moral Economy*, is the best known elaboration of this point and its political ramifications.

6. About 73 percent of the north's rural population received land. Quang Truong, *Agricultural Collectivization*, 35. For other scholarly analyses of land reform in the north, see White, "Agrarian Reform"; Moise, *Land Reform*; and Pham Quang Minh, *Zwischen Theorie und Praxis*, 87–121, 207–67.

7. An amoral familist maximizes the material, short-run advantage of the family and assumes other people will do likewise. Banfield, *Moral Basis*, 83.

8. Hy Van Luong, *Revolution*, 55–61; Kleinen, *Facing the Future*, 9–11, 65–67; and Malarney, *Culture, Ritual, and Revolution*.

helped poor villagers.[9] When villagers joined the revolution to overthrow the French, they showed they could aspire to collective goals while also fighting for the sake of their kin.

Despite a capacity for collective action, many Vietnamese villagers were suspicious of collective farming,[10] not because it required cooperation but because the cooperation was total.[11] Land, labor, money, even draft animals and plows were to be collectivized. Virtually all production was to be done collectively. Everything produced together would be shared. Red River delta villagers had never farmed that way before. If collective farming failed, the costs could be colossal for individual families and whole communities.[12] Given the extent of poverty, such a bold reorganization of agricultural production was especially dubious unless the new system could assure subsistence—a gamble, certainly, in the early stages. If collective farming could be the success leaders envisioned, then fine. But could it? This was a crucial question for many villagers.

Communist Party leaders knew that villagers were apprehensive. They expected, however, that people would gradually realize that collective farming served their families' interests as well as the cooperative's and the nation's. The approach of party leaders was different from that of their counterparts in the Soviet Union under Stalin twenty-five years earlier. The Bolsheviks, unlike Vietnam's Communist Party, had little rural support and ended up waging war against villagers to get them to collectivize.[13] Authorities in Vietnam rarely used brute force to herd people into cooperatives,

9. Ngo Vinh Long, "Communal Property," 135–37; Hy Van Luong, "Agrarian Unrest," 165–79; Scott, *Moral Economy*, 127–48.

10. Some argue that it was primarily men who were dubious of collective farming because it undermined the family economy, which was patriarchal. Collective farming, in other words, threatened men's domination over women. See especially Wiegersma, "Peasant Patriarchy." I cannot say from the material I have whether this was the case or not. My evidence does show, however, that women were also greatly concerned about the welfare of their families and the hardships collectivization frequently brought to their households.

11. A collective farm means "total agricultural cooperation," wrote Alexander Chayanov, *Theory of Peasant Co-operatives*, 207. Chayanov studied Russian peasant economies and rural cooperatives from the early 1900s until his arrest in the early 1930s. The Soviet Union police executed him in 1937.

12. As Alexander Woodside wrote about Vietnam's collectivization, "The 'management failures' of a single family affect only that family, but the 'management failures' of a [collective] cooperative cause difficulties for hundreds of families." Woodside, "Decolonization," 708.

13. In 1960, 56 percent of the Vietnam Communist Party members were from the peasantry (Elliott, "Revolutionary Re-integration," 295). For a contrast between the rural base of that party compared to the Bolsheviks in the USSR, see Tran Nhu Trang, "Transformation," 306–8. Regarding the violence against peasants and the millions of deaths during collectivization in the Soviet Union, see Conquest, *Harvest of Sorrow*, chaps. 6, 7, 11, 16; Fitzpatrick, *Stalin's Peasants*, chaps. 2 and 4; and Hughes, *Stalinism*, 129–59, 208–13.

punish those who broke rules, or confiscate their possessions. Initially they emphasized building collective cooperatives incrementally, beginning with labor exchanges among neighbors. When they encountered major problems, party leaders stressed management reforms, reorganization, and improved leadership and did not engage in the vicious campaigns against alleged subversives that occurred in other communist countries. In Vietnam's collective cooperatives, the family also remained a social unit. Unlike in Cambodia under the Khmer Rouge regime in the 1970s, families were not broken up or fused into communal living arrangements. Nor were villagers in Vietnam required to cook and eat together, as they had been in China during the late 1950s. Collective cooperatives in Vietnam even allowed families to produce a little on their own, though leaders expected this modest space for family-based production to gradually disappear.

Tensions between collective farming and the household persisted and ultimately contributed significantly to the collapse of collective cooperatives. In the end, the Vietnamese peasant's family economy, rather than disappearing, triumphed over the collective system. Other research has highlighted the friction, the generally downward trend of collectivized production, and central authorities' attempts to remedy the problems.[14] In this book I provide more evidence for all three factors and delve into the reasons. I also link those tensions to the widening discontent in the countryside and to policy shifts.

## Political Conditions for Establishing and Perpetuating Collectivization

The fact that villagers in the Red River delta had no previous history of collective farming is not sufficient to explain why collectivization ultimately failed. Nor are the tensions between the family and the collective cooperative. Organizations in which rural people share land, water, crops, and other important resources have emerged in places without previous experience. And those that survive have dealt with problems between individual members and the organization as a whole. Some reasons for success are particular to each organization. Scholars have identified other condi-

14. Vickerman, *Fate*, chaps. 4–6; Quang Truong, *Agricultural Collectivization*, 49–127; Nguyen Ngoc Luu, "Peasants, Party," chaps. 7–9; Fforde, *Agrarian Question*; Tran Duc, *Hop Tac Xa*, 1–37; Chu Van Lam et al., *Hop Tac Hoa*, 1–58; and Yvon-Tran, "Une résistible." Most of these studies also highlight the achievements of collectivization, especially its contribution to the war against the United States.

tions, however, that are necessary (though not sufficient) for these organizations to come into being and thrive. Among them are political features, which I shall use to analyze the course of collectivization in Vietnam.

The rural organizations examined in the literature I am drawing on range from those that share irrigation systems, machinery, fishing spots, or other resources to multipurpose agricultural cooperatives and communal farms. While all hold resources in common, the groups fall into two broad categories: common-pool resource organizations and common-production organizations.[15] In the former, members share a resource important for their livelihood but separately produce and consume or sell their production. An example is a cooperative of households using the same irrigation system but with each household farming its own fields and taking what it grows. In Vietnam during the mid-1950s there were groups in which people shared their labor but continued to farm separately and kept what they produced. In common-production organizations, by contrast, members not only share an important resource but work together and share what they produce. Kibbutz communities in Israel and Hutterite communities in Canada and the United States fit this model, as do Vietnam's collective cooperatives. My term for both types is "common-use agricultural organizations."

Some political conditions I use to analyze collective farming in Vietnam are necessary for the common-use agricultural organizations to emerge; others are necessary for the organizations to endure. Those necessary in the emergence of such organizations are as follows.[16] First, people see a shared serious problem regarding resources that requires a collective solution for their own individual benefit. Second, to address it, they are willing to consider collaborative ways of using or producing the resources that may involve trade-offs between their own interests and general interests. They see that moving away from individual or family-based methods of addressing the problem and toward cooperative ways may result in greater benefits for all concerned. Third, people trust each other enough to find collaborative ways to use or produce the resources. Such efforts usually involve considerable trial and error, which can strain people's willingness to continue the effort. With small successes along the way, however, trial and error can enhance people's trust in one another and in the organizational process.

15. The term "common-pool resource" comes from Ostrom, *Governing*.

16. These conditions come primarily from Ostrom, "Reformulating"; Chayanov, *Theory of Peasant Co-operatives*, 226, 244–48; Axelrod, *Evolution*, 129–38; and Morrow and Hull, "Donor-Initiated."

Fourth, people must be familiar with organizations and leadership. Prior experience in an organization can be, and usually is, unrelated to the resource problem at hand but nevertheless provides some people in the emerging common-use organization with an understanding of how individuals can join together. Forming a common-use agricultural organization also requires leadership, often from people with prior experience but sometimes from people whose leadership abilities emerge from discussing and addressing the problem. Fifth, people need to have sufficient autonomy from other entities, including the national government, to organize, make decisions about the resources, and resolve difficulties. Outside agents, such as government officials, can help people think through their resource problem and create conditions for common-use organizations to emerge. But extensive outside interference can undermine people's trust, their leaders, and their willingness to continue.

Vietnam in the early phases of collectivization had some of these preconditions. Others, however, were at best barely present. Especially deficient was the degree to which villagers could develop their own rules and experiments as they considered collaborative ways to use labor, land, and other resources. Consequently, the labor exchange groups and the early collective cooperatives were unstable. Despite these wobbly foundations, collectivization continued.

After they are under way, many rural common-use agricultural organizations encounter insurmountable difficulties and disintegrate. Others, however, survive. These durable organizations have four similarities that are particularly useful for analyzing what happened in rural Vietnam.[17] First, participants stay in the organization in large measure because they want to, not because they are compelled to. Such commitment can arise from shared ideals, goals, religious values, or ideologies. Beliefs, however, are rarely a sufficient form of commitment in common-use organizations. To survive, most of the organizations provide members with personal, familial, and material incentives to continue, which Rosabeth Kanter calls "instrumental commitment."[18] Commitment to particular individuals and groups in the organization is also often important.

---

17. I am drawing primarily on Bennett, *Hutterian Brethren*, esp. 36–45, 156–60, 245–65; Chayanov, *Theory of Peasant Co-operatives*, 212, 217–20; Kanter, *Commitment*, 61–74; Ostrom, *Governing*, esp. 58–102; Peter, *Dynamics*, 6–81; Putterman, "Extrinsic versus Intrinsic"; Wade, *Village Republics*, 179–217; Weintraub et al., *Moshava*, 68–126.

18. Kanter, *Commitment*, 69. For similar notions, see Anderson, "Between Quiescence," 503, 529; Lichbach, "What Makes," 385ff.

Second, there must be considerable trust that all members will live up to their obligations, abide by the rules, and sense the needs of others and the organization as a whole. Reciprocity is an aspect of this trust.[19] Trust is easier to develop among people who have kinship ties or other personal relationships. Regular face-to-face contact, reciprocal interaction over a range of activities, and residence in the same geographical area also engender trust. Hence, successful common-use, and particularly common-production organizations may be rather small.[20] Large ones can survive, however, if members are "nested" within smaller units that fulfill the conditions of durability.[21] The greater the trust, the easier and less time-consuming it is to monitor what members do. No organization, however, is problem free. Third, then, there must be effective monitoring of members' activities related to resources used or produced in common. Monitoring reassures members that misbehavior will be discovered and appropriately reprimanded.

Fourth, in durable common-use organizations, members have considerable confidence in how the organization is governed and how authority is exercised. This usually means that members are involved in major decisions affecting the organization. Democratic processes are not required. Indeed, authority in many durable common-production organizations is centralized. But leaders in durable organizations weigh members' views before making major decisions. The organizations also have considerable transparency regarding what leaders do and how shared resources are used. As one analyst found, "maximum flow of information" among members and between them and leaders is crucial for a healthy organization.[22] Also important for governance are conflict resolution methods that members regard as fair and minimal interference from outside agencies. Durable organizations are able to develop governing processes that work for them rather than conforming to what others say should be done.

These four political conditions overlap and are mutually reinforcing. Effective monitoring enhances trust, commitment, and confidence in how

19. The term "social capital" has become fashionable in social science circles for saying much the same thing (Putman, *Making Democracy Work*, 167–76). For my purposes, "trust" and "reciprocity" are entirely serviceable.

20. Hutterite communities, which are among the most durable common-production organizations in the world, usually have a maximum of about 120–50 people each. When a community gets larger than that, it typically divides to form two. Peter, *Dynamics*, 61; Bennett, *Hutterian*, 55.

21. Ostrom, *Governing*, 90, 102, 189. Other favorable circumstances for large common-use organizations are synthesized in Baland and Platteau, *Halting Degradation*, 298–301.

22. Nash and Hopkins, "Anthropological Approaches," 12.

the organization is governed. Proper governance facilitates commitment, trust, and monitoring. Similarly, serious weaknesses in one are likely to adversely affect the others. Bad governance undermines commitment, monitoring, and trust. Waning commitment can weaken monitoring methods, trust, and governance.

In northern Vietnam, ordinary villagers, local officials, and national authorities often knew that many collective cooperatives were weak because they lacked these characteristics. They often stressed inadequate transparency (*cong khai*), leadership (*su lanh dao*), and other matters I have clustered under governance. They also complained about low levels of trust (*long tin, tin tuong*) among cooperative members and between members and collective leaders. In the 1960s–1980s, authorities frequently revamped the organizations in hopes of meeting these political conditions. But those efforts were rarely successful.

Other researchers have emphasized that a major reason why production of paddy and other staple food crops in Vietnam fell below what authorities expected and what the nation needed was a lack of commitment among villagers, which in turn was due to the small returns individuals received for their collective work and to poor monitoring and other management problems.[23] In this book I explain why these were intractable problems, and in particular, why trust and governance were major shortcomings in Vietnam's collective farming.[24] In theory cooperative leaders were accountable to members; in practice they often were not. Frequently, higher authorities imposed unpopular changes. For example, national authorities required small cooperatives to amalgamate and production brigades to increase in size. Embezzlement, favoritism, and other abuses of power by cooperative officials were also acute problems.

It is more difficult for common-production organizations to meet the conditions for durability than for common-pool resource ones to do so. The reason, at least in Vietnam's collective cooperatives, is unresolved tensions between the organization and the family. A durable common-pool organization needs to govern and monitor the forest, fishing grounds, irrigation system, or other resource shared by all members as they go about their separate production. A durable common-production organization needs to do that and also to govern and monitor production and distrib-

23. Prime examples include Chu Van Lam et al., *Hop Tac Hoa*; Fforde, *Agrarian Question*; Tran Duc, *Hop Tac Xa*; Tran Duc, *Hop Tac trong Nong Thon*.
24. Researchers who have touched on trust and governance include Tran Nhu Trang, "Transformation," 394–99, 419–22; Nguyen Ngoc Luu, "Peasants, Party," 477–86, 505–11; Yvon-Tran, "Une résistible," 63–65, 130, 133–35, 146, 151, 195–96; Chu Van Lam et al., *Hop Tac Hoa*, 72, 74.

ution of what is produced. This requires considerably more vigilance and/or trust and commitment.

Those requirements are particularly vital in common-production orga- nizations whose members are compensated for their labor through the "remainder system" used by collective cooperatives in Vietnam and other countries.[25] After setting aside part of the cooperative's production to cover expenses and meet obligations to government agencies, leaders divided the remainder among members according to "workdays." The value of a workday—how much paddy, for instance, it was worth—was unknown until after that remainder had been divided by the total number of work- days everyone in the organization had earned.

The remainder system operates somewhat like a peasant family. In a peasant household, members share what is left of their total production after setting aside enough to plant the next season, meet other vital needs, pay expenses, and satisfy rent, tax, and other obligations. Members of peasant households, as Alexander Chayanov and others have elaborated, labor as long as there is work to be done that adds to the family's total annual income. Eyeing maximum annual remuneration for the household rather than highest remuneration per unit of labor, members endure con- siderable "self-exploitation" if necessary to earn enough for the family. They also work hard because the connection between their labor and the outcome for their family is clear and direct.[26]

In collective farming, however, with "the mediation of so many hands between plowing and harvest, no such direct link between 'drudgery' and reward can be established for any single person or household."[27] To make a connection, everyone must be confident that everyone else is working well, that shirkers will be discovered and mend their ways, and that leaders are acting properly. Meanwhile, collective farm members also still need to get sufficient annual earnings for their own households. Consequently, sat- isfying the needs of individual families and the collective is a major chal- lenge for common-production organizations using the remainder system. In addition, the collective cooperatives in Vietnam and many other com- munist countries had to meet obligations to the central government.

One way to eliminate the problem of balancing collective and family interests is to fold the family into the collective. Some common-

25. The term comes from Swain, *Collective Farms*, 42, which cogently explains its implica- tions for problems in Hungary's collective farms in the 1950s–early 1960s.

26. Chayanov, *Theory of Peasant Economy*, 5–8; Chayanov, *Theory of Peasant Co-operatives*, 35–40. Also see Netting, *Smallholders*, 59–62, 100–101; Louis Smith, *Evolution*, 42.

27. Swain, *Collective Farms*, 42.

production organizations do this well. A Hutterite community has nuclear units (with father, mother, and children), but members tend to refer to them as "home," not as family or kin. The community is each person's family. Hutterites "function as a whole, not as a group of separate nuclear families." Individuals and nuclear families rarely see their needs as separate from the community's.[28] Other efforts to dissolve the family into the community, however, have rarely succeeded.[29] When communities are forced by external agencies to keep trying, the outcome is disastrous.[30]

Another option is to replace the remainder system with wages so that members know while doing a job what they will earn. While a wage system does not guarantee success, it can help to sustain a common-production organization. Collective farms in Hungary and the Soviet Union eventually did this.[31] In effect, the shift to wages moved the organization away from collective farming toward a kind of corporation in which members were employees who also held some shares. Indeed, by the mid-1960s many Hungarian collective farms not only paid wages to members but hired outsiders to do some of the work.

A third approach is to keep the family and the remainder system but persuade people to think of collective work in the same way they think of family work. Tanzanian leaders attempted this during the "ujamaa" rural development program in the 1960s. The very word "ujamaa" means "familyhood." The program tried to "universalize the unwritten rules of living within rural households and apply them to larger social and economic forms of organization," which included communal farming and other work.[32] Vietnamese leaders sought much the same. They implored villagers to work in collective cooperatives as they would work in their own families. By and large, leaders did not succeed in either country. A large part of the reason in Vietnam (and probably in Tanzania) is that, over time, most collective cooperatives could not continue to meet the four political conditions required for durability.

28. The quotation is from Bennett, *Hutterian*, 134. See also 118–21; and Peter, *Dynamics*, 6, 21, 80.

29. Often communes in the United States during the nineteenth and twentieth centuries attempted to do this. Only 3 percent lasted twenty-five years. Wesson, *Soviet Communes*, 20; see also 30.

30. Collectivization in Cambodia under the Khmer Rouge is one of the most deadly examples of forced dissolution of the family.

31. Swain, *Collective Farms*, 42–48.

32. Hyden, *Beyond Ujamaa*, 98, also see 99, 113–15.

*Struggle and Everyday Politics*

Absent adequate political conditions for durability, Vietnam's collective cooperatives became sites of ongoing struggles.[33] Some previous studies have referred to these struggles.[34] This book examines them extensively. They occurred at several levels. Many authorities strove to make collective farming live up to their expectations. They also endeavored to stamp out corruption, instill appropriate attitudes among members, and properly manage collective resources and distribute what was collectively produced. At another level were struggles between local and higher authorities over governance of the cooperatives and distribution of paddy and other produce, among other issues. Meanwhile, ordinary villagers struggled to come to terms with collective farming. While many villagers in the Red River delta decided to give it a chance, they often remained wary. They also juggled the demands of cooperative officials and collective production with the needs of their families. Within the cooperatives there were struggles among leaders, between leaders and members, and among members themselves over work assignments, work evaluations, harvest distributions, and other matters. Finally, villagers often struggled to resist. They opposed particular leaders, specific requirements, as well as corruption and other activities they deemed unfair or wrong. People frequently opposed the cooperatives and tried to minimize their own involvement.

Aspects of these struggles surfaced in public places. Authorities issued pronouncements and directives for improving and expanding collective farming; national and local officials praised successful cooperatives and criticized errant ones; cooperative leaders and other officials emphasized at meetings what had to be done to make collective farming succeed; and ubiquitous public address systems made daily announcements and gave instructions to villagers. Dominating these public spaces and methods were officials and others who supported collectivization. Only occasionally did ordinary villagers directly challenge authorities, the management of cooperatives, or government regulations. Sometimes they did so in public

33. In both English and Vietnamese, "to struggle" (*dau tranh*) can mean to fight violently or do battle. But here it is used in another sense it has in both languages: to contest, to contend, to make great effort, to endeavor, to strive. In addition to *dau tranh* (or *cuoc dau tranh*), other words used by Vietnamese informants and in written materials include *co gang, vat lon, phan dau,* and *chong.*

34. The most substantial discussion of struggle in Vietnam is Fforde, *Agrarian Question,* which suggests that persistent conflicts in 1974–1979 weakened most collective cooperatives. Also see Yvon-Tran, "Une résistible," 107–8, 118–22, 169–79, 186–96; and Nguyen Ngoc Luu. "Peasants, Party," 425–33, 474–81, 509–11.

meetings. Or they sent petitions and letters to newspapers and to district, provincial, and national authorities. Usually villagers' public remarks complained about particular rules, abusive local officials, corruption, and government agencies' failures to deliver promised chemical fertilizer and other supplies. Rarely did people openly question, let alone condemn, collectivization itself.

Instead of being public or confrontational, most villagers' struggles were surreptitious, indirect, and entwined with their everyday lives. Consequently, daily, mundane activities were often political. To use Harold Lasswell's pithy definition of politics, they were about who gets what, when, and how.[35] They manifested lingering tensions and disagreements about the Communist Party government's rationale for how land, labor, fertilizer, time, money, and other resources in a community should be used, by whom, and to what ends. Some villagers fully or largely subscribed to that rationale. Others were unsure. Still others disagreed with parts or all of it. What the doubters and opponents thought and wanted, however, was rarely expressed publicly or directly to the proponents. Rather, their concerns, preferences, and opposition were expressed in what they did and did not do in their daily lives.

Central to politics is the distribution of important things—who gets them, in what proportion, when, how the distribution is done, and with what justifications. Politics involves actions, debates, decisions, conflicts, and cooperation by and among individuals, groups, and organizations regarding the control, allocation, and use of resources and the values and ideas underlying those activities.[36] It occurs in countless settings and forms.

Contrary to the view of many political scientists and others, politics is not restricted to activities within governments and to concerted efforts to influence them. If that were the case, then politics would involve only a minute fraction of any country's population—primarily government officials, political parties, influential individuals, and activists in organizations trying to affect what government authorities do.[37] That number would be especially tiny in a country such as Vietnam, where the opportunities for citizens to organize or speak openly about public issues are extremely limited. Such a restricted view of politics also misses a great deal of what

35. Lasswell, *Politics*.

36. For elaborations of this or similar conceptions of politics, see Leftwich, "Politics"; Kerkvliet, *Everyday*, 9–14; Ball, *Modern Politics*, 20–21; Miller, "Everyday Politics," 99–100; Stoker, "Introduction," 1995, 5–7.

37. For an elaboration highlighting the biases involved in viewing politics narrowly, see the stinging critique in Elshtain, *Real Politics*, 12–35.

is politically significant. The distribution of important resources is rarely confined to governments and related organizations. It occurs in corporations, factories, universities, religious groups, families, and other institutions. Nor is politics limited to activities aimed at influencing authorities or the processes for deciding how to allocate resources. And people need not be organized and active in public to be political.[38]

For these reasons, it is useful to distinguish three broad types of politics: official, advocacy, and everyday. Official politics has to do with authorities—whether in governments or other organizations—who contest, make, implement, change, or evade policies regarding the allocation of resources. Their activities can range from formal to informal to illegal.[39] Advocacy politics involves direct and confrontational efforts to support, criticize, or oppose authorities, policies, programs, or the entire way resources are produced and distributed. Behavior can range from friendly, civil, and peaceful to hostile, rebellious, and violent. Advocates may be individuals, groups, or organizations. Everyday politics occurs where people live and work and involves people embracing, adjusting to, or contesting norms and rules regarding authority over, production of, or allocation of resources. It includes quiet, mundane, and subtle expressions and acts that indirectly and for the most part privately endorse, modify, or resist prevailing procedures, rules, regulations, or order. Everyday politics involves little or no organization. It features the activities of individuals and small groups as they make a living, raise their families, wrestle with daily problems, and deal with others like themselves who are relatively powerless and with powerful superiors and others.[40]

Everyday politics can, in the first place, convey people's understanding and appraisal of the system in which they live and work. Take, for instance, farming activities. In the Red River delta in the 1960s–1980s, plowing, planting, tending fields, raising livestock, and harvesting were inextricably part of most villagers' lives. In the context of collectivization, how villagers

38. For clear arguments along this line, see Piven and Cloward, *Poor People's Movements*, 4–5; and Scott, "Resistance," 418–23.

39. For some analysts, the meaning of "informal politics" may be broad enough to include what I call "everyday politics." Most usage, however, restricts informal politics to types of behavior among government leaders, bureaucrats, and other public officials. See the chapters in Dittmer et al., eds., *Informal Politics*, and the articles in the special issue of *Asian Survey* (36 [March 1996]).

40. Some studies suggest that to be political, those everyday acts must aim to influence public affairs (Burns, *Political Participation*, 9–10; Tianjian Shi, *Political Participation*, 21–23; Huntington and Nelson, *No Easy Choice*, 3–7). That may be necessary for an activity to count as political participation but not for it to be political. (This view of political participation, other studies intimate, is itself too narrow. See Christiansen-Ruffman, "Women's Conceptions," 374, 382.)

did such work often expressed their views about production and distribution, the cooperatives they were in, and the authorities in charge. A villager who diligently plowed and harrowed collective fields may have been trying to please local officials or may have been expressing support for the system. Perhaps another person working in a perfunctory manner was conveying indifference, even opposition. Someone who, after being told that every household had to give the cooperative a ton of pig manure, mixed pebbles and dirt with the manure before turning it over to the organization was likely making a statement about the instruction, the leaders, and possibly the whole collective system. Closer inspection of the behavior may reveal no political message about collectivization. The diligent worker may be trying to impress his father or his girlfriend. The villager doing the sloppy work may be sick or lazy, rather than disgusted with collective farming. To ignore such activities, however, especially when they are numerous, would be to miss much of the subdued dialogue, negotiation, and contending ideas—the politics—within Vietnamese villages regarding the production, use, and distribution of resources and the control of those resources.

Everyday politics may also affect other forms of politics. It can feed into advocacy politics, which tries to influence authorities and public discourse on production and resource allocation. In Vietnam during the era of collective farming, advocacy politics was largely limited to campaigns to mobilize rural support for the government and national defense. Organizers came from the Communist Party, other organizations close to it, and the government. No movement to modify or eliminate collective farming developed among villagers. Nearly the only forms of advocacy politics among villagers unhappy with collectivization were occasional verbal and written comments expressing the frustrations and discontent normally conveyed through their everyday behavior.

Everyday politics can affect official politics whether or not people intend it to do so. For instance, daily behavior can contribute toward perpetuating incumbent leaders, existing policies, and an entire political system.[41] Other everyday activities can contribute to the demise of particular officials, to policy changes, and even to the collapse of an organization, including a government or a regime. This may be particularly true in political systems that attempt to organize people's work, where they live, their fam-

---

41. Studies have shown that German citizens' efforts to come to terms with the Nazi regime, even if they did not particularly like it, helped perpetuate it. Peukert, *Inside Nazi Germany*, 67–80, 109–10. Making a similar point in a more generalized and poignant way is Havel, "Power," esp. 35–39.

ilies, their religious practices. Such systems amplify the political aspect of small deviations from what officials expect. Initially the impact may be only local, but if those modest variations are persistent and widespread, they can have national implications.[42] For Vietnam, it is rarely clear whether villagers consciously tried to influence the government to abandon collective farming. Far more often the evidence shows that people made claims to land, their own labor, and other resources in order to support their families or because they had little confidence that the cooperative organization could properly or adequately use those resources. Those actions, in addition to making statements about how resources should be used and by whom, undermined many collective cooperatives, influenced authorities, and eventually contributed to the Communist Party government's decision to discard collective farming.

I have just indicated that everyday politics can include support for or at least compliance with authorities and how resources are used and distributed. Another form of everyday politics modifies or evades the rules and what others expect. A third form is resistance and opposition. All three occurred in Vietnam, although after the initial period of compliance and some enthusiasm, the second and third forms were more prevalent in collective cooperatives in the north. Evasion and resistance often occur together. Both involve discontent and complaints with the system and efforts to minimize adversities; both are surreptitious, nonconfrontational, and basically unorganized. The difference turns on intention and hierarchy. Resistance involves intentionally contesting claims by individuals or groups in superordinate classes, social strata, or institutions, or intentionally advancing claims at odds with what superordinates want.[43]

In Vietnam, many activities by villagers were indeed forms of everyday resistance. Other behavior, though similar in appearance, lacked the intentional and hierarchical features of resistance (or it could not be determined whether they possessed them or not).[44] For instance, people stealthily took paddy from collective fields. In some instances, they did so to quietly oppose egregious and abusive officials. Other times, however, they did it as a preemptive measure to get grain that they presumed other villagers like

---

42. For engaging elaborations, see Rev, "Advantages"; Verdery, "Theorizing Socialism"; and Creed, *Domesticating Revolution*.

43. Scott, *Weapons*, 29, 32–33; Scott, "Everyday Forms of Resistance," 7–8, 21–30; Fegan, "Tenants' Non-violent Resistance," 103–4; and Kerkvliet, *Everyday Politics*, 114–17. Another feature of resistance, which Fegan and I stress and which does figure in Scott's discussion, concerns resisters' notions of justice.

44. A similar point is made by White, "Everyday Resistance," 51–53, 59.

them would take because people did not trust one another, were continuing long-standing hostilities between neighboring villages even though they were now supposed to farm together, or were desperate for food. Both cases involve everyday politics, but only the former constitutes resistance. Similarly, villagers often secretly encroached on and used individually some land that was supposed to be used collectively. Sometimes the encroachments were acts of defiance against local or higher officials. Other times, however, people took land for themselves out of a conviction that they could farm it better individually than collectively. In short, encroachments were not necessarily a form of resistance but nevertheless were part of an ongoing, but rarely public or verbal, debate over how land should be used and by whom.

## The Power of Noncollective Action

Although villagers seldom openly expressed their views about collective cooperatives, their behavior affected leaders locally and nationally. Authorities kept making adjustments and tried to overcome problems resulting from what villagers routinely did and did not do. Ultimately, persistent everyday struggles in villages, combined with peasants' infrequent public criticisms, significantly influenced national party and government leaders to stop insisting on collectivization and to endorse family-based production.[45]

Before turning to discuss in general terms how everyday politics can sway national leaders and their policies, let me say a few words about why no protest movement against collectivization emerged.[46] Grievances, discontent, and hardships by themselves, even when widespread, are not sufficient conditions for open protest or other forms of "contentious challenges" against elites, authorities, or policies.[47] Studies of organized

45. A few earlier studies have also said that "bottom-up" pressures influenced shifts in the Communist Party government's collectivization policy: Fforde, *Agrarian Question*, esp. 80–81, 85–86, 205; Le Huy Phan, "May Suy Nghi," 14; Chu Van Lam et al., *Hop Tac Hoa*, 52, 78–79. A scarcity of evidence at the time these works were written prevented them from providing details and tracing the process.

46. I should mention that everyday resistance and other forms of everyday politics were not the reason no protest movement developed. Some analyses, such as Jean-Klein, "Nationalism and Resistance," argue that everyday resistance is separate from and even precludes organized resistance. Others, however, show that everyday resistance can and frequently does contribute to advocacy politics, including open protest. See Kerkvliet, *Everyday Politics* and "Claiming the Land"; Korovkin, "Weak Weapons"; and Gavin Smith, *Livelihood*.

47. The term "contentious challenges" comes from Tarrow, *Power*, 5.

protests show that at a micro level one of the most essential conditions is that many people conclude that possible gains from public challenges outweigh possible losses.[48] During collectivization in northern Vietnam, villagers were unsure about this or assumed that adversity resulting from open protest were greater than possible advantages. Even though many people were deeply worried about collective farming, they hoped, at least in the early years, that it would lead to improved living conditions. Moreover, until 1975, war engulfed the entire country. The government claimed that collective cooperatives were vital for national survival, a credible argument for many villagers. Others who were skeptical nevertheless thought that by tolerating collective farming they would at least be seen as doing their part for their country. Many realized that anyone who protested against collectivization would likely be deemed unpatriotic or, worse, allied with the enemy. Another factor was people's assessments of the Communist Party government. Unlike in many other countries, including several with communist governments that insisted on collective farming, relations between the state and the peasantry were reasonably good.[49] This encouraged people to think that an accommodation could be reached. Meanwhile, by engaging in low-key activities that nibbled away at collective farming, people made their lives somewhat easier than it would have been had they adhered to the rules. In other words, it is possible they saw that, given the circumstances, their everyday actions were more efficacious than open opposition to and organization against collectivization.

Macro conditions also affect the likelihood that protest organizations will develop. Several authors have stressed the pattern of political opportunities and constraints.[50] Although no single pattern fits all situations, many accounts suggest that contentious challenges are unlikely to grow in political systems that allow little legal space for people to form political organizations or to rigorously repress open dissent, and in those that are not rocked by major splits within ruling or elite circles. Individuals and groups might, of course, create and expand opportunities by taking advantage of cracks in the brickwork of highly restrictive political regimes. But this rarely happened in northern Vietnam so far as we know.

48. Lichbach, "Contentious Maps," 90–93; Melucci, "Getting Involved," 331–33, 339–41. Also see Lichbach, *Cooperator's Dilemma*; and Gamson et al., *Encounters*, 108–21. Although this last work emphasizes assessments of potential personal gains and losses, it also points to the implications of open opposition for one's family, community, or other corporate affiliations.

49. Vasavakul, "Vietnam," 266–69; White, "Everyday Resistance," 50–52.

50. Kitschelt, "Political Opportunity Structures"; McAdam, "Conceptual Origins"; McAdam et al., "Introduction"; Piven and Cloward, *Poor People's Movements*, 6–23; Tarrow, *Power*, 2–7, 18–23, 71–90.

The Communist Party dominated the political system in northern Vietnam until 1975 and in the entire nation after reunification. Party organization and government agencies reached deep and wide across the country. No competitive elections occurred. The party and government controlled all newspapers, publishing houses, and other media. Unauthorized organizations scarcely existed. In addition to a large army, the government had an internal security police force extending from Hanoi to practically every rural village and urban neighborhood. The police's principal duties were to maintain order and investigate any suspicious individuals and activities. A residential registration system (ho khau) and other regulations prevented people from traveling beyond their own subdistricts without permission. Consequently, communication, networking, or coordination among people in different parts of the country—even different parts of the same district or province—was exceedingly difficult without official involvement. Meanwhile, the government remained stable. The same person, Le Duan, was the party's top leader for twenty-five years (1960–1986), most of the collectivization era. Several peak party and government positions rotated among a small number of individuals. Leadership succession and changes in the composition of the party's Political Bureau and other key committees occurred with little disruption. Heated debates developed within high echelons of the party and in government ministries, but none resulted in major splits. All these features of Vietnam's political system put tremendous constraints on organized protests and raised considerable risks for people who might have become involved in them.

Despite no significant organized action against collective farming, villagers influenced national authorities and the course of collectivization in the 1960s–1980s. How could this happen? Here I offer a general explanation. Having considered some similar cases elsewhere, I think the explanation is not unique to Vietnam. Everyday activities that are out of line with what authorities require and expect can have considerable political clout. Testing this theory beyond Vietnam would require further study, particularly of places without communist governments in which unorganized citizens undermined major policies and of situations in which everyday politics incompatible with official policies had little or no impact.

My general explanation has five elements. The first is the degree of power that people, though in relatively weak positions, do have, at least potentially, vis-à-vis authorities and the government. In Vietnam and several other countries with communist governments pressing for collective farming, villagers' most obvious power is their labor. If villagers did not do the farming, who else would? Collective cooperative officials could not handle all the work. Nor were there enough party members and others committed to collectivization to do the job. Just as an army cannot fight without soldiers and a factory cannot produce without workers, collective farms cannot function without peasants doing the tasks they are supposed to do. Consequently, by withholding labor, using it in a manner out of sync with what is required, or in other ways "working the system" to their advantage or minimum disadvantage, peasants could exercise some power.[51]

Peasants also have another kind of power. They have alternatives or supplementary options, however limited, to what national authorities claim or want from them. Even on collective farms, villagers have retained some separate means of production. In Tanzania, the ujamaa program in the 1970s required villagers to work on the government's communal lands. Peasants still had their own fields, however, leaving them with sufficient means to subsist, which eventually contributed to the collapse of the program.[52] Households in the collective cooperatives of Vietnam and other countries had their own gardens, ponds, and small fields in which they grew a significant proportion of their basic food requirements. This was not an oversight. Authorities knew that collective farming, at least initially, could not produce every kind of crop. Hence, they left some land for members to use individually. Officials also realized that getting people into collectives would be infinitely harder if every bit of land was amalgamated, leaving none for each family's own use. But allowing households to retain some land also allowed peasants some independence from the collective system. Authorities in some countries, such as China, later tried to take away these household plots but backed down in the face of smoldering peasant opposition. Another way for peasants to remain apart from the collectives has been to leave. This was not an option for most Vietnamese. It was a possibility, however, in several Eastern European countries during collectivization there in the 1950s. And in Laos, the "haemorrhage of population" after 1975, as villagers fled across the Mekong River into Thailand to escape collective farming and other objectionable policies, was one of the main reasons why the alarmed communist government suspended collectivization in 1979.[53]

Another source of power is the importance of peasants to the government. They may be a major base of support. Or agricultural production may be vital for government programs. The latter was arguably the case in

51. In this last statement I am borrowing from Eric Hobsbawm's more general discussion of peasants' sources of power, "Peasants and Politics," 13.

52. Hyden, *Beyond Ujamaa*, 29, 31–32, 113–14, 123–24.

53. Stuart-Fox, *Buddhist Kingdom*, 168, also see 125–26.

China at the end of the 1970s, when the Deng Xiaoping government's economic program needed "record expansion in the farm sector." This increased peasants' leverage and gave the central government reason to accommodate local farming practices at odds with collectivization.[54] A somewhat similar situation developed in Poland during the 1950s. Peasants there had quietly opposed collectivization by not joining the cooperatives, by farming less, and by hiding produce. Such behavior created havoc with domestic food supplies, which aggravated strikes among urban workers, the base of the nation's United Workers Party government. To deal with workers' discontent, the government had to get peasants back to farming. To accomplish that, the party's new national leadership in 1956 retreated from collectivization.[55] In Laos and Yugoslavia, where central authorities also retreated from collectivization in considerable measure as a result of everyday political behavior, the peasantry was both a major power base for the communist governments and the muscle power for those governments' economic development programs.[56] The same was true in Vietnam. In addition, Vietnamese peasants were the backbone and arms and legs of the army, on which the very existence of the government in Hanoi depended during the war against the United States.

A second element is the extent to which authorities dare not force compliance. Although coercive when organizing and maintaining collective farming, many governments did not resort to extensive violence. As one analyst of Yugoslavia put it, the country's communist government "used all conceivable psychological, political, social, and economic pressures" to collectivize the countryside, but "it did not use brute force of the Soviet brand" to get its way.[57] Leaders in Vietnam and many other communist countries were unwilling or unable to use the full might of the state to collectivize. Consequently, unlike in the Soviet Union during the 1930s or Cambodia under the Khmer Rouge in the 1970s, these leaders' ideological commitment to collective agriculture was not lethal.[58]

54. Kelliher, *Peasant Power*, esp. 246–47.

55. Szymanski, *Class Struggle*, 27–35; Korbonski, *Politics of Socialist Agriculture*, 5, 139–40, 164, 189, 194–95, 212–14, 305; Sokolovsky, *Peasants and Power*, 65–68, 71–74, 79–80.

56. Regarding Laos, see Evans, *Lao Peasants*, 53–54, 122, 133–37, 146–47; Stuart-Fox, *Buddhist Kingdom*, 117–26. For Yugoslavia, see Bokovoy, "Peasant and Partisans," 116–17, 125–29, 132; R. F. Miller, "Group Farming," 165; Rusinow, *Yugoslav Experiment*, 36–40; Tomasevich, "Collectivization," 174, 177–79.

57. Tomasevich, "Collectivization," 172.

58. I am thinking here of the discussion in Scott, *Seeing*, 5, about authoritarian states that are willing to use all means to get "utopian social engineering schemes" implemented. For references on the Soviet Union, see above, n. 13. Regarding collectivization by the Khmer Rouge, see Kiernan, *Pol Pot Regime*, 456–60, and chaps. 5 and 6; and Martin, *Cambodia*, chap. 7.

The third element is the magnitude of everyday politics at odds with what national authorities prescribe. If only a few people in a village were skirting the collective farm's claims on their time and labor, the impact on the organization would be slight and the effect on national policy zero. Even errant behavior in several villages would have a trivial effect on national authorities. If, however, such behavior were widespread and similar across numerous collectives, the impact would be considerably greater.[59] Under collectivization in several countries, many people in many places did the minimal required work for the collective, farmed collective land with little enthusiasm, resented local officials, and diverted labor and other resources away from collective production to household production. One analyst likened the phenomenon in China to an unorganized yet extensive "invisible 'sit-in.' "[60] The behavior also reflected similar preferences among villagers across the countryside—away from collective farming and toward family farming. Countless similar actions by the peasantry persisted despite authorities' efforts to counter them.

By what they did and did not do and how they used their labor and other resources over which they retained some control, peasants in collective cooperatives were essentially manipulating collectivization policy. Their intent may have been to provide for their families and exact concessions or immediate benefits. The consequence, however, was to alter the application of policy in their own villages. Similar behavior in countless places across the countryside meant that many collective cooperatives turned into organizations different from what central authorities had wanted.[61] In Hungary, according to one study of the country's rural situation, peasants

59. For other sectors of society or for other policies, the behavior need not encompass a large portion of an entire country. The pertinent requirement is that a significant percentage of people vital for the policy to be implemented or for the institution to function is not complying.

60. Xueguang Zhou, "Unorganized Interests," 67. He also calls it "collective inaction" that is "a form of collective action" (66). That, however, is befuddling language. Such conduct is politically potent but cannot sensibly be called collective action. People are acting more or less privately, surreptitiously, and with little or no organization. I agree with Daniel Kelliher, *Peasant Power*, 246, that the behavior is only collective "in the sense of being duplicated and multiplied on a massive scale."

61. Kelliher, *Peasant Power*, 239–42, makes this point regarding China. It applies as well to Vietnam and several other countries with Communist Party governments. Some China scholars disagree with Kelliher and others, who contend that local arrangements at odds with central authorities' preferences were widespread and influenced the direction of national policy. Such occurrences, they say, were rare and usually took place in remote parts of China. Decollectivization, they argue, was a mixture of top-down and bottom-up pressures, and that most of the bottom-up ones were from provincial and other lower-level offices, not ordinary villagers. For a thoughtful presentation of this argument, see Unger, *Transformation*, 95–115.

"just lived their lives and their way of living gradually changed the political system around them."[62] There, and in Bulgaria and Romania, such everyday practices cumulatively led authorities to temporarily back away from collectivization drives and later to give more scope to family production and in other ways modify collective farming.[63] Analogous changes occurred in Vietnam, except there, as in Yugoslavia, Poland, Laos, and possibly China, the process continued until decollectivization was complete.

Collectivization itself is largely responsible for generating extensive antagonistic everyday activities that moved in the same direction.[64] The collective farming system put all villagers in northern Vietnam in the same boat. Of course, that did not mean they were homogeneous. They lived in different parts of the country, produced different things, and had various customs. Within the same village, some were better off than others, some had strong connections to local authorities while others did not, and some had revolutionary credentials that gave them an advantage over others. Nevertheless, because they were in collective cooperatives, villagers far and wide faced similar circumstances and did similar things to deal with the system, provide for their families, and resist where they could. To behave alike, they did not need another organization. The collective cooperative itself was enough to get people thinking and acting in similar ways.

A fourth element in the explanation of how small activities can have large consequences is the very nature of those acts.[65] Because it was nonconfrontational and leaderless, behavior out of line with collective farming provided no organizations for authorities to crush and no obvious individuals to arrest. Being largely hidden, often atomized or only loosely coordinated among neighbors, yet spread across numerous provinces, such activities were extremely costly to stop. Vietnamese authorities tried repeatedly to monitor collective farming members. They rewarded villagers who complied with rules and penalized those who did not. These efforts, however, were not enough. Authorities could have resorted to force and physically punished, incarcerated, or even killed some errant peasants. But that could have been even more costly, would probably have proven no more effective in the long run, and would have been highly counterpro-

---

62. Rev, "Advantages," 348.

63. Creed, *Domesticating Revolution*, 3, 184–87; Kideckel, "Dialectic," 52–58; Kideckel, "Socialist Transformation," 321, 326, 328; Rev, "Advantages," 343–44; Swain, *Collective Farms*, 25–26, 41–42, 60–66.

64. Others have also made this argument: Kelliher, *Peasant Power*, 247; Xueguang Zhou, "Unorganized Interests," 56–58, 67.

65. Emphasizing the same point for China is Kate Xiao Zhou, *How the Farmers*, 243–44. Also see Kelliher, *Peasant Power*, 248; and Rev, "Advantages," 343, 345, 347.

ductive. Perhaps violent repression is more likely if authorities conclude—on the basis of delusion or some hard evidence—that villagers are challenging or trying to overthrow the government.[66] But authorities in Vietnam were not delusional, and peasants there had considerable goodwill toward the party, or at least were not particularly hostile toward it.

A fifth element is the extent to which officials, particularly local ones, knowingly or unwittingly spread everyday political activities at odds with national prescriptions. In agricultural collectives, leaders, because of incompetence or lack of resources, were sometimes unable to stop the violations. Others gave tacit approval. Still others explicitly endorsed the deviations. Motivations among authorities varied. Collective officials in Vietnam, China, Hungary, and other countries negotiated different arrangements with villagers and turned a blind eye to practices out of line with the rules, simply to get the work done.[67] Officials also granted favors to relatives and friends. Some used their positions to steal and in other ways illegally serve their own interests.[68] In addition to directly undermining collective farming, such favoritism and corruption allowed other villagers to justify their own deviations from what leaders were exhorting them to do. Some officials made concessions, initially small but later larger, because they concluded that changes were necessary for the cooperative to function, albeit differently from the way the central government prescribed. Sometimes such local accommodations were later endorsed by higher authorities, particularly when better production resulted.[69]

These five elements help to explain how and why everyday politics had local and national repercussions in Vietnam. The everyday behavior of villagers as they struggled to deal with collectivization affected local officials' efforts to organize and run the cooperatives according to higher authori-

---

66. Part of what drove the violent and murderous methods of collectivization in the Soviet Union under Stalin and Cambodia under the Khmer Rouge were authorities who read any sign of deviation from what people were told to do as treason and opposition to the regime.

67. Even in the Soviet Union, bargaining between ordinary members and collective leaders and managers over jobs to be done was "so widespread as to be simply the way things work." Humphrey, *Karl Marx Collective*, 305.

68. For a detailed analysis of favoritism and other aspects of clientelistic relationships that frequently developed between local collective leaders and ordinary members in China, see Oi, *State and Peasant*, chap. 7. A study that stresses the adverse consequences of local corruption for collectivization in China is Kate Xiao Zhou, *How the Farmers*, esp. 53–56, 239, 242.

69. A study of China that tends to dismiss the influence of bottom–up pressure against collectivization nevertheless points to peasants and local authorities who developed ways of farming out of line with official policy. Then splits within high echelons of the Communist Party over collectivization and other policies provided an environment in which local experimentation spread. Fewsmith, *Dilemmas*, 19, 27–29. Also see Kate Zhou, *How the Farmers*, 60–62, 70.

ties' expectations. Villagers' everyday activities, combined with their rare public criticisms and expressions of discontent, also influenced party and government debates and decisions about how to improve collective farming. And in the late 1980s they significantly influenced national decisions to back away from collectivization and encourage instead family-based farming, the very thing most villagers had wanted.

I am not saying that everyday politics is the only explanation for the direction collective farming took in northern Vietnam. Other factors were at work, which also constrained or enhanced the impact of everyday politics. There was the war against the United States, food aid from other countries, other communist countries' influence on the Vietnamese leaders' stance on collectivization, and severe problems with the nation's centrally planned economy in the late 1970s to early 1980s.

## Understanding Vietnam's Political System

Two main interpretations of Vietnamese Communist Party rule synthesize important aspects of the country's political system, but neither can accommodate well how and why collectivization policies changed.

The first is the "dominating state" interpretation.[70] It says that rules and programs governing Vietnam are monopolized within the state. According to one analyst, Vietnam is a "vast and coordinated party-state which preempts alternative and autonomous societal organizations from the national center down to the grassroots of the village and the workplace."[71] Another contends that "Vietnam's system is mono-organizational socialism" in which "there is little scope for the organization of activity independent of the party-led command structures."[72] With regard to policy making and implementation, this interpretation grants importance only to the state institutions. Gareth Porter is clearest on this: "The model of the *bureaucratic polity*, in which major decisions are made entirely *within* the bureaucracy and are influenced by it rather than by extra-bureaucratic forces in society—whether parliamentary parties, interest groups, or mass move-

70. The publications to which I refer in this section by no means exhaust the literature. Also, a reference to a particular scholar's work does not mean that everything that person has written about Vietnam fits within one interpretation. The study of politics in contemporary Vietnam is young and evolving, hence an individual scholar can come to a tentative conclusion at one stage and later change it.

71. Womack, "Reform in Vietnam," 180.

72. Thayer, "Political Reform," 111–12.

ments—aptly describes how the Vietnamese policy system works."[73] To understand those internal processes, scholars analyze debates and factions within the Communist Party, government ministries, the military, and other components of the state.[74] The only noteworthy influences outside those official policy-making circles that the dominating state interpretation acknowledges are international ones.[75]

A second interpretation modifies the first by arguing that forces in society can influence policy through authorized organizations. Some analysts call this phenomenon "mobilizational authoritarianism," others, "state corporatism." I use the term "mobilizational corporatism." This interpretation highlights organizations that the Communist Party government has established. Among them are organizations for peasants, workers, youth, women, Buddhists, and other sectors of society. Through them, the party and government ministries can mobilize people to support programs and policies, maintain channels of communication between authorities and each sector of society, and manage social and economic groups that otherwise might become unruly. William Turley argues that because other organizations independent of the state are prohibited, and because the Communist Party retains considerable legitimacy, "the power elite has been able to invite popular involvement under its supervision without much fear that things will get out of control." At the same time, people's concerns expressed through these authorized channels can influence policy debates.[76]

Both interpretations focus on the formal institutions of policy making and implementation. The first emphasizes the Communist Party, the government, and other agencies of the state that fit squarely into what I call "official politics." The second adds authorized state organizations, arguably leaning toward what I call "advocacy politics." These institutions and organizations are indeed major players in the story of agricultural collectivization and decollectivization. It was national leaders who decided the country had to collectivize. Through structures extending from Hanoi into most villages, party and government agencies built the collective cooperatives, carried out numerous campaigns to train leaders, improve management, and teach villagers how to farm together, and conducted other programs to bolster collectivization. Meanwhile, local branches of national organizations

73. Porter, *Vietnam*, 101, emphasis in the original.
74. Thai Quang Trung, *Collective Leadership*; and Stern, *Renovating*. Also see Kolko, *Vietnam*, 119–25, 130–32.
75. Porter, *Vietnam*, 96; Kolko, *Vietnam*, 29–30, 133–37.
76. Turley, "Party, State, and People," 269–70; Turley, "Political Renovation," 330–31. For state corporatist arguments, see Jeong, "Rise," 152–71; and Stromseth, "Reform and Response."

for peasants, youth, and women persuaded, encouraged, and coerced fellow villagers to work hard to make collective farming a success.[77] The cooperatives, local branches of the party, and other authorized organizations also conveyed villagers' concerns and criticisms to higher levels, where discussions and debates addressed how to improve production and strengthen collectivization. From those deliberations in national circles came decisions in the 1960s and early 1970s to enlarge collective cooperatives, revamp their management, and make other changes aimed at reinforcing and improving collectivization. In the late 1970s those agencies authorized modest shifts away from collective farming. More debate in national party and government offices during the 1980s led to decisions that endorsed family farming.

Mobilizational corporatism can account for how villagers in Vietnam voiced concerns and criticism through official channels. But neither it nor the dominating state analysis includes what villagers did outside those channels that affected how cooperatives actually functioned and stymied authorities' persistent efforts to make cooperatives operate according to official rules and regulations. In other words, those two interpretations do not acknowledge the significance of differences between what the Communist Party government stipulated and what villagers did. Nor do they recognize that what peasants did influenced national policies. Through their everyday practices and ongoing contestation and negotiation among themselves and between them and local officials, villagers created methods of production and distribution that did not jibe with national policies. Higher authorities were often aware of these unauthorized practices. Indeed, numerous measures to improve collective farming in the 1960s and 1970s were aimed at eliminating such deviations as well as corrupt and incompetent leadership within the cooperatives. Officials in party and government circles pondered how to deal with the shortcomings they saw in most collective cooperatives, the falling food production, and other crises in the nation's economy. Gradually, national authorities began to look differently at deviant local arrangements, which featured family-based farming and yields that were significantly better than collective farming achieved. Between the late 1970s and late 1980s, the Communist Party government incrementally adjusted its collectivization policy to accommodate aspects of those unauthorized practices instead of trying to expunge them. Initially, authorities did so in hopes of confining family-based farming to a small

77. The Peasants' Association, said one of its reports, is a "prop" (*cho dua*) of the Communist Party government and a force for implementing "the policies and undertakings of the party and the state." BCHTU, Hoi Nong Dan Viet Nam, "Bao Cao," 12.

proportion of the land or to a few tasks, while many others continued to be done collectively. By the late 1980s, however, officials gave up and redistributed collective land and other means of production to individual households.

The impact of everyday politics on collectivization policy bolsters a third interpretation in the study of Vietnam's political system. It picks up on a point Brantly Womack makes about the Communist Party during Vietnam's revolutionary period, before its government ruled the country. At that time, he says, the party had to be "mass-regarding" to garner popular support, especially among the peasantry. "Upon victory," however, the "imperative for mass-regarding politics is lost and the authoritarian internal structure" tends to take over. The masses no longer have any significant influence on the party.[78] The third interpretation, which I call "dialogical," posits that the interaction between the party and the masses does not stop with the end of the revolution. Dialogue, in the broad sense of communicating ideas and preferences, continues between authorities and various sectors of society and is an important aspect of the political system.[79] The views and demands of authorities are often public. Those of the masses rarely are. Peasants and workers do use the narrow authorized avenues to voice their views and concerns. Sporadically, such as in demonstrations and uprisings, they also venture beyond those avenues to challenge authorities publicly. Generally, however, they express their views through nonconfrontational actions involving little or no organization. This dialogical interpretation of the political system recognizes that the communist government's capacity to coordinate programs and implement policies is considerably weaker than what a dominating state or mobilizational corporatist view would argue. Activities not under the state's control remain afoot and introduce discrepancies between what authorities claim and what actually occurs. Indeed, social forces and groups beyond the state can contribute to shifts in policies. This interpretation also points out that authorities can adjust and change policies in the face of realities beyond their control.

78. Womack, "Party and the People," 486. Womack applies his argument to China as well. A similar view about Vietnam emerges in Woodside, "Peasants and the State," 284–85, 289–90.

79. Earlier studies highlighting dialogue of this kind in Vietnam include Post, *Revolution*, 14, 212; Pelzer, "Socio-Cultural Dimensions"; Hy Van Luong, "Marxist State"; and Kerkvliet, "Dialogical Law Making." Without using the term, others make the same point: Beresford and Fforde, "Methodology"; Fforde, *Agrarian Question*; Koh, "Wards of Hanoi"; O'Rourke, "Community-Driven Regulation"; Thrift and Forbes, *Price of War*; and White, "Agricultural Planning."

# CHAPTER 3

# Building on Wobbly Foundations, 1955–1961

Vietnam's Communist Party government began to build collective cooperatives on foundations composed of labor exchange groups. In that way, authorities believed, villagers would see the benefit of collaborative work and want to create collective farms. But the approach was slow and most villagers remained wary of the collective cooperatives. This provoked debate within the party about how to proceed. National leaders ultimately decided to push villagers rapidly into collective farming.

## Perceiving Shared Problems

To emerge anywhere, common-use organizations require, among other things, that five political conditions be met. First, individuals must realize that they share a serious problem requiring a collaborative solution. This condition existed in the Red River delta and other parts of northern Vietnam in the mid-1950s. Devastation from years of war was a widely shared predicament. Many houses burned and damaged during the war were still unfit for habitation in 1955–1957. Because a large percentage of water buffaloes and oxen had been killed, many villagers had to pull their own plows and harrows to prepare their fields. Numerous families no longer had basic farming tools and were too impoverished to replace them.[1]

---

1. UBHC Ha Nam, "BC Chung Nien, 1956" [Ha Nam province, "1956 report"], 8 February 1957, 8 (P UBKCHC LK 3, hs 125, vv); TCT VH HTX Hung Tien, Vinh Bao, Kien An, BVH, "BCSK CT, 1-10/8" [MC group, Hung Tien subdistrict, Vinh Bao district, Kien An province, "Assignment report"], 13 August 1958, 4 (P BVH, hs 911, vv)

Getting enough food was a major worry. Famine was still a recent memory. Ngo Van Tinh, for instance, was orphaned at age thirteen in 1945, when his parents died of hunger. All together, seven close relatives had starved to death that year.[2] Other families in his village and the neighboring villages of Dao Duc subdistrict suffered similarly. In 1944–1945, between one-fifth and one-tenth of the north's population perished from hunger.[3] The famine was most severe in several delta provinces. While living conditions were not so horrific by the mid-1950s, many villagers, like Ngo Van Tinh, then in his early twenties and just married, were anxious about how to provide for their families. One out of six villagers in Ha Nam province, for example, was hungry.[4] People there and elsewhere in the delta in 1954–1958 frequently lived "hand-to-mouth" (an dong). Many ate only rice gruel (chao) and mixtures (don) of rice with corn or sweet potatoes with cassava. So destitute were some that they lived on vegetables and bran (cam).[5] During 1958, desperate people in parts of Ta Ngan zone in the Red River delta sold their paddy while it was still growing to have money for food.[6]

In this context, arguments about the need to help one another and work together made sense to many villagers. Otherwise, advocates of collective cooperatives predicted, an increasing proportion of villagers would grow hungrier and more desperate, and would ultimately be so deep in debt that they would sell their fields. They would end up working for the few remaining landowners. Already in 1957–1958, only a few years after land reform, impoverished peasants in Ha Dong, Ha Nam, Hanoi, and Kien An, among other provinces, were mortgaging and selling their land.[7] Villagers, these

2. Interview, Dao Duc, Vinh Phuc, 17 August 2000. One or both parents of other people I met in Dao Duc and elsewhere in Vinh Phuc also had starved to death in the mid-1940s. Please note that pseudonyms are used for this and other rural informants cited in this book.

3. The higher percentage is from White, "Agrarian Reform," 103–4, and Cao Van Bien, "Ve Nan Doi," 25. The lower one is from Marr, *Vietnam 1945*, 104.

4. UBHC Ha Nam, "BC Chung Nien" [1956 report], 8 February 1957, 8.

5. TCT Thuc Te Son Tay, "BC TH To Can Bo, CT Thuc Te, 29/7–5/8" [Field study, Son Tay, "Report, MC team"], 5 August 1958, 3 (P BVH, hs 911, vv); TCT VH, "BCSK" [Assignment], Hung Tien, Kien An, 13 August 1958, 3; TCT, BVH, Gia Tan, Gia Loc, Hai Duong, "BC So Luoc TH CT" [MC team, Gia Tan subdistrict, Gia Loc district, Hai Duong province, "Report"], 7 August 1958, 3 (P BVH, hs 911, vv); and UBHC, Ha Dong, "BCTK, 1956" [Administrative Committee, Ha Dong province, "Report, 1956"], 20 January 1957, 2 (P UBKCHC LK 3, hs 125, vv).

6. Le Huy, BCH Khu Ta Ngan, DLDVN, "BCCT Sau Thang, 1958" [Le Huy, Executive Committee, Ta Ngan zone, VWP, "Six months, 1958"], 23 July 1958, 9 (P UBHC Khu Ta Ngan, hs 40, vv).

7. TCT VH, "BCSK" [Assignment], Hung Tien, Kien An, 13 August 1958, 6; Pham Cuong and Nguyen Van Ba, *Nam Hong*, 34; Tran Duc Cuong, "Nhin Lai," 14–15.

advocates argued, also needed to share the scarce draft animals and farming implements and to pool their labor and other resources in order to repair damaged irrigation canals and build new ones.

## Organizational Experience and Local Leadership

A second condition for common-use groups to form is that prior organizational experience must exist among the people potentially involved in a cooperative effort. In this regard, villages in the Red River delta and many other parts of northern Vietnam had two advantages. The first was that in the early 1900s it was "filled with communalistic peasants."[8] They were not involved in collective farming. Nor were people living in "closed, corporate" communities, though many villages in the Red River delta were more cohesive than were villages in southern Vietnam.[9] But people had strong loyalties to their community, beginning with their hamlet and neighborhood and extending to their village.[10] There was not complete harmony. Conflicts and rivalries within villages and between them were legion. Divisions among family lineages were common, though kinship and villageship could be complementary. Socioeconomic inequities, which French colonial rule aggravated, were also divisive. Nevertheless, the idea of community remained. By the 1940s, when yet another foreign occupier—the Japanese—and war turned their lives topsy-turvy, rural people felt a tremendous need "for a new means of social integration."[11] In the 1950s local Communist Party leaders drew on this sentiment when explaining the value of collective farming. As Adam Fforde writes, "The strong collective sense in traditional thinking" among peasants in northern Vietnam, when applied to agriculture, "somehow pointed towards the appropriateness of the co-operative form" of production and distribution.[12]

Villagers also had experience with organizations. In the 1920s–early 1950s most villagers in the delta belonged to associations and engaged in collaborative activities for matters ranging from the supernatural to the practi-

8. Woodside, *Community*, 154.

9. Regarding Vietnam, see Rambo, *Comparison*. Regarding "closed" and "open" villages, see Eric Wolf's seminal articles, "Types" and "Closed Corporate Peasant Communities."

10. For a discussion of attachment to neighborhood and hamlets in rural villages, see Nguyen Tu Chi, "Traditional Viet Village," 60–67.

11. Woodside, *Community*, 148.

12. Fforde, "Historical Background," 93.

cal.[13] There were often associations to care for Buddhist temples, Catholic churches, and village shrines; to prepare for celebrations and festivals; to maintain irrigation canals; and to lend money. There were also organizations among families with similar trades (ceramic making, wood carving, weaving, etc.) and organizations to administer communal land. Perhaps most ubiquitous were groups in which members helped one another with various tasks. Some specialized in mutual assistance for weddings or funerals. Others were more general. One man in Ha Tay province recalled: "When I was growing up [in the 1940s], my parents and neighbors helped each other do farm work, repair houses, and cook during ceremonies." An elderly villager in rural Hanoi said of the mutual assistance group he and his family were part of: "If I were fixing my house and needed some help to carry sand and brick, then people in the exchange group would assist. I'd also help anyone else in the group."[14]

In addition to a history of organizations and mutual exchange, many delta villages had a deep involvement in resistance and revolution against colonial rule, particularly the protracted war against the French army (1946–1954). Out of that era also emerged most of the local leaders for the early years of collectivization. The Communist Party itself had only about 168,000 members by the late 1940s. Over half were from the peasantry. While the party grew slowly, the military force opposing the French increased rapidly, from several thousand soldiers in 1945 to about four hundred thousand by 1954. Supporting those forces in the early 1950s were two million or more guerrillas and local militia.[15] Several times as many men, women, and youngsters supplied food, shelter, hiding places, and information to allies and denied the same to opposition forces. Consequently, probably more than one-third of rural households in the delta were directly involved in organized efforts to defeat the French and support the revolution.[16]

13. Studying villagers in the 1930s in northern Vietnam (then called the Tonkin), the French ethnographer Pierre Gourou wrote, "The most outstanding characteristic of the social life of the Tonkinese village is the tendency that the peasants have to form groups." Gourou, *Peasants*, 312; also see 313–17. Also see Nguyen Tu Chi, "Traditional Viet Village"; To Lan, "On Communal Land," 173–89; Tran Duc, *Hop Tac trong Nong Thon*, chap. 1; and Nguyen Duc Nghinh, "Lang Xa," 436–39, 441.

14. Interviews, Nghiem Xuyen, Ha Tay, 12 May 1993, and Da Ton, Hanoi, 22 March 1996.

15. Figures are from Fall, *Viet-Minh Regime*, 35, 72; Elliott, "Revolutionary Re-integration," 295; and Van Tao, "Vai Net," 22.

16. Many commissioned local histories recount what villagers did during the upheavals of 1945–1954. Scholarship on the subject in English is sparse. Two informative examples are Hy Van Luong, *Revolution*, chap. 4; Kleinen, *Facing*, chap. 4.

*Addressing Shared Problems Collectively*

A third condition is that people be willing to cooperate to develop solutions for common problems. People in the Red River delta were willing to address collaboratively food shortages and other vexed issues. The Communist Party government's prescription, however, involved cooperation that went far beyond what villagers had done in the past. Collective farming meant that production and distribution went from being primarily household-based to being communal. Many people had doubts about this shift. As discussion about collective cooperatives spread across the delta in 1957–1958, many villagers grew concerned. Would they be free to do something other than work for the cooperative? Women wondered: If they were doing collective work every day, would they have time to spend with their families, to care for their kids and look after the sick? How would people too young or too old to work be supported? Would people still be permitted to raise pigs and grow vegetables in yards? Would they have to give their gardens, fruit trees, and fish ponds to the cooperative? Some had heard that being in a cooperative meant having to ask permission just to kill and eat one's own chicken. Teenagers asked if they would still have time to play. Villagers also wondered whether they could endure working all day next to people they disliked. Farmers who were also carpenters, weavers, and blacksmiths worried that they would not be able to practice their other trades. Farming households who also sold products at markets or had other small businesses feared that the cooperative would snuff out those sources of their income.[17]

The main question rural families pondered was how collective farming would affect their incomes. Poor peasants' economic priority was to assure their subsistence. Which was less risky, they wondered, farming separately or collectively? The question families, including those with party members, were asking, said a 1958 report from Ta Ngan zone, was if they formed cooperatives, "would they have enough to eat." In Kien An province within the zone, peasants worried that harvests in a cooperative might "be small," resulting in people being "hungry or short of food."[18] In places where living conditions had started to improve, people wondered whether the

17. TCT Co So Ty VH Son Tay, "BCSK, 1 Thang, Tham Gia Lao Dong" [Assignment team, Cultural office, Son Tay, "Joining workers"], 31 August 1958, 3 (P BVH, hs 911, vv); Le Huy, "BCCT" [Six months], Ta Ngan, 23 July 1958, 4; and TCT VH, "BCSK" [Assignment], Hung Tien, Kien An, 13 August 1958, 6–7.

18. Le Huy, "BCCT" [Six months], Ta Ngan, 23 July 1958, 4; TCT VH, "BCSK" [Assignment], Hung Tien, Kien An, 13 August 1958, 7.

trend would continue. Paddy production had markedly increased and food was more available than it had been for years (see appendix 1, table 1). For these improvements many villagers credited land reform and the Communist Party government.[19] But would collective farming make things even better?

## *Trust*

A fourth political condition is that people have sufficient trust in themselves and in their leaders to attempt a collaborative approach to addressing shared problems. Vietnamese authorities were acutely aware that villagers were dubious about collective farming. To engender greater trust among villagers in one another and the collective method, national and local authorities purposefully took an incremental approach. "Don't be impatient, don't make cooperatives quickly and hastily," Ho Chi Minh instructed a May 1955 conference organized by the party's national headquarters. Statements from that meeting stressed that "agricultural transformation must pass through a very long stage and be made step by step." In August the party's Central Executive Committee resolved that creating socialism in the countryside required "passing through each form of mutual help and cooperation, from low level to high, gradually getting peasants voluntarily to go down the road of collective work."[20]

The foundations on which to gradually build collective cooperatives, party leaders decided, would be three types of work exchange groups. In the basic group, villagers would exchange labor for a particular task or during a particular season (*to doi cong tung vu, tung viec*). This was similar to old mutual assistance, which party leaders believed contained a "germ of socialism" from which collective farming would sprout.[21] With practice, this basic group was supposed to evolve into a "regular labor exchange team" (*to doi cong thuong xuyen*) in which members helped one another season after season. From this villagers would then establish groups based on work points (*to doi cong binh cong cham diem*). Members would award "work points" (*cong diem*) for the work each person did. That way, everyone would

19. Cuc Xuat Ban, "BC, Net Chung ve Cong Viec, 18/11/58–15/3/59, huyen Dong Quan, Thai Binh" [publishing unit, "Assignment, Dong Quan district, Thai Binh"], n.d. [circa March 1959], 2 (P BVH, hs 911, vv).

20. The quotations appear in Nguyen Quang Hong, "Tu Tuong," N2–N3, one of several reports on collectivization done in the early 1990s at the Communist Party's school, Hoc Vien Nguyen Ai Quoc.

21. Bui Cong Trung and Luu Quang Hoa, Hop Tac Hoa, 8.

contribute and benefit more or less equally. Authorities expected that better harvests and other positive experiences flowing from this progression of work exchanges would deepen people's trust in one another and show them the benefits of close collaboration.

Then, authorities said, villages would construct the initial form of collective farming, called a "low-level agricultural production cooperative" (*hop tac xa san xuat nong nghiep bac thap*).[22] Households would pool their land, water buffaloes, oxen, and labor, then collectively farm, raise livestock, and produce other things. The quality and quantity of each member's labor would be measured in work points. Each member would receive a share of net collective earnings according to the number of points earned. Because fields still belonged to the members, the cooperative would also pay each one for the use of the land (*hoa loi cho ruong dat*). It might also pay for using members' draft animals. Once production had improved, the fully collectivized "high-level agricultural cooperative" (*hop tac xa san xuat nong nghiep bac cao*) would be established. Fields would no longer be identified with individual families; payments for use of land and draft animals would no longer be made. Members would earn a share of collective earnings only through work points.

Even while the nation was still at war with the French, Communist Party leaders had encouraged labor exchange teams and agricultural cooperatives. In 1950, northern Vietnam had about 7,700 exchange teams that the party claimed it had organized.[23] At about that time, approximately 980 cooperatives dotted the countryside in northern Vietnam, 81 percent of them in Interzone 3 (*Lien Khu 3*), which included several provinces in and around the Red River delta.[24] The cooperatives in Interzone 3 averaged sixty-one people (roughly ten to twelve households) farming about one hectare of land (3.15 *mau*).[25] Information about these cooperatives is sparse, but apparently members contributed some land, money, and labor to farm and, in some places, to fish and do other work together. They also retained land for their own use and farmed it separately.

It was difficult to sustain these young cooperatives during wartime. Those in Interzone 3 that managed to endure often had to "operate secretly in

22. Also planned were cooperatives for other activities. I have not investigated them but am told they were usually folded into the farming cooperatives.

23. Bui Cong Trung and Luu Quang Hoa, *Hop Tac Hoa*, 9. This source also says that south-central Vietnam had about 3,700 and southern Vietnam in 1949 had about 11,600.

24. Ibid., *Hop Tac Hoa*, 9.

25. Kinh Te LK 3, "TH HTX, 1949" [Interzone 3, Economics, "Cooperatives, 1949"], 7 February 1950, table after page 15 (P UBKCHC LK 3, hs 2187, vv). The interzone had 884 agriculture (and fish culture) cooperatives; 443 were in Thai Binh province.

very narrow spaces and in disguised forms."[26] When the fighting ended in mid-1954, few of these cooperatives had survived. One reason besides the war, according to reports, was that the understanding of collective work was "very superficial." Moreover, because land reform had not yet been done, land inequality and the old class structure undermined the cooperatives.[27]

In mid-1955, the Communist Party government began a concerted effort to form work exchange groups, often in conjunction with the land reform that was still under way. In August, following the Central Executive Committee's conference, the party's national leadership also decided to experiment with cooperatives in order to accumulate experience, train organizers, and establish good examples so that peasants could see the advantages of graduating from exchanging labor to farming together.[28]

Labor exchange groups in 1955–1957 usually started when local party members convened village meetings to stress the merits of collaborative work and production. Delegations from higher party offices and government ministries also met with local authorities, party cells, and units of the Women's Association, Peasants' Association, and Youth League to explain policies for "rebuilding the countryside" and farming together. The Ministry of Culture sent staff to villages to explain how and why labor exchanges and, later, cooperatives should be formed. Such activities, the Ministry of Culture believed, would "destroy backward thinking and hesitation" and "push the movement forward."[29] Ministry employees organized skits and plays and showed films about work exchange groups and cooperatives. Initially the films were from China, despite complaints that they were inappropriate for Vietnam. Eventually the government produced its own.

Events in Da Ton, rural Hanoi, illustrate what occurred in many places in the delta. Basic work exchange groups teams began in 1956 after land reform in the subdistrict had been completed and at the instigation of local officials, usually party members. Each group had five to twenty families, usually in the same neighborhood (*xom*). Anyone except former landlords could join.[30] Each group had a leader (*to truong*) and some had an assistant

26. Giam Doc Khu Kinh Te 3, "BCTK, 1950" [Economy director, "Report, 1950"], 8 February 1951, 4 (P UBKCHC LK 3, hs 2219, vv).

27. Kinh Te LK3, "TH HTX" [Cooperatives], Interzone 3, 7 February 1950, 14; and Bui Cong Trung and Luu Quang Hoa, *Hop Tac Hoa*, 9.

28. Cited in Nguyen Quang Hong, "Tu Tuong," N2, also N7.

29. Le Thanh Cong, Bo Truong BVH, "BCCT, NT, NN, 3 Nam" [Le Thanh Cong, Minister's Office, MC, "Three-year report"], 13 February 1959, 2–3 (P BVH, hs 934, vv).

30. In 1955, thirty-four families in the subdistrict had been classified as landlords. When mistakes were corrected in 1957, four were reclassified as rich peasants and six were verified as prorevolution landlords, leaving twenty-four when labor exchange groups began (Tran Quoc

(*to pho*), but members did not go through the leader to arrange exchanges, and being in one exchange group did not prevent someone from exchanging labor with people in different groups. Exchanges were simple. "No money changed hands, no evaluation of work was done," recalled one man. "We just helped each other. . . . No counting up the hours, no thinking of the pluses and minuses" (*khong suy nghi hon thiet*). For instance, said another, "if you worked for someone for three days, then that person would, in return, work three days for you. Other than that, each would just feed the other rice and vegetables on the day work was done."[31]

Basic labor exchange groups spread quickly. By the end of 1956, half of rural northern households were in them. During 1957, however, the proportion fell to about 20 percent (appendix 1, table 2). A major reason for the decline was the excesses of land reform.

Redistributing land had involved classifying households according to such criteria as their property, whether they had hired people or used tenants, and whether they had lent money for profit. Those deemed to be landlords—the class most vulnerable in these circumstances—were further differentiated. The worst were "wicked and tyrannical" (*cuong hao gian ac*). The least abhorrent had supported the revolution and fought against the French (*dia chu khang chien*). They still had to surrender land and other major possessions but were not supposed to be punished or killed. Not only landlord families were vulnerable. So were "rich peasants" (*phu nong*) who had paid low wages to hired laborers or charged high interest when lending money.

The process was divisive and violent. Some villagers made false accusations against neighbors for reasons having nothing to do with land ownership, tenancy conditions, or usury. Many who had joined the revolution were not recognized as having done so. Party members sometimes accused one another of wrongdoing. Superiors instructed land reform teams to find abusive landlords and rich peasants even when villages had none. Many people were wrongly classified and punished. In a subdistrict in Son Tay province, for instance, fifty-two of the fourteen hundred households were classified as landlords: fifteen as wicked, thirty-six as regular, and one as prorevolution. After corrections, it had but twenty-two landlords, only five

---

Vuong et al., *Da Ton*, 87, 89). Just prior to land reform, residents said, the subdistrict had approximately one thousand households and about fifteen hundred *mau* of agricultural land, one-third of which landlords owned.

31. Interviews, Da Ton, 20 January and 22 March 1996.

of whom were wicked.[32] For the country as whole, more than half of those who had been called landlords were reclassified.[33]

While correcting classifications helped to calm growing discontent and restore confidence in the party and its government, the excesses and the correction project itself hampered other programs, particularly the creation of labor exchange groups and cooperatives. To rectify land reform excesses as expeditiously as possible, many personnel were diverted from other projects. Teams from the Ministry of Culture assigned to establish libraries or stage performances, for instance, were sidetracked for months to correct land reform mistakes.[34] People sent by provincial offices to help villages organize mutual exchange groups ended up instead dealing with land reform problems. Village officials and party members were preoccupied with reclassifying households, attending to complaints, and resolving altercations among villagers. In some places quarrels among officials and party members over mistakes made during land reform prevented anything else from being done. Consequently, as a report on provincial administration in Ha Nam concluded, authorities in 1956 gave little attention to mutual exchange groups.[35] Not until mid-1957 were local leaders in the north able to concentrate on organizing or reviving labor exchange teams.[36]

In many villages, lingering wrath and animosity greatly handicapped organizers' efforts to get people to work together. Villagers in Ha Dong province, for example, who had been falsely accused and unjustly punished were "indignant" (uat uc). It was little comfort, at least initially, that Ho Chi Minh and other prominent authorities had acknowledged the mistakes. "Heated arguments continued to break out between wrongly accused and their accusers, between wrongly punished and those who had punished them." Villagers argued over fields that had been divided, asserting claims and counterclaims as to who had rights to the land. Some altercations became violent. At least three people in the province were killed. While hostilities had declined by late 1956, animosities still "smoldered" (am y). Many villagers could not farm in peace, fearing their fields would be overrun or their crops destroyed by others claiming the land. Getting people to farm together was virtually impossible.[37]

32. TCT Thuc Te Son Tay, "BC TH To Can Bo" [Report, MC team], 5 August 1958, 2.
33. Moise, Land Reform, 261–62.
34. Reports from MC assignment teams, 1956–1957 (P BVH, vv).
35. UBHC Ha Nam, "BC Chung Nien" [1956 report], 8 February 1957, 10.
36. "BCTK CT Xay Dung Thi Diem HTX SXNN, du thao" ["Experimental cooperatives"], n.d. [circa September 1957], 32 (P UBKHNN, hs 616, tt). The report was probably prepared by the party's BCTNT for an October 1957 conference.
37. UBHC, Ha Dong, "BCTK," 20 January 1957, 1–2.

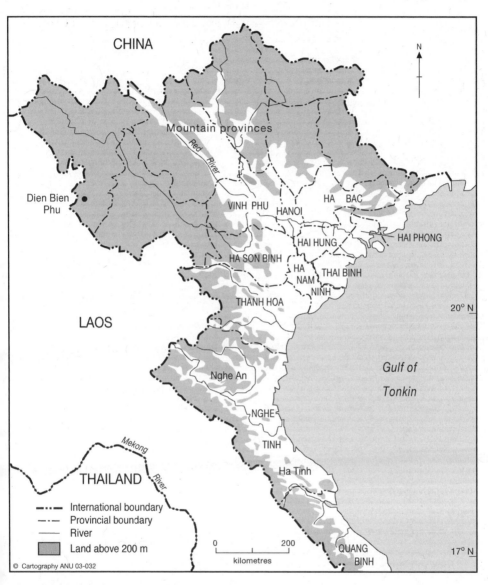

*Map 1.* Northern Vietnam, circa 1990.

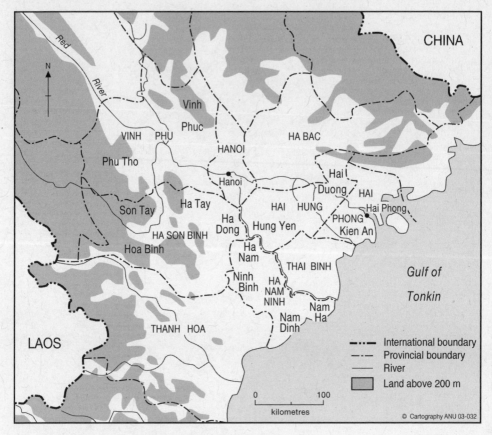

*Map 2.* Provinces in and around the Red River delta; circa 1990.

Because of discord and the diversion of resources away from labor exchange groups, many collapsed. Ninh Binh province in January 1957 had 8,333 groups, but as a result of land reform mistakes and subsequent difficulties, the groups were nearly inactive.[38] In much of Ha Nam province, labor exchange groups had "virtually disintegrated" (*hau nhu tan ra*) because officials were preoccupied with correcting land reform mistakes and villagers were no longer enthusiastic.[39] A 1957 report concluded that through-

38. Tran Tinh, UBHC Ninh Binh, "TK, Ket Qua, Thieu So, Ke Hoach Nam 1956" [Tran Tinh, Administrative Committee, Ninh Binh province, "Results, limitations, 1956 state plan"], 20 January 1957, 4 (P UBKCHC LK 3, hs 125, vv).

39. UBHC Ha Nam, "BC Chung Nien" [1956 report], 8 February 1957, 10.

out the north the "labor exchange movement . . . has deteriorated a lot."
While some groups were recovering, "many others remain very weak."[40]

Adversities due to land reform excesses continued beyond 1957. In mid-1958, the zone of Ta Ngan, for instance, had to send forty staff members
to help officials in several villages who were still weighed down by prob-
lems arising from the land reform mistakes.[41] In August 1958, "basically
good people" in a subdistrict of Hai Duong province were "talking non-
sense" against cooperatives "because they were dissatisfied" with the land
reform process.[42] Throughout the province, said a September 1958 report,
"unity . . . even after mistakes are corrected is not solid." "At times peasants who were reclassified to lower [more acceptable] categories verbally
attack and abuse the core cadres" who had misclassified them in the first
place, even though the individuals in question no longer had any authority. "The masses" in several places still thought little of authorities and party
members who had badly implemented land reform yet remained in office.
This atmosphere undermined Hai Duong authorities' efforts to persuade
people to join cooperatives.[43]

Although some families remained silently angry about the whole episode
for decades, officials reported that animosities dissipated after 1957. The
"seething complaints and unease" (thac mac soi noi) among villagers and
many local officials that initially confronted error correction teams in Ha
Nam province, for instance, were "gradually" replaced with "feelings of
unity" as misclassifications were corrected and people falsely accused or
imprisoned were cleared of wrongdoing. Officials in another province
observed that while some residents remained bitter in 1958, generally they
"no longer complain[ed] very much" about land reform.[44] As rural conditions settled down, according to several other accounts in late 1957 and
1958, many work exchange groups recovered and authorities could focus
on expanding them and building cooperatives.

In Ha Dong province, for instance, during the first half of 1957 the work
exchange movement had proceeded in a "plodding" and "scattered" fashion.

40. "BCTK" [Experimental cooperatives], circa September 1957, 32.

41. Le Huy, "BCCT" [Six months], Ta Ngan, 23 July 1958, 11. Earlier that year, Ta Ngan
officials found that half of the hundred-plus petitions from people objecting to their classifi-
cation or punishment were justified, 30 percent were not, and 20 percent needed further study.
Ban Thuong Vu, BCH Khu Ta Ngan, "NQ Hoi Nghi, Khu Uy" [Standing Committee, Ta Ngan
zone, "Resolution"], 21 February 1958, 1 (P UBHCKTN, hs 40, vv).

42. TCT, BVH, "BC So Luoc," Gia Tan, Hai Duong, 7 August 1958, 2.

43. TCT Hai Duong, BVH, "BC, 10/8/–31/8/1958, TCT" [Hai Duong Group, MC, "Assignment report, Hai Duong province"], 6 September 1958, 2 (P BVH, hs 911, vv).

44. UBHC Ha Nam, "BC Chung Nien" [1956 report], 8 February 1957, 4; TCT, BVH, "BC
So Luoc," Gia Tan, Hai Duong, 7 August 1958, 2.

Even many hamlet and village officials had not joined. In the second half of the year, however, the number of exchange groups rose significantly after officials, assisted by local chapters of the Peasants' Association (Nong Hoi), mobilized 210 of the province's 228 subdistricts to hold education and training sessions on how work exchange teams could overcome equipment and water buffalo shortages and address other farming problems.[45] Similarly, in a subdistrict of Kien An province the number of labor exchange teams, which had dropped from fifty-nine in 1956 to twenty-two in 1957, rebounded to sixty-four by August 1958. Already 67 percent of households were members; soon, said the report, it would be 80 percent.[46] In the four delta provinces within Ta Ngan zone, 40 percent of households were in exchange groups in mid-1958, nearly as many as a year before. Villagers, said a Ta Ngan official, particularly appreciated working together to repair irrigation canals and recover from a recent drought.[47] Across the north, 66 percent of northern Vietnam's rural households were in work exchange groups by the end of 1958, triple the 1957 percentage and more than the 1956 figure (appendix 1, table 2).

Meanwhile, authorities increased the number of "experimental cooperatives" to thirty-three by mid-1957. All but two were "low-level." They averaged thirteen households and fifty-two people each. The smallest (in Phu Ca, Phu Tho province) had but three households. The largest (in Yen Dong, Thanh Hoa province) had forty-four. The average land area per cooperative was nearly ten hectares.[48] By mid-1958, the number of cooperatives had risen to one hundred and thirty-four and they were sprinkled across most provinces in northern Vietnam.

Villagers in these early collective cooperatives had apparently come up through the ranks, so to speak. They had first been members of simple work exchange groups, then regular ones, followed by work point–based ones before forming "low-level" collective cooperatives. A hamlet in the poorest part of one subdistrict in Hai Duong province provides an example of this progression. Most of the hamlet's families before land reform had "fished a little and were wage laborers." After land

45. Ngo Van Thin, pho chu nhiem, UBKH Ha Dong, "BCTK, KHNN, 1957" [Ngo Van Thin, vice chair, Planning Committee, Ha Dong province, "Report, 1957 plan"], 14 March 1958, 2 (P UBKCHC LK 3, hs 127, vv).

46. TCT VH, "BCSK" [Assignment], Hung Tien, Kien An, 13 August 1958, 4.

47. Le Huy, "BCCT" [Six months], Ta Ngan, 23 July 1958, 3.

48. "BCTK" [Experimental cooperatives], circa September 1957, 2, 11. By region, province (and number of cooperatives per province): Red River delta, Ninh Binh (2), Thai Binh (2); midlands, Phu Tho (10), Vinh Phuc (3); mountain areas, Moc Chau (1), Thai Nguyen (4); central, Ha Tinh (1), Nghe An (1), Thanh Hoa (9).

reform, several families formed labor exchange teams. By early 1957, some of those teams were using work points. By May 1958, twenty-six families combined their 11.5 hectares to create a collective cooperative. Shortly thereafter the members expanded their collective work to include pork production by borrowing money from a government bank to purchase thirty-five pigs.[49]

Generally speaking, people classified during land reform as "poorest peasants" (*ban co nong*, about half of rural northern Vietnam) and "lower middle peasants" (*trung nong duoi*) were more interested than "middle peasants" (*trung nong*) in joining the experimental cooperatives.[50] In some instances, however, such as the first cooperative in Kien An province, more middle peasants signed up than poor ones.[51] Early joiners expected collective cooperatives to better assure their subsistence. They reasoned that cooperatives would provide them with enough to eat even if they fell ill or for some other reason could not work. Peasants who had already sold their land because they were in such dire straits joined in order to have a way to make a living. Others assumed that a cooperative would save them from having to sell their land should they fall into debt. They reasoned that if they were in a cooperative in which their fields, though collectively farmed, still belonged to them, their land would be safe.[52] By pooling their resources, early joiners also expected to have plows, carts, and other equipment that individually they could not afford; water control systems for droughts and floods; and higher production.[53] Moreover, the cooperative's payment for the use of their fields would help them meet their basic needs.

The payment for land was either a fixed or a variable percentage of the crop. Available evidence does not indicate which method villagers preferred but does suggest that they tried to get as high a figure as possible. Early cooperatives typically paid between 35 and 40 percent of the gross harvest for use of members' fields, percentages that authorities subsequently deemed too high. Some peasants reportedly calculated that "without doing any work they could have enough to live on just from payments for their

49. TCT BVH, "BC So Luoc," Gia Tan, Hai Duong, 7 August 1958, 3.
50. "BCTK" [Experimental cooperatives], circa September 1957, 9. People classified as "rich peasants" and landlords were not permitted to join until the early 1960s.
51. The cooperative had eighteen middle peasant households and sixteen poor ones. TCT VH, "BCSK" [Assignment], Hung Tien, Kien An, 13 August 1958, 5.
52. TCT VH, "BCSK" [Assignment], Hung Tien, Kien An, 13 August 1958, 6; interviews, Nghiem Xuyen, Ha Tay, May 1993, and Da Ton, Hanoi, April 1993, January–April 1996.
53. TCT VH, "BCSK" [Assignment], Hung Tien, Kien An, 13 August 1958, 7–8; Le Huy, "BCCT" [Six months], Ta Ngan, 23 July 1958, 4; "BCTK" [Experimental cooperatives], circa September 1957, 9.

land and water buffaloes."[54] Similarly, a 1958 study in Kien An province found many villagers were far more concerned about being paid for the use of their fields than about doing collective farming.[55]

While some villagers readily joined the early cooperatives, many others remained ambivalent or decided not to join. Large numbers of people in villages with these cooperatives had "divided minds" (ban khoan). They sat on the fence, "arguing with themselves and one another" about the "individual, private way of work, which was familiar to them, compared to the collective and public good way of thinking, which was still immature and green."[56] Some households quit soon after joining. As of mid-1957, 541 families had joined experimental cooperatives but 226 (42 percent) had left again. Eighty percent of the quitters were poor peasants, amounting to nearly half of the poor who had joined. The rest were middle peasants, who accounted for 38 percent of joiners from that class. Also among the quitters were 41 percent of the 112 Communist Party members who had joined. The large percentage of people leaving, combined with other problems, resulted in the disintegration of at least one-fourth and possibly up to one-half of the forty-two experimental cooperatives that had existed in 1956. Several were revived, bringing the number back up to thirty-three by mid-1957. But nine (21 percent of the forty-two) had completely collapsed, despite repeated efforts to reestablish them.[57]

People left or decided not to join mainly because they thought their economic situation would be better if they did.[58] To many villagers, giving their fields, water buffaloes, oxen, and other means of farming to the cooperative meant surrendering their livelihood. They doubted that cooperatives could continue to pay them for their land or decided that the payment was too small. Many feared that after working all season in a cooperative, they would receive little in return, especially during the initial years when this new way of farming would face numerous problems. Often villagers reasoned that being a cooperative member meant losing their freedom to do other work. After observing the cooperatives in their area, they calculated that they made more as hired workers and through other means than cooperative members earned. Many people insisted that, were they to enter a cooperative, they would have to be allowed to keep for themselves their

54. "BCTK" [Experimental cooperatives], circa September 1957, 13, also 12, 16, 24.
55. TCT VH, "BCSK" [Assignment], Hung Tien, Kien An, 13 August 1958, 7.
56. TCT Hai Duong, "BC, 10/8–31/8/1958" [Assignment], 6 September 1958, 3; TCT VH, "BCSK" [Assignment], Hung Tien, Kien An, 13 August 1958, 12.
57. "BCTK" [Experimental cooperatives], circa September 1957, 6–7, 26.
58. Ibid., 7, 9, 10, 30.

gardens, fish ponds, and hilly areas because those areas were vital for their livelihood.[59] In a subdistrict of Son Tay province, residents told officials "sullenly and resentfully" (doi) that if their tea gardens (vuon che) had to be put into the cooperative, "then one may as well put everything in there just to make things neat and tidy" (cho gon chuyen).[60]

A key issue affecting villagers' assessments of cooperatives was production results. According to a lengthy 1957 study, "Whether peasants join a cooperative or not depends on whether the cooperative can increase harvests and assure members a higher income."[61] Similarly, a report from Ta Ngan zone observed that if people did not have a higher income from farming collectively than from farming individually or in labor exchange groups, they did not want to join.[62] Skeptical villagers typically stood back and observed "the work and yields of cooperative farming, waiting to see real, concrete advantages before they joined."[63] One or two seasons of good results from cooperatives convinced some watchful people to sign up. Others wanted more evidence, saying that "proof would be in seasons yet to come."[64] One disappointing experience could reinforce people's skepticism. Let us take a village in Hai Duong as an example. Results from the local experimental cooperative's first harvest in August 1958 were "not yet really high" but were promising. Later that year, the cooperative failed to find water even after members had invested time and money drilling for it. Consequently, vegetables and sweet potatoes planted as subsidiary crops could not be adequately irrigated. The yields were meager. Meanwhile, households in a nearby village who were not in a cooperative had bountiful harvests of tomatoes, kohlrabi, and other vegetables. The contrast prompted many villagers to question the value of a cooperative in which members "work like crazy, transplant seedlings densely, follow a schedule,

59. TCT BVH, "BC So Luoc," Gia Tan, Hai Duong, 7 August 1958, 3; TCT Co So, "BCSK" [Joining workers], Son Tay, 31 August 1958, 3; Dang Huy Thong, To Truong, TCT, Cam Thuong, "BCSK, 1–1959, Tham Gia Lao Dong, Thi Diem, Cam Thuong, Son Tay" [Dang Huy Thong, leader, project team, Cam Thuong subdistrict, "Experimental work, Cam Thuong, Son Tay province"], 29 January 1959, 2 (P BVH, hs 942, vv).

60. Dang Huy Thong, "BCSK" [Experimental work], Cam Thuong, Son Tay, 29 January 1959, 2.

61. "BCTK" [Experimental cooperatives], circa September 1957, 30, see also 6.

62. BCH Khu Ta Ngan, DLDVN, "Nhiem Vu Xay Dung, Cung Co HTX SXNN 6 Thang, 1958" [EC, Ta Ngan zone, VWP, "Cooperatives, second half 1958"], 19 September 1958, 2 (P UBHCKTN, hs 40, vv).

63. Tran Lam, To Truong, VH, UBHC Hai Duong, Ty VH, "BCSK, 21/11–25/12/58, Tham Gia Lao Dong, Thi Diem, Hai Duong" [Tran Lam, group leader, Cultural office, Hai Duong province, "Joining workers, experimental cultural work"], 17 January 1959, 2 (P BVH, hs 942, vv).

64. TCT Hai Duong, "BC, 10/8–31/8/1958" [Assignment], 6 September 1958, 2.

and are coerced and not free to relax [*go ep khong duoc tu do thoai mai*], yet harvest little."[65]

What villagers saw or heard regarding cooperative farming compared to household farming was probably often inconclusive. Cooperatives in Ta Ngan zone, for instance, reportedly had higher yields than households. In Son Tay province, however, household farming usually surpassed cooperative farming.[66] The one comparative study I located for the early cooperatives found it difficult to draw clear conclusions. Numerous variables—weather, quality of land, health and strength of farmers, quality and quantity of draft animals—could account for differences. Isolating the key variables—collective farming and household farming—was virtually impossible. The best the report writers could conclude was that in well-managed cooperatives in which labor and draft animals were efficiently used and members worked well together, total production and members' income compared favorably to what households farming individually or in work exchange groups accomplished. A significant problem, however, was that few cooperatives had those qualities.[67]

In most cooperatives, shortcomings were numerous. A prominent weakness was discord among members. "Even brothers in the same family can not work together," villagers said, "so how can many different families possibly farm together?"[68] In a district of Thanh Hoa province, cooperative members were quick to criticize and "envy" one another, often "over the smallest things" (*ken cua, ganh ty*). Even leaders squabbled. The heads of two production teams in a cooperative of Kien An province, for example, scuffled over a tin can used for measuring rice.[69] Cooperative members often argued over who should do what work, how it should be done, or why it was not done. So prevalent were such disputes that a saying spread: "Wherever many people are working, there's a cooperative; wherever people are arguing, that's also a cooperative."[70]

65. Tran Lam, "BCSK" [Joining workers], Hai Duong, 17 January 1959, 2; also TCT, BVH, "BC So Luoc," Gia Tan, Hai Duong, 7 August 1958, 3–4.

66. Le Huy, "BCCT" [Six months], Ta Ngan, 23 July 1958, 4; TCT Co So, "BCSK" [Joining workers], Son Tay, 31 August 1958, 2.

67. "BCTK" [Experimental cooperatives], circa September 1957, 2–6.

68. "Chi may anh em mot nha ma khong lam chung duoc voi nhau thi lam the nao ma co the giai quyet so dong gia dinh lam chung voi nhau duoc." "BCTK" [Experimental cooperatives], circa September 1957, 24.

69. Le Nguyen Thanh, Ty VH, Thanh Hoa, "BCSK, Thuc Te Hoang Quy" [Le Nguyen Thanh, cultural office, Thanh Hoa province, "Field study in Hoang Quy"], 26 January 1959, 2 (P BVH, hs 942, vv); TCT VH, "BCSK" [Assignment], Hung Tien, Kien An, 13 August 1958, 5.

70. "Cho nao lam dong la hop tac xa ma cho nao to tieng cung la hop tac xa." "BCTK" [Experimental cooperatives], circa September 1957, 19.

Getting members to work diligently was another vexing problem. Before cooperatives, people "put in a lot of energy, hard work, capital, and fertilizer; whether the harvest was big or small, it didn't matter," said one provincial study. "But now in the cooperative, peasants calculate each time they carry fertilizer to the field, each bit of work done, each measure of rice. And when the share of the harvest that ends up in their hands is small they complain and think that by joining a cooperative they're suffering a loss."[71] When people saw no connection between doing a task (or not doing it) and a personal benefit (or harm), they might well ignore it. A study on experimental cooperatives complained that when cows grazed in paddy fields or when irrigation water was not going where it should, cooperative members did not remove the cows from the fields or dam the water. "Leave it to the administrative committee," people would say. Villagers also frequently worked sloppily in collective fields; they were "primarily interested in getting the job done quickly so as to earn more work points." Doing the job well was not a high priority in their thinking. A common attitude among members was "vie for the easy work, avoid the heavy work."[72] And they neglected collectively owned property. According to a 1958 account, before joining cooperatives, peasants "cleaned and nicely cared for their farming tools. . . . But now [as cooperative members], they leave the equipment topsy-turvy, lying about, and dirty. They don't yet see the cooperative as belonging to them."[73] Members also hid grain. When threshing, for instance, they intentionally left kernels on stalks, which later their children gleaned and took home, thereby increasing the family's supply but diminishing what was divided among all members. Because they knew that these things were happening, people became suspicious of one another.[74]

Snitching grain, shirking work, and the like are also typical ways agricultural workers and tenants in other agrarian settings resist landowners, landlords, or others who underpay them, abuse them, or charge excessive land rent.[75] Whether Vietnamese cooperative members in the mid-1950s saw their actions as resistance is unclear given the available evidence. But the case of one poor peasant suggests they sometimes may have. According to a 1958 report from Hai Duong province, he spoke for others when he complained that "working for the cooperative day in and day out is like

71. TCT Co So, "BCSK" [Joining workers], Son Tay, 31 August 1958, 3.
72. "BCTK" [Experimental cooperatives], circa September 1957, 19, 24.
73. TCT VH, "BCSK" [Assignment], Hung Tien, Kien An, 13 August 1958, 7.
74. "BCTK" [Experimental cooperatives], circa September 1957, 23, 24.
75. Scott, Weapons; Kerkvliet, Everyday Politics.

working for a landlord without even knowing what the result will be."[76] Many people, according to another source, thought cooperative managers were "like landlords" of the past—always telling them what to do and "criticizing them for their shoddy work." A "rather common" attitude among cooperative members was that "they are laborers hired by the cooperative, hence they have no concern for how work was done and no respect for discipline."[77] People also often complained that they had little voice in governing the collective cooperatives. Possibly, therefore, when members took grain while harvesting or shaved time from their workday—tactics they had probably used when laboring as tenants and hired laborers—they thought they were not hurting themselves or other members but were getting some advantage for themselves at the expense of this new entity to which they felt no obligation and may have felt some resentment.

The underlying reason why villagers shirked collective work, lamented a 1957 study of the experimental organizations, was that the "consciousness among members that they are working to build a cooperative remains deficient."[78] In Son Tay, for instance, villagers entered cooperatives "without really believing in them, still dragging their feet, keeping their ears perked, in anticipation, ready to leave if harvests are poor."[79] The 1957 study concluded that the "socialist consciousness" of many villagers, including several Communist Party members, "remains very weak whereas their orientation for individual production and private property [tu tuong rieng le tu huu] remains very strong."[80] Even in cooperatives with many enthusiastic members, "collective consciousness is still feeble" while "individual production and private property thinking is common."[81]

Overall, the collective cooperative experiments had proved by late 1957 or mid-1958 that considerable time and effort was required to allay villagers' doubts and create trust among them and in the new organizations. Even though most early cooperatives had been built on the foundation of advanced forms of labor exchange, several had collapsed. And in the

76. TCT Hai Duong, "BC, 10/8–31/8/1958" [Assignment], Hai Duong, 6 September 1958, 3.

77. "BCTK" [Experimental cooperatives], circa September 1957, 19, 24.

78. Ibid., 19.

79. TCT Co So, "BCSK" [Joining workers], Son Tay, 31 August 1958, 2.

80. "BCTK" [Experimental cooperatives], circa September 1957, 26.

81. TCT BVH, "BC So Luoc," Gia Tan, Hai Duong, 7 August 1958, 4. See also TCT VH HTX Vinh Bao K. An, "BC TH CT Buoc Hai, Bo Xung" [Cultural affairs team, Vinh Bao cooperative, Kien An province, "Second stage"], 10 September 1958, 1 (P BVH, hs 911, vv).

remaining ones, many members were unsure about staying. From the side-
lines, other villagers watched, curious but showing little enthusiasm for collective farming.

Labor exchange teams had a much broader appeal. Their problem for
collective farming advocates, however, was that most did not mature.
In a few places, such as Hung Tien subdistrict of Kien An province,
a majority of teams went beyond the basic forms. One of the most
impressive had fifteen households that helped one another farm as well as
raise and sell pigs, chickens, ducks, and other livestock. The group's
work point system had become so elaborate that in 1958 members
were fine-tuning how many points to give those who cooked for others
laboring in the fields.[82] That was the sort of standard that party leaders
wanted teams everywhere to achieve prior to establishing cooperatives. The
great majority of teams, however, were far less developed. In the entire
north by the end of 1958 only 28 percent were regular. The proportion
that used work points is unclear but it was probably less than 10 percent.[83]
In population terms, 66 percent of northern agricultural households
were in labor exchange groups by late 1958, but only 21 percent were in
regular ones and 8 percent were in groups using work points (appendix 1,
table 2).

Organizers encountered considerable difficulty persuading villagers to
switch from intermittent to regular labor exchanges. A subdistrict in Hai
Duong province, for instance, had sixty-four work exchange teams as of
August 1958, composing 87 percent of all households. Although the first
groups had begun in 1950, not until 1957 did a few become regular. A
year later, "most" were "still seasonal and piecemeal." And most of those,
complained observers, were "slack" (*long leo*)—"sometimes people joined
together, other times not" and "members' consciousness, generally speaking, remained low."[84] There and elsewhere, such as villages in Tam Dong
subdistrict of Vinh Phuc province, people were "ebullient" (*ram ro*) to
exchange labor at harvest time and on some other occasions but the rest
of the year they were uninterested.[85] In several provinces, exchange of labor
occurred so infrequently that many teams existed "in form only" (*hinh thuc*).

82. TCT VH, "BCSK" [Assignment], Hung Tien, Kien An, 13 August 1958, 5.
83. TCTK, "Nhung Chi Tieu, NN, 1955–1967" [GSO, "Agriculture, 1955–1967"], 1968, table
25, and table beginning "Tinh Hinh Doi Cong" (P UBKHNN, hs 1258, vv).
84. TCT BVN, "BC So Luoc," Gia Tan, Hai Duong, 7 August 1958, 3.
85. Tran Gia Bang, Truong ty, ty VH, Vinh Phuc, "BCTK, To Thi Diem, VH, Tam Dong,
11/58–2/59" [Trang Gia Bang, head, Cultural office, Vinh Phuc, "Cultural team, Tam Dong
subdistrict"], 31 March 1959, 2–3 (P BVH, hs 942, vv).

These teams were also described as "corpses without souls" (*chi co xac ma khong co hon*).[86]

## Autonomy

A fifth condition for the emergence of agrarian common-use organizations is that there be minimal interference from outsiders such as government agencies. This condition was not met in the Red River delta during the 1950s. If it had been, labor exchange teams might have continued and other forms of cooperation would likely have developed, though probably few of these would have been collective cooperatives.

Villagers in Vietnam were not the ones who decided how to proceed. Communist Party and government leaders, particularly in provincial and national circles, made the decisions. The prevalent view among leaders in late 1957, exemplified in an October conference convened by the party's Secretariat to assess the experimental cooperatives, was to continue the gradual course.[87] Thus far, said the conference report, neither production nor income was impressive, many management problems remained, and peasants were unenthusiastic. Consequently, it continued, the next few years should be focused on improving existing cooperatives, establishing advanced labor exchange groups, and training additional organizers and local officials to carry out these tasks. The report proposed that 234 cooperatives be built in 1958. Goals for 1960, it said, were to have labor exchange groups everywhere, to have 20 percent of farming households in "low-level" cooperatives, and to start experiments with "high-level" ones.[88]

By late 1958, however, the party's leaders had abandoned the gradual approach. Even though the extent to which "peasants had been won over to socialism" was "still low," a November 1958 resolution from the party's Central Executive Committee emphasized that collective farming had to proceed quickly. Specifically, by the end of 1960 collective cooperatives

86. "BC TH mot so Xa, Dong Quan (Thai Binh)" ["Report, Dong Quan district, Thai Binh," apparently from an MC team], 1958, 1–2 (P BVH, hs 911, vv); and Doan Can Bo Tham Gia Lao Dong,VH, Hai Phong, "BC Tham Gia Lao Dong, Nong Thon" [delegation, Hai Phong province's Cultural office, "Joining workers"], 28 March 1959, 1 (P BVH, hs 942, vv).

87. The Secretariat (*Ban Bi Thu Trung Uong*) together with the Political Bureau (*Bo Chinh Tri*) form the inner core of the Communist Party's national leadership circles.

88. Dang Tho Xuong et al., "Tong Thuat," 17. Also, Nguyen Quang Hong, "Tu Tuong," N7, N12–N14.

were to be established throughout the north and some were to be "high-level" ones.[89] An interim goal was to have 40 percent of all farming households in cooperatives and the rest in labor exchange teams using work points by the end of 1959. After completing cooperativization in 1960, all cooperatives were to be converted to "high-level" ones during 1961.[90]

Rushing to reach these goals, national authorities in 1959–1960 accelerated programs to train cooperative organizers.[91] National organizations for peasants, women, and youth mobilized members to aggressively support the "agricultural cooperativization movement" (*phong trao hop tac hoa nong nghiep*). Branches of the Peasants' Association, for instance, competed with one another to get villagers to enter cooperatives.[92] In ordering all education, culture, and science agencies to bolster the movement, the prime minister's office said that peasants were obliged to know the purpose of cooperatives, "to distinguish clearly the difference between the socialist road and the capitalist road for agriculture, to accept the essential correctness of the cooperative way to making a living over the private way of working," to be "won over to socialism," and to enter cooperatives for "love of country" and in order "to build a life for themselves with adequate food and clothing."[93]

Meanwhile, provincial and district authorities set local targets and mobilized resources accordingly. Officials in My Duc district of Ha Dong province, for example, decided in early 1959 to have at least 20 percent of rural households in cooperatives by mid-year. For the first three months, they worked with village leaders to strengthen and expand labor exchange groups, train villagers how to form and manage cooperatives, and establish ten experimental cooperatives. In April, while simultaneously helping villages to protect crops against an insect infestation and a drought, district officials stepped up the training of future cooperative leaders, sent some trainees to observe well-established cooperatives, and assisted villages in creating new cooperatives. By late May, officials claimed to have formed

89. BCHTU, DLDVN, "NQ, Hoi Nghi Trung Uong, lan thu 14," 6, 20–21.

90. Nguyen Quang Hong, "Tu Tuong," N17. Also see BCHTU, DLDVN, "NQ, Hoi Nghi Trung Uong, lan thu 16."

91. Nguyen Quang Hong, "Tu Tuong," N30–31, N34. Numerous articles in *Nhan Dan* also convey the urgency of cooperativization.

92. BCHTU, Hoi Nong Dan, va Vien Lich Su Dang, "De Cuong Chi Tiet," 52–53; interviews, Dao Duc, Vinh Phuc, 18 August 2000.

93. Thu Thuong Phu, "Cac Nganh Van Giao, HTHNN Nhu The Nao" [PMO, "Culture, education, cooperativization"], 29 June 1959, 2, also 1–7 (P BVH, hs 934, vv).

132 collective cooperatives with over 4,000 households, 27 percent of all farming families in the district.[94]

Collective cooperatives were often set up within weeks. Deputy Prime Minister Truong Chinh recommended "about 20 days"; a Communist Party assessment in mid-1959 said "15 to 20 days."[95] Typically, the process had three phases. The first was "propaganda, education, and training." A "mobilizing committee" (ban van dong) composed of a few villagers—usually party members—and district officials convened meetings, frequently at night, to explain to residents the purposes of cooperatives, elaborate the government's policy, distribute application forms, and answer questions. The second phase was an evaluation of the quality and worth of draft animals, tools, and land that the new members contributed to the cooperative. The final phase was the election of officers by members of the new organization, usually by nominations and a show of hands or balloting, and the drafting of rules based on a model provided by the mobilizing committee. Elected officers included a chairperson, vice-chair, accountant, and members of a managerial board. Soon after election, some or all of these officers had a few days of training in the district or provincial capital.[96]

In some places, nearly all eligible villagers joined cooperatives simultaneously. For example, in certain hamlets within Dao Duc and Quat Luu subdistricts, Vinh Phuc province, most households signed up during the first "wave" (dot) of mobilization. Elsewhere, including in some other parts of Dao Duc and Quat Luu, only some households initially joined.[97] But usually within the next few months, virtually all eligible households became members. In Da Ton subdistrict, for instance, a cooperative in Thuan Ton village began in 1959 with about thirty households. By mid-1960, after three waves, all peasant households in that village had joined. The collectivization drive also enlarged cooperatives established earlier. Da Ton's first cooperative had begun operations in February 1958 with seventeen or eighteen households in Dao Xuyen village. The flurry of meetings and other mobilizing activity in 1959 resulted in nearly every Dao Xuyen household joining.[98]

94. Nhan Dan, 18 September 1959, 2.

95. Truong Chinh, Resolutely, 73; BCTNT, "BCTK, HTHNN, 1958, 6 thang 1959, du thao" [RAC, "Cooperative movement, 1958, first half 1959"], n.d. [circa July 1959], 16 (P UBKHNN, hs 1258, vv).

96. Interviews, Da Ton, Hanoi; Nghiem Xuyen, Ha Tay; and Dao Duc and Tien Thang, Vinh Phuc.

97. Interviews, Dao Duc, 15–19 August 2000, and Quat Luu, 3 and 7 August 2000, Vinh Phuc.

98. Interviews, Da Ton, Hanoi, 1 and 10 February 1996.

Government statistics portray a highly successful campaign. By the end of 1958, the number of collective cooperatives had jumped to 4,720, a thirty-five-fold increase within a mere six months. Five percent of agricultural households were now in the cooperatives. A year later, 45 percent of farming households were members, and by the end of 1960, 86 percent had joined (see appendix 1, table 3). Most were in collective cooperatives the size of hamlets and neighborhoods. In July 1961 national party leaders deemed that the "cooperativization of agriculture at the low level" had "essentially been completed." Now, they said, the revolution in agricultural production could move to a new phase: enlarge the cooperatives to "village size of 150–200 households each" in the delta and midlands and convert them to "high-level" ones.[99]

### Debates over Timing and Process

To explain why this rapid collectivization occurred, I must begin with debates in 1958–1959 among national policy makers and local implementers. Those discussions were an early consequence of ordinary people's reactions to the government's collectivization policy. Largely because of peasants' lack of enthusiasm for collective farming and contrary behavior inside the experimental cooperatives, many local leaders wondered how to proceed. Was it realistic, they asked, to expect collective farming to evolve from simple labor exchange groups to complex ones and then to become cooperatives by the end of 1960? Many national party and government authorities realized that something had to give. It was not possible to lay solid foundations *and* erect thousands of cooperatives by 1961. There had to be a trade-off between quality and quantity.

During 1958, Communist Party leaders in numerous villages opposed a rapid increase in cooperatives. Some acknowledged that they themselves or members of their families did not wish to join the cooperatives. Instead, they said, the party should strengthen the labor exchange groups. Many also argued that most villagers preferred to farm separately and were not ready to pool land and other assets. Against those views were other local leaders who contended that villagers were eager to join cooperatives. Hence, they insisted, the party leadership needed to move quickly to keep up with "jubilant masses." Still others argued that even if villagers were not entirely happy with farming collectively, the party had to be in the fore-

99. BCHTU, DLDVN, "NQ, Hoi Nghi Trung Uong, lan thu Nam," 5, 6, 36.

front as it had been in the successful drive for independence, the war against the French army, and land reform. The masses, they predicted, would follow.[100]

Even though the party's Central Executive Committee resolved in November 1958 to complete low-level cooperativization by the end of 1960, dissension persisted. A mid-1959 national study found local party leaders and members who wanted to abandon the collectivization campaign and leave the cooperatives they were in. "There are even comrades who still suggest that the party's agricultural cooperativization line should be reconsidered, that maybe it is premature" to farm collectively.[101] In late 1960 and early 1961, reports, such as one from Ha Dong province, complained that too many local leaders and party members were "pessimistic and negative" about collective farming and other aspects of socialism, apparently because production increases were modest, people's incomes were small, and numerous cooperative members "did not yet really believe in or feel attached to cooperatives."[102] As late as 1962, a few government officials and party members wondered why they ought to insist on collective farming when assisting family farming might better increase production and raise villagers' real income.[103]

To give up on building collective cooperatives or to postpone them indefinitely was out of the question for most authorities, particularly those in national offices of the Communist Party and its government. They were convinced that collective cooperatives were inevitable.[104] That position is succinctly captured in a 1959 report from the party's central Rural Affairs Committee (Ban Cong Tac Nong Thon Trung Uong). Peasants, it stressed, "want to eliminate exploitation." That could not be done with private farming; "exploitation will resurface." Nor could advanced technologies be

100. TCT VH "BCSK" [Assignment], Hung Tien, Kien An, 13 August 1958, 4, 6; Ty VH Son Tay, "BCTK, Xuong Co So, Thi Diem, Son Tay" [Cultural office, Son Tay province, "Grassroots, cultural work"], 26 March 1959, 7 [P BVH, hs 942, vv). Several *Nhan Dan* articles mention dissension among party members and local officials about cooperatives and the rate at which they were being formed. See, for instance, 8 June 1958, 3; 17 January 1959, 2; 11 February 1959, 2; 18 February 1959, 3.

101. BCTNT, "BCTK" [Cooperative movement], circa July 1959, 7; see also 6.

102. Ha Dong, "BC Bo Sung, Dai Hoi, Ha Dong" [Ha Dong, "Ha Dong province party congress"], February 1961, 47, 50 (P UBKHNN, hs 352, vv).

103. Dang Tho Xuong et al., "Tong Thuat," 27.

104. Vickerman, *Fate*, 118, 141. In "North Vietnam's Collectivisation," 29–30, Alec Gordon writes that although collectivization was party policy, the leadership "dragged its feet" on implementation until "pushed into action" in 1958 by its left wing "in response to groups of peasants," particularly poor ones, "setting up their own cooperatives." His argument, based on the limited material obtainable at the time he wrote, is not substantiated by evidence available now.

used to increase production and raise rural living standards. The "only direction to take the peasantry," despite difficulties now and likely ones in the future, was "down the collective road; there is no other road." It was also a road, the report indicated, that other socialist countries, especially China and the Soviet Union, had already blazed, facilitating Vietnam's journey.[105]

The prominent debate in 1958–1960 was about how quickly to build cooperatives. Prompted by its Rural Affairs Committee, the party's Secretariat in December 1958 convened a national conference in Thanh Hoa province to "come to a united assessment" (thong nhat nhan dinh) and prepare proposals for the Central Executive Committee conference to consider in early 1959. According to secondary accounts that draw on records from that conference, delegates were divided over two questions: Did peasants want cooperatives, and how much preparation was necessary before establishing them?[106] Representatives from twelve provinces, four of them in the Red River delta, said cooperatives "had become a request of the masses."[107] But delegates from another thirteen provinces, including five in the delta, said only in some areas were villagers or indeed party members and local government officials enthusiastic. For the most part, the masses and party members were "not yet sympathetic to entering cooperatives."[108]

Debate over preparations required for establishing cooperatives erupted over a slogan used in the campaign: "Zealously lead with sure-footed steps" (tich cuc lanh dao, tien buoc vung chac).[109] Some Thanh Hoa conference delegates wanted less inhibitive language. The words "sure-footed steps," they argued, encouraged local organizers to be overly cautious, thereby slowing down the campaign. Others, however, wanted no rewording. They feared that local activists would zealously form cooperatives without first explaining to villagers the purposes of collective farming. Similar arguments emerged when delegates discussed the organizational guideline that a coop-

105. BCTNT TU, "Phong Trao HTH, SXNN, 1958, Dong Xuan 1959" [RAC, "Cooperativization, 1958, 1959"], n.d. [circa mid-1959], 3–4 (P UBKHNN, hs 1258, vv).
106. Dang Tho Xuong et al., "Tong Thuat," 17–18; Nguyen Quang Hong, "Tu Tuong," N15–N17. These reports note documents in the party's archives about conflicting assessments.
107. Dang Tho Xuong et al., "Tong Thuat," 18. The places listed are Hai Duong, Hai Ninh, Hoa Binh, Hung Yen, Khu Thai Meo, Kien An, Lien Khu 4 (Ha Tinh, Nghe An, Thanh Hoa, Vinh Linh), Son Tay, and Thai Binh.
108. Dang Tho Xuong et al., "Tong Thuat," 18. Listed are Bac Can, Bac Giang, Bac Ninh, Cao Bang, Ha Dong, Ha Nam, Ha Noi, Hai Phong, Khu Lao-Ha-Yen, Ninh Binh, Phu Tho, Tuyen Quang, and Vinh Phuc. Representatives from Hong Quang said it was premature to assess villagers' reactions but noted that the number of labor exchange groups had recently dropped 20 percent. Nguyen Quang Hong, "Tu Tuong," N16.
109. Nguyen Quang Hong, "Tu Tuong," N16–N17.

erative could be created within fifteen to twenty days. Several contended no time frame should be specified because conditions varied from village to village. Some argued that a cooperative could be established in a shorter time. Others insisted it would take much longer.

During the campaign to build cooperatives, leaders often disagreed over the proper balance between "zealously leading" and taking "sure-footed steps." Organizers seen to be emphasizing the latter were often regarded as "conservative and timid" (*bao thu rut re*), as overwhelmed by difficulties, especially by peasants' predilection for private property and household farming. Those who emphasized leadership were regarded as "hasty and impatient" (*nong voi*), giving little importance to labor exchanges or other preparations. As the campaign accelerated during 1959 and into 1960, those favoring more "zealous leadership" came to dominate.

Consider the outcome of "seething discussion and debate" among party officials in Thai Binh province, which the party's national newspaper, *Nhan Dan*, began to investigate in March 1959. Thai Binh leaders were ridiculing one another for being either too reticent or too eager to start cooperatives. Officials in one district, for instance, sarcastically likened the forming of cooperatives in a neighboring district to "launching satellites" that "disappear into the atmosphere" without a trace because their quality was poor. Others accused those critics, however, of being overly cautious and failing to lead peasants to establish cooperatives. Organizers in districts that had quickly established numerous cooperatives argued against provincial leaders who defended a slow pace for cooperativization because only 12 percent of Thai Binh farming households were in regular work exchange groups and even fewer were in work point–based ones. The defiant district officials insisted that villagers were eager to form cooperatives but required leadership.[110]

By May 1959, leaders who favored fast-tracking cooperatives had prevailed in Thai Binh. Concerns about the small number of advanced labor exchange teams and other shortcomings were pushed aside when the province's top party leader wrote that Thai Binh was now on course to have at least 20 percent of farming households in cooperatives by mid-year and a larger percentage before 1960.[111] The reasons for this shift are not evident from available information. One may have been the *Nhan Dan* accounts' implicit criticism of the cautious approach. Probably an even more influential factor was that central offices of the party were pressur-

110. *Nhan Dan*, 30 and 31 March and 1 April 1959, 3.
111. Ibid., 19 and 20 May 1959, 3.

ing officials all across northern Vietnam to form cooperatives more quickly.

A major dilemma for local authorities was that they had to build cooperatives everywhere before 1961, but only after laying the foundation of regular and work point–based labor exchange groups. Because most groups were still basic, organizers would need to create advanced ones quickly and then immediately change them into cooperatives. This scenario posed difficulties. Many villagers were unenthusiastic about complicated labor exchanges. Second, resources were inadequate to do everything that was demanded of local officials: form advanced exchange groups, build cooperatives, introduce new farming methods, improve irrigation, establish and staff schools, build health centers, and so on. Third, quickly forming advanced labor exchange groups and immediately converting them into cooperatives defeated the purpose of exchange teams in the first place. Villagers would have no experience farming together and using work points. Consequently, many village and district leaders concluded that the time for work exchange groups "had passed" (*da den luc het*). They wanted to concentrate on establishing cooperatives.[112]

Indeed, few of the forty thousand cooperatives built between mid-1958 and 1960 rested on the foundations of mature labor exchange groups. Although two-thirds of rural households were in labor exchange groups by late 1958–early 1959, few were in advanced ones. In April 1959, the peak of the groups' development, only 11 percent of households were in work point–based teams (appendix 1, table 2).

In December 1958, the party's Secretariat criticized the spreading practice of "skipping over" labor exchange phases and turning simple exchange teams into cooperatives without first becoming work point–based. Cooperatives built that way, warned the Secretariat, "will not be able to satisfy the needs of the masses nor advance production well." A cooperative, it insisted, should be built on labor exchange groups using work points. Only after the cooperative movement had reached a "high tide" might this no longer be necessary.[113] The party's Rural Affairs Committee was also alarmed. Not only had few cooperatives emerged from advanced labor exchanges, but organizers no longer tried to form such groups. They had been "sucked into" (*bi hut vao*) building cooperatives without first

112. BCTNT TU, "BC Kiem Diem, HTHNN, Thu 1959, PHNV" [RAC, "Critical report, cooperative movement"], 7 December 1959, 4 (P UBKHNN, hs 1258, vv).
113. Nguyen Duy Trinh, Ban Bi Thu, BCHTU, DLDVN, "118 CTTW, HTHNN, San Xuat" [Nguyen Duy Trinh, Secretariat, CEC, VWP, "Instruction 118, cooperative movement, production"], 8 December 1958, 1, 2 (P UBHCKTN, hs 40, vv).

strengthening labor exchange teams, complained the committee in mid-1959.[114] Organizers, it insisted in December 1959, "absolutely cannot take lightly or flinch from strengthening the labor exchange movement and guiding labor exchanges to become regular and have members evaluate one another's' work and assign points. This even applies in areas where the party cell is firmly in charge, where there is already a good cooperative [nearby], and where the proportion of cooperatives [in the vicinity] is relatively high."[115]

Shifts in national pronouncements earlier in 1959 suggest, however, that the Rural Affairs Committee's view no longer prevailed in the party's leadership. In April, the Central Executive Committee declared that "generally speaking" the step-by-step method of building cooperatives still applied, but "places that already have some really good cooperatives, have a strong mass movement, and have experienced leaders may accept into cooperatives peasants who have no work exchange team background." Other places should start a cooperative with "at least one" work point–based labor exchange team. Afterwards the statement intimated, villagers who had not been in such teams could also join.[116] In May, Truong Chinh, deputy prime minister and member of the party's Political Bureau, told the National Assembly that "it is not absolutely essential for every peasant household, hamlet, and village" to be in work exchange groups before forming a cooperative. Under certain conditions, "a number of peasant households working individually can organize an elementary [low-level] or advanced [high-level] cooperative without necessarily proceeding" through labor exchange phases.[117]

In November, an editorial in Nhan Dan acknowledged that two methods for increasing the size and number of cooperatives had emerged. The first was to strengthen and enlarge the early experimental cooperatives and establish new ones after advanced labor exchange teams had developed. The second was to form cooperatives "without any longer developing those teams." Although the editorial deemed the first method better, it did not dismiss the second. Indeed it indicated that the second would spread with the rush to bring all households into cooperatives.[118] In August 1960, the

114. BCTNN, "BCTK" [Cooperative movement], circa July 1959, 5. Also, Tran Van Dai, BCTNT TU, "BC TH, HTH, San Xuat 6 thang, 1959" [Tran Van Dai, RAC, "Cooperativization, half of 1959"], 30 July 1959 (P UBKHNN, hs 1258, vv).
115. BCTNT, "BC Kiem Diem" [Critical report], 7 December 1959, 4.
116. BCHTU, DLDVN, "NQ, Hoi Nghi Trung Uong, lan thu 16," 29–30.
117. Truong Chinh, Resolutely, 67–68.
118. Nhan Dan, 10 November 1959, 1, 4.

party Secretariat itself announced that peasants without any work exchange experience could join cooperatives. This departed significantly from its December 1958 position.[119]

## Reasoning behind Acceleration

One reason national leaders' abandoned the graduated approach was that they had resolved in late 1958 to make a centrally planned socialist economy by 1960–1961. For that to happen, collective farming cooperatives were vital. In addition to increasing production, cooperatives would control consumption and trade of agricultural products and direct a proportion of agricultural earnings to state agencies in charge of building factories and other parts of the economy.[120] Another reason for fast-tracking collectivization was that officials increasingly worried that rural living conditions were eroding. Unless collectivization was vigorously pursued, argued leaders such as Truong Chinh, "land will be concentrated little by little in the hands of a few persons, and class differentiation will be accentuated."[121] Third, to many leaders rapid collectivization seemed to be working. Cooperatives were not only spreading quickly, but were applying new agricultural techniques and helping the government's program to expand irrigation.[122]

The need for leadership provided another argument for rapid collectivization. While agreeing that organizers had to understand people's reluctance to farm collectively, advocates of a fast approach stressed that negative attitudes should not deter leaders from doing what was best for peasants specifically and the country generally.[123] The main restraint on rural development, many claimed in late 1958 and 1959, was within the Communist Party itself. Peasants, they said, had already come much further than seemed possible in late 1957 when the experimental cooperatives were assessed. What was lacking now was decisive and effective party leadership. For instance, an April 1959 resolution of the party's Central Executive Committee argued

119. Ban Bi Thu, "Chi Thi 221" [Party Secretariat, "Instruction 221"], 18 August 1960, cited in Dang Tho Xuong et al., "Tong Thuat," 21.

120. BCHTU, DLDVN, "NQ, Hoi Nghi Trung Uong, lan thu 14," 15–25; Nguyen Ngoc Luu, "Peasants, Party," 389–92; Tran Nhu Trang, "Transformation," 20, 311–13.

121. Truong Chinh, Resolutely, 29.

122. Nguyen Quang Hong, "Tu Tuong," N17–N18.

123. TCT VH, "BCSK" [Assignment], Hung Tien, Kien An, 13 August 1958, 11. See also Doan Can Bo Tham Gia Lao Dong, "BC Tham Gia Lao Dong" [Joining the workers], Hai Phong, 28 March 1959, 2, 4.

that "some party members and cadres still do not fully see the importance of cooperatives for our entire revolutionary cause and have yet to accept their responsibilities in leading peasants to take the road of agricultural cooperativization."[124] About a fifth of the pages in the resolution are devoted to elaborating why this leadership was crucial. Assertive leadership, said this and other party pronouncements that year, could bring peasants into collective farming and develop socialism throughout the countryside.

Another reason was the wave of optimism about socialist, especially collective, production.[125] Particularly influential were developments in China. Frequently during 1958, the party's First Secretary Le Duan and other national leaders marveled at the extraordinary high yields collectivized peasants in China had reportedly achieved.[126] One summary of the November 1958 conference in Thanh Hoa province said that rapid economic development in other socialist countries, "especially the gigantic targets of the Soviet Union's seven-year plan and China's great leap campaign, influenced us a great deal. In particular, one can say that China's ability to increase productivity using simple technology, which our own people also have, was an extremely favorable new factor for the cooperative movement."[127] In addition to China's and the Soviet Union's economic performance, the rate of progress in other socialist countries also influenced the February 1959 Central Executive Committee conference, which prepared a timetable to complete cooperativization by the end of 1960.[128]

Finally, political conditions for quickly forming cooperatives were auspicious.[129] National leaders believed that a large proportion of the

124. BCHTU, DLDVN, "NQ, Hoi Nghi Trung Uong, lan thu 16," 9, see also 36–43.
125. Vickerman, Fate, 141.
126. Ibid. See also, "May Kinh Nghiem Trung Quoc ma Chung ta nen hoc" [Chinese experiences we need to study], a series by Ho Chi Minh published in Nhan Dan (28 articles, 1 July to 23 August 1958). That the author was Ho Chi Minh is revealed in Nhan Dan, 17 May 1980, according to Vickerman, Fate, 315. For a list of pen names Ho Chi Minh used when writing in this party newspaper, see Nhan Dan, 10 March 1991, 3. I am grateful to Russell Heng for bringing this list to my attention.
127. Comrade Tran Huu Duc, quoted in Nguyen Quang Hong, "Tu Tuong," N14. See also Le Duan, On the Socialist Revolution, 1:96.
128. Nguyen Quang Hong, "Tu Tuong," N18, referring to records in the party's archives. I do not know whether Vietnam's leaders in 1958–1959 had any inkling of the disastrous consequences of China's "Great Leap Forward" policies. Food production and consumption in China were relatively good in 1956–1958 but fell sharply in 1959–1961, when millions of people starved to death. Selden, Political Economy, 17–21.
129. They feature in a 1961 party resolution on how collectivization was completed by the end of 1960. They also figure in the resolution's argument for quickly converting "low-level" cooperatives into "high-level" ones (BCHTU, DLDVN, "NQ, Hoi Nghi Trung Uong, lan thu Nam, 6–7, 13–15, 46ff.). I have no evidence they were prominent in the 1958–1959 debates but I am guessing they were.

peasantry trusted the party and that noticeably improved rural living conditions in 1956–1960 had reinforced this support, despite whatever doubts
villagers had about collective farming. Moreover, no significant opposition
to collectivization had emerged. Land reform had eliminated the influence
of former landlords and rich peasants in the countryside. Opposition from
other peasants was mild. Although I have no evidence of this, prominent
party leaders may have worried that serious opposition would surface unless
collectivization was swift.[130] Meanwhile, leaders argued, the pervasive party
organization in the countryside could efficiently implement national
policies. A political factor lurking in the background was the situation in
southern Vietnam. In the event of war to defend the north against the
government in Saigon or to reunify the country, collective farming was
expected to be "very advantageous" for strengthening the home front and
bolstering national defense.[131]

In short, the arguments that prevailed in the late 1950s for accelerating
collectivization emphasized advantageous circumstances and the party's
responsibility to lead. If it did not live up to its responsibility, what had
been achieved since 1954 would be jeopardized and socialism would not
flourish.

## Explaining Peasants' Participation

Beginning in late 1958, over 2 million families seemingly flooded into
the collective farming cooperatives within two years, with the result that
86 percent of agrarian households in the north were members by the end
of 1960. In the Red River delta, the figure was nearly 90 percent (appendix 1, table 4). Public pronouncements from the Communist Party's central
leadership frequently claimed that peasants "eagerly" and "enthusiastically"
wanted cooperatives.[132] Internal reports at both the national and local level
often said otherwise. In December 1959, a year into the concerted drive
for collective farming, the party's Rural Affairs Committee concluded with

130. One fear might have been that the longer peasants farmed their own fields, the more
reluctant they would be to farm collectively. Such concerns were cited in arguments for rapid
collectivization following land reforms in other Communist Party governments. Pryor, *Red*,
112–13.
131. BCHTU, DLDVN, "NQ, Hoi Nghi Trung Uong, lan thu 14," 12, 21. Also see Nguyen
Ngoc Luu, "Peasants, Party," 387.
132. For example, BCHTU, DLDVN, "NQ, Hoi Nghi Trung Uong, lan thu 16," 6; BCHTU,
DLDVN, "NQ, Hoi Nghi Trung Uong, lan thu Nam," 9.

disappointment that, by and large, "cooperative members and the masses still do not really have confidence in cooperativization" and retained a "strong sense of private ownership."[133] More than a year later, in February 1961, the party's Political Bureau also reportedly concluded that peasants "actually were not enthusiastic" (*khong thuc su phan khoi*) about cooperatives.[134] This and the speed at which they were built, reports said, were significant reasons why many cooperatives were "of low quality" and by mid-1961 were "not yet really steady."[135] Provincial reports, such as one in early 1961 from Ha Dong, noted that villagers were "still not confident about or deeply attached to cooperatives" and that "most peasant households now in cooperatives"—about 90 percent of the province's farming families—"were there as a result of being drawn in and pushed up by the movement. . . . Few joined with a sense of volunteering."[136]

What many peasants experienced was *go ep* (pressure and coercion) a term used in several documents from the 1959–1961 period.[137] A national report in mid-1959, for instance, said when discussing how villagers were recruited into cooperatives that "*go ep* and commanding people [to join] were rather common and took many different forms."[138] Rarely violent, pressure and coercion were usually verbal and included hints of adverse consequences if people did not join.[139] Organizers sometimes used study sessions more to scare villagers than to persuade them. During some sessions in Vinh Phuc and Phu Tho provinces, for instance, people were asked to vote: "All those who support socialism should raise their hands and join the cooperative." Those who did not raise their hands risked being seen as opponents of cooperatives and of the regime itself. Villagers who held back

133. BCTNT, "BC Kiem Diem" [Critical report], 7 December 1959, 8.

134. Dang Tho Xuong et al., "Tong Thuat," 23.

135. BCTNT, "BCTK" [Cooperative movement], circa July 1959, 5; BCTNT, "BC Kiem Diem" [Critical report], 7 December 1959, 9; and BCHTU, DLDVN, "NQ, Hoi Nghi Trung Uong, lan thu Nam," 7–8.

136. " . . . do phong trao loi cuon va thuc day ma tham gia." Ha Dong, "BC Bo Sung" [Ha Dong party congress], February 1961, 7.

137. *Go ep* is "to press in such a way as to conform or be in accordance with a certain size, shape, framework, established order or established practice." *Tu Dien Tieng Viet*, 429. A Vietnamese-English dictionary translates it as "compel, force, constrain, coerce." Bui Phung, *Tu Dien Viet-Anh*, 662.

138. BCTNT, "BCTK" [Cooperative movement], circa July 1959, 16.

139. The one documented use of armed force I have read about is when militia "intervened" to stop people who wanted to leave a cooperative and take with them cattle and land they had contributed. Apparently they were eventually able to leave. The sense of "intervened" is unclear. Hy Van Luong, *Revolution*, 199.

were "invited to come to district offices and explain their objections," a prospect few villagers would have wanted.[140] In Tien Thang subdistrict of Vinh Phuc, local party leaders rarely took no for an answer. They repeatedly returned to reluctant villagers' homes, sometimes staying until ten or eleven o'clock at night, for days and even weeks on end to urge the households to sign up. In this and other ways, recalled one resident, about "thirty percent of cooperative members were pressured and coerced to join."[141] Intimidating tactics elsewhere included mock funerals mourning the "death of individualism" staged in front of the houses of people who had not yet joined, songs and verses ridiculing individuals who had not yet signed up, and villagewide broadcasts announcing the names of people who had not become members. Villagers in Da Ton who had not joined recall neighbors who "looked down" on them. As more people became members, the ostracism intensified. In some places youth organizations and schools required children to urge their parents to join. If the parents refused, the youngsters had to criticize themselves in public. Families not in a cooperative had to pay higher taxes. Nonmembers also often encountered obstacles when trying to send their children to village schools, get health services, and farm their own fields.[142] In Thinh Liet subdistrict, Hanoi, nonmembers with fields surrounded by collective land were prevented from crossing to reach their fields or to channel irrigation to their crops.[143]

Some people in 1958–1961 defiantly objected to cooperatives. One person in a local drama group, for example, refused to play the role of a cooperative member in a skit because he disliked cooperatives. Slogans on banners and walls imploring people to join cooperatives were sometimes secretly destroyed and replaced with statements calling for the "overthrow of the work exchange teams and cooperatives." Sometimes the new slogans even exhorted: "Overthrow the Communist Party government, support Ngo Dinh Diem" (the president of the Saigon-based government). Some opponents uprooted plants in collectively farmed fields and torched the houses of cooperative officers and local police. Villagers who could not escape joining occasionally sold their draft animals rather than let the coop-

140. *Nhan Dan*, 15 May 1959, 3.

141. Interview, Tien Thang, Vinh Phuc, 26 August 2000.

142. BCTNT, "BCTK" [Cooperative movement], circa July 1959, 16–17; Dang Tho Xuong et al., "Tong Thuat," 21; interviews, Da Ton, Hanoi, 25 January 1996; Chaliand, *Peasants*, 146–47, 151, 161; Yvon-Tran, "Une résistible," 54–58.

143. Shaun Malarney, personal communication, 5 July 1997, based on his interviews in Thinh Liet in 1990–1991.

erative have them.[144] In some predominantly Roman Catholic areas, villagers initially opposed collective farming on religious grounds.[145] In 1960–early 1961, the number of people asking to leave the cooperatives they had recently joined was "increasing daily." Among them were forty women from one village who protested at the Phu Xuyen district head-quarters in Ha Dong province. In sampled areas of five provinces, the party's Rural Affairs Committee found in 1961 that between 3.5 and 15 percent of households had petitioned to return to individual farming. A few coop-eratives established in 1959–1960 collapsed because so many members wanted out. What people disliked specifically is not reported, except that their incomes had decreased since joining cooperatives.[146]

More instances of open opposition probably occurred and was not reported. Officials may have missed much. They may have also known far more than they conveyed to their superiors. Even so, I suspect that oppo-sition was rarely vigorous. When it was, those involved could be dismissed as old enemies of the regime or supporters of the regime in southern Vietnam. Villagers may have been too frightened to object strenuously. Many had heard about the 1956 *Nhan Van Giai Pham* matter in which the party's national leadership repressed artists and writers in Hanoi who had criticized certain policies and the government. Yet a large number of vil-lagers had complained a few years earlier against the way land reform was implemented. Their objections and those of many local party members had prompted the national leadership to pause, apologize, and redo it. Had a significant proportion of villagers deemed cooperativization unacceptable, they probably could have said so, one way or another, and their objections would appear in surviving material or in what has been revealed subsequently.

For many villagers, entering a cooperative came down to doing what authorities obviously wanted them to do. Several villagers who recalled this period said they joined because "it was the state's policy."[147] This expres-

144. Truong Doan, Doan Chi Dao, Thach Dai, Ty VH Ha Tinh, "BCSK, Tham Gia Lao Dong, Thi Diem, Thach Dai" [leader, Guidance group in Thach Dai, Ha Tinh province, "Joining workers, experimental work, Thach Dai subdistrict"], 20 February 1959, 2 (P BVH, hs 942, vv); Tran Van Dai, "BC TH, HTH" [Cooperativization], 30 July 1959, 9; BCTNT, "BC Kiem Diem" [Critical report], 7 December 1959, 6.

145. Houtart and Lemercinier, *Hai Van*, 169–70; Nguyen Ngoc Luu, "Peasants, Party," 429–30; and Grossheim, *Nordvietnamesische*, 227–29.

146. Tran Van Dai, "BC TH, HTH" [Cooperativization], 30 July 1959, 7, 9; Dang Tho Xuong et al., "Tong Thuat," 23; Tran Duc, *Hop Tac*, 79–80.

147. Interviews, Da Ton, Hanoi; Nghiem Xuyen, Ha Tay; and Dao Duc, Quat Luu, Tam Canh, and Tien Thang, Vinh Phuc.

sion conveys two messages. The first is a sense of resignation toward a government committed to collective farming. Vietnam, leaders repeatedly stressed, had to choose between capitalism (specifically, for the countryside, private property and individual farming) and socialism (collective owner-ship and collective farming). Capitalism was linked to land concentration, foreign domination, extreme inequality, and an elite that lived well at the expense of poor, illiterate peasants and laborers. Socialism was linked to land reform, equality, nationwide programs in education and health care, and a better life for the vast majority of Vietnamese. Capitalism was also associated with French colonialism, Vietnam's recent past. Socialism was equated with Vietnam's future.[148] Theoretically, peasants had a choice; officials verbally endorsed the "principle of voluntary membership" in cooperatives (nguyen tac tu nguyen). But in light of the government's determination, many villagers saw no real choice.

The second message is that people often trusted the party; they gave the party and its policies the benefit of the doubt. For instance, according to an August 1958 report, despite ambivalence and opposition to the cooper-atives in Kien An province, "the majority of people are resolved to build them." The report quoted one villager: "The party in the past and until now has looked after our interests; never has it taken us down into a big hole. Helping to advance socialism [with cooperatives] is an honor, even though there are many problems which we must try hard to overcome."[149] When I asked people for the reasons why they had become members of cooperatives in the late 1950s, the frequent reply was "following Ho Chi Minh," "confidence in the party," and "gratitude to the party." A woman who had joined with her husband in 1960, a few years after they had married, recalled how poor they were and how they agonized over sur-rendering the fields they had obtained during land reform. Both her parents and her husband's parents had been landless. Ultimately, she and her husband decided to join because they "believed in the government."[150] At village meetings in Hai Duong province during 1959, those skeptical about collective farming suggested that the party, not peasants, wanted it. Propo-nents agreed but said it was still in the peasants' interest. Look at the other

---

148. See Nhan Dan, esp. in 1959; for example, 17 June, 3; 3 October, 1 and 2; 19 October, 2.

149. TCT VH, "BCSK" [Assignment], Hung Tien, Kien An, 13 August 1958, 7. Similar sentiments are summarized, for example, in Ban Thuong Vu Khu Uy, BCH Khu Ta Ngan, DLDVN, "BC TH, Thi Xa trong Khu" [Standing Committee, EC, Ta Ngan zone, VWP, "Situation, regional towns"], 18 January 1958, 11 (P UBHCKTN, hs 40, vv).

150. Interview, Da Ton, Hanoi, 3 February 1996.

projects the party had undertaken, they said—from land reform to the drainage culverts installed in the vicinity. Initially many people had objected or had been reluctant to get involved. Afterward, however, even those people acknowledged the improvement. It would be the same with cooperatives, these advocates said.[151]

Another reason peasants joined was the prospect of a better life. Even though living conditions since 1954 had improved for a large proportion of villagers, most remained poor. About a third occasionally went hungry.[152] Peasants in many places were like those in Thai Binh, who in 1958–1959 "went in and out, in and out" of cooperatives like "ants crawling around the rim of a basket," not sure whether inside or outside was better for their livelihood.[153] Meanwhile organizers and government officials warned that unless the country continued to follow the Communist Party, rural conditions would deteriorate. Crop failures and other misfortunes could quickly cast most peasants into debt, landlessness, and profound misery.[154] Villagers could readily imagine that. They had lived it only a few years earlier. The alternative, officials and cooperative organizers promised, was that living conditions would continue to improve. For that to happen, everyone had to combine their land and work together. In that way they would share the costs and risks instead of shouldering them individually. Moreover, they could afford to use more fertilizers, buy tractors, and invest in other methods to raise production and diversify. All the while the government would help by levying fewer taxes on members than on nonmembers, sending the army to assist with irrigation and flood control projects, and providing new farming technologies.[155]

Bolstering this argument for joining were signs of improved agricultural production and higher incomes as the number of cooperatives mushroomed. Villagers with whom I spoke remember having more rice to eat during the first few years of the cooperatives than they had had during the 1940s and early 1950s. Reports from the period suggest this was true. For instance, most cooperative members in Nam Sach subdistrict, Hai Duong province, had higher incomes after joining than before. In Ha Dong province, cooperative members had higher living standards in 1960 than before they had joined.

151. *Nhan Dan*, 9 October 1959, 2. Also see Vickerman, *Fate*, 152.

152. A 1960 survey of peasant households found 29 percent had more food to eat than they needed, 34 percent had enough, and 37 percent had too little. TCTK, "Nhung Chi Tieu, NN, 1955–1967" [Agriculture, 1955–1967], 1968, table 284.

153. Elliott, Transcript, 121.

154. Chaliand, *Peasants*, 98–101; Hy Van Luong, *Revolution*, 196–97.

155. See villagers' accounts in Chaliand, *Peasants*, 99–100, 140, 187, 191, 194.

In Ha Nam province, stable prices and much greater purchasing power in 1960 compared to 1957 strengthened the masses' confidence in the party and government.[156] Meanwhile, health centers and schools were more numerous and more accessible, especially to cooperative members. Across northern Vietnam, food production per capita was rising, exceeding what it had been even in the peacetime of the late 1930s, and was particularly high in 1959 (appendix 1, table 1). Growth in the value of agricultural production averaged 5.6 per cent per annum between 1957 and 1960.[157]

It is unclear whether collective cooperative members were better-off than nonmembers. Two available comparisons in 1960 of gross monetary income and paddy show nonmembers did somewhat better. But in one of the comparisons, net income was slightly higher for all cooperative members than for nonmembers; and in both, net income was greater for members from a poor peasant background than for nonmembers from that background.[158] One can imagine that many peasants estimated there would be only a marginal difference in their income if they joined a cooperative. After adding other apparent benefits of cooperatives, especially protection in the event of personal tragedies, however, they could see advantages to spreading the risks of farming across an entire group.[159]

Women reportedly saw additional benefits to joining the cooperatives. Because they carried more than half the workload of supporting their families, they looked on collective production, said one early joiner, as a way "to ease their burdens."[160] In cooperatives, men would have to do more work than they had before. Also, combining the limited resources of several families and farming together would make life easier for men and women. These sentiments and analyses were particularly pronounced in places with active chapters of the national Women's Association. Organizers from this association also emphasized gender equality, one of the themes in the socialist revolution campaigns of which collectivization was a part.

156. *Nhan Dan*, 9 October 1959, 2; Ha Dong, "BC Bo Sung" [Ha Dong party congress], February 1961, 6; Cao Van Chuc, Pho Chu Nhiem, UBKH, Ha Nam, "BCTK, SXNN, 3 nam" [Cao Van Chuc, vice chair, Planning Committee, Ha Nam province, "Agricultural production, 1958–1960"], 1961, 6–7 (P UBKHNN, hs 279, vv).

157. BCHTU, DLDVN, "NQ, Hoi Nghi Trung Uong, lan thu Nam," 9.

158. TCTK, "So Lieu, Doi Song Nong Dan, 1960" [GSO, "Peasants' living conditions"], n.d. [circa 1960], tables 3, 4, 6, 10 (P UBKHNN, hs 1282, vv). The two comparisons use data from surveys of 617 households in twelve provinces, seven in the Red River delta.

159. Chaliand, *Peasants*, 219, 223–34.

160. Cited in Werner, "Cooperativization," 84, and 83, 85. Some analysts say that collective farming was more attractive to women than to men because it increased their social standing and gave them more independence from the male-dominated family economy. Wiegersma, "Peasant Patriarchy," 188–89.

Yet another reason peasants joined is that they could keep some land. The knowledge that they would receive a portion of the crops grown on fields turned over to the collective cooperative frequently "encouraged" (*khuyen khich*) villagers to join.[161] In many places, however, this payment was already shrinking by 1960–1961 and was thus less of a consideration for new members. Besides, they usually knew that the payment would be expunged when their cooperative became "high-level." More important were the small amounts of land they could keep for themselves. Generally, that land had two components. Usually the larger was some farmland, typically two hundred to four hundred square meters, that each household was allowed to use as its own. The other was the yard around a family's house, which often had a garden and pond and could be used for raising vegetables, chickens, ducks, and fish. With these bits of land, however modest in size, villagers could enter cooperatives knowing that their livelihood would not depend entirely on collective farming.

Party leaders and cooperative organizers had concluded early on that they would let villagers keep some land. They knew that Communist Party governments elsewhere allowed this and understood it would assuage peasants' desire for land and thus help collectivization occur. Leaving villagers some land on which to grow things for themselves, said one party circular in 1960, was compatible with rural "custom" and "human nature."[162] Having land to farm individually was good for peasants' "psychology" (*tam ly*), said a party analyst. It gave them satisfaction and a "good feeling" (*tinh cam*), which in turn helped them make the transition from private to collective production and be cooperative members with a "positive attitude" (*tinh tich cuc*).[163] Also, authorities acknowledged, income from collective farming during the first few years would be insufficient. Hence, peasants needed some land for themselves to earn additional income. The combined earnings from collective work and family work would mean that living conditions would "continuously improve. Consequently, peasants cannot help but believe in the party, be close to the regime, and strive to strengthen cooperatives."[164] Finally, authorities knew that not everything could be produced collectively, especially at first. Even later, many vegetables and fruits

161. Interviews, Tam Canh, 10 August 2000, and Dao Duc, 15 August 2000, Vinh Phuc. Also, Elliott, Transcript, 122–23.

162. Extract from circular (*thong tri*) 32 of the party's central Rural Affairs Committee, 5 May 1960, in *Duong Loi, Chinh Sach*, 91.

163. Le Trung Viet, *Kinh Te Phu Gia Dinh*, 6, 20–21, 24. Duong Quoc Cam, *Kinh Te Tap The*, 10–11, hints at similar reasoning.

164. Le Trung Viet, *Kinh Te Phu Gia Dinh*, 20–21. See also Duong Quoc Cam, *Kinh Te Tap The*, 6–7, 15–16, 23.

and some livestock—chickens and ducks, for instance—could not be all be raised collectively.[165] Pig farming, weaving, mat making, traditional medicine making, and some other production would temporarily remain with the individual household. To do those things, families needed land of their own. The family economy, authorities repeatedly said, would be an important "subsidiary" to the collective economy.

Regulations specified that "up to 5 percent" of agricultural land within a collective cooperative could be set aside for households to use privately.[166] The area was then divided equally among everyone in the organization, including children. Each cooperative had to decide whether to go all the way to 5 percent and which fields would be used. I have found no documentation on the process. Villagers, including local officials at the time, recall that during meetings people wanted "the best land" for household plots. And that is what happened, at least in the places I visited. Leaders did not object because, as cooperative members, they too were entitled to such land.[167] Household plots were typically close to residential areas and pathways, making it easy for people to tend their crops regularly and transport fertilizer to and produce from the fields. The plots were also usually among the easiest in the cooperative to irrigate. As for the amount of land reserved for households plots, 5 percent was extremely common. Places where organizers allocated much less or even no area for household plots encountered significant problems getting villagers to enter or stay in the cooperatives. Alarmed that the collectivization campaign might collapse over the issue, central authorities reportedly had to insist in the late 1950s and early 1960s that local organizers allow the full 5 percent.[168]

165. See, for instance, comments by two prominent officials: Duong Quoc Cam, *Kinh Te Tap The*, 8, 10–11, 18–19, 31, 36; and Nguyen Chi Thanh, "May Kinh Nghiem," 18–19. Also see the rationale in "Dieu Le Mau" [Regulations, low-level cooperatives], n.d. [circa late 1959], 9, in *Chinh Sach, Luat Le*. In the early 1960s, Duong Quoc Cam was head of the Bureau of Agricultural Cooperativization (Vu Truong, Vu HTHNN) within the MA. By the mid-1970s, he was showing up in government documents as the assistant head of the Council of Ministers' CACMC (BQLHTXNNTU). Nguyen Chi Thanh held key positions in the party in the late 1950s–early 1960s, including Political Bureau member and head of the party's Agriculture Committee (BNNTU).

166. "Dieu Le Mau" [Regulations], circa late 1959, 9. A common Vietnamese term for the household plots is "5 percent land" (*dat nam phan tram*). The regulations allowed households in mountain villages somewhat more than 5 percent.

167. Interviews, Da Ton, Hanoi; Nghiem Xuyen, Ha Tay; Dao Duc, Quat Luu, Tam Canh, and Tien Thang, Vinh Phuc province. Many acquaintances in Hanoi who had lived in the countryside during the collective period also told me that household plots were usually located in the cooperative's best fields.

168. Elliott, Transcript, 146–47; Duong Quoc Cam, *Kinh Te Tap The*, 27–28. As of 1967, according to surveys, household plots amounted to 5.5 percent of agricultural land in the Red

## Summary

According to official figures, the intense campaign to collectivize agriculture in northern Vietnam was extremely successful. By the end of 1960, nearly 90 percent of farming households were in collective cooperatives—not quite the goal set by the national leaders in November 1958 but close enough. By early 1961, leaders were moving rapidly to enlarge the cooperatives and convert them to "high-level" ones.

The extent of collectivization far surpassed what the preconditions analyzed in the first sections of this chapter justified. The accomplishment was largely the result of the Communist Party government's resolute determination. Although done without recourse to vicious measures, the rapid building required leaders to discard the graduated plan of easing peasants toward collective production through three types of labor exchange groups. By late 1957–early 1958, peasants were willing to exchange labor occasionally but showed little sign of wanting to be involved in more elaborate arrangements. Their cool reactions to extensive labor exchanges and experimental cooperatives sparked vigorous debate among government and party officials about whether to stay with the plan or not. The answer that emerged was no. During the ensuing two-year collectivization campaign, organizers quickly established some forty thousand cooperatives, most of them resting uneasily on wobbly foundations.

Villagers by and large went along with what party and government leaders wanted. Few did so enthusiastically. Coercion was one reason people complied. Another was considerable trust in the Communist Party government, which had already done more for the majority of peasants than any regime they had seen before. Third, families could keep some land and thus not be entirely dependent on collective farming. Finally, people joined expecting, primarily because of what officials had promised, that the cooperatives would mean better living conditions. The combination amounted to a tacit agreement between them and authorities. They would work collectively so long as their lives improved, or at least did not get worse, and so long as leaders continued to merit their respect. Time and additional experience in the new organizations would show what the ultimate result would be.

---

River delta. Authorities had a serious problem keeping households from using more land than 5 per cent (see chapter 4). Nguyen Duc Duong, Tong Cuc Truong, "BC, Dieu Tra Dat Nong Nghiep" [Nguyen Duc Duong, head, GSO, "Land surveys"], 22 February 1968, 8 (P TCTK, hs 801, vv).

# Coping and Shoring Up, 1961–1974

National authorities in the early 1960s knew that many collective cooperatives were unstable. And they acknowledged that "socialist consciousness and a spirit of cooperative ownership" was not yet high. Nevertheless, they were confident that effective leadership could achieve complete collectivization and socialist agricultural development.[1] In 1961–1962, they hastened the drive to bring into the cooperatives those villagers who had not yet joined, to enlarge the organizations in the delta and midlands so that each corresponded to at least one entire village, and to convert them from "low-level" to "high-level" types. By 1965, according to official statistics, 90 percent of northern Vietnam's farming households were in collective cooperatives (appendix 1, table 4). Seventy percent of the organizations in the Red River delta and 60 percent in the entire north were "high-level." Three years later, when nearly every farming family was in a cooperative, 97 percent of the cooperatives in the delta and 80 percent across the north were "high-level."[2]

Below the surface of these achievements, however, were pervasive shortcomings, beginning with a failure to meet the four political conditions necessary for durable collective farming.

1. BCHTU, DLDVN, "NQ, Hoi Nghi Trung Uong, lan thu Nam," 9, 46, 53.
2. TCTK, *12 Nam Phat Trien*, 60, 557–58.

*Commitment and Incentives*

If significantly more villagers became ideologically committed to collective farming in the 1960s than had been in the late 1950s, no evidence of it has surfaced. Not only did many ordinary villagers remain dubious, many local party members were also uncertain.[3] A major reason for the cooperatives' problems, concluded the head of the government agency overseeing collectivization in 1963, was that "cadres, party members, and cooperative members did not yet possess a consciousness for actively strengthening and reinforcing the collective economy."[4] This remained a serious problem despite persistent training, education, and mass media programs to make villagers embrace collective farming. An assessment in Hai Hung in December 1968 aptly summarizes what was often reported there and in other provinces during the late 1960s and early 1970s: "Cooperative members are not yet really inspired to work enthusiastically nor are they fully devoted to the collective economy."[5]

But collective action—and collective farming in particular—can be sustained without participants first having a deep-seated faith. More important in many cases is commitment that grows as a result of benefits arising from the collective action. Those benefits are often personal and material in nature but may also be public and impersonal.

Party and government leaders in Vietnam understood the importance of personal and material benefits, or what scholars have called "instrumental commitment" and "selective incentives." The fundamental aim of socialism emphasized in the party's Rural Affairs Committee in the early 1960s was to "raise unceasingly" (*nang cao khong ngung*) the quality of people's lives.[6] A principal purpose of collective production was to do precisely that.

3. For instance, at a large July 1962 meeting to discuss the collectivization campaign, several provincial delegates argued that collective farming was premature. Dang Tho Xuong et al., "Tong Thuat," 26–27; Chu Van Lam et al., *Hop Tac Hoa*, 21.

4. Duong Quoc Cam, *Mot So Kinh Nhiem qua Dot I*, 42.

5. Hai Hung, "Du Thao: Cai Tien To Chuc QL KT, Hai Hung, NQ Phan Cap" [Hai Hung province, "Hai Hung's economy"], 20 December 1968, 7 (P UBKHNN, hs 641, vv). Examples of similar accounts include Pham Van Cac, UBHC, Ha Bac, "BC TH CT, 1969, PHNV, 1970" [Pham Van Cac, Administrative Committee, Ha Bac province, "Report on 1969, tasks for 1970"], 8 April 1970, 4, 6 (P BNN, hs 25, vv); Hoang Quy, Pho Bi Thu, BCH, Dang Bo, Vinh Phu, DLDVN, "BCTK CT, 1969, Vinh Phu" [Hoang Quy, deputy party secretary, EC, Vinh Phu, VWP, "Summary, Vinh Phu"], 12 January 1970, 22 (P UBKHNN, hs 698, vv); Thai Binh, "Du Thao, Huong Dan, Xay Dung KH, 1970" [Thai Binh province, "Draft, planning guidelines, 1970"], n.d. [circa late 1969], 2 (P UBKHNN, hs 762, vv).

6. BCTNT, *Cai Tien Cong Tac*, 19.

Failure, warned the deputy prime minister and other top leaders, would result in a loss of interest by cooperative members.[7]

In some respects, living conditions did improve. Villagers in Da Ton in rural Hanoi and Nghiem Xuyen in Ha Tay province remember with pride the schools opened in their subdistricts by the early 1960s, which provided an education that had been impossible a decade earlier.[8] After primary school, some youngsters from poor peasant families entered secondary schools—again, something that would have been unimaginable during the colonial period. Each subdistrict also had a health clinic, staffed by one or two nurses and regularly visited by a doctor who provided medical services and medicines at little or no cost. Similar improvements developed in many other subdistricts.[9] Whereas only two or three hundred Vietnamese—nearly all of them male—out of every ten thousand had gone to school during the 1930s and 1940s, the proportion in the north climbed to nearly eight hundred of every ten thousand by 1956, doubled to seventeen hundred by 1960, and reached nearly twenty-five hundred by 1970. And 47 percent of those schooled were women. The number of health clinics and local hospitals increased from about 750 throughout north Vietnam in the early 1940s (about six beds for every ten thousand people) to 4,800 in 1960, and exceeded 7,500 by 1970 (thirty-three beds per ten thousand).[10] Funds for these educational and medical services came from national and provincial governments but cooperatives also contributed, especially toward costs for buildings, teachers, and nurses.

In other respects, however, living conditions during the 1960s were stagnating or even regressing. Notable increases in material goods in the late 1950s and early 1960s had ameliorated somewhat the harshness of rural life.[11] At least, recalled one Da Ton woman, "we had enough rice." She and her husband had married in 1960 and were just starting a family. Having grown up in the households of dirt-poor tenant farmers, both she and her husband appreciated now having enough food. She also expected conditions to improve further, as did government officials. Instead,

7. Pham Hung, Pho Thu Tuong, "HN TK NN, 1961" [Pham Hung, deputy PM, two speeches to conference on agriculture 1961], 8 March 1962, second speech, 1 (P BNN, hs 07, vv).

8. Interviews, Da Ton, Hanoi, 1993 and 1996, and Nghiem Xuyen, Ha Tay, 1993.

9. For another example, see Houtart and Lemercinier, *Hai Van*, 80–93.

10. TCTK, *Kinh Te Van Hoa*, 60, 64, 67, 68.

11. See remarks of Pham Hung, "HN TK NN" [conference], 8 March 1962, first speech, 5–6; and report on Ha Dong, To Thao, Chi cuc truong, CCTK, Ha Dong, "BC TH Doi Song Nong Dan" [To Thao, Statistics branch, Ha Dong province, "Peasants' conditions, 1961"], 20 July 1962, 10 (P TCTK, hs 2579, vv).

six or seven years later, "we couldn't afford enough rice. We had to mix our rice with corn or cassava." Even then, she sighed, "we were often hungry."[12]

Reports from many areas indicate a regression in living conditions. Take, for example, Ha Tay province. A 1962 sample survey in eight subdistricts found improvements compared to two years earlier, though the average person's monthly paddy consumption was only 16.4 kilograms.[13] The comparable figure in 1965, according to a study of twenty-one cooperatives in fifteen subdistricts, was 15.2 kilograms. By other measures, too, conditions had deteriorated. Villagers, the study found, "are still in such a state of hardship, poverty, and misery [thieu thon] that they are always worrying about their material needs—how to get sufficient food and clothing [lam the nao duoc an no mac am]."[14] A similar study done in 1970 found further decline: the average person had only about 13.5 kilograms of paddy to eat.[15] The most arduous times of the year for Ha Tay villagers were between harvests (giap hat) when the average person often had fewer than fourteen kilograms per month of paddy and other staples, well below what was considered necessary for basic nutrition. During one such period in 1966, 38 percent of Ha Tay's villagers were malnourished by local standards. During a comparable time three years later, half the people were underfed.[16] People most desperate dug up immature cassava roots to eat, begged door to door, sold paddy still growing in their household plots, and sold their immature pigs and household belongings. A few parents even sold their children or gave them away to others who could feed them.[17]

Surveys of cooperatives across the north found that average net real monthly per capita income for villagers in collective cooperatives was lower

12. Interview, Da Ton, Hanoi, 20 January 1996.

13. To Thao, "BC TH" [Peasants' conditions], 20 July 1962, table 1. Note that in the mid-1960s Ha Dong became part of Ha Tay province.

14. To Thao, Chi Cuc truong, CCTK, Ha Tay, "BC, Doi Song Nong Dan Ha Tay, 1965" [To Thao, Statistics office, Ha Tay province, "Peasants' conditions, Ha Tay, 1965"], 15 June 1966, 15, 17 (P TCTK, hs 2840, vv).

15. Vu Van, Chi Cuc truong, CCTK, Ha Tay, "BC TH Doi Song Nong Dan, 1970" [Vu Van, Statistics office, Ha Tay province, "Peasants' conditions, 1970"], 8 April 1971, 5 (P TCTK, hs 3092, vv). Because the report does not include paddy consumption, I estimated it at between 85 and 90 percent of total paddy income, a figure derived from other reports in the late 1960s.

16. Ha Tay, "PHNV KH, KT, VH, 1967–1968, KH 1967" [Ha Tay province, "1967 plan, planning for 1967–1968"], 19 December 1966, 8 (P UBKHNN, hs 621, vv); Van Phong Tinh Uy, Ha Tay, "Tom Tat So Lieu, TH SX, Doi Song" [Provincial committee office, Ha Tay, "Living conditions, statistics"], 30 September 1966, 4 (P UBKHNN, hs 528, vv); "BC KH, Phat Trien KT Dia Phuong, Ha Tay, du thao" ["Draft, 1970 plan Ha Tay"], 12 October 1969, 3a (P UBKHNN, hs 749, vv).

17. Van Phong Tinh Uy, Ha Tay, "Tom Tat So Lieu" [Living conditions], 30 September 1966, 4–5.

in the 1960s than in 1959.[18] A more telling indicator of living conditions is food consumption, particularly rice, the most important food for virtually all Vietnamese. During the 1960s–1970s, the government's desired minimal level of staple foods (*luong thuc*), measured in "paddy equivalents," was twenty kilograms per person per month.[19] This was achieved in the late 1950s and early 1960s, but the average dropped to about nineteen in 1962–1964, then ranged between seventeen and eighteen until the early 1970s (appendix 1, table 5). The proportion that was paddy, the preferred staple, dropped from 96 to 82 percent between 1960 and 1964, then averaged about 85 percent in 1965–1968, when the United States was intensively bombing northern Vietnam. By 1971, it still had not returned to the 1960 level. Without corn, potatoes, and cassava, the food situation would have been even worse, though even those rice substitutes were less available than they had been in 1959–1960. What increased in people's diets were vegetables, by more than 60 percent in the late 1960s and early 1970s compared to 1960. The only other foods to increase, according to available data, were sauces; the amount consumed doubled during the decade. As poor people in Asia often do, Vietnamese villagers reached for more soy and fish sauce to break the monotony of starchy foods and vegetables.

This bleak food situation did not vary much from region to region.[20] Within a village, some families had more food, better houses (tiled rather than thatched roofs, for instance), and more money than the majority. The differences, however, were modest.[21] As Vietnamese often say of their collective farming experience, the aim to make everyone equal succeeded: nearly everyone was equally poor (*ngheo ngang nhau*). Those who had lived

18. 11.90 dong in 1959 compared to 11.41 dong in 1966. TCTK, "Nhung Chi Tieu, NN, 1955–1967" [GSO, "Agriculture, 1955–1967"], 1968, table 286 (P TCTK, hs 760, vv). I found no real income figures beyond 1967.

19. *Luong thuc* includes paddy and other basic foods such as corn, potatoes, and cassava. Its weight is expressed in "paddy equivalents" (*quy thoc*). For instance, three kilograms of potatoes equaled one kilogram of paddy; whereas one unit of corn was equivalent to one unit of paddy. TCTK, "So Lieu Cung Cap, Van Phong Trung Uong" [GSO, "Data for central office"], June 1968, table 1 (P TCTK, hs 751, vv).

20. The small quantity of survey data I have that is broken down by region or province indicates that producers in the southernmost provinces of the north, an area usually referred to in government records as the Old Fourth Zone (*Khu 4 cu*), usually had one or two kilograms less per person per month than their counterparts elsewhere. TCTK, "So Lieu, TH SX, Phan Phoi, LT, Mien Bac" [GSO, "Staple foods, production, distribution"], 30 March 1969, tables 44, 45 (P TCTK, hs 761, vv).

21. The three reported "classes," as categorized during the 1950s land reform, and their net monthly nominal income in dong (1964 and 1970) were upper middle peasant (16.10, 21.12); middle peasant (14.77, 18.70); and poor peasant (13.50; 16.29). Vu Van, "BC TH Doi Song" [Peasants' conditions], Ha Tay, 8 April 1971, 3.

through the 1940s and early 1950s, however, had the consolation that conditions were not as bad as they had been.[22]

Living standards declined because overall production and production per capita decreased. A major reason was the war. The United States bombed northern Vietnam continuously from February 1965 to March 1968 and then again, with even greater intensity, from March to December 1972, destroying crops, dikes, and other farming infrastructures; killing and maiming villagers; and hindering farming and other production. People who could have been farming had joined the army or were otherwise directly involved in the war. Another, often related, reason was a shortage of chemical fertilizers, fuel, farming implements, and other inputs from the government. A third reason was the little incentive villagers often had to work hard and well for the collective. The value of their work points (*cong diem*) and workdays (*ngay cong*) was not known until the end of each season. Moreover, the values decreased during the 1960s and 1970s. Consequently, the average cooperative member worked more days but did not necessarily have more rice, money, or other tangibles at the end of the season.[23] Villagers also had difficulty linking an individual's work to the outcome that many people had a hand in producing. This problem is not peculiar to collective farming. Corporations, universities, and bureaucracies around the world face it. Solutions or at least partial solutions involve periodic assessments of employees, the possibility of dismissal, and competitive recruiting. In Vietnam's cooperatives, dismissal and competitive recruiting were impossible. Indeed, few people were permitted to leave the cooperatives. Assessments were made but the rewards and penalties were insignificant because the cooperative's produce was distributed according to the quality of each person's work but through a method that minimized inequalities and assisted those who were ill, weak, or too young or old to work (see appendix 2).

Such conditions suggest there was no reason for villagers to commit to collective cooperatives and no incentive to stay. This, however, is not the whole story. Other dynamics from the early 1960s to the mid-1970s engen-

22. Sikor, "Political Economy," 90, has a similar assessment.
23. Many documents indicate that as the size of collective cooperatives increased, the value of a workday decreased. Vinh Phuc villagers I interviewed recalled that a workday equaled two to three kilograms of paddy when cooperatives were the size of a hamlet or two in about 1960–1961, but dropped to one kilogram or less when cooperatives encompassed one or more villages in the mid- and late 1960s. The only available general figures, which compare workday values (measured in currency unadjusted for inflation) for selected years between 1960 and 1970, show that while the number of workdays per cooperative member increased from 166 in 1960 to 215 in 1970, the value per workday dropped from 0.61 to 0.49 dong. TCTK, *12 Nam Phat Trien*, 578, 582.

dered considerable emotional commitment to fellow villagers and to the aim of collective farming for the nation. Until about 1964 or 1965, most cooperatives were still composed of people in the same neighborhood or hamlet (*xom*) within a village. Relationships among people there had helped in the forming of cooperatives in the first place and encouraged people to make the best of collective farming, considering that, at least for the time being, no realistic alternative existed. Kinship and friendship ties were strong. A large percentage of spouses were from the same or adjacent neighborhoods. Neighborhoods and hamlets in the Red River delta also often shared communal halls, shrines, and rituals. This is not to say that everyone got along, but they did know one another.

That knowledge made it easier for people to keep an eye on those reputed to be shirkers. It also meant that social pressure against such behavior could be effective and that individuals would do their share to avoid embarrassing themselves. This situation is probably one reason production per capita on collective land in the early 1960s tended to be higher than later, when cooperatives became larger. Being reasonably close to one another also made sharing produce more acceptable than it would have been otherwise. Many villagers saw the value, albeit sometimes reluctantly, of assuring a minimum amount of income to everyone. This was not just altruism. The person giving today could be the one receiving tomorrow.[24]

As the collective cooperatives grew, however, personal relations among members became fewer, weaker, and hence less useful for engendering commitment, incentives, and trust. As one villager recalled, people could "understand and appreciate" (*thong cam*) the importance of sharing paddy with those who were too sick or old to work, but not with those who were "lazy" (*luoi*). Knowing who was what became more difficult as production brigades and cooperatives became larger. A theme in documents, publications, and interviews is that individuals often believed that devoting a great deal of their energy to collective production would benefit "everyone" much more than it would benefit them. If everyone were equally industrious, then there would be more returns for all to share. In practice or in people's fears, however, many members failed to do their share yet still had a claim on what was produced. Villagers also became alienated from the organizations and the work they did. They looked on the collective cooperatives not as theirs but as "everyone's," meaning no one's or somebody else's.[25]

24. Interviews, Da Ton, Hanoi, and Nghiem Xuyen, Ha Tay, 1992, 1993.
25. The oft-heard expression *cha chung khong ai khoc*, "no one cries for the father of everyone," captures this problem, namely, that what belongs to everybody is no one's concern, or everybody's business is nobody's business.

Wartime conditions compensated for some of this loss. Local and national officials stressed that the cooperatives were key units in the nation's war to "fight the United States and save the country" (*chong My cuu Nuoc*), a popular slogan at the time. Usually cooperatives rather than subdistrict governments were the agencies that recruited young men for the army, mobilized grain and other produce to feed the troops, and organized local militia. Although some villagers did not support the war, far more believed that their work in the cooperatives would support Vietnam's army and help defeat the United States.[26] An elderly villager put it this way: "The cooperative and the war were glued together. Without the cooperative, what was required on the home front and on the fighting front could not have been accomplished."[27] As they farmed collective fields, often at night and in the wee hours of the morning to avoid U.S. bombers, villagers were not just mindful of the nation's struggle in the abstract. They were thinking of relatives and friends. Sixty percent of families in Vinh Phuc and Phu Tho provinces had husbands, sons, brothers, or sisters who were directly involved in the war effort, many of them in the army.[28] The situation was similar elsewhere. Knowing their country's survival and their own relatives' lives were at stake, villagers tended to pull together and endure hardships more than they might otherwise have done. Meanwhile, for the people directly involved in the war effort, the cooperatives were assurance that their families back home would have something to eat precisely because produce was divided not just according to one's work but also according to need.

26. Scanty information about those who did not support the war or who evaded army recruiters suggests they ranged from former landlords and French partisans to average villagers who had earlier fought against the French. Nguyen Xuan Truong, Bi Thu, BCH Dang Bo, DLDVN, Ha Tay, "Qua Ba Nam Chong My, Xay Dung CNXH" [Nguyen Xuan Truong, party secretary, EC, VWP, Ha Tay province, "Three years, fighting United States, building socialism"], December 1967, 12, 129 (P UBKHNN, hs 553, vv); Pham Van Cac, "BC TH CT, 1969," Ha Bac, 8 April 1970, 6; Huyen Tien Lang, *Lich Su*, 139–40; DiGregorio, "Iron Works," 254–55.

27. "Khang chien gan voi hop tac xa. Khong co hop tax xa se khong lam duoc viec hau phuong va mat tran." Interview, Tam Canh, Vinh Phuc, 10 August 2000. Other informants in Vinh Phuc and elsewhere also believed the cooperatives helped the war effort. Documents from the period say the bombing and the war prompted cooperative members to work harder. For instance, a 1969 report on rural Hanoi, which discussed weak collective cooperatives and villagers' doubts about the honesty and abilities of local leaders, says the war inspired people to persevere. Vu Hoa My, So NN, UBHC Ha Noi, "BC TH CT, 1969" [Vu Hoa My, Agriculture office, Hanoi administrative office, "Conditions, 1969"], 20 March 1970, 2 (P BNN, hs 25, vv). See also Tran Thi Que, *Vietnam's Agriculture*, 21; Nguyen Ngoc Luu, "Peasants, Party," 483, 564; Luu Van Sung, "Nhung Hinh Thuc," 422–23; Chaliand, *Peasants*, 139, 140, 147, 156, 235.

28. From a report by Kim Ngoc, provincial party secretary, *Vinh Phu*, 21 October 1975, 2.

*Trust*

In durable rural common-use organizations, mutual trust enhances cooperation and reduces monitoring costs. In northern Vietnam trust in the government helped get people to join cooperatives, but the prolonged and mutually beneficial interaction often needed for bonds to develop among members was rare.[29] A major reason was that the collective cooperatives were rapidly enlarged, hindering people's efforts to enhance old or build new relationships. An example is Bach Tru village (*thon*) in Tien Thang subdistrict of Vinh Phuc. In 1960 the village had four hamlet-sized cooperatives. In 1964, those four became two. By 1969–1970, those two had become one cooperative for the entire village of about 280 households. The pace of amalgamation was similar elsewhere. The several hamlet- and neighborhood-sized cooperatives in Tam Canh subdistrict, Vinh Phuc, in 1960 were replaced in 1962 with three village-sized ones. By 1966–1967, two of those three were joined into one.[30] In Da Ton subdistrict, Hanoi, the several hamlet-sized cooperatives that existed by 1961 were reconfigured in 1962 to form five cooperatives, one for each village. By 1965, these five were forged into one subdistrict-sized cooperative with over 600 households.[31] Although such subdistrict-sized cooperatives were unusual in the mid-1960s, by then the majority in the delta were village-sized.[32] Between 1960 and 1970, the number of cooperatives dropped by half, from 40,400 to 19,900, yet the number of rural households in them increased by 30 percent.[33] As small ones were combined to form larger ones, the average size of Red River delta cooperatives doubled, from 77 households in 1960 to 123 in 1964. By 1968, the average had more than doubled again, to 299 households, and continued to increase during the 1970s. For northern Vietnam as a whole, the increase was smaller but nevertheless nearly

29. Axelrod, *Evolution*, 129–30, provides a general argument about the importance of prolonged interaction.

30. Interviews, Tien Thang and Tam Canh, August 2000.

31. Interviews, Da Ton.

32. Having found no data on this point for the delta as a whole or the entire north, I base this on information about particular places. For instance, informants recall that cooperatives in the Vinh Phuc subdistricts of Dao Duc, Quat Luu, Tam Canh, and Tien Thang corresponded to entire villages by 1962–1965. In Ha Dong province, 54 percent of the cooperatives were village-sized by 1962 (assorted tables in P TCTK, hs 456, vv). In Hai Hung, 90 percent of the province's cooperatives encompassed a village or multiple villages (*lien thon*) by early 1968. The other 10 percent encompassed entire subdistricts. BCH, Dang Bo, "PHNV, KH, 1968, Hai Hung" [EC, party provincial office, "Hai Hung, 1968 plan"], 25 April 1968, 4 (P UBKHNN, hs 641, vv).

33. Rounded figures from TCTK, *12 Nam Phan Trien*, 557, 559.

tripled between 1960 and 1971, from 60 households per cooperative to 160 (see appendix 1, table 6).

It was not impossible to establish trust and cooperation among people who were not previously close. But it was difficult, particularly when people were brought together from different villages with a history of suspicion and animosity between them. Often, as one man recalled, "those in one village were dubious [nghi ngo] about those in the next."[34] Even among hamlets, said a former cooperative leader in Vinh Phuc province, "jealousies and envy" (suy bi ti nanh) worked against good farming in large cooperatives.[35] There and elsewhere, such as a village in Hai Hung province, families in hamlets with more or better-quality land felt wronged when they were merged with less advantaged hamlets.[36] Leaders of small cooperatives were known to hide or disperse accumulated funds and sell or even consume their cooperative's pigs and draft animals rather than surrender them to the enlarged organization. After mergers, members squabbled over equipment, funds, and other resources that had previously belonged to the smaller cooperatives.[37]

To significantly reduce distrust, durable large common-use agrarian organizations usually build on small units, each composed of people with long associations and with a track record of accomplishments. These small units typically come first. Later they join together to create larger organizations in which they are then "nested."[38] While such a building process corresponds to what the Communist Party in Vietnam outlined when embarking on collectivization in the 1950s, it did not occur in most areas. The initial small units themselves were often wobbly. And when cooperatives were amalgamated in the 1960s and 1970s, the small ones were not retained as units within the larger ones.

China's collectives had something closer to nested units than did Vietnam's. Collectives in China, created and enlarged even more hastily than in Vietnam, by 1958 often encompassed several villages, each with about five hundred to a thousand households. After various attempts to encourage trust and give members more incentive to work well, the "production team" became the key work and social unit by 1961–1962.

34. Interview, Tien Thang, Vinh Phuc, 25 August 2000.
35. Interview, Quat Luu, Vinh Phuc, 5 August 2000.
36. Pham Toan, "Ngo Xuyen," 212.
37. Hai Hung, 30 March 1972, 2; CCTK, Ha Tay, "BC TH, HTX, 1966" [Statistics office, Ha Tay province, "Cooperatives, 1966"], 7 January 1967, 3, 9 (P TCTK, hs 743, vv); Nguyen Ngoc Luu, "Peasants, Party," 522.
38. Ostrom, Governing, 90, 102, 189.

Averaging thirty-three households in 1976, each team had considerable autonomy from the next-higher unit, the brigade, to which it had to turn over some of its produce to meet tax obligations and crop quotas.[39] In addition to having its own leaders, a team owned the land, draft animals, and other resources it used. Usually each team also had its own cashier and storehouse and could establish its own funds. Many teams were composed of people in the same hamlet or neighborhood, linked together through "a complex skein of loyalties, social pressures, and shared beliefs and commitments that go beyond anything mere economic cooperation could engender."[40] Others deviated from traditional hamlet and neighborhood boundaries to create teams with more than one family lineage, for instance, while respecting other social continuities.[41]

The nearest comparable unit in Vietnam's collective cooperatives was the production brigade (*doi san xuat*). It too was the basic unit of production and its leaders were in charge of setting daily farming schedules and assigning and overseeing work. But brigades owned no land, draft animals, tractors, or other means of production. These resources belonged to the cooperative and were distributed only provisionally to the brigades by the managerial board. Nor were brigades supposed to have their own funds. In practice, struggles between brigade leaders and cooperative managers over land, crops, funds, and other resources were ubiquitous. Nevertheless, the underlying principles governing brigade-cooperative relations made the brigade more subordinate to the cooperative's top leaders than the production team was in China.

Moreover, the size and composition of brigades frequently changed. The trend was to merge small brigades to form larger ones. For instance, in the early 1960s Dao Xuyen village in Da Ton had twelve brigades, each averaging fifteen households that were in the same neighborhood. During the next dozen years, the number of brigades decreased and their size increased. By 1976, the village had only four, each with about sixty to eighty households farming twenty to twenty-two hectares.[42] Villagers in Vinh Phuc province also recall that brigades decreased in number and increased in size as cooperatives were enlarged.[43] Officials justified the changes by saying they were to improve production, minimize inequalities in land and income among brigades in the same cooperative, and shake up brigades that author-

39. Oi, *State and Peasant*, 5; Kelliher, *Peasant Power*, 9.
40. Unger, "Collective Incentives," 585.
41. Potter and Potter, *China's Peasants*, 98.
42. Interviews, Da Ton, Hanoi, January–April 1996.
43. Interviews, Vinh Phuc, August 2000.

ities thought were deviant. In practice, the changes often undermined informal relationships and other connections that might have engendered more trust among members and greater incentives to work hard for the good of everyone in the brigade, if not for the cooperative as a whole.

## Monitoring and Sanctions

In successful common-pool organizations, monitoring and sanctions are largely a by-product of the personal, usually material interests members have in seeing that all members follow the rules. In an irrigation organization, for instance, the individuals most concerned with cheating are typically "in direct contact with each other." Consequently, each person deters others from taking too much water. Members also have an interest in reporting violations and imposing sanctions on violators.[44] Such simple mechanisms may be less viable in common-production organizations, which share what has been collectively produced, because the connection between how each member uses the shared resource and the result for that member is difficult to see. Two people in the same production brigade of a Vietnamese cooperative assigned to irrigate a collective field could not readily connect how each used the water with how much each received of the harvest.[45]

Some durable common-production agrarian organizations rely on simple monitoring and sanctioning methods. Hutterite collectives, whose members have a high degree of mutual trust and ideological commitment, operate on the assumption that everyone will do her or his best for the community. These collectives do not keep track of how much time people spend working nor do they measure labor productivity nor is there elaborate surveillance. Peer pressure to work and behave properly goes a long way toward disciplining members. Anyone who thinks someone is letting down the community is expected to tell the Elders, who generally resolve the matter in a low-key but often public manner. Sanctions are usually "gentle and persuasive, not physical or drastic." The reprimanded person has considerable confidence that other members in the same situation would have been treated similarly.[46]

44. Ostrom, Governing, 95–99. Also see Wade, Village Republics, 90, 216.

45. It was easier for them to see advantages to preventing water for their brigade's field from being used by a different brigade. Dinh Thu Cuc, "Qua Trinh," 349–50; and Truong Huyen Chi, "Changing Processes," 56–57.

46. Bennett, Hutterian Brethren, 136, 200–201, 259.

Social pressures and obligations did affect how Vietnamese worked in collective fields, but more so while cooperatives were hamlet- or village-sized than when they became larger. Within brigades, lazy members were sometimes embarrassed before fellow workers. Wartime conditions also influenced villagers to do the jobs assigned to them as well as possible. Neither social pressure nor the war, however, was enough to assure that people would do what they were supposed to do.

Vietnam's cooperatives used various methods to monitor and assess work. In the early years, brigade members assessed one another and assigned points (*binh cong cham diem*). The people doing a particular task also sometimes assessed one another's work. Brigade leaders could oversee the work and determine how many points it was worth. Villagers, however, often criticized such methods. Self-assessments, they complained, favored people who exaggerated and penalized people who were modest or shy. Similarly, "loudmouths" and others who were pushy and grumbled received more points than people who just did the work.[47] Some people routinely tried to get more work points by taking longer to complete a job than was necessary. Dilatory work, exaggerated claims about its quality, and other such behaviors were dubbed "prolonging the work, inflating the points" (*rong cong phong diem*), an expression widely known among cooperative members. Another criticism was that women were given harder tasks but fewer points than men.[48] Villagers also believed that brigade leaders often played favorites, awarding more points and easier jobs to people they liked and discriminating against those they disliked.[49]

Trying to address such complaints and improve production, national authorities began to insist in the early 1960s that cooperatives develop "work norms" (*dinh muc lao dong*) and "work ratings" (*bac cong viec*).[50] The norms specified the amount and quality of work to be completed within a stipulated time period. Ratings categorized each task according to physical effort, complexity, and importance to the end product. The objective was to systematize the allocation of work points. If there were norms and corresponding points for each phase of work, the official thinking went, there would be no arbitrariness and less discrimination, favoritism, and

47. One expression for this was *cong lung an chao, lam lao an com* (those who bend over get gruel, those who are cheeky and insolent get rice). *Vinh Phu*, 25 February 1969, 2.

48. Nam Ha, *May Kinh Nghiem*, 10, 20.

49. A common expression captured this: *Doi truong yeu nen tot, ghet nen xau* (a brigade leader's love brings good things, hate brings bad). Vinh Phu, *Hoc Tap va Thi Dua*, 20.

50. These were supposed to be developed with the "three contracts" system (see appendix 2).

"stealing of work points" (*an cap cong diem*). Initially, the norms and ratings were based on estimates. Later, authorities pressed cooperatives to develop them through tests that took into account "well-grounded technical criteria."[51]

Establishing and then applying the norms and ratings were complex operations. It was not simply a matter of determining, for instance, that the norm for planting paddy was three *sao* (1,080 square meters) per day per transplanter or that the standard for plowing was four *sao* per day per plowman (or plowwoman). Other factors were supposed to count: condition of the soil, elevation of the land, the field's distance from the village, age and health of the draft animal, type of plow used, and so on. Not only authorities added factors; villagers themselves insisted on them.[52] Ratings required additional distinctions. For instance, plowing to prepare a seedling bed could have a different rating than plowing to prepare a paddy field. Plowing a vegetable patch could be different still. The logic of the system dictated that norms and ratings be established for every phase of work: not only plowing and planting but harrowing, preparing seedlings, pulling seedlings, carrying seedlings to the fields, carrying manure to the fields, spreading the manure, irrigating fields, scooping water into irrigation canals, weeding, standing paddy plants upright after they had been flattened by floods, spreading chemical fertilizer, reaping, threshing, drying, packing, and so on. The list was virtually endless. Theoretically, each task needed to be suitably modified by such variables as soil conditions, distance, and quality of draft animals. All of this was just for paddy farming. A similarly elaborate process was supposed to be done for every other aspect of collective work.

The result was hundreds of norms, each classified into several ratings. When compiled, one villager in Vinh Phuc recalled, they formed "fat books." Dong Xuan, a cooperative in Vinh Phuc province that national authorities said was exemplary, had over five hundred work norms in 1967–1968: three hundred for farming and more than two hundred for other kinds of work. A year later it had six hundred. Some cooperatives had more. The one in Yen Lo, a village of Dao Duc subdistrict in Vinh Phuc, had thirteen hundred and twenty-nine in 1969.[53] Still these were inadequate. "They had to be combined with judgment based on experience," recalled a man who had been a brigade leader (*doi truong*) in Da Ton

51. *Management of Cooperatives*, 100–101. See also Tran Ngoc Canh, *Cai Tien*, 15–38.
52. See list of villagers concerns in *Vinh Phu*, 25 October 1968, 2.
53. Vinh Phu, *Hoc Tap va Thi Dua*, 12, 20; *Vinh Phu*, 1 April 1969, 3.

for more than thirty years.[54] Thus even cooperatives such as Da Ton, which used this complex system better than most, did not eliminate discretion and possible discrimination. In numerous places the system barely got started. In many others it collapsed under its own weighty bookkeeping and complexity. Cooperatives frequently reverted to the system where brigade leaders and members assessed the work—a method that depended on trust and commitment and was vulnerable to favoritism, bargaining, and cheating. One consequence, according to a 1972 survey in rural Hanoi, was the resurgence of "prolonging the work, inflating the points" and other poor work habits.[55]

## Governance

Many aspects of how Vietnam's collective cooperatives were supposed to be governed and managed corresponded well to how durable agrarian common-use organizations are governed. As members of the cooperatives, ordinary Vietnamese villagers were supposed to be the "masters of the house."[56] Statutes and official pronouncements emphasized "democracy" (*dan chu*) and "democratic management" (*quan ly dan chu*). The overall governing body of each cooperative was supposed to be a "congress" composed of all members (*Dai Hoi Xa Vien*) or a "congress of delegates" representing the members (*Dai Hoi Dai Bieu Xa Vien*). That body would decide financial and production matters, set work standards, establish brigades, elect the managerial board and other leaders, and make all other important decisions.[57] Financial and other sorts of records were supposed to be transparent (*cong khai*). Leaders were to be honest and dedicated cooperative members as well as experienced farmers. They were supposed to listen and to be accountable to members, encourage discussion about the cooperative's affairs, and lead by example rather than by order.[58]

54. Interview, Da Ton, Hanoi, 23 April 1993.
55. Hanoi, *Bao Cao Ket Qua*, 110.
56. A well-known slogan of the time, attributed to Ho Chi Minh, was *Hop tac xa la nha, xa vien la chu* (a cooperative is the house, a member is the master).
57. Drafts and other versions of statutes for cooperatives appeared in the 1960s–1970s. At least three have been translated into English. Fforde, "Law," 323–36; "Constitution of High-Level Co-operative Farms," in *Vietnamese Studies* no. 27 (1971), 253–86; and "Agricultural Co-operatives Statute," in *Summary of World Broadcasts*, 30 October 1974, FE/W799/C1–C14.
58. As one early instruction said, "For cooperatives to be managed well, the principle of democratic management must be comprehended." BCTNT, *Cai Tien Cong Tac*, 25. A published list of "dos and don'ts" for cooperative leaders said, "Work alongside the masses, live with and

Many leaders had these attributes and enjoyed the respect of fellow villagers. And numerous collective cooperatives were governed well. Among them were some village-sized cooperatives and later the subdistrict-wide cooperative in Da Ton of rural Hanoi. Such cooperatives were held up as models for others to emulate.[59] One indication of good governance in Dong Xuan of Vinh Phuc province was that the sixteen bicycles awarded to it for greatly increasing its production and sales to state agencies were given to the cooperative's best workers. Officials did not take any of the bicycles for themselves.[60] Villagers in another cooperative in Vinh Phuc praised their chairperson for his honesty and evenhanded treatment of all members, whether they were related to him or not.[61] Good brigade leaders in a village in Hoa Binh province worked in the fields along with everyone else, skillfully resolved problems among members, and were dutiful parents and attentive caretakers of their elderly relatives.[62] A village in rural Hanoi boosted production when managers sought villagers' advice, encouraged their participation in major decisions, and shared financial information about the cooperative.[63]

Poorly managed and governed cooperatives, however, were also numerous. Many chairpersons, brigade leaders, and other cooperative officials acted like "mandarin" or "white collar" officials (*tha trung quan*). They shunned physical labor and "commanded" (*menh lenh*) people to do things. Some belittled women and others they deemed inferior. Although such behavior often angered villagers, most were too intimidated to complain. Those who did sometimes suffered more. Their work points were mysteriously reduced, for instance, or their children were dismissed from school for no apparent reason. Authorities tended to treat complainers, as a 1967 Ha Tay provincial report said, with "extreme prejudice" (*thanh kien sau sac*). From such evidence of a "lack of democracy" (*thieu dan chu*) and of other failings in management, the report concluded that only 40 percent of cooperative chairpersons in the province were doing their job properly, that 35 percent were not but with training could improve, and that 25 percent

listen to the masses, discuss all tasks with the people, be a model for implementing policies, don't reserve the easy work for yourself, look after the fruits of collective labor, and resist any tendency to disregard or ignore the masses." *Vinh Phu*, 17 September 1968, 3.

59. Interviews and observations in Da Ton, Hanoi.

60. Vinh Phu, *Hoc Tap va Thi Dua*, 15.

61. *Nhan Dan*, 5 January 1967, 3. Such leaders are also depicted in novels and short stories written in the 1960s–1970s. See "Trong Lang Nho" [In a small village], written in 1969 and republished in Le Luu, *Truyen Ngan*, 27–50.

62. *Nhan Dan*, 10 August 1969, 2.

63. Ibid., 24 November 1970, 2.

should be removed.[64] No assessment was made of other cooperative leaders, though the report did say that 24 percent of the local party secretaries and 22 percent of subdistrict presidents ought to be removed as well. Figures for other periods and provinces are not available. But the many accounts of such problems in particular villages and the frequent rectification campaigns suggest that poorly governed cooperatives were widespread.[65]

Another serious failing was corruption—officials illicitly using their positions to benefit themselves and their families. Often the amounts taken were small—a few sacks of paddy or a few hundred dong. Or an official might credit himself with days of work that had not been done. In the context of scarcity and war, these seemingly modest amounts often exceeded what villagers could forgive. The amounts could also be large. In one subdistrict in Phu Tho province, the cooperative chairperson, local party secretary, and subdistrict president took about 2,300 dong each and much of the 8,675 kilograms of paddy missing from the cooperative's granary.[66] Officials in about a third of eighty-two surveyed cooperatives in the 1960s "borrowed" money and paddy from the cooperative but did not repay it or did so only after being discovered. Outright embezzlement was less common yet occurred at least once in 70 percent of the party cells within the surveyed cooperatives between 1964 and 1970.[67] By forging receipts and using deceptive accounting methods, leaders created "black

64. Nguyen Xuan Truong, "Qua Ba Nam" [Three years, fighting U.S.], Ha Tay, December 1967, 104–12. Other material I am drawing on includes Lai Huy Tien, DB Thai Binh, "TL, QL HTX, Ky Thuat" [Lai Huy Tien, delegate, Thai Binh province, NA, "Technology, management of cooperatives"], 8 May 1963 (P QH, hs 272, vv); "Phuong Huong, KT Dia Phuong, 1969–1975, Vinh Phu" ["Economic development, Vinh Phu province, seven years], 10 January 1969, 10–12 (P UBKHNN, hs 698, vv); and several articles in *Nhan Dan*, 1967–1971.

65. Some of those campaigns are discussed in Tran Nhu Trang, "Transformation," 422–29; and Post, *Revolution*, 190–94. Also, a ranking party member, Hoang Quoc Viet, said in "Kien Quyet," 35–41, that bureaucratic and undemocratic leaders were significant problems in the collective cooperatives during the late 1960s.

66. TCTK, "BC: Mot So Net, TH Lang Phi, Tham O, HTXNN" [GSO, "Waste, embezzlement, cooperatives"], 1 March 1967, 4–5 (P TCTK, hs 791, vv). At that time, one dong was worth about 3.2 kilograms of paddy (interviews, Vinh Phuc, August 2000).

67. "BCKQ Dieu Tra, TH QL HTXNN" [Management survey], n.d. [circa 1971], 4, 25–26 (P TCTK, hs 993, vv). This is the title I have given to five reports in a folder labeled "BCKQ Dieu Tra Dien Hinh TH QL HTXNN, 4 Huyen thuoc Khu 4, 1960–1970, TCTK" (page numbers are those that archive staff penciled on each sheet). The folder's label is misleading. Only one of the four studied districts, Do Luong (Nghe An province), is in "Khu 4," the southernmost region of northern Vietnam. The others are Chiem Hoa, Tuyen Quang province, in the mountainous north; Thanh Ba, a midlands area in Vinh Phu; and Xuan Thuy, Nam Ha, in the delta. Some reports in the folder also draw on surveys of collective cooperatives in all four regions of the north. The five reports apparently are part of a larger study, which I could not find.

funds" (*quy den*) for their own use. Officials in charge of money and produce, such as chairpersons, accountants, storehouse managers, and granary custodians, were especially tempted. Detection by auditors was often difficult, especially when several key authorities were "in cahoots" (*moc ngoac*).[68] Accomplices sometimes included district authorities.

Corruption began in some areas not long after collective cooperatives were established. A former Thai Binh official said a cooperative chairperson had stolen a sizable proportion of newly harvested paddy in 1960.[69] Assisted by relatives not yet in the cooperative, the chairperson managed to sell the grain, then bought a radio and a motorcycle and renovated his house.[70] Although an investigation failed to prove he had done these things, he was removed from office. In Ha Dong province, embezzlement and "waste and squander" (*lang phi*) were already "fairly common" (*kha pho bien*) by early 1962.[71] Villagers recall that corruption worsened as cooperatives grew larger and required accounting and managerial skills beyond the abilities of those in charge.[72] Suspicions of corruption, if not the misdeed itself, afflicted "nearly 100 percent" of cooperatives in Thai Binh province by 1963.[73] A 1966 survey of two hundred collective cooperatives in Ha Tay province found that 78 percent had at least one leader, often a party member, who embezzled cooperative assets and in other ways illicitly profited from his or her position (*loi dung*).[74] Reports from other provinces in the late 1960s also criticized prevalent corruption.[75] The General Statistics

68. As a former villager from Vinh Phuc province said, "If the chairman, the chief accountant, and the audit commissioner go into collusion, no cadres from outside the village can detect the corruption and embezzlement." Tran Nhu Trang, "Transformation," 508.

69. Elliott, Transcript, 126–28.

70. More commonly, corrupt officials avoided conspicuously consuming their illicit gains. They might, for instance, use the paddy for pig feed, increase the number of pigs they raised, and then sell the mature animals. Large amounts of stolen paddy or cash could be converted into gold or other precious items and hidden until safe to use.

71. Ngo Van Thin, pho chu nhiem, UBKH, Ha Dong, "BC Thuc Hien KH Nha Nuoc, 1961" [Ngo Van Thin, vice chairperson, Planning Committee, Ha Dong province, "Implementing state plan"], 15 February 1962, 11 (P UBKHNN, hs 353, vv). Documents often refer to *lang phi* (waste, squander), which can cover a range of things but frequently referred to food and privileges that officials indulged in at the expense of collective resources.

72. Interviews, Nghiem Xuyen, Ha Tay province, and four subdistricts, Vinh Phuc province. A similar explanation appears in official histories of the period. For instance, Huyen Chuong My, *Lich Su Dang Bo*, 61.

73. Elliott, Transcript, 128.

74. The average amount missing or stolen per cooperative was 3,900 dong and 476 kilograms of paddy. CCTK, Ha Tay, "BC TH HTX" [Cooperatives], 7 January 1967, 3.

75. UBHC, Vinh Phu, "Phan Thu Nhat, TH, Vinh Phu" [Administrative Committee, Vinh Phu province, "Vinh Phu features"], 12 December 1968, 6 (P UBKHNN, hs 698, vv); "May Van De, KT, Hai Hung" ["Economic problems, Hai Hung," probably from the province's planning office], April 1970 (P UBKHNN, hs 751, vv).

Office found that corruption, waste, and lack of transparency in budgets and accounting records were "widespread and rather serious" (*pho bien va kha nghiem trong*) across the countryside.[76] In late 1969, disappointed that corruption persisted, the government and the party's Central Executive Committee called for a redoubling of efforts to fight it.[77]

None of the campaigns to fight corruption and improve management addressed another governance shortcoming: cooperatives had little room to run their own affairs. While emphasizing democracy and villagers' roles as masters of the cooperatives, the Communist Party government insisted on "socialist democracy" and "collective mastery." These concepts embraced transparency and ordinary villagers' involvement in decision making, but they also required creating a social, political, and economic order in line with the party's overall vision. "Democracy" and "mastery" without the "socialist" and "collective" attributes were not acceptable.

As the head of the Ministry of Agriculture's Bureau of Agricultural Cooperativization and other authorities stressed, this meant that the local Communist Party organization was to be in charge of production brigades and collective cooperatives.[78] Party members, authorities believed, were more committed to collective farming and other aspects of socialism and better prepared to raise the awareness of fellow villagers. National leaders also expected party members to be more disciplined and public service–oriented than other people. And if some party members were not, then the party organization would make them shape up. With party members in charge of cooperatives, the implementation of national policies and programs was also supposed to be assured.

In the early 1960s, numerous rural areas had no or very few party members, a situation that hampered the party's efforts to dominate collective cooperatives. Recruitment drives rapidly broadened the party's reach, however.[79] For example, most villages in Ha Tay without party cells (*chi bo*)

76. TCTK, Vu Pho, Vu NN, "BC TH SX, HTHNN, 1966" [GSO, Agriculture bureau, "Agricultural cooperativization, production, 1966"], 15 January 1967, 22 (P TCTK, hs 734, vv). The GSO found 836 embezzlement cases in 967 cooperatives surveyed across the country in 1970, 187 cases in 425 sampled cooperatives in 1972, and 432 cases in 378 sampled cooperatives in 1973. TCTK, *Bao Cao Phan Tich*, 31.

77. BCHTU, DLDVN, "TT, Nguoi Cach Mang, Chong Lam Dung, Tham O," so 242-TT/TW [CEC, VWP, "Fighting embezzlement," circular 242], 21 November 1969, in Bo Noi Vu, *Van Kien Dang*, 219–21.

78. Duong Quoc Cam, *Mot So Kinh Nghiem qua dot I*, 44–45. A training manual for party cadres says, "The principle of democratic management in the cooperatives aimed at mobilizing all members to participate in managing the collective and to bring into play their creativity is to be combined with the party's leadership and the organizational and implementation work of the cooperative's managerial office." *Cong Tac Quan Ly*, 11.

79. Porter, *Vietnam*, 70.

early in the decade had them by 1967. By that point 2.3 percent of the province's population—and 4.2 percent of all cooperative members—were in the party. Nearly one-third of the party members in the rural areas were women. Although 25 percent of cooperatives still had no party cells, all had members. Half of the province's brigades, however, had no members. Such gaps, insisted provincial and national leaders, required serious attention if the party's influence over the collective cooperatives was to grow.[80]

In theory, any member could be elected brigade leader or member of the cooperative's managerial board. In practice, few people other than those the party supported—by the mid- to late 1960s, they were often party members themselves—held key positions.[81] The managerial board (*ban quan tri*) was elected by the cooperative member's congress or, in most cases, their congress of delegates, which chose from a list of nominees. The local party organization invariably made nominations. Anyone else could also submit names. Rarely, however, were nonparty nominees chosen. No one was required to vote for them, but it was difficult to do otherwise. In speeches and by other methods, party members pressed for their nominees. Nominees without party support had no such advantage. Moreover, party nominees usually came across as better informed, better prepared, and more concerned with the general welfare. After being chosen, the managerial board selected one of its members to chair the board and, thus, the collective cooperative. Often the chairperson (*chu nhiem*) was not only a member of the party but the secretary (*bi thu*), the highest officer in the local party organization. Brigade leaders, though usually elected directly by brigade members, were sometimes appointed by the managerial board. In either event, if party members were available, they were likely to head the brigades.[82]

Higher authorities made the major decisions, not cooperative members or even their leaders.[83] National authorities were the ones who insisted on

80. Nguyen Xuan Truong, "Qua Ba Nam" [Three years, fighting U.S.], Ha Tay, December 1967, 110–22; Van Phong, BCHTU, DLDVN, "TB, BBT Gop Y Kien, Uy Ha Tay, PHNV, KT, 1968–1970" [Office of CEC, VWP, "Secretariat with Ha Tay leaders, economy 1968–1970"], 27 August 1968, 2 (P UBKHNN, hs 705, vv).

81. In Hai Hung province, for instance, 66 percent of managerial board members in collective cooperatives sampled in 1972 were in the party; 93 percent of the chairpersons and deputy chairpersons were party members. Pham Quang Minh, *Zwischen Theorie und Praxis*, 278.

82. Interviews, Vinh Phuc, August 2000; Elliott, Transcript, 131, 149. See also Tran Nhu Trang, "Transformation," 479–85 passim.

83. One big mistake, wrote a man who had worked from 1966 until the early 1990s in the Ministry of Agriculture's units concerned with collectivization, was that all the major steps along the way were taken "because cadres and top officials wanted them, not because cooperative members asked for them." Nguyen Huu Tien, "Phong Trao," 28.

maintaining the cooperatives despite the many deficiencies they themselves acknowledged. Few areas got away with not having cooperatives.[84] National and provincial party and government officials organized the drives to enlarge the cooperatives. They also decided to convert "low-level" cooperatives to "high-level" and eliminate payments to villagers for the land they had given up. Those payments, villagers recall, ended within two or three years after the cooperatives were established. The directive came from above in the early 1960s when the "management improvement" campaign (*cai tien quan ly*) began and when external authorities required small cooperatives to merge.[85] As some villagers said about this top-down method of decision making, "the province pressures the district, which pressures the subdistrict, which pressures the cooperative, which pressures the brigade, which pressures the members."[86]

National authorities regularly issued instructions and rules about running the cooperatives. Often these were reactions to reports and surveys about arrangements within cooperatives that were out of line with national prescriptions. Those arrangements frequently emerged from understandings reached between dissatisfied cooperative members and local officials who were trying to follow national instructions while dealing with villagers' concerns and other realities on the ground. Few national party and government authorities, at least until the mid-1970s, regarded these modifications as healthy signs that members were exercising their "ownership" rights over "their" cooperatives. They saw them instead as weaknesses and failings, which needed to be rectified through better management, training, discipline, and additional regulations and directives from Hanoi.

The Communist Party government's "three contracts" policy (*ba khoan*), which was supposed to be a major feature of collective farming after about 1961, spawned some of the most threatening local modifications. The contracts, drawn up between a cooperative's managerial board and its brigade leaders, specified the inputs and labor a brigade would use and the amount of paddy and other products it would produce. Brigade leaders were

---

84. Among the few were some villages in Chuong My district, Ha Tay province, in which less than 15 percent of households had formed cooperatives by 1967. CCTK, Ha Tay, "BC TH HTX" [Cooperatives], 7 January 1967, 3.

85. Interviews, Da Ton, Hanoi, and four subdistricts in Vinh Phuc province.

86. "Tinh tan huyen, huyen tan xa, xa tan hop tac xa, hop tac xa tan doi, doi tan xa vien." Villagers were playing with the Vietnamese word for metric ton, *tan*, and a government campaign in the 1960s imploring cooperatives to produce at least five tons of paddy per hectare per year. The word *tan* can mean assail, pressure, or impose. Hence the demand for "five tons" becomes the "five pressures" enumerated in the expression. Villagers' use of the expression is reported in TCTK, "BC TH SX" [Agricultural cooperativization], 15 January 1967, 21.

responsible for seeing that villagers worked collectively to fulfill the contracts. In many brigades, however, households, rather than the teams
appointed by brigade leaders, did the work. Such household-based production violated the spirit and objective of collective farming. Even more
upsetting to higher authorities were arrangements in which a household
was not doing merely particular tasks but most, if not all, of the work on
fields it had taken over.[87] After harvest, it gave the brigade some of what
had been produced and kept the remainder. In effect, farming and other
production had reverted to households. As one party member said about
such arrangements discovered in 1963 in Thai Binh province, on the outside
they had "the appearance of people working for the collective cooperative,
but the inside was composed entirely of family economic activity."[88]

Often neither national nor even provincial or district authorities knew
about such arrangements. Villagers dubbed them "sneaky contracts" (khoan
chui) or "household contracts" (khoan ho). When higher officials found out,
they did not necessarily have the capacity to eliminate them. A few deviant
arrangements reportedly continued with the blessing of higher authorities.
The party secretary in Hai Phong in about 1963 is said to have had the
approval of Nguyen Chi Thanh, then the head of the party's Agriculture
Committee, to allow household contracts that had spontaneously emerged
in some cooperatives to continue as closely monitored experiments.[89]

Around that time, some production brigades in Vinh Phuc allowed
individual households to do farming tasks and other work.[90] By 1965,
provincial authorities, including the party secretary Kim Ngoc, knew and
investigated. They were impressed with production levels and villagers'

87. See, for instance, the critical remarks of the head of the Ministry of Agriculture's Bureau
of Agricultural Cooperativization, Duong Quoc Cam, Mot So Kinh Nghiem qua dot I, 29–30,
and Ha Tay province's party leader, Nguyen Xuan Truong, "Qua Ba Nam" [Three years, fighting U.S.], Ha Tay, December 1967, 29.

88. Elliott, Transcript, 145.

89. Tran Duc, Hop Tac trong Nong Thon, 93; and Dang Phong, "Lo Trinh," 6–7, which explains
the arrangements developed in 1962 in some cooperatives within Vinh Bao and Kien Thuy
districts, Kien An province. When Kien An became part of Hai Phong province in 1963, the
local arrangements continued "secretly" but had "the sympathy" of district authorities. Provincial leaders found out later.

90. This account draws on interviews in Hanoi, July 1996, with two people who knew well
Kim Ngoc, the party secretary of Vinh Phuc province in the mid-1960s; "Collectivization of
Agriculture in Vinh Phu Province," a summary of materials collected by a team of researchers,
1993; Tran Thi My Huong, "Buoc Dau Tim Hieu," 2000; an interview with a former cooper-
ative leader in Tam Canh, Vinh Phuc, 8 August 2000; an interview in Dao Duc, Vinh Phuc, 15
August 2000; and an article, with which Martin Grossheim kindly provided me, by Van Chinh,
a Vinh Phuc official during the mid-1960s, published in the newspaper Nong Nghiep Viet Nam
[Vietnam agriculture], 15 August 1995, 4.

enthusiasm. They also determined that the arrangements were within the bounds of how brigades were supposed to implement the "three contracts" policy. Kim Ngoc authorized further "experimentation."[91] The results were favorable. In September 1966, a resolution from the standing committee of the province's Communist Party branch authorized all brigades to make contracts with individual families to do specific tasks.[92] Kim Ngoc and his colleagues were attempting to arrest the falling levels of production in the province, which they attributed largely to lack of interest among villagers. They were also trying to put all available people to work. Because of the escalating war against the United States, young workers, especially men, were going off to defend the nation. Household contracts encouraged everyone in the family, including children and grandparents, to labor in the fields.

By trying to use the family as a production unit but within the framework of collective farming, Kim Ngoc and his colleagues were acting in ways similar to what Hungarian officials were doing at about the same time. Struggling to keep collective farming from disintegrating in the early and mid-1960s, Hungarian leaders made concessions to family-based production. They even allowed a form of sharecropping in which families were assigned certain fields to farm and then paid a portion of the crops to the collective after harvest.[93]

By 1967–1968 many collective cooperatives in Vinh Phuc were going in the same direction, though the Vietnamese villagers and local leaders did not know about Hungary.[94] Households were using collective fields to raise crops and pigs much as though the land was their own. Some of the work, such as plowing, was still done collectively. Mostly, however, each household worked separately. Each family paid the cooperative (through the brigade) a share of the grain or pork that it produced and kept the rest for its own use.[95] In many places, this went on for several seasons. Villagers

91. Sources name Thon Thuong cooperative in Tuan Chinh subdistrict (Vinh Tuong district), three cooperatives in Dai Dong subdistrict (also in Vinh Tuong), and Dong Xuan cooperative in Xuan Hoa subdistrict (Lap Thach district).

92. BCH, Vinh Phuc, DLDVN, "Nghi Quyet cua Ban Thuong Vu."

93. Swain, Collective Farms, 46–48; Volgyes, "Dynamic Change," 387.

94. National party leaders probably knew what was happening in Hungary. If they did, they chose not to emulate the program.

95. Vinh Phuc villagers I met in August 2000 called this arrangement a type of "household contract" (khoan ho). Documents from the period use that term as well as "output contract with a household" (khoan san luong cho ho), "product contract with each household" (khoan san pham cho tung ho), and "blank (white) contract" (khoan trang). The last sometimes means households gave nothing to the cooperative. See, for instance, BCH, Vinh Phu, DLDVN, "PHNV, Cong NN, 1969–1970" [EC, Vinh Phu province, VWP, "Agricultural, industrial development, Vinh Phu, 1969–1970"], 3 September 1968, 7 (P UBKHNN, hs 698, vv).

preferred this new arrangement to the way they had been required to farm before, and production increased.[96]

The arrangements that emerged in parts of Vinh Phuc resemble the "product contract" system that Vietnamese authorities endorsed in 1981. But in the late 1960s, provincial and national officials did not like what was taking place.[97] Vinh Phuc by then had been combined with Phu Tho to create Vinh Phu province, with Kim Ngoc as its party secretary. Kim Ngoc later wrote that he and other provincial authorities "could not keep a firm grasp on" what was happening on the ground. Villagers, often aided by brigade leaders, were pulling the implementation of the 1966 provincial resolution much further in the direction of family farming than officials had intended. The resolution allowed each household to work as a unit to do assigned tasks. In practice, however, individual households were farming entire fields. Collective farming was vanishing. Meanwhile, splits within the provincial party leadership developed.[98] Some provincial authorities pressed to stop the disintegration of collective work but to still treat households as work units. Others opposed households being allowed to work together. National authorities were also alarmed. To them, work assigned to families undermined collective production. They also claimed that these problems contributed to falling production and the province's inability to deliver paddy and other products required for troops at the battlefront.[99] In November 1968, one of the party's most senior leaders, Truong

96. Interviews, Dao Duc, Vinh Phuc, where family-based production arrangements in Yen Lo village occurred between about 1965 and 1969. Newspaper accounts in *Vinh Phuc* and *Vinh Phu* in 1966–1968 also tell of higher production and greater enthusiasm in collective cooperatives with "household contracts." Only a few accounts explicitly say land was turned over to villagers (for example, *Vinh Phu*, 26 April 1968, 2; 7 May 1968, 2). In most, "household contract" refers to specific work assignments done by individual families.

97. BCH, Vinh Phu, "PHNV, Cong NN" [Agricultural production], 3 September 1968, 7; *Vinh Phu*, 1 November 1968, 2.

98. Kim Ngoc, "Quyet Tam," 40–42. The party secretary reportedly wrote this as part of the self-criticism. His superiors did not remove him from office or hold him responsible for the deviations in Vinh Phuc province, contrary to what many Vietnamese and foreigners, myself included (Kerkvliet, "Village-State," 407), have said. He remained Vinh Phu's party secretary until late April 1977, when he retired, apparently because of the illness from which he died in May 1979, a few months before his sixty-second birthday. *Vinh Phu*, 3 May 1977, 1, and 29 May 1979, 1. Van Chinh wrote in *Nong Nghiep Viet Nam*, 15 August 1995, 4, that Kim Ngoc continued in office because Truong Chinh and Pham Van Dong, two of the party's highest officials, were his comrades in arms during the war against the French. Dang Phong and Melanie Beresford, *Authority Relations*, 61–62, suggest that Kim Ngoc continued because Le Duan, the first secretary of the party, thought that by 1968 criticisms of him had already gone too far.

99. Vu Tong Hop Van Phong TU Dang, "May Nhan Xet Lon, TH, Vinh Phu" [General Bureau, Central Party Office, "Observations regarding Vinh Phu"], 10 September 1968, 3–4 (P

Chinh, went to the province to insist that the three contracts system be implemented in a fully collective manner. Soon afterward the party's Central Executive Committee sent a letter to all party branches that forbade cooperatives from allowing households to farm fields on behalf of the brigade. With rare exceptions, brigades were not even allowed to assign specific jobs to a family. They were to rely on groups and teams formed to do each task.[100]

*What to Do?*

For most villagers by the mid- and late 1960s, economic conditions in the Red River delta were deteriorating and the Communist Party, in which they still had considerable trust, seemed to be going in a different direction than they wanted to go. The collective cooperatives were becoming larger; the fields villagers farmed, even the people they worked with, kept changing; rules and regulations about production and distribution of what had been produced were complicated and too often unfairly implemented; villagers' role in governing the cooperatives was small; and leaders were prone to be heavy-handed and self-serving. Meanwhile, the country was at war yet again, after less than a decade of relative peace. Under these circumstances, many villagers wrestled with the question, "What can we do?"[101] The political environment greatly influenced their answers.

*Open Dissent*

In other countries, villagers disgusted with collective farming moved away. Tens of thousands did so in the Soviet Union in the 1920s–1930s and

UBKHNN, hs 659, vv); BCHTU, DLDVN, "TB, BBT, Y Kien, Dai Hoi DB Dang Bo, Vinh Phu" [CEC, VWP, "Secretariat meeting in Vinh Phu"], 8 October 1968, 2–3 (P UBKHNN, hs 705, vv). These and other available documents provide little evidence for either allegation. Production levels and quantities of grain given to the state did decrease between 1965 and 1968, but that was true for every other province in the delta as well. Charges and counter-charges of "revisionism" within the party at that time may also have influenced central authorities to clamp down on what was happening in Vinh Phuc (Vinh Phu). For an analysis of that dynamic, see Heng, "Of the State," chap. 4.

100. BCHTU, DLDVN, "TT," 12 December 1968, 1 and 2. The newspaper *Vinh Phu*, 22 November 1968, 1, 4, has a bland account of Truong Chinh's visit. His criticisms of what was happening in the province are clearer in Truong Chinh, *Kien Quyet Sua Chua*.

101. Interview, Nghiem Xuyen, Ha Tay, 12 May 1993.

in Eastern Europe during the 1950s.[102] Many of them found employment in urban areas, often making a better living than if they had stayed on the collective farm. In East Germany, rural families fled to West Germany. In Laos, the government's insistence on collective farming in the late 1970s and the adverse economic consequences that followed contributed to a mass exodus of villagers, who crossed the Mekong River into Thailand.[103]

In Vietnam, moving to another country or to southern Vietnam was not an attractive option even if it had been feasible. Moving to towns or cities was scarcely an option at all. Only about 15 percent of northern Vietnam's population was urban, and manufacturing or other employment opportunities were scarce. Moreover, leaving one's village without official authorization was enormously difficult. By the early 1960s, the state's "registration system" (*he thong ho khau*) was in place. Only with proper documentation could a person realistically move or even travel. A villager who went without proper papers to Hanoi or Hai Phong city, for instance, would face immense obstacles getting employment, housing, and food. Imposing on relatives and friends was at best a stopgap measure. Among the only ways to leave one's village, apart from joining the army, was to be among the select people recruited to work in factories and government departments or to move from the delta to "new economic zones," which the government was creating. But they too were supposed to have cooperatives.[104]

Abandoning (or never starting) collective farming but staying in the village and farming one's own land was an option, at least theoretically. Between 1961 and 1964, thousands of cooperative members asked to quit. In some cooperatives, such as Cam La in Hai Phong province and Vu Thang in Thai Binh, 40–70 percent of members wanted out.[105] Available materials do not say what the levels were generally. Official statistics for the north do show, however, that the proportion of rural households in cooperatives decreased from 89 percent in 1961 to 85 percent in 1964, probably pri-

102. Fitzpatrick, *Stalin's Peasants*, chap. 3; Sokolovsky, *Peasants and Power*, 132–33, 143–44, 163; Swain, *Collective Farms*, 32, 41; Vasary, *Beyond the Plan*, 57–65, 74; Adams and Adams, *Men versus Systems*, 177, 182; Myant, *Czechoslovak Economy*, 53, 93; Baring, *Uprising*, 17; Francisco, "Agricultural Collectivization," 68, 70. In Hungary, alternative employment opportunities put some pressure on cooperative managers and the state to make farmwork more attractive and allow families to have some members working in other sectors of the economy, a rare situation in Vietnam.

103. Stuart-Fox, *Buddhist Kingdom*, 85, 126, 168.

104. For an engaging study of migration to those economic zones in the 1950s–1980s, see Hardy, *Red Hills*.

105. Huyen Tien Lang, *Lich Su*, 115; Nguyen Manh Huan, "Hop Tac Xa," 35.

marily because people demanded they be allowed to leave. The sharpest drop was in two Red River delta provinces, Ha Tay and Thai Binh, down 10 and 9 percentage points, respectively (see appendix 1, table 4).[106]

People left or tried to leave for economic and political reasons. One woman in Vinh Phuc province encapsulated them as "hunger" and "to be free."[107] Married in 1955, she and her husband, both from poor peasant families, had seen nearly every household join their village's collective cooperative by the early 1960s. But during that time, her initial enthusiasm and that of many other members had dissipated. Falling production and income were the main economic reasons for disgruntlement. Some villagers were also upset that cooperatives no longer compensated them for the fields they had surrendered. Knowing that they and others did collective tasks haphazardly, villagers believed they would produce more and live better if they farmed separately. People also wanted to be free from "imperious" (hong hach) officials and "unjust" (khong cong bang) treatment. They complained, for instance, that brigade leaders "gave heavy work but few work points to some people but easy tasks and many points to their wives and other relatives." Consequently, the distribution of the harvest "lacked democracy" (thieu dan chu). Many people objected to the merging of small cooperatives, the "lack of transparency" (thieu cong khai) in financial matters, and the embezzlement and other corruption among leaders.

Quitting a collective cooperative, however, was difficult, which probably explains why few people did so. Quitting required the managerial board's approval. Otherwise, a quitter received no land. Cooperative leaders were extremely reluctant to agree, even if only a few people wanted out, for fear

---

106. Scattered reports suggest that the leavers came from several class backgrounds. Those with poor peasant backgrounds (co nong; ban nong) were in the majority, just as they were the majority of rural people. In Ha Tay province, for instance, 63 percent of the noncooperative members in 1966 had poor peasant backgrounds and 28 percent had middle peasant backgrounds, percentages similar to the overall class distribution at the time of land reform. CCTK, Ha Tay, "BC TH HTX" [Cooperatives], 7 January 1967, 2.

107. Thieu, doi, and tu do. Interview, Quat Luu, Vinh Phuc, 7 August 2000. This paragraph and the next two draw on other interviews in Quat Luu, 3 and 5 August 2000, and in the Vinh Phuc subdistricts of Dao Duc, 15 and 18 August 2000, and Tien Thang, 23 August 2000, as well as on the following documents: Ngo Van Thin, pho chu nhiem, UBKH, Ha Dong, "BC TH, KH 9 Thang, PHNV 3 thang" [Ngo Van Thin, vice chairperson, Planning Committee, Ha Dong province, "Implementing the plan"], 23 October 1962, 7 (P UBKHNN, hs 387, vv); CCTK, Nam Dinh, "BC TH HTHNN, 1964" [Statistics office, Nam Dinh province, "Cooperativization, 1964"], 11 September 1964, 3–4 (P TCTK, hs 619, vv); CCTK, Ha Dong, "BC TH, HTX den 1/7/1964" [Statistics office, Ha Dong province, "Cooperatives' situation"], 30 September 1964, 4 (P TCTK, hs 619, vv); CCTK, Ha Tay, "BC Phan Tich TH, HTH SX NN, 1969" [Statistics office, Ha Tay province, "Cooperatizing agriculture"], 15 January 1970, 3–4 (P TCTK, hs 927, vv).

that many more would then ask to leave. A request to leave usually prompted an investigation; and the requesters had to attend educational sessions on the importance of collective farming. By this stage, many would-be leavers decided to stay because their complaints had been addressed or the pressure to remain was too intense. If allowed to leave, a household was allocated some of the worst land in the area—land that was far from irrigation with poor soil and other bad features. Some people were allowed to quit but not to take with them the plows and draft animals they had contributed to the cooperatives. Leavers and those who had yet to join were often discriminated against, despite official pronouncements condemning the practice. For example, they had to pay very high taxes and could not use the local health clinic. Given these adversities, quitters and families who had not joined often concluded to their dismay that it was better to be inside than outside. It was a situation, recalled an elderly villager in Vinh Phuc, in which people were "not forced but partly forced" (khong bat ep ma hoi bat ep) to be in the cooperative. Consequently, by 1968 membership was at 95 percent of farming households and thereafter climbed even higher.[108]

The war was another reason membership stopped declining and then increased from about 1965, the first full year of U.S. bombing. Given the collective cooperatives' responsibilities for mobilizing food and troops for national defense, local officials were even less inclined to permit disgruntled members to leave. For the same reason, many people decided to stay and villagers who had not been members decided to join. Either they were being patriotic or they feared being perceived as unpatriotic. For the good of the country and their relatives and friends in the army, villagers boosted their resolve to make the cooperatives better.

Apart from efforts to quit the cooperatives, the only other significant public expressions of discontent toward collective farming were verbal and written complaints. In late 1968–early 1969, for instance, ordinary villagers as well as brigade leaders in Vinh Phu province objected during meetings and in local government offices to national authorities' prohibition on households doing tasks on collective land.[109] In Nam Dinh province in May–July 1964, one district office received twelve written complaints from villagers that their cooperative's leaders were embezzling paddy and selling

108. See appendix 1, table 4. Nevertheless, in a few villages, there were many households that did not join. Michael DiGregorio, Iron Works, 246–59, depicts one village in which about half of farming households never joined collective cooperatives. Note that most former landlords and rich peasants (phu nong) were not permitted to join until after about 1964.

109. Vinh Phu, 25 April 1969, 2.

it on the black market. In 1967, the Hai Duong provincial office received 419 written complaints, 185 of them from peasants, most alleging corruption and undemocratic procedures within cooperatives.[110] In 1974, corruption, poor leadership, and improper distribution of harvested paddy were among the concerns villagers expressed in letters to the Hai Hung provincial newspaper.[111]

Such complaints sometimes got results. Allegations of corruption and other infractions were often investigated. When charges were borne out, officials were reprimanded, removed from office, or even imprisoned. Villagers' persistent complaints against particular leaders sometimes also meant that an offensive brigade leader, managerial board member, or even a cooperative chairperson was not reelected.

So far as I know, dissatisfied villagers in the north confined their open acts of discontent almost entirely to those just described. It is not that Vietnamese villagers had such a meager "repertoire" for protesting. They had a history of demonstrating, marching on government buildings, capturing police officers, and burning officials' residences. The only such instances during collectivization in the north that I know of occurred in 1959–1961 (see chapter 3) and 1986 (see chapter 6). If there were others, they were few and far between and never approached the scale of unrest that occurred during collectivization in the Soviet Union.[112] The reasons have to do with political conditions and villagers' assessments of their situation. Travel restrictions hampered any unauthorized organized activity beyond one's village. So did surveillance. The police, on the lookout for any signs of hostility and disloyalty, would have regarded open opposition to collectivization as an action against the regime or for the Saigon government and the United States.[113] Then there were villagers' own inclinations. Despite their grievances about collectivization, a large proportion of vil-

110. CCTK, Nam Dinh, "BC TH HTHNN, 1964" [Cooperativization], 11 September 1964, 4; Hoang Son, Pho Chu Tich, UBHC, Hai Duong, "BC TH, SX, Chien Dau, 1967, Hai Duong" [Hoang Son, vice president, Administrative Committee, Hai Duong province, "Production situation"], 6 January 1968, 20 (P UBKHNN, hs 597, vv).

111. *Hai Hung*, 29 May 1974, 3; 26 June 1974, 3.

112. Viola, *Peasant Rebels.* Thinking I had overlooked other open protests, I asked informants in Hanoi who had held party and government positions and would have known of such things. They knew of none.

113. Such surveillance and concerns appear in reports from Hoang Son, Pho Chu Tich, Uy Ban Hanh Chinh, tinh Hai Duong [Hoang Son, vice president, Administrative Committee, Hai Duong province]: "BC TH, Chien Dau, SX, 1965, UBHC, Hai Duong" ["Situation, 1965"], 15 January 1966, 20 (P UBKHNN, hs 497, vv); "BC TH, Chien Dau, SX, 1966, Hai Duong" ["Situation, 1966"], 7 January 1967, 17 (P UBKHNN, hs 531, vv). Also, Nguyen Xuan Truong, "Qua Ba Nam" [Three years, fighting U.S.], Ha Tay, December 1967, 19–20.

lagers still had considerable goodwill toward the Communist Party government, personified especially by Ho Chi Minh, Vo Nguyen Giap, and some other admired leaders. Political and economic conditions were still much better than most adults had known before that government had come to power. Haughty and corrupt leaders were usually regarded as individual failures, not a failure of the regime itself. Consequently, people who openly expressed discontent did so through avenues that authorities could tolerate.

## Everyday Politics

Pictures in Vietnamese newspapers from the mid-1960s to early 1970s suggest that village life was serene and filled with people happy and smiling even while they planted paddy, hoed weeds, and spread manure. Not shown were the U.S. planes bombing homes, fields, dikes, roads, schools, hospitals, and people. Even if their own villages were not attacked, smoke on the horizon and distant artillery fire regularly reminded villagers that their country was under siege. Between 1965 and 1972, the United States dropped nearly three bombs for every person on Nam Sach, a rural district of Hai Duong province.[114] "Many more" U.S. planes attacked the whole province in 1966 than had done so in 1965 and "eleven times as many" dropped bombs in 1967 compared to 1966.[115] In numerous areas, such as Vinh Tuong district in Vinh Phuc province, the United States hit a large proportion of villages with bombs and rockets.[116] Many villages, such as those near the town of Viet Tri in Phu Tho province, were bombarded several times.[117] All told, between 1965 and 1972, the United States bombed 70 percent of all subdistricts in the north and "obliterated" (huy diet) 5 percent of them.[118]

The other major aspect of political life not portrayed in newspaper photos was the perpetual struggle within collective cooperatives over the use and distribution of resources. The primary resources were time, labor,

114. *Hai Hung*, 6 February 1974, 2.

115. In 1967, there were 394 attacks involving nearly two thousand airplanes. Hoang Son, Hai Duong, "BC TH Chien Dau" [Situation, 1966], 7 January 1967, 1; Hoang Son, Pho Chu Tich, UBHC, Hai Duong, "BC TH, SX, Chien Dau, 1967, Hai Duong" [Hoang Son, vice president, Administrative Committee, Hai Duong province, "Situation, 1967"], 8 January 1968, 1 (P UBKHNN, hs 597, vv).

116. *Vinh Phu*, 22 November 1968, 3.

117. Vinh Phu, *Hoc Tap va Thi Dua*, 27–28.

118. Bo Truong, BNN, "TH, Phat Trien NN, VN" [minister, MA, "Agricultural development"], 17 December 1976, 7 (P BNN, hs 61, tt).

means of production (especially land), and what was produced. The main claimants were households, production brigade leaders, cooperative managers, and state agencies. Their interests both overlapped and clashed. Households included the families of brigade and cooperative officials. Brigade leaders and members might work together to protect resources from other claimants but might also compete with one another. Brigade leaders had to deal with cooperative managers, who had to come to terms with the brigade and with district and provincial agencies of the state. State agencies pressured cooperative officials to hand over grain and other resources and to make brigade leaders and households work effectively.

In the 1960s–1970s, national party and government campaigns implored villagers to devote more time to collective work. Villagers did. The average number of workdays per cooperative worker rose from 90 in 1959 to 215 in 1970 and reached 236 by 1975, just short of the 250 days targeted by the government in 1973.[119] Villagers did this work in addition to serving in the local militia, making bomb shelters, repairing roads, expanding irrigation canals, and performing other public works.

Some villagers, primarily those committed to the socialist ideal and those who benefited most from a cooperative's output (often people in households with few able-bodied members), labored energetically for the cooperative.[120] Generally, however, the quality of collective work was below people's abilities. Many cooperative members calculated how many workdays they needed to satisfy local leaders and to reach the level of paddy or other staple food to which they were entitled, then labored in a manner often described as "a few hours each day and a little work each hour."[121] This was particularly likely when no one was supervising, a common situation as the brigades and cooperatives enlarged.

Villagers recalled, often with amusement, how they and others cut corners in order to maximize their points with the least effort. A spry

119. The figures are average workdays per cooperative member between the ages of sixteen and sixty for males and sixteen and fifty-five for females. Cuc Thong Ke TU, "So Lieu Dieu Tra HTHNN 1959 [Central Statistics Office, "Agricultural cooperativization, 1959"], 1959, 13 (P UBKHNN, hs 1258, vv); TCTK, *Nien Giam Thong Ke, 1975*, 295. The target figure is from BQL HTXSXNN, "KH, HTX, Cai Tien QL HTX, Dong Bang va Trung Bo 1973–1975" [Managerial Committee, Agricultural Cooperatives, "Consolidating cooperatives, strengthening management, 1973–1975"], 26 July 1973, 3 (P UBNNTU, hs 105, vv).

120. Such people were celebrated in the mass media and literature. See, for instance, the characters Ha and Le Van in the short stories "Trong Lang Nho" [In a small village; 1969], and "Nguoi Ve Dong Coi" [Returning to the field of reeds; 1970], in Le Luu, *Truyen Ngan*.

121. "Ngay lam it gio, gio lam it viec." The expression was probably a play on a 1960s slogan: "Do the proper number of days each month, the proper hours each day, and lots of good work each hour" (*thang lam du ngay, ngay lam du gio, gio lam nhieu viec tot*).

elderly lady, who had been the chairperson of a village-sized cooperative in Nghiem Xuyen subdistrict during the late 1960s, pantomimed how people spread fertilizer.[122] Barely stepping into each paddy field, she said as she daintily lifted her feet, "they'd dump a bunch of manure in one spot, then another bunch in another spot." Without stopping to spread the manure, they went to another field and did the same thing. "They were simply trying to finish their assigned task as quickly as possible." They harrowed flooded fields in such a manner that, rather than the harrow going deep into the soil to break up the clogs, it scarcely penetrated at all. It was as though, she said laughingly, "they were harrowing water." Paddy transplanters, who earned work points based on how many bundles of seedlings they planted, made the bundles small. Leaders wised up to that tactic and required that bundles be a uniform size, each wrapped with a bamboo strip (lat). Points were then allocated according to how many strips each transplanter presented at the end of the day. Some villagers in Vinh Phuc responded by presenting more strips than the number of bundles actually planted. They surreptitiously added strips they had made. When work points for harvesting paddy were calculated according to weight, cooperative members cut the entire stalk rather than only a short portion. To counter that, cooperative leaders gave points instead based on the area harvested. Then villagers often cut just the tips that held the grain and thus harvested the area quickly. That cutting method, however, caused more grain to fall out during transport. Without proper monitoring or self-control, deceit by a few could spread to more and more people, however uncomfortable they might feel about it. "People who worked diligently would go hungry," explained a villager who had been a brigade leader from the mid-1960s until the early 1970s, "because others who lied [about work done] and cheated [by sloppy work] received many points."[123]

One main reason for such lackadaisical work was dissatisfaction with how collective cooperatives were governed. A man in Nghiem Xuyen recalled that because people were too intimidated or otherwise unable to complain openly about these matters, they expressed their disquiet by "foot dragging" (lan cong), a description villagers interviewed in Vinh Phuc province also used.[124] Believing that a cooperative really belonged to its officials, many members frequently saw no benefit for themselves to farm

122. Interview, Nghiem Xuyen, Ha Tay, 12 May 1993. This paragraph also draws on other interviews with villagers and on Tran Quang Ngan, "Phan Tich," 37.
123. "Nguoi lam ky se bi doi vi nguoi lam doi se duoc nhieu diem." Interview, Tam Canh, Vinh Phuc, 11 August 2000.
124. Interview, Nghiem Xuyen, Ha Tay, 14 May 1993.

well, a sentiment they sometimes expressed by ridiculing government slogans. One slogan, attributed to Ho Chi Minh, implored "everyone to work as hard as two" in order to provide supplies to both the home front and the war front. A satirical take-off went:

> Everyone work as hard as two
> so that the chairperson can buy a radio and bicycle.
> Everyone work as hard as three
> so that the cadre can build a house and courtyard.[125]

Known or suspected corruption adversely influenced villagers' attitudes toward collective work. As Ha Tay provincial reports in the late 1960s concluded, lack of enthusiasm was due not only to villagers' inadequate appreciation of socialism but to leaders' lack of "moral qualities" (*pham chat dao duc*), manifested in "rather widespread and long-standing" (*kha pho bien va keo dai*) theft, waste, and embezzlement of collective property.[126] Leaders' corruption and other improprieties, according to surveys across the north, made cooperative members "uneasy, indignant," and they went about their work "in a negative way" to the point that many villagers were asking, "Does working properly bring more than does embezzling or being lazy?"[127]

Another, related reason was the conclusion many villagers drew that diligent work had, at best, tiny rewards. A well-prepared field still might not result in a decent crop if cooperative managers had not arranged for enough seed or if required fertilizer did not arrive. Such problems were understandable when U.S. bombing caused them, but not, as too often happened, when incompetent or corrupt officials were the cause.[128] Careful plowing might also be for naught if brigade leaders failed to arrange for sufficient transplanters or if the transplanters did not plant well or if the people responsible for subsequent fertilizing, weeding, and irrigating did sloppy work. In other words, careful farming by an individual had a chance

125. "Moi nguoi lam viec bang hai, de cho chu nhiem mua dai mua xe. Moi nguoi lam viec bang ba, de cho can bo xay nha xay san." For another version, see Tran Nhu Trang, "Transformation," 420.

126. UBHC, Ha Tay, "PHNV KH, KT Dia Phuong, 1969" [EC, Ha Tay province, "Developing local economy, 1969"], 12 December 1968, 9–10; and UBHC, Ha Tay, "BC TH CT, 1969 PHNV KH, KT VH, 1970" [EC, Ha Tay province, "Work done 1969, responsibilities 1970"], April 1970, 10, 16 (Both documents are in P UBKHNN, hs 675, vv).

127. "Tich cuc cong tac co gi hon nhung ke tham o luoi bieng." "BCKQ Dieu Tra" [Management survey], circa 1971, 5, 31.

128. Interviews, Da Ton, Hanoi, 20 April 1993, 3 February 1996, 22 March 1996; *Hai Hung*, 6 February 1974, 3; 15 February 1974, 3; 20 November 1974, 3.

of paying off only if brigade and cooperative leaders coordinated labor and other requirements and all or nearly all members in the brigade worked well, not just one day but every day and every step along the way. Even then, the rewards were modest. When the harvest was divided, "the good worker and the bad worker were basically alike," said a Vinh Phuc villager, because each received nearly the same amount, as various surveys confirmed.[129]

Work habits were good in collective cooperatives with many firm believers in socialism. Such cooperatives, however, were few. Social pressure and mutual monitoring could also minimize lackadaisical behavior, but the trend to larger cooperatives lessened their effectiveness. Brigades that created adequate cohesion among members despite the obstacles were fairly numerous. Some managed to take advantage of kinship ties without turning production over to family units. If plowers in a brigade knew that close relatives would be planting the field, for example, they were more likely to prepare the ground well.[130] Often brigades achieved favorable results for members by deviating from national regulations—hiding land and other resources from higher authorities and allowing households to farm among themselves more as family units than as collective workers, similar to what was occurring on a large scale in Vinh Phuc province.

Villagers preferred to work as households. The connection between one's labor and the results for one's family was clearer. Moreover, doing a task that way was easier than arranging for many other people to do it.[131] Indeed, families worked on their own as much as possible. Virtually every family, according a popular saying, had "one leg inside and the other outside" the cooperative. For many, the "the leg outside was longer than the one inside," meaning that people did more and worked harder outside the collective cooperative than they did inside. When working "outside," villagers "assiduously make use of every minute, whereas when working for the cooperative, they did the opposite."[132]

Authorities during the 1960s and 1970s continued to affirm that the "subsidiary family economy" (*kinh te phu gia dinh*) was necessary. Consequently, as in many other collective systems in Communist Party

129. Interview, Dao Duc, Vinh Phuc, 17 August 2000. Also, BLTTP, "BC, TH CT LT 10 nam qua, PHNV, Thoi Gian Toi" [Ministry of Staple Foods and Foodstuffs, "Staple food situation past 10 years, tasks the coming years"], October 1970, 9 (P BLTTP, hs 506, vv); and BQLHTXNNTU, *Khoan San Pham*, 15–17.

130. Hanoi, *Mot So Kinh Nghiem*, 40.

131. Interviews, Nghiem Xuyen, Ha Tay, May 1993, and four subdistricts in Vinh Phuc, August 2000.

132. Hanoi, *Bao Cao Ket Qua*, 110.

states, collective and private production were "complementary," according to Le Duan and other high-ranking Vietnamese officials.[133] While some party leaders feared the family economy would lead to capitalism, the head of the party's Rural Affairs Committee and others argued that was unlikely because household production was embedded within the cooperative.[134] National leaders even encouraged cooperative officials to assist in household economic activities, such as advising families about raising pigs and allowing villagers to plow household plots with the cooperative's draft animals (usually for a fee). The result, they said, would benefit the cooperative as well as individual households. More households raising pigs, for instance, would mean more manure for the collective fields.[135]

At the same time, authorities frequently fretted that villagers devoted too much labor and other resources to their household plots and other "subsidiary" economic activities. Many newspaper accounts tell of villagers who worked day and night on their household plots while doing minimal work on collective fields. Finding in 1968 that villagers in one cooperative of Quat Luu subdistrict devoted more attention to their household plots than to collective fields, Vinh Phu provincial authorities concluded that "nearly all the cadres and party members there sympathized with the villagers and were themselves also running after their own families' material interests."[136] In the early 1970s, many villagers in Tien Thang subdistrict concentrated on their own vegetable and fruit crops, which they sold in nearby Phuc Yen town, a gateway for such products going to Hanoi. When the peak season for these crops clashed with intensive labor requirements on collective land, local officials had trouble getting villagers to do the collective work and resorted to intercepting villagers as they carried their produce to town.[137] The government's Agriculture Commission reported in 1974 that during harsh economic times, villagers were so preoccupied with providing for their families that leaders in many cooperatives in Hai Hung,

133. Le Duan, *On the Socialist Revolution*, 2:148–54. Also see Duong Quoc Cam, *Kinh Te*, 23–29. Regarding the family economy in the Soviet Union's collectives, see Wadekin, *Private Sector*.

134. Nguyen Chi Thanh, *Ve San Xuat*, 111–15. For an elaboration on this discussion, see Beresford, "Household and Collective."

135. Accounts about Hai Hung province in *Nhan Dan*, 2, and 4 June 1968, 2; interview, Tam Canh, Vinh Phuc, 12 August 2000; and Nguyen Xuan Truong, "Qua Ba Nam" [Three years, fighting U.S.], Ha Tay, December 1967, 29.

136. "hau het can bo, dang vien cung dong tinh voi xa vien, chay theo loi nhuan gia dinh." *Vinh Phu*, 29 November 1968, 2.

137. Interviews, Tien Thang, Vinh Phuc, 26 August 2000.

Thai Binh, and other unspecified provinces could mobilize only 30–40 percent of the people necessary for collective work.[138]

In the early 1960s, about 38 percent of an average cooperative member's net income came from collective work. The rest came from household economic activities and other private earnings. National officials predicted the proportion from the cooperative would reach at least 60 percent by the mid- or late 1960s, and that collective farming would provide all the rice a villager needed.[139] That did not happen. Instead, the percentage from collective work decreased. By 1971, it was only 30 percent; the remaining 70 percent, according to surveys, came from private earnings (see appendix 1, table 7), a rate higher than in China, the Soviet Union, and possibly other countries with collective farming.[140] Roughly 45–60 percent of an average Vietnamese cooperative member's private earning came from raising livestock (especially pigs); 35–40 percent from growing paddy, potatoes, cassava, and vegetables; and the remainder from working for wages, selling things made at home, and engaging in other activities.[141]

In short, what central authorities regarded as a "subsidiary" economy was to most villagers crucial for their survival.[142] Household plots, in particular, were "very precious" (quy lam), as one woman described them. Having raised four children during the height of collectivization, she speculated that her family would have perished without their household plot and other private ways to earn income. Those activities, she stressed, "saved our lives" (cuu song).[143] Collective farming could not even provide an average household in northern Vietnam with sufficient rice. Like poor peasants in other countries, one of the things Vietnamese villagers were primarily con-

138. UBNNTU, "TB" [CAC, "Bulletin"], 5 April 1974, 1 (P UBNNTU, hs 83, vv).

139. Duong Quoc Cam, Kinh Te, 35, referring to an untitled December 1961 official study.

140. For China and the Soviet Union, see Lu, "Household and Collective," 152–53; Zweig, Agrarian Radicalism, 133; Wadekin, Private Sector, 193. Vu Tuan Anh and Tran Thi Van Anh, Kinh Te Ho, 79–81, argue that Vietnam's statistics significantly understate the value of income from collective work. Their argument turns on how exactly official figures were compiled, which remains unclear. In any event, the decrease in the portion from collective work and the increase in that from private earnings would probably remain. So would the gap between what national officials expected and what occurred.

141. CCTK, Vinh Phuc, "BC, TH Doi Song Nong Dan, Vinh Phuc, 1961" [Statistics office, Vinh Phuc, "Peasants' living conditions"], 8 August 1962, 6 (P TCTK, hs 2569, vv); To Thao, "BC, Doi Song" [Peasants' conditions, Ha Tay], 15 June 1966, 8; Vu Van, "BC TH Doi Song" [Peasants' conditions], Ha Tay, 8 April 1971, 3; Post, Revolution, 211.

142. And, paradoxically, without the family economy, the collective system could not survive. It needed peasants but could not produce enough food for them, hence it needed them to produce a significant amount of their own food. This situation is not peculiar to collectivization in Vietnam. Lev Timofeev, Soviet Peasants, argues the Soviet Union was much the same.

143. Interview, Nghiem Xuyen, Ha Tay, 10 May 1993.

cerned with was securing their basic needs. Laboring as much as possible on their own seemed a more likely way to achieve that goal than working diligently in collective production. "Peasants have brains of their own," emphasized an elderly lady when recalling the difficult straits confronting her and other villagers during the late 1960s. "They figure out ways to avoid what brings them little benefit."[144]

Like collective production, the farming of household plots and other private economic activities were vulnerable to bad weather, pests, and U.S. bombs. In that shared environment, each hour of labor, kilogram of manure, and drop of sweat expended in the private economy was usually more remunerative to a villager than what was spent in collective production. Villagers recall their households getting "more from less" than their co-operatives could.[145] Paddy yields on household plots were frequently two and three times those on collective land.[146] Surveys in the 1960s showed that while collective work consumed between 50 and 67 percent of a typical villager's work life, private work took 12–25 percent yet produced considerably greater results. One 1966 study calculated that an average day of collective work in Ha Tay province was worth 0.85 dong whereas a day earning private income was worth 2.69 dong, more than three times as much.[147]

144. Interview, Tien Thang, Vinh Phuc, 22 August 2000.

145. A common view in Tien Thang, Vinh Phuc, one man recalled, was "120 square meters of [household] gardens equaled 720–1,080 square meters of the cooperative's land" (nam thuoc rau xanh bang vai sao dat cua hop tac xa), interview, 22 August 2000. Household plots were usually farmed year-round. A 1971 survey in rural Hanoi found that 70 percent of the household plots, compared to only 3.5 percent of collective fields, were planted three times a year. Hanoi, Bao Cao Ket Qua, 109. The most comprehensive statistics I have found on this subject are for Ha Tay province in 1969. Collectively farmed land was 115,399 hectares, which was planted 1.5 times that year. The area of all household plots was 5,743 hectares, which was farmed 3.4 times that year. CCTK, Ha Tay, "BC, So Lieu Gieo Trong, Dong Xuan, 1968–1969" [Statistics office, Ha Tay province, "Crop data for winter/spring"], 14 June 1969, unnumbered tables (P TCTK, hs 904, vv); CCTK, Ha Tay, "BC Phan Tich TH" [Cooperatizing agriculture], 15 January 1970, table 18.

146. Interviews, Da Ton, Hanoi; Nghiem Xuyen, Ha Tay; and four subdistricts in Vinh Phuc. For instance, during the mid- and late 1960s villagers in Quat Luu and Tam Canh, Vinh Phuc, frequently raised 100–120 kilograms of paddy per sao in a season, while the cooperative's averages were in the 40–70 kilogram range. Many villagers in Da Ton recall getting 180–200 kilograms per sao in the early and mid-1970s while yields from collective fields rarely exceeded 120 kilograms.

147. CCTK, Vinh Phuc, "BC, TH Doi Song" [Peasants' conditions], 8 August 1962, 6; Do Van Hanh, Chi Cuc pho, CCTK, Ha Noi, "BC, Lao Dong NN, Dieu Tra, 15/08/1965" [Do Van Hanh, Statistics office, Hanoi, "Agricultural labor survey"], 28 January 1966, 13 (P TCTK, hs 971, tt); To Thao, "BC, Doi Song" [Peasants' conditions, Ha Tay], 15 June 1966, 10; CCTK, Vinh Phu, "BC, Dieu Tra Dien Hinh, SX, Thu Nhap, Phan Phoi, HTXSXNN, 1969" [Statistics office, Vinh Phu province, "Surveys of agricultural cooperatives"], 9 May 1970, table 7 (P TCTK, hs 932, vv).

In addition to their economic significance, private earnings were also important politically. Household plots and other income sources gave peasants, as one account put it, "peace of mind" while they did collective work.[148] Authorities may also have believed that private sources of income made villagers less likely to raise objections or become too openly critical of the entire collective system. Yet authorities also saw the private economy threatening the "socialist thinking" and "collective spirit" they were trying to nurture. To most villagers, "outside" sources of income made collectivization more tolerable. Private earnings were a partial "exit" from a situation in which actual departure was impossible or made life worse.[149] Moreover, the superior results of their own labor within the family and among relatives and friends were further evidence to many villagers that collective farming was deeply flawed. Increasingly, their own experience was at odds with officials' persistent claims that collective farming, rather than household farming, would improve their living conditions and produce more per unit of land and labor.

## Sites of Negotiation and Resistance

The deepening conviction that collective production was inferior to what they could produce on their own was one reason for many peasants' ongoing negotiation and resistance within the cooperatives.[150] Two additional factors were the drive to provide for one's family and the discontent with officials and how cooperatives were governed. Across the countryside, season after season, year after year, negotiation and resistance in numerous forms occurred at several junctures during production. Three primary "sites" were livestock raising, land usage, and harvests.

The best way to raise pigs and draft animals (water buffaloes and oxen), according to national government and party policies, was collectively. Collective piggeries and herds of draft animals would result in more animals, enable state agencies to control markets for these animals, and help cooperatives to collect manure for fertilizer.[151]

---

148. *Vinh Phu*, 1 May 1968, 2.

149. Drawing on Hirschman, *Exit*, Stefan Hedlund, "Private Plots," 223–25, describes private economic activities in the Soviet Union's collectives as "soft exits."

150. A similar realization among Hungarian peasants contributed to resistance against collective farming. Rev, "Advantages," 345.

151. In northern Vietnam, manure was the principal source of fertilizer, followed by azolla and other locally grown plants, and distantly, by chemicals.

When collective cooperatives were established, villagers were allowed to keep their pigs. National policy, however, urged cooperatives to establish piggeries and expected collectively raised pigs to soon compose a sizable proportion of the nation's total.[152] The number of pigs did increase by about 67 percent between 1960 and 1974. Households, however, not cooperatives, were raising nearly all of them. Collective pigs in 1974 composed only 10 percent.[153] The peak in the proportion of collectively raised pigs had already passed—11 percent in 1967–1968. From then to the end of collective farming, the proportion continued to drop despite authorities' efforts to reverse the trend.[154] Many cooperatives managed to raise collectively only a few of the animals. Collective pigs were often neglected, and consequently many were underweight and died prematurely. Another frequent problem was that the people minding the animals took piglets, especially the females, for themselves or sold them illegally.[155]

Meanwhile, families raised their own pigs. The animals were like savings accounts. In emergencies, one could be sold for desperately needed cash. To families who could afford to keep more than one or two, pigs were an important source of additional income. A woman in Ha Tay, for example, recalled selling pigs in the late 1960s and 1970s on the "black market" (cho den), where prices were much higher than in state markets, in order to buy additional food and other necessities.[156] Together with chickens and ducks, pigs were also the main source of whatever meat a household could indulge in. And pig manure was crucial for household plots and gardens.

152. The head of the Agricultural Cooperativization Bureau summarizes the official stance in Duong Quoc Cam, Mot So Kinh Nghiem qua dot I, 11–12.

153. There were 3.81 million pigs (two months old or more) in 1960 but 6.36 million in 1974, of which only 646,000 were collectively raised. TCTK, Nien Giam Thong Ke 1975, 276, 278.

154. By 1980, only 5 percent of the pigs in northern Vietnam were raised collectively. Two years later, according to one provincial account, the proportion was "not worth mentioning" and indeed it is scarcely brought up in available documents and news reports. Ha Son Binh, 2 June 1982, 2. Also see Vinh Phu, 2 January 1987, 2. Figures for collective pigs during the 1960s–1970s are from TCTK, 12 Nam Phat Trien, 531; and Tong Tran Dao, Thu Truong, BNN, "BC TH, Chan Nuoi Lon, HTXSXNN, Quoc Doanh NN" [Tong Tran Dao, MA, "Pig raising in cooperatives"], 14 March 1981, 2 (P BNN, hs 548, vv).

155. Ban Thuong Vu, Tinh Uy Hai Hung, "BC, Du An KH, KT Dia Phuong 1968–1975" [Standing Committee, Hai Hung province, "Local development plan"], 10 August 1968, 6 (P UBKHNN, hs 641, vv); UBHC, Vinh Phu, "BCTK CT, 1969, UBHC, Vinh Phu" [Administrative Committee, Vinh Phu province, "Summary report"], 2 February 1970, 5 (P UBKHNN, hs 698, vv); TCTK, "BC TH NN, 1970" [GSO, "Agricultural situation"], 2 February 1971, 36–37 (P TCTK, hs 938, vv); Hai Hung, 25 September 1974, 3; and interviews, Nghiem Xuyen, Ha Tay; Da Ton, Hanoi; and Tien Thang, Vinh Phuc.

156. Interview, Nghiem Xuyen, Ha Tay, 10 May 1993.

To get more pork into the state's market system and more pig manure into collective fields, national policies by the mid-1960s required households to deliver annually a certain weight of each to their cooperatives. This became another site of contention. Although villagers were paid for the pork and manure, the prices were usually low. Vinh Phuc villagers recall, for instance, that the price for a kilogram of pork (live weight) in the late 1960s–early 1970s was only one-fourth that on the "free" and "black" markets. Outright refusal to comply, however, could mean penalties such as reduced work points and rice rations. Instead, many villagers sold inferior pigs to the cooperative. Or they sold their best ones illegally, getting prices that more than compensated for any penalties their cooperative imposed. To minimize the amount of manure actually sold to the cooperative, villagers frequently mixed it with chopped banana stems, other unusable foliage, sand, or gravel.[157]

Unlike pigs, draft animals were supposed to be collectivized from the outset. Households in collective cooperatives were not to have their own water buffaloes or oxen. Few households managed to keep them after joining a cooperative.[158] But the number of draft animals decreased as collectivization took hold. Prior to collectivization, the draft animal population in northern Vietnam had risen from 1.252 million head in 1955 to 1.637 million in 1958. But after collectivization began in earnest, the number of draft animals in the north declined. By 1963, the number had dropped to 1.589 million.[159] Alarmed at this trend and usually blaming cooperative members for improperly minding the animals, national and local leaders searched for solutions. Some cooperative leaders sold the animals back to individual households. This measure did not go over well with higher authorities and had to be retracted.[160] More commonly, cooperatives stopped keeping the animals in collective sheds and corrals. Instead, they allocated each animal to an individual household to mind for the cooperative. This method, though regarded as less socialistic, was neverthe-

157. Interviews, Quat Luu, Vinh Phuc, 7 August 2000; Da Ton, Hanoi, 23 April 1993; and Van Hoang, Ha Tay, 30 October 1992. Also see *Nhan Dan*, 5 January 1967, 3.

158. The exceptions I am aware of were in Hoa Binh province. In 1967, households within cooperatives still retained 19 percent of the draft animals. A year later, that had dropped to 5 percent. My calculations are based on CCTK, Hoa Binh, "BC, Dieu Tra, Co Khi Nho HTXNN" [Statistics office, Hoa Binh province, "Survey of agricultural cooperatives"], 6 December 1967, 6–7 (P TCTK, hs 799, vv); CCTK, Hoa Binh, "BC Nhan Xet, TH, HTX, 1968" [Statistics office, Hoa Binh province, "Situation of cooperatives"], 20 December 1968, unnumbered tables (P TCTK, hs 870, vv); and TCTK, *12 Nam Phat Trien*, 410.

159. TCTK, *Nien Giam Thong Ke 1975*, 271, 273.

160. Post, *Revolution*, 211.

less endorsed by provincial and national authorities. It quickly became the most common way to raise the animals and helped reverse the trend.[161] By 1965 there were 1.660 million head in northern Vietnam.[162]

Lax care of draft animals by cooperative members working in the collective stockyards had influenced local officials to shift responsibility for these important animals back to individual households. This method did not, however, allow households to own the animals. Each household entrusted with a water buffalo or ox was to feed, shelter, and clean it on behalf of the cooperative. Failure to do so would result in fines or the animal's being assigned to a different family. The entrusted household received additional work points, an allocation of straw after each harvest for the animals to eat when pasturing was not possible, assistance in building a stable, and other compensations such as bonus work points for each newborn calf.

Soon several nodes of negotiation and resistance appeared within this new system.[163] One centered on who would be entrusted with each animal. Numerous households wanted the opportunity. The additional work points alone could equal two-thirds of what a typical cooperative member earned annually from collective work. One major criterion for a carer household was that it have several people, including youngsters, to share the chores of maintaining the animal. This still left more qualified households than animals. Some cooperatives annually rotated the animals among these households. Too often, however, this undermined care. Long-term allocations to a few families, on the other hand, sometimes aroused suspicions that personal relationships and even party membership more than proper animal care had influenced the assignments. Another node of contestation was the animal's use. Fearing the animal would be overworked or injured, which would result in penalties, the carer sometimes refused to let others use the animal. Yet when the carer household used it, the animal was underworked, at least in the opinion of brigade supervisors. Also contentious was the straw given to a carer household for silage. Straw was valuable for

161. Accounts during the 1960s and early 1970s in provincial newspapers *Hung Yen, Hai Hung, Vinh Phuc, Vinh Phu*. An early endorsement came in April 1964 from Nguyen Van Binh, a National Assembly delegate, who said that significant numbers of draft animals were dying from neglect. Nguyen Van Binh, DB Ha Bac, "TL, Chan Nuoi Trau Bo, Dong Bang" [Nguyen Van Binh, delegate, Ha Bac province, NA, "Water buffaloes and oxen"], 6 April 1964, 1–6 (P QH, hs 279, vv).

162. TCTK, *12 Nam Phat Trien*, 427, 463.

163. The following is based on interviews in Quat Luu, Tam Canh, Dao Duc, and Tien Thang, Vinh Phuc; and articles in the provincial newspapers *Hai Hung*, 1974, *Hung Yen*, 1962–1963, and *Vinh Phu*, 1968–1969, 1972.

thatching, bedding, fuel, and other uses around a peasant family's house and yard. Like grain, it was supposed to be divided fairly. While carers typically pressed for more straw, brigade and cooperative leaders suspected them of using it for other purposes and even of selling it. Manure was also controversial. All that the animal produced was supposed to go to collective fields. Many carer households, however, used some for their own purposes. To minimize this problem, numerous cooperatives created standards for how much manure each kind of water buffalo and ox (young, mature, old; strong, weak; male, female) produced, then required the carer to deliver that amount. The standards were partly based on how much excrement the carers themselves had previously reported. Some cooperative leaders later realized that the standards were significantly below the real amount because carers had been hiding not just a little but a great deal of manure to use on their own plots and gardens and those of close relatives.

In many cooperatives, assigning draft animals to selected households proved not to be a lasting solution. In addition to the problems just discussed, the number of work points paid to carers escalated yet the quality of care frequently deteriorated. Looking for better ways to husband the collective animals, officials in some places created specialized brigades to mind all water buffaloes and oxen belonging to the cooperative. Other cooperatives required each production brigade to form a team to look after animals assigned to it. No one solution worked for all places or even for particular cooperatives. Many cooperatives went from one method to another. Some tried combinations, letting each brigade try a different method.[164] Meanwhile, the number of draft animals in the north declined, particularly in the Red River delta where, after peaking in 1964, the population fell 12 percent by 1974.[165] U.S. bombs killed thousands and inflicted other hardships on animal husbandry. Another major cause, however, was neglect (see figure 1).

Land and how to use it constituted another site of negotiation and resistance, beginning with the household plots. In Vietnam, unlike in some other Communist Party regimes, authorities did not try to eliminate these lands, reshuffle them, or retrieve them if villagers failed to work a prescribed number of days in collective production.[166] They did try, however,

164. *Hai Hung*, 25 September 1974, 3; *Vinh Phu*, 5 November 1968, 2; 7 January 1969, 2; 27 June 1969, 2; 21 April 1972, 2.

165. Calculated from data in TCTK, *12 Nam Phat Trien*, 427, 463, and TCTK, *Nien Giam Thong Ke 1975*, 275.

166. Regarding China, see Zweig, *Agrarian Radicalism*, 122ff., and Potter and Potter, *China's Peasants*, 110–12; regarding the Soviet Union, see Wadekin, *Private Sector*, 23–25.

Trâu than :
*Dông về sương lanh tê minh.*
*Hõi oi ! Ông chủ thấu tinh cho chăng ?*

*Figure 1.* An ox with protruding ribs says to itself, "Winter has turned to freezing, numbing, moist air. But, my goodness, does the guy in charge care?" Drawn by Nguyen Quang Ve; published in *Vinh Phu*, 7 July 1969, 2.

to dictate what people planted. National regulations in the late 1950s and 1960s stipulated that villagers use the plots only for vegetables, fruit, and other "secondary crops" and for pigs, other small livestock, and fish.[167] Paddy, corn, and other staple food was to come from collective farming. Nevertheless, by about 1963–1964, according to most villagers I asked in Hanoi, Ha Tay, and Vinh Phuc provinces, people were growing as much paddy as possible in their household plots because, as one woman explained, what they received from their collective work was "far from enough." Officials, though acknowledging paddy from collective production was insufficient, were distressed. A 1965 Ha Tay report showing that paddy was being grown on 44 percent of the household plot area in the Ha Dong section of this new province argued that villagers "have not yet

---

167. See statute provisions: "Dieu Le Mau" [Regulations, low-level cooperatives], n.d. [circa late 1959], 9, in *Chinh Sach, Luat Le*; Fforde, "Law," 325–26; "Constitution of High-Level Co-operative Farms," 271.

been adequately guided" to raise only vegetables and livestock.[168] In Hung Yen province, where 68 percent of household land area grew paddy in 1967, authorities insisted that villagers needed to be "mobilized" (van dong) to grow vegetables and livestock fodder.[169] Those efforts swayed few villagers. How could they afford to grow food for livestock, people wondered, when they were hungry themselves?[170] Gradually officials gave up. An early 1967 Ha Tay report raised no objections even though 42 percent of household plot area in the province was still growing paddy. Instead it explained that because collective farming provided only "daily rice needs at a meager level, people have to plant paddy on their household plots to get additional rice, to address the hard times confronting them."[171] Rarely any longer did even national authorities criticize villagers for growing paddy.[172]

National and provincial authorities remained highly critical, however, of villagers who used as their own land what was supposed to be collectivized. Some were fields that villagers had managed to avoid surrendering to cooperatives when they joined.[173] Others were parcels that individuals or small groups of villagers secretly "encroached on" (lan chiem), as official reports often put it. People planted areas reserved for cemeteries and future buildings, strips along riverbanks and roadways, and other underused lands belonging to the collective cooperative. Some people dug ponds in remote fields rarely visited by brigade leaders. There they raised fish and grew water spinach (rau muong). Some villagers enlarged their household plots, creeping little by little into adjacent collective fields. Some, in the dead of night, built bamboo huts on collective land adjoining residential areas, then started planting their own crops. Others used these makeshift structures as leverage for claiming house lots, which were in short supply.[174]

168. CCTK, Ha Tay, "BC TH, HTX NN 6 thang, 1965" [Statistics office, Ha Tay province, "Cooperatives first half 1965"], 20 October 1965, 3–4 (P TCTK, hs 673, vv).

169. Nguyen Van Thanh, Ban Dieu Tra, Hung Yen, "BC, Dat Dai, 1967, Hung Yen" [Nguyen Van Thanh, investigating bureau, Hung Yen province, "Hung Yen's land statistics"], 12 September 1967, 8 (P TCTK, hs 808, vv).

170. Interviews, Nghiem Xuyen, Ha Tay, May 1993. Also, UBHC, Vinh Phu, "BCTK CT," 2 February 1970, 5.

171. CCTK, Ha Tay, "BC TH HTX" [Cooperatives], 7 January 1967, 5.

172. By 1974, if not earlier, even regulations for cooperatives no longer specified what villagers were to plant on the household plots. See "Agricultural Co-operatives Statute," C10.

173. Duong Quoc Cam, Mot So Kinh Nghiem qua dot I, 42; "BCKQ Dieu Tra" [Management survey], circa 1971, 10.

174. Duong Quoc Cam, Mot So Kinh Nghiem qua dot III, 2–4, 14–16, 21; Nhan Dan, 8 July 1969, 2; Vinh Phu, 21 March 1969, 3; 18 April 1969, 2; Hanoi, Bao Cao Ket Qua, 14–15; Hai Hung, 18 September 1974, 3.

On being discovered, people had to surrender the land, though sometimes they were allowed first to harvest what they had planted.[175] Many
cooperatives retrieved land only to lose it again a season or two later. In
some, such as several Son Tay cooperatives in 1964, not long after officials
had taken back parcels in one location "villagers took for themselves some
land in another place" or in anger "dug up the potatoes" in collective
fields.[176] Neighboring Ha Dong and other provinces had similar experiences.[177] Many reports convey subdued tussles over land as villagers tried
to get for themselves a piece here, a piece there. Authorities never brought
this struggle to an end. Accounts in the late 1960s and 1970s were still
complaining about villagers "holding" and "encroaching on" land belonging to the cooperatives.[178]

The private use of fallow collective land was another contentious point.
In the early 1960s, national policy allowed cooperative managers to set aside
small amounts of land that temporarily could not be farmed collectively.[179]
Commonly, this involved allowing households to raise their own potatoes,
kohlrabi, vegetables, and other "secondary crops" (hoa mau) during the
winter, when the primary crop of the region (usually paddy) could not be
grown. By about 1963–1964, as part of the campaign to improve management of the cooperatives, national authorities required that the practice be
stopped. That was easier said than done. In September 1964, Ha Dong
provincial officials reported with pride that nearly all collective cooperatives whose management had been revamped no longer lent land to
members to raise secondary crops. Six years later, however, leaders of Ha
Tay province, which then included Ha Dong, were pressing collectives to
retrieve all land that villagers were not supposed to have, including fields

---

175. This provision appears, for instance, in BBT, TU Dang, "TT 224, BBT TU Dang, 3 K,
QL HTX" [Secretariat, VNWP, "Circular 224, 3 contracts"], 18 November 1969, in *Cam Nang
Quan Ly*, 115.

176. BCH, Son Tay, "BCTK Dot III, Cai Tien QL HTX, Cai Tien KT, NN" [EC, Son Tay
province, "Third wave, campaign to improve cooperatives"], 20 August 1964, 10 (P TCTK, hs
609, vv).

177. CCTK, Ha Dong, "BC TH, HTX" [Cooperatives' situation], 30 September 1964, 4;
Bo Xuan Luat, DB Hung Yen, "TL, Cai Tien QL HTX, Ky Thuat" [Bo Xuan Luat, delegate,
Hung Yen province, NA, "Improving cooperatives' management"], April 1964, 3 (P QH, hs 279,
vv).

178. Examples include BBT, TU Dang, "TT 224," 18 November 1969, 112–16; UBHC, Ha
Tay, "Thong Tu," 15; Vu Cong Hau, DB Nam Ha, "TL Tang Cuong, XHCN, CT QL Ruong
Dat" [Vu Cong Hau, delegate, Nam Ha province, NA, "Land management"], 24 March 1972,
4–5 (P QH, hs 771, vv).

179. Duong Quoc Cam, *Mot So Kinh Nghiem qua dot I*, 23; Duong Quoc Cam, *Kinh Te*, 21,
38–41.

that local leaders had lent them for secondary crops.[180] Throughout the 1960s, Vinh Phuc villagers recall, the borrowing of collective land to use temporarily—typically for growing vegetables and potatoes in the winter— varied from cooperative to cooperative and even brigade to brigade, depending on how stringent local leaders were and perhaps on how pressured those leaders were to toe the official policy line.[181]

Another way to get land was for villagers and local leaders together to deviate from national policy. Numerous Red River delta cooperatives had more area for household plots than the permitted 5 percent. While sometimes due to erroneous calculations, it was also the result of officials succumbing to local influence. Regulations in Vietnam, unlike in some other communist countries, prohibited the area for household plots to increase as the population grew. Consequently, households established after cooperatives had been formed were expected to share their parents' plots or go without. Disgruntlement frequently resulted in the creation by cooperative officials of additional plots for new households, so that plots exceeded the stipulated 5 percent.[182] Contracts were given in several places to families to farm sections of collective land even after national and provincial authorities had clamped down on such practices in Vinh Phu in late 1968. Even in that province, several collective cooperatives had revived such arrangements by 1969.[183] In Hai Hung province, authorities in 1973–1974 had to launch a concerted campaign against brigades that "contracted directly" (*khoan thang*) and "leased" (*phat canh thu to*) land to households.[184] Authorities in other provinces had similar problems.[185] At about that time, the national government's Cooperative Management Committee called for vigilance to stop and guard against such practices.[186]

By hiding or not reporting land to higher authorities, villagers also used more land or took more produce from it than they were supposed to. A 1967 report from Thai Binh province said efforts to get accurate figures from local authorities revealed "one basic thing: reported areas of land were

180. CCTK, Ha Dong, "BC TH, HTX" [Cooperatives' situation], 30 September 1964, 4; UBHC, Ha Tay, "Thong Tu," 2–3.

181. Interviews, Dao Duc, 16 and 17 August 2000. Also, *Vinh Phu*, 21 March 1975, 2.

182. UBHC, Ha Tay, "Thong Tu," 2; Vu Cong Hau, "TL" [Land management], 24 March 1972, 4; *Hai Hung*, 20 March 1974, 2; Nguyen Khai and Le Van Bam, "May Y Kien," 30–31.

183. *Vinh Phu*, 16 May 1969, 2; 21 March 1973, 2; Hoang Quy, "BCTK CT" [Summary, Vinh Phu], 12 January 1970, 22.

184. *Hai Hung*, 20 March 1974, 2; and 16 November 1974, 3.

185. *Nong Nghiep Ha Bac*, April 1976, 2–4, 13, 34.

186. BQLHTXNN, UBNNTU, "KH Cung Co, HTXNN Mien Nui, 1974–1975" [ACMC, "Strengthening cooperative, mountainous region"], 26 July 1973, 3 (P UBNNTU, hs 105, vv).

inevitably less than the actual amounts."[187] Some underreporting, studies found, resulted from arithmetic and measurement errors. Other instances, however, were intentional. "Falsified reports" on land, expenses, and production, one informed observer wrote years later, "became 'an art form' among cooperative leaders."[188] When production brigade leaders in Thai Binh, Ha Tay, Hai Hung, and other provinces thought that collective managers were too busy or lazy to monitor them, they reported planting less than they actually had. Records from brigades and sometimes entire cooperatives were known to show land as having buildings, irrigation canals, or roads when the sites were actually planted fields. Areas reported as having been eroded by rivers or inundated by rains were found instead to be producing crops.[189] Such unreported areas might be farmed collectively, but some or all could instead be divided among households to farm individually.

Through such techniques, villagers, as a 1972 investigation in rural Hanoi said, were "nibbling and gnawing" (gam, nham) at collective land.[190] One major motive, it suggested, was economic necessity. A 1971 survey also said that a primary reason for illicit land use was "that the collective economy is not yet strong and not yet really the principal place villagers can rely on and because living conditions improve very slowly and the availability of staple food is decreasing. So cooperative members, worried and filled with anxiety, have to make a living on their own."[191] By taking additional land for themselves, ordinary villagers were also doing what numerous local party members and officials did. Indeed, leaders tended to take more land. The Hanoi study found that land appropriators who were local officials or party members averaged between 267–316 square meters of appropriated land each compared to an average of 232 square meters usurped by an ordinary villager.[192] The 1971 survey found that whereas an average villager

187. Ban Lanh Dao Dieu Tra Dat NN, Thai Binh, "BCTK CT Dieu Tra Dat NN, Thai Binh" [Committee investigating agricultural land, Thai Binh province, "Investigating land, Thai Binh"], 21 October 1967, 7 (P TCTK, hs 808, vv).

188. Nguyen Huu Tien, "Phong Trao," 30.

189. CCTK, Ha Tay, "BCTK Dieu Tra Dat Dai, NN" [Statistics office, Ha Tay province, "Investigating land"], 9 September 1967, 4, 6 (P TCTK, hs 809, vv); Phan Tu, Vu NN, TCTK, "BCKQ, Kiem Tra Dien Tich, Nang Suat, Lua, CT, LT, 1969, Thai Binh, Hai Hung" [Phan Tu, Agriculture bureau, GSO, "Inspecting paddy area and yields, autumn 1969, Thai Binh and Hai Hung provinces"], 25 February 1970, 2–4 (P BNN, hs 38, vv). Also pertinent is Ban Lanh Dao Dieu Tra Dat NN, "BCTK CT Dieu Tra" [Investigating land, Thai Binh], 21 October 1967, 7; and Bo Xuan Luat, QH, "TL" [Improving cooperatives], April 1964, 3.

190. Hanoi, Bao Cao Ket Qua, 15.

191. "BCKQ Dieu Tra" [Management survey], circa 1971, 10.

192. Hanoi, Bao Cao Ket Qua, 1972, 13.

illegally had between 100 and 200 square meters of land, party members who had taken land averaged 390 square meters.[193] Seeing party members and cooperative leaders getting land for their own use, other villagers thought they could do the same. Consequently, in a cooperative where households had appropriated many collective fields, villagers told provincial investigators in Vinh Phu that they basically did what local leaders themselves were doing.[194]

Many reports indicate that unreported land or land not being farmed collectively were acute problems in "average" and "weak" collective cooperatives, which constituted about three-fourths of the total. How much land was involved, however, is impossible to pin down. Figures vary. A 1970 investigation in fourteen sampled cooperatives in Hai Hung and nine in Thai Binh found only 1 to 2 percent more land area than the cooperatives had reported. The largest discrepancy was 7 percent in one Hai Hung cooperative; the lowest was practically zero.[195] Other accounts found large differences. A 1967 report said that the area planted and harvested in Ha Tay was 18 percent greater than local officials had revealed.[196] A report on Hai Hung concluded that a significant reason for a 12 percent decline in official figures for paddy area between 1964 and 1969 was production brigades "allocating land to members to farm on a rental basis."[197] As for land that villagers appropriated, with or without assistance from local officials, in one striking case 68 percent of supposedly collective land in a Hai Hung cooperative was farmed for years by individual households.[198] More typical was another Hai Hung cooperative in which 15 percent of the collective land had "disappeared" between 1964 and 1974. Although new irrigation canals had consumed some of the land, villagers, including some officials and party members, had taken most of it for their own use.[199] A 1974 newspaper report indicated that households in many cooperatives across the country farmed as their own 8 to 9 percent of cultivated land.[200]

193. "BCKQ Dieu Tra" [Management survey], circa 1971, 4, 10, 23.
194. *Vinh Phu*, 21 March 1969, 3.
195. Phan Tu, "BCKQ" [Inspecting paddy area], 25 February 1970, 2–3.
196. Making up the difference was land that was reported as nonagricultural but that was planted and land that was reported as farmed once or twice a year but was actually farmed more often. CCTK, Ha Tay, "BCTK Dieu Tra Dat Dai" [Investigating land], 9 September 1967, 10 and tables.
197. Other reasons offered were flooding, waste, and lack of seedlings. "May Van De" [Economic problems, Hai Hung], April 1970, 3. To calculate the percentage, I used the data in this report and in TCTK, *12 Nam Phat Trien*, 111, 115.
198. *Hai Hung*, 6 July 1974, 3.
199. *Hai Hung*, 18 September 1974, 3.
200. *Nhan Dan*, 1 August 1974, 1, 2.

The most comprehensive figures appear in two studies done in the early 1970s. In thirty sampled cooperatives of rural Hanoi, about 6 percent of land theoretically farmed collectively was instead being farmed "contrary to policy" by 65 percent of the households.[201] The other study, done in seventy-two cooperatives in four districts, each in a different province and region of the country, found that individual families farmed between 9 and 20 percent of supposedly collective land.[202]

Harvests were yet another site of contestation. While reaping, carrying sheaves of paddy to collective yards, threshing and drying it, and carting it to storerooms, individual villagers were often tempted to sneak some grain for themselves. In places that allowed youngsters to glean fields, mothers were known to give their children tips about where to look for grain, some of which they had "accidentally" dropped or forgotten. When threshing, a task usually done in yards belonging to the cooperative, a man might beat the stalks lightly, leaving several clinging kernels. Later, after hauling the stalks home, the fellow could strip them clean, thereby getting additional grain for himself. Most cooperative leaders quickly wised up to this ploy and prevented individuals from taking home the stalks they had threshed.[203] The straw allocated as fodder to households minding collective draft animals inevitably had some remaining kernels, which the carer households could keep. Villagers who were not entrusted with the animals sometimes complained that the equivalent to what the carers gleaned should be deducted from what those households earned from work points. Methods were devised to estimate how much grain that would be. In some places, carers convinced cooperative managers for years that the amounts gleaned were only about half what close investigation eventually proved to be the case.[204]

Other ways to keep more grain involved collaboration between ordinary collective cooperative members and leaders, usually within production brigades. Brigade leaders might give some grain to fellow members without recording it, thereby reporting to cooperative managers a smaller amount than had actually been harvested. Some brigades set aside grain without reporting it for meals prepared for all harvesters.[205] To guard against such practices, cooperative managers assigned people from other brigades to

201. Hanoi, *Bao Cao Ket Qua*, 5, 12–13.

202. "BCKQ Dieu Tra" [Management survey], circa 1971, 9.

203. Interviews, Quat Luu, 7 August 2000, Tam Canh, 11 August 2000, Dao Duc, 18 August 2000, and Tien Thang, 25 August 2000, all in Vinh Phuc.

204. *Hai Hung*, 17 August 1974, 3.

205. Phan Tu, "BCKQ" [Inspecting paddy area], 25 February 1970, 10.

supervise, especially while grain was being threshed, dried, and divided. Such measures also reduced opportunities for fellow brigade members to agree among themselves to thresh stalks sparingly in order to leave more kernels for them to glean later.

Another node of contention during paddy harvests involved the allowances for shrinkage. Often the allowances exceeded actual shrinkage. For instance, some brigades in a cooperative in Hai Hung in 1969 allowed 9 or 11 percent or even more for shrinkage even though the real figure was lower. One family given 214 kilograms to dry for the cooperative returned 162 kilograms, the amount required based on the permitted weight loss of 24 percent. Actually, however, the dried paddy had weighed 192 kilograms because it had shrunk only 9 percent.[206] The 30 kilogram difference was the family's gain and the collective granary's loss. To counter such practices, cooperative officials improved methods for determining shrinkage. Also, rather than allowing villagers to dry newly harvested grain at home, officials had the drying done in a few public places, making monitoring easier. This, however, was not much protection against a cooperative leader's overstatement of the degree of shrinkage in reports to higher authorities, which reduced the amount the cooperative was obligated to give to state granaries. Cooperative officials were also known to deduct more than regulations allowed for wastage, seed, and fodder.

I have no comprehensive data, only isolated estimates, on the amount of grain cooperative members and officials hid from higher authorities. In Da Ton, rural Hanoi, the most anyone drying collective paddy at home might be able to snitch or to get by virtue of inaccurate drying allowances was 1 percent.[207] A study of ten collective cooperatives in Hai Hung concluded that villagers were able get about 4.7 percent more paddy than they were actually entitled to, mainly by manipulating drying methods and shrinkage allowances. The same report indicates that deliberate underreporting, honest mistakes, stealing, excessive allowances for shrinkage, and other measures meant that actual paddy production in seven sample cooperatives in Hai Hung and six in Thai Binh was 4 to 5 percent higher than had been reported to higher authorities.[208] These estimates do not include paddy that individual households produced on land that was supposed to be farmed collectively.

Although villagers' justifications for getting more grain than rules allowed are not entirely clear, some do emerge from available information.

206. Ibid. See also *Hung Yen*, 28 November 1962, 3.
207. Interview, Da Ton, 22 March 1996.
208. Phan Tu, "BCKQ" [Inspecting paddy area], 25 February 1970, 9, 10.

"Taking private property," explained one villager, "was shameful. Taking common property was not shameful, and indeed some people encouraged it."[209] The reasons relate to trust and commitment, or the lack thereof. Informants claim that paddy and other jointly produced or owned property rarely disappeared when the collective cooperatives were small. They recall villagers carrying newly harvested paddy home to dry and afterward returning all of it to the collective granary for distribution according to work points. "Taking" (lay) would have been "stealing" (an cap; an trom) and would have attracted shame and chastisement. Such inhibitions against appropriating common property for oneself dissipated as the collective cooperatives grew larger. Mutual trust became harder to sustain, and monitoring became more necessary but less reliable. Aggravating these tendencies were hostilities and suspicions among people from different hamlets and villages. Moreover, the hardships of war and deteriorating economic conditions made mothers with hungry children and other desperate people resort to taking grain from collective fields and storehouses.[210] If villagers saw cooperatives not as theirs but as belonging to the managers and other officials, then that helped them to justify taking collective paddy, fertilizer, or other property. They were not stealing from their neighbors, people reasoned, but from authorities who gave them little consideration, bossed them around, and probably took far more from the cooperative than they did.[211] Embezzlement and other corruption among local leaders not only set poor examples for villagers but helped them justify the taking they did.[212]

People could readily distinguish between "taking" and "corruption," and not simply by the fact that it was officials who were corrupt. Officials also had families who might, out of desperation or for other justifiable reasons, appropriate common property for themselves. In that event and if the amounts were small, such taking was likely understandable and forgiven.

209. Interview, Tien Thang, 22 August 2000. Other material in this paragraph and the next comes from additional interviews in Tien Thang as well as in Dao Duc and Tam Canh, Vinh Phuc, August 2000.

210. One destitute woman who stole to feed her children reportedly was so racked with guilt that she could not sleep and made a public confession. *Hai Hung*, 17 July 1974, 2. See also *Vinh Phu*, 25 June 1968, 1.

211. "If a party member takes one sliver of wood, a cooperative member will carry off the entire bundle" (*Dang vien lay mot cay dom, xa vien se vac ca bo cui*). Vinh Phu, *Hoc Tap va Thi Dua*, 19. Many leaders did not take to heart this party saying. My sense is that the proportions were frequently the reverse; party members and other leaders in cooperatives were more likely to take bundles while ordinary villagers took slivers.

212. BCH, Vinh Phu, "PHNV, Cong NN" [Agricultural production], 3 September 1968, 7; UBHC, Ha Tay, "PHNV KH" [Developing local economy], 12 December 1968, 8–10 passim; UBHC, Ha Tay, "BC TH CT" [Work done], April 1970, 3, 16.

Leaders who hid or underreported land or grain in such a way as to benefit everyone else under their charge were not seen by those villagers as corrupt, even if the leaders themselves also personally benefited and even though higher authorities might deem such behavior corrupt.[213] If such activities, however, were done in such a way that only the leaders themselves and perhaps a few other individuals close to them benefited, then this was clearly corruption and an abuse of power in the eyes of most other people in the cooperative.

## What Were National Authorities to Do?

The daily struggles within collective cooperatives in the Red River delta and elsewhere in northern Vietnam affected the central government and party leaders' collectivization program. Despite no open demonstrations and few public displays of discontent, authorities knew that agricultural collectivization was not popular with the masses. Reports from district and provincial offices and studies by central government and party agencies themselves provided the indirect evidence—poorly farmed collective fields, grain that had disappeared, collective land that was hidden and that individual households farmed, inadequate care of draft animals, and the importance of family-based economic activities for villagers' livelihood. Those reports and studies also showed that collectivization had not lived up to the central authorities' expectations.

Collectivization, national authorities said, had had successes. During the war to defeat the United States and save the country, collective cooperatives "proved to be vital and powerful," a national party secretary stressed in 1974, an assessment many of his colleagues shared.[214] The cooperatives had mobilized not only food and other supplies for the military but also a large proportion of the men who went to the front.[215] The result of these

213. Nguyen Ngoc Luu, "Peasants, Party," 479, makes a similar point.

214. Hoang Anh, "TCL SX, Cai Tien, QL NN, SX Lon Xa Hoi Chu Nghia" [Reorganize agricultural production toward large-scale socialist production], August 1974, in Nhan Dan, 30 September 1974, 2. In addition to being a party secretary, Hoang Anh was also the government's deputy prime minister at the time.

215. BCHTU, DLDVN, "NQ, Bo Chinh Tri, Dan Chu, Che Do lam Chu Tap The, SX NN Phat Trien" so 197-NQ/TW [CEC, VWP, "Political Bureau resolution 197, collective mastery of cooperative members"], 15 March 1970, in Van Kien cua Dang, 6; editorial, Nhan Dan, 12 February 1971, 1. See also White, "Interview," 127; Chu Van Lam et al., Hop Tac Hoa, 27, 35; Quang Truong, Agricultural Collectivization, 125. Some Vietnamese analysts, however, have said that the role of collective farming in the war effort was overstated.

other factors was that cooperatives often became de facto units of local government, which significantly diminished the formal governing institutions in subdistricts.[216] National officials also credited collective farming, together with expanded irrigation and improved paddy seeds, for advancing agricultural production. Land planted in staple crops had increased from an annual average of 2.4 million hectares in 1957–1958 to nearly 2.7 million in 1970–1972. In that same period staple food production had risen from about 4.5 million metric tons per year to 5.3 million; paddy production had grown from an annual average of 4.1 million to nearly 4.5 million metric tons. And yields of paddy and other staple foods were higher (see appendix 1, table 1).

At the same time, accumulated evidence in national offices showed serious problems with collective farming. The amount of land planted in paddy and other staple crops had peaked in the mid-1960s. By 1971, it was 16 percent less than it had been in 1964. Paddy and total staple food production had also been higher in the mid-1960s than in the later part of the decade (see appendix 1, table 1). Annual production of paddy and all staple food was lower in 1960–1965 than in 1959, when collectivization was accelerating. By 1968, paddy production was 27 percent *lower* than in 1959; production of all staple foods was 17 percent lower. Not until 1974 did production exceed what it had been in 1959. From 1960 to 1971, paddy yields were lower than during the late 1950s. Meanwhile, production costs in cooperatives across the north increased, consuming on average nearly 43 percent of what a cooperative produced in 1971–1972 compared to 26 percent in 1960.[217] Villagers' living conditions had deteriorated since the early 1960s. One of the most distressing statistics for national authorities was staple food production per capita—an indicator as important to them as interest rates and the Dow Jones index are to government leaders in capitalist countries today. In 1959, the figure was 360 kilograms (325

216. The cooperative chairperson, said villagers I interviewed, had considerably more responsibilities and resources than the president of the subdistrict (*chu tich xa*). Cooperative leaders frequently interacted directly with district government agencies rather than going through subdistrict officials. See Pham Cuong and Nguyen Van Ba, *Nam Hong*, 63–68; Phan Dai Doan, "May Suy Nghi," 54–55; Nguyen Van Khang and Thang Van Phuc, "Bo May Quan Luc," 118–19; and Nguyen Ngoc Luu, "Peasants, Party," 457–62.

217. TCTK, *12 Nam Phat Trien*, 580; BQLHTXNN, UBNNTU, "BC, Mot So Net, HTX SXNN, 1975" [ACMC, CAC, "Major features of cooperatives"], 10 February 1976, 14 (P UBNNTU, hs 160, vv). In sampled Red River delta cooperatives, production costs in 1974 (the only year available) averaged 48 percent. Ban Nghien Cuu CS NN, BNN, "BC, Gia Mua Thoc, Thit, San Pham, Gia Ban, Tu Lieu SX NN, KH 1976–1980" [Agricultural Policy Research, MA, "Purchase prices, selling prices, agricultural inputs"], 10 December 1976, unnumbered table showing costs and distributions (P BNN, hs 115, vv).

kilograms of which was paddy). The trend thereafter was downward, hitting a low in 1971 of 233 kilograms (195 kilograms in paddy) (see appendix 1, table 1).

Three other clusters of evidence disturbed national leaders. First, the quality of collective cooperatives had scarcely advanced. In 1962—the beginning of the campaign to enlarge cooperatives, make them "high-level," and improve their management—29 percent were reasonably good (*kha*), 49 percent were average (*binh thuong*), and 22 percent were weak (*yeu kem*). By the end of 1965, after a majority of cooperatives had gone through the campaign's training sessions, there was progress: 41 percent of the cooperatives were rather good, 48 percent were average, and only 11 percent were weak.[218] By 1973–1974, however, the situation had deteriorated: 25 percent of the cooperatives were "advanced and rather good" (*tien tien va kha*), 42 percent were average, and 33 percent were weak. Why, after more than thirteen years of building collective cooperatives and campaigns to improve them, asks a 1974 report from the government's Agriculture Commission, "can't [the proportion of] advanced and rather good cooperatives increase or at least hold steady? Why can't the weak and average ones be strengthened?"[219] Although weak cooperatives were reportedly most common in the mountainous region, delta provinces were not much different. In Ha Tay, for instance, 28 percent of the province's cooperatives were rather good, 45 percent were average, and 27 percent were weak in 1963. The profile improved during the next two years, and in late 1966

218. Vu NN, TCTK, "So Lieu 5 Nam HTX, 1960–1965" [Agriculture bureau, GSO, "Five years' data on cooperatives"], February 1966, table 6 (P TCTK, hs 661, vv).

219. UBNNTU, "De Cuong Cung Co HTC, CT QL HTXSXNN, 1974–1975" [CAC, "Strengthening management of cooperatives"], 2 June 1974, 1 (P UBNNTU, hs104, vv). Criteria for evaluating collective cooperatives are rarely spelled out and probably shifted over time. Apparently, in "advanced" ones, collective production was well developed, provided members with adequate food and other benefits (for example, good schools and health clinics), rewarded industrious workers with additional shares, invested in infrastructure and new technologies, met obligations to the state, and had enough produce left to sell at the higher price allowed after other obligations were met. "Rather good" cooperatives met several, possibly all, of these criteria but not as fully. In "average" ones, the collective economy grew slowly and erratically, provided members barely adequate amounts of food and other benefits, gave small rewards for industrious workers, and had difficulties meeting obligations to the state and investing in infra-structures. In "weak" ones, the collective economy was poorly developed, could not provide members with sufficient food, and had significant trouble investing in better infrastructure and meeting obligations to the state. Womanizing, excessive drinking, gambling, and other vices were also common in weak cooperatives, says Duong Quoc Cam, *Mot So Kinh Nghiem qua dot III*, 5–6. Other sources include Nguyen Huu Khieu, "Phat Trien," 33; Vo Thuc Dong, Chu Nhiem UBNNTU, "Thong Tu, Phan Phoi LT, HTXSXNN" [Vo Thuc Dong, chairperson, CAC, "Distributing staple foods in cooperatives"], 30 April 1975, 2–3 (P UBNNTU, hs 161, vv); and *Post, Revolution*, 89.

provincial authorities predicted that, as a consequence of a continuous management improvement drive, Ha Tay would have no weak cooperatives and 80 percent "advanced" ones by 1968. That never happened. By 1974, the province's profile had regressed and nearly paralleled the national picture: 27 percent advanced and rather good, 45 percent average, and 28 percent weak.[220]

Second, a frequent complaint in official reports during the 1960s and early 1970s was that the collective cooperatives failed to meet annual production expectations. Consequently, incomplete data suggest, agricultural targets were rarely reached. In the late 1960s, Vinh Phu and three Red River delta provinces for which I have information produced 15–25 percent less paddy and other staple crops than was planned. In 1970–1972, the shortfalls for those provinces ranged between 5 and 20 percent.[221] For the entire north, staple food production was below expectations by 9 percent in 1965 and 7 percent in 1970 and 1972 (the only years for which such data are available).[222]

The shortfalls relate to a third grave shortcoming: collective cooperatives were not reliable sources of commodities. Cooperatives' disappointing production, their inability to tap much of what villagers produced on their own, and a policy that permitted economically strapped cooperatives not to sell food to the state meant that agencies procured less from the countryside than expected.[223] One indication is the volume of staple foods,

220. Vu NN, TCTK, "So Lieu 5 Nam" [Five years' data], February 1966, table 6; Ha Tay, "PHNV KH" [1967 plan], 19 December 1966, 33; and Nguyen Xuan Truong, Bi Thu, BCH, Ha Tay, DLDVN, "BC Trinh BBT TU Dang, TH, Dang Bo Ha Tay" [Nguyen Xuan Truong, secretary, EC, Ha Tay province, VWP, "Central secretary, report from Ha Tay"], 26 September 1974, 4 (P UBKHNN, hs 998, vv).

221. The delta provinces are Hai Hung, Hanoi, and Ha Tay. The information is incomplete and scattered among documents in the National Archives, Hanoi. The most systematic is a report for 1970 and another for 1972. They list production targets and results for every northern province. Several figures there are different from data in TCTK, 12 Nam Phat Trien, and TCTK, Nien Giam Thong Ke 1975. The two reports are Nguyen Duc Duong, Tong Cuc Truong, TCTK, "TB TH, KH Nha Nuoc, 1970, cac Tinh, Thanh Pho" [Nguyen Duc Duong, head, GSO, "Implementation of 1970 plan"], 22 June 1971 (P UBKHNN, hs 747, vv); and Vo Van Doan, Chanh Van Phong, TCTK, "TB TH, KH Nha Nuoc 1972, cac Tinh, Thanh Pho" [Vo Van Doan, office chief, GSO, "Implementation of 1972 plan"], 20 February 1973 (P UBKHNN, hs 849, vv).

222. Nguyen Tien Hung, Economic Development, 84; Nguyen Duc Duong, "TB TH, KH" [Implementation of 1970 plan], 22 June 1971, passim; Vo Van Doan, "TB TH, KH" [Implementation of 1972 plan], 20 February 1973, passim.

223. By 1968 and possibly earlier, the national government, recognizing the unsatisfactory conditions in the countryside, no longer required cooperatives to sell food commodities if the average amount of staple food per member was fifteen kilograms per month or less. Phu Thu Tuong, "Chi Thi (68-TTg/TN)," 6; Tong Cuc Luong Thuc, Chinh Sach, 5.

including paddy, paid in taxes and sold to state agencies. In 1959–1960, the state procured 18 percent of all staple food production (including 19 percent of the paddy). The proportions then declined: 16 percent (19 percent of paddy) in 1961–1964 and 15 percent (17 percent of paddy) in 1965–1971. Given that annual production also drifted downward between 1961 and 1971, state agencies obtained a smaller percentage of a smaller volume.[224] Even in 1972–1974, when production started to recover, the state's annual collection was only 16 percent of staple crops (18 percent of the paddy).[225] To make up some of the difference between what state agencies could extract from the countryside and what was expected or needed, the central government increasingly relied on foreign assistance. Northern Vietnam's exports of staple food had virtually ended by 1961. Imports, however, rose from 55,300 tons of paddy and other staple food (measured in paddy equivalents) in 1961 to 562,200 in 1967 to 787,600 in 1970. The 1970 imports equaled 15 percent of all domestic staple food production recorded that year.[226] Most of the imports were loans and grants from China, the Soviet Union, and other socialist countries. By the early 1970s China alone was sending northern Vietnam 500,000 tons of staple food each year.[227] That equals about 10 percent of what was officially produced in the north.

Meanwhile, the central government was putting more resources into the countryside than it had expected. Programs to help cooperatives with hungry people reportedly provided the average villager with about one kilogram paddy or paddy equivalent per month between 1961 and 1967.[228] I found no data for total amounts but details for Ha Tay and Hai Hung

---

224. These percentages and the reported volume of staple food production (see appendix 1, table 1) can be used to calculate the annual averages of state collections (in metric tons) for each of the three periods: 1959–1960, 926.5 tons staple food (877.1 tons paddy); 1961–1964, 836.1 tons staple food (822.6 tons paddy); 1965–1971, 762.8 tons staple food (708.0 tons paddy).

225. What the government agencies collected included the staple food that cooperatives and state farms (which produced only a tiny amount) sold to the state and paid as taxes. The percentages are based on figures for 1955–1974 in TCTK, *Nien Giam Thong Ke 1975*, 281. Slightly different data for fewer years are in TCTK, *12 Nam Phat Trien*, 401–402. See also Nguyen Ngoc Luu, "Peasants, Party," 529–39; Fforde, *Agrarian Question*, 22–23; and Beresford, *National Unification*, 219.

226. TCTK, "So Lieu, TH SX, Phan Phoi" [Staple foods], 30 March 1969, table 53; Nguyen Huy, *Dua Nong Nghiep*, 95. In 1967, about 45 percent of the total imported was rice, 30 percent was wheat flour, and the remainder was corn and other grains.

227. Dong Chi B, "Am Muu," 5. Comrade B (Dong Chi B) is reportedly Le Duan, the first secretary of the party. Regarding the importance of foreign aid to the DRV's economy and government, see Beresford, *Vietnam*, 143–44, and Spoor, "Finance," 343. For the quantity of food the Soviet Union exported to northern Vietnam between 1961 and 1976, see Fforde, *Agrarian Question*, 214.

228. TCTK, "So Lieu, TH SX" [Basic foods], 30 March 1969, tables 44, 45.

provinces suggest that in the second half of the 1960s, the amount of paddy and other staple foods received from the state equaled 50–60 percent of what the provinces had relinquished.[229] During the 1960s–early 1970s, the state lent more money to cooperatives, sold at subsidized prices more chemical fertilizers and insecticides, and devoted about 20 percent of the national budget to agriculture.[230]

During the late 1960s–early 1970s, party and government analysts were trying to explain these disappointing results of collectivization. One reason, many agreed, was the war, especially U.S. bombing. A national summary of the bombing's impact during 1965–1966 said, "Water buffaloes and oxen have been killed, some land can't be plowed and planted, various public works have been damaged, transportation is difficult, the delivery of materials and inputs (such as chemical fertilizers, pesticides, and farming implements) has been delayed, healthy workers have had to be mobilized to defend the nation, etc. All of these have adversely affected agricultural production."[231] Provincial reports make the same point for subsequent years. Reports also worried about the young male labor force, which was shrinking because of the war: 60–70 percent of young workers were women.[232] The destruction of flood control and irrigation systems, largely due to bombing, was another major setback. By 1968, "hardly any irrigation works,

229. In 1964, 1967, and 1969, Hai Hung provided state agencies with 316,219 tons of paddy but received 167,755 tons of paddy and other staple food (weighed in paddy equivalents) ("May Van De" [Economic problems, Hai Hung], April 1970, tables 1–6). In 1966, 1968, and 1969, Ha Tay province provided 97,254 tons of paddy and other staple food (measured in paddy equivalents) but received 59,950 tons. These figures I pieced together from Nguyen Xuan Truong, "Qua Ba Nam" [Three years, fighting U.S.], Ha Tay, December 1967, 66; UBKH, Ha Tay, "May Van De, KT, Ha Tay" [Planning Committee, Ha Tay province, "Economic problems"], August 1970, 3 and tables (P UBKHNN, hs 749, vv); and TCTK, 12 Nam Phat Trien, 401.

230. For example, state agencies supplied cooperatives with chemical fertilizers (mainly nitrogen, phosphorous, and phosphate) amounting to 111 tons in 1960, increasing to 313 tons by 1965, declining to 224 tons by 1968, then rising to 590 tons by 1971. Insecticides amounted to 110 tons in 1961, 4,424 in 1965, 6,913 in 1968, and 6,500 in 1971. Calculated from TCTK, 12 Nam Phat Trien, 82–83. For loans to cooperatives, see TCTK, Nien Giam Thong Ke 1975, 205; for budget expenditures on agriculture, see Nguyen Tien Hung, Economic Development, 123.

231. TCTK, "BC TH SX" [Agricultural cooperativization], 15 January 1967, 12.

232. BCH, Vinh Phu, "PHNV, Cong NN" [Agricultural production], 3 September 1968, 3; Nguyen Xuan Truong, "Qua Ba Nam" [Three years, fighting U.S.], Ha Tay, December 1967, 6–7; UBHC, Ha Tay, "PHNV KH" [Developing local economy], 12 December 1968, 12–13; CCTK, Hoa Binh, "BC, Dieu Tra" [Survey], 6 December 1967, 3. According to 1969 figures for Ha Tay province, for instance, 68 percent of the agricultural laborers in the sixteen-to-thirty-year-old age bracket were women. CCTK, Ha Tay, "BC, Dieu Tra Lao Dong NN, 01/07/1970" [Statistics office, Ha Tay province, "Agricultural labor survey"], 20 November 1970, table 2 (P TCTK, hs 990, vv). Yvon-Tran, "Une résistible," 113, claims that during the second half of the 1960s, about 70 percent of the people in the eighteen-to-twenty-five-year-old age bracket, most of them males, went into the army or took other war-related assignments.

large or small, remained intact" in northern Vietnam.[233] When the air attacks on the north were halted in March 1968, provincial leaders hoped that recovery could begin.[234] But in early 1972, just as authorities thought production was beginning to improve, the "American invaders," said a report from Vinh Phu, "resumed violent destruction and disruption" across the north.[235]

No documents I have seen, however, blame the war exclusively for problems in the cooperatives. Many scarcely mention it. Most cite it as one among several factors. Investigations into diminishing cultivated land, for instance, found that hardships and destruction due to the war were part of the explanation. A larger part was construction, which consumed more agricultural land, wasteful practices in the cooperatives, and households that were encroaching on collective fields. These, in turn, the report stressed, were due to bad management and administration within cooperatives and in the government agencies responsible for monitoring land use.[236] Indeed, mismanagement and poor leadership are the primary explanations running through official analyses from the mid-1960s, especially following the 1968 condemnation of household contracts in Vinh Phu, and into the 1970s. Other frequently cited reasons include villagers' low commitment to collective farming, lack of democracy within the cooperatives, and insufficient technology.[237] Often these are traced back to deficient management and leadership. Even "too little or too much state investment" is not the problem, said a Ministry of Finance official. "The problem is organization and leadership of production."[238] Hoang Anh, the deputy prime minister and a national party secretary, echoed many studies and reports when he

233. Phan Khanh, *So Thao Lich Su*, 104, see also details 103–18. I am grateful to Drew Smith for bringing this publication to my attention.

234. "BC KH, Phat Trien KT" [draft, 1970 plan], Ha Tay, 12 October 1969, 1b; Hoang Quy, "BCTK CT" [Summary, Vinh Phu], 12 January 1970, 18.

235. UBKH, Vinh Phu, "BC TH, KH 6 Thang, PHNV KH, 1972, Vinh Phu" [Planning Committee, Vinh Phu province, "Implementing 1972 plan"], 25 June 1972, 1 (P UBKHNN, hs 812, vv).

236. Le Xuan Tai, Pho Chu Nhiem, UBNNTU, "BC, Hop Thu Truong, Thuoc UBNNTU, CT QL Ruong Dat, Su Dung Ruong Dat" [Le Xuan Tai, deputy chairperson, CAC, "Unit chiefs' meeting on agricultural land"], 25 April 1975, 1–2 (P UBNNTU, hs 157, vv).

237. Notice that authorities, unlike their counterparts in some other Communist Party governments, were not searching for subversives and class enemies to blame for problems with collective farming. The contrast between the moderate class struggle in Vietnam and the strident one in China is a theme in Abrami, "Self-Making."

238. Hoang Van Diem, Thu Truong, Bo Truong, Bo Tai Chinh, "Phat Bieu Y Kien, Bo Tai Chinh, KH, KT, VH, 1975, Ha Noi" [Hoang Van Diem, deputy minister, Ministry of Finance, "Ministry's views on Hanoi's 1975 plan"], 30 October 1974, 3 (P UBKHNN, hs 997, vv).

spoke in Thai Binh at a major conference in August 1974 on collectivization in delta and midland provinces. "Organization and management" in a "large proportion of cooperatives" remained inadequate and this was the root cause of "undisciplined and uncoordinated production," "low productivity," "illogical and inequitable" distribution of harvests, "slack care of land" and other common property, and the perpetuation of "family-based subsistence" farming. Also afflicting the weak cooperatives, he stated, were "land encroachment," "embezzlement," and "blank contracts" to individual households to use collective property. Despite the fact that "most cooperatives in the delta and midlands appear to be production units with hundreds of hectares," they actually "are broken into individual brigades, each arranging on its own the use of land, labor, implements, and draft animals and each deciding how to distribute what is produced."[239] In short, concluded a February 1974 editorial in the party's national newspaper, the drive to improve management "had yet to achieve what was required."[240]

Three additional specific points emerge from national authorities' assessments. Land was inefficiently distributed among production brigades. Typically, each brigade used some of each type of land in the area—good, bad, high, low, near the village, far from the village, and so on. The result, analysts argued, was wasteful scattering and irregular configurations. Second, cooperatives had too many responsibilities, in part because of the war. A high-level party study concluded that, because cooperatives recruited soldiers, mobilized villagers for public works, and did "other work for the state," their leaders "have not been able to concentrate on what they should be doing," namely, improving production and villagers' living conditions, and increasing sales to the state.[241] Third, most cooperatives did not have enough land and people to use irrigation and new agricultural technology properly or to develop groups of specialized workers.

National-level analyses resulted in decisions that underscored authorities' resolve to make collective cooperatives perform better. In August–September 1974, party leaders launched a major campaign to "reorganize production and improve agricultural management."[242] In particular,

239. Hoang Anh, "TCL SX, Cai Tien" [Reorganize], August 1974, 1, 2.
240. Nhan Dan, 27 February 1974, 1.
241. Ban Chi Dao Lam Thu Xay Dung Cap Huyen, BCHTU, DLDVN, "BC, Chi Dao Thi Diem Xay Dung Cap Huyen Thanh, KH, NN, Tieu Thu Cong" [Steering committee to test the creation of district levels, CEC, VWP, "Turning districts into planning levels"], 12 January 1973, 3 (P UBNNTU, hs 44, tt).
242. "To chuc lai san xuat va cai tien quan ly nong nghiep." The decisions emerge in resolutions from three party CEC plenums (Third Party Congress)—the nineteenth in February 1971, the twentieth in April 1972, and the twenty-second in March 1974—and directive 208

authorities insisted that each cooperative's managerial board had to control collective land and other resources, allocate labor, determine the value of work points, set production schedules, and tightly monitor brigades and households. To this end, most production brigades were to be phased out. They would be replaced by specialized brigades (*doi chuyen*), which authorities expected to be more efficient because each would perform a discrete task, such as preparing seedlings, plowing, transplanting, or irrigating. These new brigades would also be composed differently. Whereas members of the previous production brigades typically lived in the same neighborhood or hamlet, people in these new brigades would come from throughout the cooperative. These changes, authorities predicted, would solve the problem of brigades trying to wrest control of land and other resources from the managerial board. The campaign also required larger cooperatives, each averaging about 200 hectares and 350 households (compared to 89 hectares and 156 households in 1970). Cooperatives in the Red River delta and midlands would be larger still. The ideal was one cooperative, rather than several, in each subdistrict. Subdistrictwide cooperatives, authorities vowed, would improve planning and the use of resources and reduce administrative costs. Instead of several cooperatives, each with a managerial board, a subdistrict would now have only one set of leaders for the entire area.

This new system was a core component of the central authorities' plan to accelerate "large-scale socialist production."[243] A closely related policy was to give each district (*huyen*), the unit of government below the province, more responsibilities. Working with the enlarged, usually subdistrict-sized cooperatives, district officials were to plan and coordinate all economic matters within their jurisdiction, thereby ensuring "balanced production."[244] The district would also relieve cooperatives of responsibilities not associated with economic activities. Another related component was to clamp down on free markets, especially in rice (or paddy) and other staple foods. Previous efforts to concentrate the buying and selling of all staple foods in cooperatives and government agencies had "exceeded the state's and cooperatives' capacity." By redoubling vigilance and "reorganizing pro-

from the party's Secretariat, 16 September 1974. The latter apparently resulted from consultative conferences such as the one held in Thai Binh province in August 1974. See *Nhan Dan*, 29 September 1974, 1, 3; and Le Duan, "Ra Suc." For more on these decisions and the campaign to revamp the cooperatives, see Fforde, *Agrarian Question*, chap. 4; and Vickerman, *Fate*, 238–58.

243. White, "Debates"; White, "Alternative Approaches."

244. Excerpt from directive 208 from the party's Secretariat, 16 September 1974, in *Nhan Dan*, 29 September 1974, 3.

duction and improving agricultural management," the government would eliminate the free market (*thi truong tu do*) for staples.[245]

Why, instead of pressing ahead with collectivization, did leaders not decide to back away from it? They would not have been the first Communist Party government in the socialist world to have done so in the face of poor performance and rural opposition. Their counterparts in Yugoslavia and Poland had taken that measure in the 1950s. Four reasons, I think, go a long way toward explaining their decision. First, party leaders in Vietnam, unlike in Poland and Yugoslavia, still believed, despite setbacks, that collective farming was central to improving rural living conditions and production.[246] Few officials in Vietnam's national party and in government circles questioned this.[247] Most argued for bolstering collective farming. The model of socialist production in Marxist-Leninist thought, and their counterparts in China, the USSR, and Eastern European countries other than Yugoslavia and Poland, probably influenced them. They also believed collectivization could result in prosperity. One of the clearest presentations at the time was the speech by Le Duan, the first secretary of the party, to the August 1974 conference in Thai Binh. The nub of his argument was that Vietnam had to find a way to develop the country despite its underdeveloped industrial sector. That meant combining "collective ownership, the science of labor organizing and economic management, and the sciences dealing with irrigation, fertilizers, seeds, and tools." The agricultural sciences and collective ownership were in place. Application of the "science" of management and organization remained to be done.[248]

This relates to a second reason: party leaders had confidence in managerial and leadership solutions. Party authorities reasoned that local leaders and ordinary villagers alike could learn how to manage and organize collective property, labor, and other resources so as to create large surpluses for their own families as well as the state. This would take time, persever-

245. HDCP, "QD 75" [Eliminating free market for staple foods], 8 April 1974, in *Cong Bao*, 15 April 1974, 61–65; also CEC, resolution, nineteenth plenum, as reported in *Nhan Dan*, 2 February 1971, 1–2, 12 February 1971, 2. The quotation about previous attempts is from BLTTP, "BC, TH CT LT" [Staple food situation], October 1970, 7.

246. For Poland and Yugoslavia, see Korbonski, *Politics*, 138–42, 146–49, 168–71, 235; Sokolovsky, *Peasants*, 65, 78–80; Rusinow, *Yugoslav*, 36–40; and Tomasevich, "Collectivization," 174, 179.

247. Among the few dissenters were some officials in the government's Ministry of Agriculture and the party's Agriculture Committee. Interview with a well-placed informant, October 1995, Hanoi.

248. Le Duan, "Ra Suc," 23–24, 29–31. For further analysis of the importance of collectivization to the economic, technical, ideological, and social revolutions envisioned by Vietnam's leaders, see Fforde, *Agrarian Question*, 72–76.

ance, and training. Collective cooperatives, after all were brand-new. There were bound to be setbacks. Villagers were used to farming individually. Many local leaders, even party members, did not yet understand how to farm collectively. They would, however, through more training and political education, which would result in better-governed and -managed cooperatives, higher production, and greater support among villagers for collective farming.[249]

Third, some collective cooperatives by the early 1970s had greatly improved and were living up to central leaders' expectations. Because some could do it, Le Duan said, "there is no reason why other weak cooperatives cannot do the same."[250] Similarly, the Agriculture Commission answered its own question in 1974 as to why most cooperatives had not reached the advanced stage, essentially saying the weak ones had not yet emulated the successful ones.[251] A theme in presentations to the 1974 conference in Thai Binh was that large, productive, well-managed model cooperatives already existing in every province proved that others could also succeed.[252]

Finally, the United States had stopped bombing the north and had signed a peace accord with the government in January 1973. The last U.S. ground forces left South Vietnam in March. Peace in the north and the looming prospects of the same in the south and a reunited country encouraged party leaders to try again to make collective farming succeed. In 1974 Hoang Anh said that the campaign to reorganize production and improve management should have been completed ten years earlier, implying that war and other circumstances had inhibited the effort. Now, he added, "we must vigorously carry it out to make up for lost time."[253]

## Summary

One theme in this chapter is that the four political conditions for durable common-use agrarian organizations were weak in most collective cooper-

249. Views such as these appear in numerous pronouncements and news items. Examples are BCHTU, DLDVN, "NQ, Bo Chinh Tri" [Political Bureau resolution 197], 15 March 1970; and an editorial in Nhan Dan, 14 April 1972, 1, 2.

250. Le Duan, "Ra Suc," 21. He also said that the successful cooperatives had no special advantages such as additional state funding (19), a claim that was untrue (see chapter 5).

251. UBNNTU, "De Cuong Cung Co HTC" [Strengthening management], 2 June 1974.

252. Nhan Dan, 29 September 1974, 1, 2.

253. Hoang Anh, "TCL SX, Cai Tien" [Reorganize], August 1974, 2. The raised hopes for improving cooperatives as wartime conditions receded are also discussed in Dang Tho Xuong et al., "Tong Thuat," 36, and in interviews I had with knowledgeable people, Hanoi, October 1995 and June 1996.

atives in the Red River delta during the 1960s and early 1970s. Governance in some cooperatives was of high quality; in many others, however, officials were heavy-handed or corrupt and villagers had little say. Trust among cooperative members was often marginal, particularly when, at the insistence of provincial and national authorities, small cooperatives were merged to form larger ones. Enlarged cooperatives and low levels of trust also overburdened methods for monitoring members' work. Authorities had expected higher production and other economic improvements to compensate for villagers' skepticism about collective farming and hence to boost commitment, the fourth condition. As things turned out, however, economic circumstances worsened during the 1960s. The one significant boost to commitment was the war against the United States. For the sake of their homeland and their loved ones, many people tried harder to make collective farming succeed.

A second theme is the low-key, everyday struggles over resources. Broadly speaking, the struggles were over collective farming itself. Seen close up, they were over mundane yet vital issues: how pigs and draft animals should be raised and who would get their manure; how small bits of land should be used and by whom; and how paddy should be reaped, threshed, and dried. Officials tried to enforce regulations about these matters. Through pronouncements, national campaigns, and the Communist Party's extensive organization, authorities pressed villagers to conform to the official vision of how collective farming was to be done. They condemned leaders who were corrupt, misused their positions, or allowed villagers to deviate from how collective cooperatives were supposed to function. They implored villagers to work together energetically and criticized those who failed to do so. Few villagers, however, worked in collective fields with great enthusiasm. For most, the reality of collective farming was far from what had been promised. A major shortcoming was the improper way leaders often ran the cooperatives, applied rules, and treated people. Another was that collective farming could not provide enough food. Better, they concluded, to produce as family units, not collective ones. Indeed, they earned a sizable portion of their meager incomes on their household plots and through other family-based activities.

Another theme is that villagers' everyday practices were politically significant in two respects. First, how they farmed and harvested collective fields, used their labor, raised pigs, tended their own land, and did other things conveyed their sentiments about collective farming. By and large, their behavior indicated that most villagers disliked collective cooperatives and wanted to return to family farming. Second, everyday politics affected official politics. Through their daily practices and without any organization other than some coordination among neighbors, villagers influenced collectivization policy and implementation. In most cooperatives they foiled authorities' plans for how pigs and draft animals should be raised. They ignored prohibitions against planting paddy, corn, and other staple food crops in their gardens and household plots to the point that those regulations became meaningless. Villagers' modifications of the "three contracts" policy, sometimes with support from local officials, provoked national leaders to intervene directly to stop them. In considerable part because villagers' everyday activities were out of line with how cooperatives were supposed to function, the results of collective farming by the early 1970s so greatly disappointed Communist Party and government officials in Hanoi that they launched a major campaign to reverse the trend and bring collective farming up to the standards they expected.

# CHAPTER 5

# Collapsing from Within, 1974–1981

In the Red River delta, the campaign to reorganize and improve the collective cooperatives lasted from late 1974 to early 1978. After the war against the United States and for reunification ended in April 1975, the Communist Party government also began to develop collective cooperatives in the southern half of the country. By 1979–1980, however, national authorities were significantly modifying the collective farming policy. They were scrambling to solve terrible agricultural and food conditions. Political conditions necessary for durable collective farming were even weaker than before, and intense everyday struggles over vital resources were, willy-nilly, removing collective farming structures. In the face of collapsing cooperatives, widening rural discontent, and the worsening economy, policy makers debated what to do. Gradually they decided that, to save collective cooperatives, they would have to make further concessions to family farming.

## National Campaign to Reorganize and Expand Collective Cooperatives

As one implementing agency summarized the task, "reorganizing production and improving agricultural management" in each northern cooperative involved "consolidating dispersed land and work under centralized instructions and guidelines keyed to an integrated plan." This, said the agency, would transform weak cooperatives into strong ones. Specifically, the campaign entailed retrieving land that households had usurped, reallocating land among brigades so as to enlarge fields and minimize waste areas, reorganizing labor into specialized brigades and teams, linking remaining production brigades to the specialized ones, and taking advantage of improved seeds and other technological advances.[1] Following directives from Hanoi, provincial and district authorities mobilized teams of officials to fan out across the countryside and run training and information sessions, initially for cooperative and brigade leaders and then for ordinary members. By mid-1975, Hai Hung authorities claimed, over half a million people—practically all adults in the province's cooperatives—had attended these sessions.[2] By early 1976, the Ministry of Agriculture reported, 75 percent of cooperative members in the north had been trained.[3] In the sessions, officials explained how to form brigades and work teams that would specialize in land preparation (plowing and harrowing; also caring for draft animals), fertilizer preparation (collecting manure and producing azolla and other natural fertilizers), irrigation, seed and seedling preparation, and pig raising, among other farming tasks.[4] They stressed the importance of forming larger cooperatives, preferably a single one for all land and villagers within each subdistrict. In that way, the number of production brigades would be reduced and therefore the size of each increased. The land assigned to each brigade would be divided into as few fields as possible to minimize unproductive area and all fields would be contiguous. No attention was to be paid to village boundaries.

By early 1976, about one thousand collective cooperatives (about 7 percent) had been reorganized. Two years later, it was nearly four thousand (about one-fourth of all cooperatives).[5] In some provinces, especially those in mountainous areas, the process was slow. It was faster in the Red River delta, where nearly 70 percent of cooperatives reportedly had been revamped by early 1978. By then, all cooperatives in Hanoi, Ha Nam Ninh, Hai Hung, Thai Binh, and Vinh Phu provinces had been reorganized.[6] One result was that land villagers had been using illicitly was often retrieved. In some places, such as a cooperative in Thanh Ha district, Hai Hung province,

1. BQLHTXNN, UBNNTU, "BC, Mot So Net, HTXSXNN, 1975" [ACMC, CAC, "Major features of cooperatives"], 10 February 1976, 5 (P UBNNTU, hs 160, vv).

2. Hai Hung, 19 July 1975, 2. In about 1976, the province had 555,400 adults working in agricultural cooperatives. Vu Nong Nghiep, So Lieu, 54.

3. BNN, "Phong Trao, LD SX, Phuc Vu SX, NN, 1975, 1976" [MA, "Worker emulation, agricultural production"], n.d. [circa 1976], 8 (P BNN, hs 70, tt).

4. One published list indicates that each agricultural cooperative could have as many as eleven specialized brigades and teams. Hai Hung, 22 March 1975, 2.

5. BQLHTXNN, "BC, Mot So Net" [Major features], 10 February 1976, 4; BNN, "BC Kiem Diem TH, Van Dong TCL SX, Cai Tien QL Nong Lam Nghiep, Co So" [MA, "Reorganizing production, improving agricultural and forestry management"], 13 May 1978, 2 (P BNN, hs 174, vv).

6. BNN, "BC Kiem Diem" [Reorganizing production], 13 May 1978, 2.

the amount of land recovered was two-fifths of the total amount suppos-edly controlled by the cooperative.[7] On average, according to a 1975 survey of nearly two thousand cooperatives across eight provinces, each coopera-tive recovered over three hectares, or about 3 percent of the land under its jurisdiction.[8] For authorities, this land, though small, represented a signifi-cant breakthrough in their drive to solidify collectivization. What most impressed authorities was the extent to which cooperatives were enlarged, especially in delta and midland provinces. At the outset of the reorganiza-tion campaign, few delta and midland cooperatives encompassed an entire subdistrict. By February 1978, "nearly all" did.[9] To national leaders, this meant each cooperative could be better managed and more productive. To them, large cooperatives were also a giant step toward integrating all sub-districts into districtwide economic activities. The Ministry of Agriculture was even encouraging some districts to form cooperatives that combined two or more subdistrictwide ones (*quy mo lien xa*).[10] Because of consoli-dation, the number of cooperatives in the north declined nearly 40 percent within four years, from 17,000 in 1975 to 10,529 in 1979. The average size nearly doubled, from 199 households and 115 hectares to 378 households and 202 hectares. Red River delta figures for those years are unavailable, but in 1971 an average delta cooperative had 328 households; by 1976, it had 528 and by 1979, it had 918—nearly three times as many as it had had eight years earlier. The average land area in 1979 was 357 hectares, com-pared to an estimated 200 hectares in 1975.[11]

When cooperatives were consolidated, production brigades were usually enlarged as well. For instance, the five cooperatives in rural Hanoi's Da Ton subdistrict had a total of twenty-five production brigades, each with twenty-five to thirty adult workers. After all five were combined in 1976 into one cooperative for the whole subdistrict, only sixteen brigades remained, averaging fifty workers each.[12] In one unnamed province (prob-ably in the Red River delta), the number of brigades in rice-growing areas

7. *Hai Hung*, 28 May 1975, 2.

8. BQLHTXNN, "BC, Mot So Net" [Major features], 10 February 1976, 7.

9. Tran Ngoc Canh, Pho Ban, BQLHTXNNTU, BNN, "BC Kiem Diem CT, 1977" [Tran Ngoc Canh, deputy head, CACMC, MA, "Activities 1977"], 24 February 1978, 5 (P BNN, hs 105, vv).

10. Duong Quoc Cam, Pho Truong Ban, BQLHTXNNTU, BNN, "TB TH, Quy Mo HTXNN, Thoi Gian Qua" [Duong Quoc Cam, deputy head, CACMC, MA, "Enlarged coop-eratives"], 19 July 1976, 1 (P BNN, hs 73, tt).

11. TCTK, *Tinh Hinh Phat Trien*, 110–11; TCTK, *12 Nam Phat Trien*, 557, 559; Vu Nong Nghiep, *So Lieu*, 20, 61, 73.

12. Tran Quoc Vuong et al., *Da Ton*, 97, 104; interviews, Da Ton, February–April 1996.

declined 45 percent between 1973 and 1976, while the average number of workers in each rose over 80 percent, from sixty-four to one hundred and eighteen, and the land area increased 75 percent, from twenty hectares to thirty-five.[13] By 1979, the average cooperative in the delta had only eight production brigades, each averaging one hundred and twenty-six workers and forty-four hectares.[14] The number of specialized brigades also rose, though not as much as national leaders had wanted, from an unknown small number to 3,182 in 1977 and 18,041 in 1979 (about two brigades per cooperative).[15] Many cooperatives also had teams within the production brigades that specialized in plowing and other tasks.

Meanwhile, the Communist Party government began to build collective cooperatives in the south, starting in 1976–1977 with experimental ones in seven provinces. Similar to what had been envisioned in the north twenty-five years earlier, cooperatives in the south were to be constructed in stages. The plan was as follows: first, establish simple work exchange groups; second, get the groups to cooperate across numerous activities; third, turn those groups into a "production team" (*tap doan san xuat*), similar to the earlier "low-level" cooperatives in the north except that less land and fewer draft animals belonging to members were to be pooled for collective use. The final stage was a collective cooperative that encompassed all production teams and all means of production within a village or subdistrict. By 1978, organizers and trainers, including hundreds of cadres sent from the north, were mobilizing villagers to form these organizations. By mid-1980, 36 percent of southern peasant households were reportedly members of production teams and collective cooperatives. In the central coast and central highlands, 70–90 percent of households were in production teams and cooperatives. In the more heavily populated southeast and Mekong delta area, about 30 percent of peasant households on 23 percent of the agricultural land had joined.[16] To many officials, these results were certainly encouraging.

## Impact on Political Conditions for Durable Collectivization

At the national level the drive to reorganize and enlarge collective cooperatives in the north appeared to be going well. In most cooperatives them-

13. Le Trong, *To Chuc Lao Dong*, 156.
14. BNN, "Bao Cao ve Cung Co," 9. An amended version of this report, is BNN, "Cung Co HTX SX NN, Day Manh CT K," in Le Thanh Nghi, *Cai Tien Cong Tac Khoan*, 32–78.
15. Nguyen Sinh Cuc, *Thuc Trang*, 20.
16. The statistics are from *Nhan Dan*, 14 July 1980, 1; Chu Van Lam et al., *Hop Tac Hoa*, 46–47; and Nguyen Huy, *Dua Nong Nghiep*, 113.

selves, however, villagers were even more apathetic than before. We can assess this situation by analyzing the campaign's impact on the four political conditions for durable common-use agricultural organizations and what many villagers did to deal with their predicament. Ultimately, the success of reorganizing and enlarging cooperatives depended on villagers' compliance. Deviation created problems. Consequently, what villagers did mattered.

The four political conditions for durability, let us recall, are trust, effective monitoring of members, commitment, and good governance. Let us turn to trust and take one example to illustrate a pervasive problem. Tri Tri and Trung Lap, two collective cooperatives in Phu Xuyen district, Ha Son Binh province, were combined in 1976 to form one cooperative that encompassed an entire subdistrict, with two hundred and thirty hectares and four hundred households.[17] People lived in separate areas within the subdistrict and the two places had had meager interaction with each other. Now suddenly they were expected to work together and share their fields, labor, draft animals, and harvests. Worse, the brigades in which people had been working were abolished. Local leaders, doing as district authorities had instructed and what had been taught in training seminars, assigned households to new, much larger brigades, each with over one hundred workers and about thirty-six hectares. The changes destroyed whatever effective relationships among the villagers had developed during the previous years when brigades were small. In their place grew suspicions and doubts. Within each large brigade, some members suspected that others simply went through the motions of farming in order to collect work points. They were "scratching and wiping" a paddy field (*cay gai bua chui*), for instance, rather than properly plowing and harrowing it; or "raking by stirring the water" (*cao co khua duc nuoc*) instead of actually raking the field. When brigade leaders were present, people worked diligently. When not being watched, however, many people slacked off—or were suspected by fellow workers of doing so. Increasingly, people asked themselves, why work carefully when others work carelessly?

Thousands of villagers in the north had similar views, one researcher later concluded, summarizing studies from numerous cooperatives.[18] People weeding paddy fields, for instance, often doubted that the others who had prepared the land or who had transplanted the seedlings had done their best. Believing that the crop was fundamentally flawed already, these people

17. My account is based on *Ha Son Binh*, 17 December 1980, 2.

18. *Nhan Dan*, 18 December 1980, 2. The article is by Le Nhat Quang of the Economics Institute (*Vien Kinh Te Hoc*).

tended to weed hastily. At harvest time, people suspected, rightly or wrongly, that others were hiding and snitching grain. Such suspicions justified their own stealing. A basic problem, in short, was that villagers in the reorganized and larger cooperatives often had little confidence in one another.

Distrust and suspicion among fellow members had been persistent problems. When villages were required to form one cooperative for the entire subdistrict, the situation frequently worsened. Let us consider Dao Duc, a subdistrict in Vinh Phuc province.[19] Beginning in the mid-1960s, when several hamlet-sized cooperatives were joined together, Dao Duc had three cooperatives, each corresponding to one of the subdistrict's villages (*thon*). None of the cooperatives was particularly cohesive. The one in Yen Lo village had even reverted for a while to five hamlet-sized cooperatives because of interminable conflicts among members and leaders. Some hamlets in Yen Lo were located three or four kilometers away from the others and had their own identities. In 1976, the three village-sized cooperatives in Dao Duc were combined into a single subdistrict-sized cooperative with nearly one thousand households and over six hundred hectares. The three villages had even weaker foundations on which to build trust and cooperation than the hamlets within each village. Although administratively linked for years, people in the different villages had rarely interacted. Intermarriage was highly unusual, hence family ties across the three villages were few. Moreover, one village had considerably more land than the other two and people in the larger village resented having to subsidize those in the other villages when harvests were divided among everyone in the cooperative.[20]

In time, concerted effort and exemplary behavior by local leaders and other villagers eager to make the collective farming viable helped some enlarged cooperatives reduce problems arising from unfamiliarity and distrust. But often good leadership was not sufficient to contend with other weak political conditions. Monitoring people's work, for example, was more difficult in the larger brigades and cooperatives.[21] The cumbersome system

---

19. Interviews, Dao Duc, Vinh Phuc, 16, 18, and 19 August 2000.

20. A similar situation prevailed in Quat Luu, another subdistrict in Vinh Phuc, when all hamlet and village-sized cooperatives there were folded into one big one in 1976 or 1977. Interviews, Quat Luu, 3–7 August 2000.

21. Interviews, four subdistricts, Vinh Phuc province, August 2000; Doan Truong DHNN I, "BC, Khao Sat, CT K trong HTXNN, Ha Nam Ninh" [team, Agricultural College 1, "Investigating contracts in cooperatives, Ha Nam Ninh province"], n.d. [circa October 1980], 3–4 (P BNN, hs 380, vv); Vu Trong Khai, "Ve Van De 'Khoan,'" 25–26; BQLHTXNNTU, *Khoan San Pham*, 18–19.

of work standards and work ratings became more complicated with additional norms and ratings to conform to the specialized brigades and the revamped production brigades. And larger brigades often meant that leaders knew less about what workers actually did. They were discouraged from adding more assistants, which would have increased administrative overhead. Brigade leaders often ended up assigning points based on what those doing the work told them. This often attracted two kinds of criticisms. Villagers unhappy with the number of points they had received believed that the leaders were biased against them and favored others. They may not have complained to the leader but their thinking adversely affected how they did collective work. Second, if brigade leaders gave all members of the cooperative what they claimed, managers criticized them for being too accommodating to the workers, thereby allowing the number of points to be inflated which, in turn, deflated the points' value at harvest time.

Commitment and incentives, a third condition for durability, also further weakened during the second half of the 1970s. Few villagers had ever been ideologically attached to collective farming. The war against the United States and to reunite the country, however, had given many cooperative members an incentive to do their best. By May 1975, the war had ended and the country was being reunited. Hence those reasons for collectivization had vanished.[22] Later wars between Vietnam and China in 1979 and with the Khmer Rouge from December 1978 until the early 1980s were not enough to revive the linkage between collective farming and patriotism.

The end of the war with the United States also greatly diminished the validity of certain requirements within the cooperatives. One was the duty (nghia vu) to sell a certain amount of their produce to state agencies at low government prices. During that war, many villagers could see some justification for this. Afterward, however, few could, particularly given that on the free market those products could fetch several times more than the official price.[23] Another was the system of rations (dinh suat) and adjustments (dieu hoa) for distributing a cooperative's earnings among those who had worked. Even during the war, people complained about this system, though they were able to "put up with it."[24] After the war ended, however,

22. Years later, national leaders publicly acknowledged this. See Le Duc Tho, "On the Question," C6. Leaders in Da Ton made similar observations during interviews, 12 October 1992.

23. BNN, "BC, Kien Nghi, CS Gia Mua, Nong San, Gia Ban, Tu Lieu SX, NN" [MA, "Purchase prices for agricultural products and selling prices of agricultural inputs, 1976–1980"], 15 February 1977, 9 (P BNN, hs 115, vv); Nguyen Sinh Cuc, Thuc Trang, 33–34.

24. Interviews, Da Ton, 20 and 23 April 1993, Nghiem Xuyen, Ha Tay, 12 May 1993, Quat Luu, Vinh Phuc, 7 August 2000.

the system made less sense. It was even less acceptable in the newly enlarged brigades and cooperatives. Small adjustments to members' earnings in order to share among neighbors, especially in times of adversity, were understandable. But being required to share across several villages among hundreds of households who neither knew one another well nor trusted one another was not.

Had the reorganized and enlarged cooperatives improved their lives, villagers' commitment might have been boosted. Indeed, this happened in the Da Ton cooperative.[25] Most villagers there recall having more to eat in the late 1970s than they had had earlier in the decade, when each village had its own cooperative or after all five villages were combined into a single cooperative in 1969, an arrangement that lasted only one year because production was badly organized and living conditions had drastically deteriorated. After forming the subdistrictwide cooperative in 1976, paddy production improved, to many villagers' surprise. In a typical season during the late 1970s, yields were one hundred to one hundred and twenty kilograms per *sao* compared to seventy to ninety in the first half of the 1970s. The value of work points also increased, which meant more earnings from collective work. This helped people take collective farming tasks more seriously. "There was still sloppy work," remembered one woman, "but less than before."

Most revamped collective cooperatives, however, provided less of what members needed than the smaller ones had. Consequently, said a 1977 Ministry of Agriculture report, "it is impossible for people to give themselves over to collective work."[26] Recalling the 1970s, several villagers in Vinh Phuc province said that "the bigger the cooperative, the more hungry people were."[27] Leaders could not properly organize and manage land, labor, seeds, fertilizers, draft animals, water, and other resources. Production costs rose while output fell. Hence, villagers' earnings from collective farmwork were at their lowest in the late 1970s. A workday was often worth only four hundred to six hundred grams of paddy and sometimes less than one hundred and fifty grams. A workday payment never reached one kilogram, the value it sometimes had in the late 1960s–early 1970s. Even if an adult had 236 workdays a year, the average in northern Vietnam in 1975, at five hundred grams per workday that would come to only 118 kilograms

25. This paragraph draws on interviews, Da Ton, April 1993, February–March 1996; and Tran Quoc Vuong et al., *Da Ton*, 104–5.

26. BNN, "BC, Kien Nghi" [Purchase prices], 15 February 1977, 7.

27. The remainder of this paragraph draws on interviews, four subdistricts, Vinh Phuc, August 2000.

of paddy a year.[28] Yet, according to research at the time, a working-age villager needed about 240 kilograms a year, plus some cash, to provide adequately for his or her needs.[29] More was required if the person was supporting a dependent who could not work. No wonder villagers in Vinh Phuc remember one or more years in the late 1970s as being a "year of hunger" (*nam doi*). Rice became a luxury, eaten only on special occasions, like a death anniversary. Otherwise people ate corn, potatoes, and cassava. "Every year in 1976–1980," recalled one woman, "I went to distant places to get cassava" because the family did not have enough rice to eat. Her husband, four children, and she had to share "one or two small bowls of rice a day."[30] She mixed it with cassava, corn, or potatoes. A common recipe was one part rice to ten parts something else. "We ate slowly," trying to savor every morsel, she said. "Our children often cried from hunger." Frequently she had nothing to feed them other than boiled water with a few vegetables.

Accounts from Vinh Phuc correspond to evidence from elsewhere. People in Nghiem Xuyen subdistrict, Ha Tay province, also associate the 1970s with hunger. One man who lived through that decade estimated that 70 percent of households lacked food 30 percent or more of the time. The war was one reason. But even after the war ended, conditions did not improve. "People were even hungrier," said one woman. She and others blamed the 1976 formation of one cooperative for all villages in the subdistrict. People did not want it and leaders could not manage it, others recalled. They also blamed the state price system, which paid little for what people produced.[31] In a nearby subdistrict, food availability fell from twenty-six kilograms per person per month before the three village-sized cooperatives there were folded into one large cooperative in 1976 to six kilograms per person in 1980.[32]

A mid-1976 report from the Ministry of Agriculture acknowledged that rural living conditions across the north had declined and cooperative members were dissatisfied. It predicted, however, that once the reorganized cooperatives had stabilized, people's earnings from collective farming would

28. TCTK, *Nien Giam Thong Ke 1975*, 294.

29. Le Trong, "Ve Thu Lao," 27. A similar figure of 233 kilograms of paddy per year can be calculated from 1976–1980 data in Vu Quang Viet et al., "Kinh Te Nong Thon," 115.

30. Interview, Dao Duc, 17 August 2000.

31. Interviews, Nghiem Xuyen, 10, 12, and 14 May 1993.

32. Kilograms of paddy and other staple food (measured in paddy equivalents). Nguyen Ngoc Khoa, Chu Nhiem, HTX Binh Minh, "BC, 3 nam Thuc Hien KSP LD, Nguoi LD [Nguyen Ngoc Khoa, chair, Binh Minh cooperative, "Implementing product contracts"], 20 February 1984, 1 (P BNN, hs 548, vv).

improve and people would produce enthusiastically.[33] But average earnings from cooperatives did not rise. At best they remained constant, amounting to less than half of minimal needs.[34] Total income for most villagers continued downward. According to surveys, the average real income for rural people in 1966–1975 was 78 percent of what it had been in 1959; that average dropped to 68 percent in 1976–1980.[35] Cooperative members who consumed less than fifteen kilograms (in paddy equivalents) of staple food per month, said a January 1981 report, were in bad straits.[36] That probably included most members. In numerous cooperatives in 1977–1980, people consumed less than eleven kilograms each.[37] Cooperatives such as Cam Phuc in Hai Hung province and Hoa Binh and Yen So in Ha Tay province, which raised the average above thirteen kilograms per person in 1979, were heralded for making big improvements.[38] Across the entire north, the average monthly consumption per person dropped from seventeen kilograms of paddy equivalent staple food in 1974 to about fifteen in 1976. By 1980 it fell to under ten (appendix 1, table 5 and graph). Although these official data do not indicate how much people actually ate, since villagers hid information from authorities, they do indicate that living conditions were grim.

Good governance, the fourth condition for durable common-use agrarian organizations, includes minimal outside interference, members' participation in major decisions, fair rule making and enforcement, transparent use of resources, and confidence in leaders. In most of Vietnam's coopera-

33. Duong Quoc Cam, "TB TH" [Enlarged cooperatives], 19 July 1976, 5.

34. According to government surveys, the average workday was worth 0.60 dong in 1974 and between 0.50 and 0.70 dong in 1979–1980. Studies showed that each worker required at least 1.50 dong from cooperative earnings. In terms of paddy, the most important commodity to villagers, 0.60 dong equaled about 2 kilograms in 1974 but only 1.15 kilograms in 1979 by government-stipulated prices (0.30 dong in 1974, 0.52 dong in 1979). A villager who used that money on the free market, as often happened because official outlets had nothing to sell, could purchase much less because paddy prices were five times the official one in 1974 and seven to ten times more in 1979–1980. Some cooperatives paid members not in paddy but in currency, thus requiring villagers to buy paddy and other necessities, often on the free market. Ban Nghien Cuu CS NN, BNN, "BC, Gia Mua Thoc, Thit, San Pham, Gia Ban, Tu Lieu SX NN, KH 1976–1980" [Agricultural policy research, MA, "Purchase prices, selling prices, agricultural inputs"], 10 December 1976, 4, 8 (P BNN, hs 115, vv); Ha Noi Moi, 29 November 1979, 3; Le Trong, "Ve Thu Lao," 26–27, 29; and BQLHTXNNTU, "Bao Cao ve Van De Khoan," 4.

35. "Sau 30 Nam," 48.

36. BNN, "Bao Cao ve Cung Co," 19.

37. See examples in Ha Son Binh, 1 May 1982, 2; Xa Vong Xuyen, Lich Su, 127; and Vu Van Nam, "Mot So Bien Doi," 6.

38. HTX Yen So, "Bao Cao Tong Ket," 4; Hai Hung, 19 December 1979, 4; Ha Son Binh, 27 May 1981, 2.

tives, these were even more problematic after enlargement and reorganization than they had been before. Ordinary villagers had little say in the enlarged collective cooperatives. "Forming the subdistrict-sized cooperative was the policy of the state," said one man in the Vinh Phuc subdistrict of Tien Thang. "No one in the villages wanted it." Villagers recalled that at meetings, "people were simply informed." "They weren't permitted to vote" or really discuss the matter. Several did dissent. Even some local party members and cooperative leaders objected. In Dao Duc of Vinh Phuc, party members argued over the question, especially whether one cooperative for all three villages in the subdistrict could be managed well. A leader in one of the village-sized cooperatives in Dao Duc said that he "was never able to understand why subdistrict-sized cooperatives were required."[39]

Despite lingering misgivings, local party leaders followed instructions from higher authorities. And "most villagers went along," explained a party member in Dao Duc, "because our party held power and monopolized the leadership."[40] In many places, consequently, the gap between ordinary villagers and leaders widened further. Even more than before, villagers felt that the cooperatives were not run by and for them, but by and for the leaders. Households were assigned to brigades with leaders they neither knew nor necessarily trusted. Often dominating a cooperative's managerial board were individuals from the largest one or two villages in the subdistrict, because those had the most delegates at sessions where board members were chosen. Frequently, the chairperson was from the biggest village. Such leadership configurations upset residents of smaller villages. In some places, such as Dao Duc in Vinh Phuc and Hoa Thach in Ha Tay, villagers had to accept leaders whom district officials imposed. These men, though originally from the subdistricts, had been working elsewhere before superiors assigned them to chair the enlarged cooperatives.

Da Ton cooperative minimized these leadership problems, which helps explain why that subdistrictwide cooperative was more successful than most.[41] The chairperson, Le Van Bui, lived in Ngoc Dong, the third largest of the subdistrict's five villages. Bui had led Ngoc Dong's cooperative since 1970 and was considered fair. Incomes for households there and in Dao

39. Interviews, Dao Duc, 15, 17, and 18 August 2000, and Tien Thang, 25 August 2000.

40. "Dai da so lam theo vi dang chung toi la dang cam quyen, doc quyen lanh dao." Interview, Dao Duc, 17 August 2000. The rest of this paragraph draws on other interviews in Dao Duc, Tam Canh, Quat Luu, and Tien Thang, Vinh Phuc province, August 2000; Duong Quoc Cam, "TB TH" [Enlarged cooperatives], 19 July 1976, 4; and Xa Hoa Thach, Lich Su, 184.

41. This paragraph relies on interviews, Da Ton, April 1993, January–April 1996; and Tran Quoc Vuong et al., Da Ton, 92–93, 103–4.

Xuyen, another village-sized cooperative, were higher than in the other three villages. When Bui became the head of the enlarged cooperative, the change eased the minds of people in Ngoc Dong and Dao Xuyen who had objected to the enlargement in 1976, fearing their situation would deteriorate. Bui chaired the cooperative in Da Ton for many years. Da Ton residents do not have fond memories of collectivized agriculture, but they credit Bui and some other leaders for making conditions there less severe than in many other places. They particularly commend him for not being excessively partial to people from his home village.

Corruption and other abuses of power, which were significant problems before, did not abate and probably became worse in the late 1970s despite persistent campaigns to counter them. The "five transparencies" campaign instructed local leaders to publicize their cooperative's expenditures and taxes, its income, its use of production inputs, details of special funds, and each members' work points and earnings. The "five prohibitions" campaign told leaders not to embezzle, engage in feasts and parties, borrow from the cooperative, engage in collusion, or encroach on land. Yet in the late 1970s, a board of investigation found embezzlement and other corruption in one-fourth of Hai Hung province's 416 subdistricts. Embezzled paddy averaged more than one ton in each of those corrupt subdistricts.[42] Trying to correct such transgressions, several cooperatives and districts across the Red River delta punished or removed 30 to 60 percent of the local officials.[43] Not long after, some new leaders were misbehaving. For instance, party leaders in a cooperative of Ha Son Binh province were entangled in various shady deals prior to a big shake-up in 1975–1976, after which relations between villagers and new leaders improved and production increased. By 1979, however, villagers' criticisms about lack of transparency and accountability had prompted another round of weeding out errant officials and party members.[44]

Some of the dishonesty involved brigade leaders and managerial board members who assigned themselves more work points than they deserved, used fertilizer that belonged to the cooperative on their own household plots, "borrowed" money indefinitely from the cooperative, falsified receipts and other documents in order to benefit themselves, and stole collective property outright (see figures 2–5).

42. *Hai Hung*, 23 May 1981, 1.
43. Dam Mai, "Nhung Chuyen Bien," 95; *Ha Son Binh*, 26 August 1978, 5; 1 November 1980, 3; and 27 May 1981, 2; *Nhan Dan*, 31 October 1980, 2; Hoang Ham, "Buoc Phat Trien," 38–39.
44. *Ha Son Binh*, 24 June 1978, 5; 26 August 1978, 5; 7 May 1980, 2.

*Xe của hợp tác xã nhưng ông chủ nhiệm nhờ tôi chở giúp hộ về xây nhà của ông ấy!!!*

Tranh : LÊ PHÂN

*Figure 2.* The man driving a tractor pulling a load of bricks and cement mix says, "This tractor-trailer belongs to the cooperative but the chairman told me to carry this stuff to help build his house." Drawn by Le Phan; published in *Ha Noi Moi,* 31 October 1979, 2.

*— Có lẽ ta phải ‹nghiên cứu› chi thành món ‹đồ rác› hay ‹tổng vệ sinh›, chị nhỉ ?*

Tranh : TRẦN QUYẾT THẮNG

*Figure 3.* The chairman of cooperative says to the accountant while holding list of expenses for a banquet: "Perhaps we need to 'research' how to convert these expenses into items for 'garbage disposal' or 'sanitation,' okay?" Drawn by Tran Quyet Thang; published in *Ha Noi Moi,* 11 January 1975, 2.

Đội trưởng : — Có ít thóc mới, cậu đem xay giã
làm bữa « bồi dưỡng cho lỗ sân kho ».
                              TRANH : HÀ NGỌC

*Figure 4.* A brigade leader tells another guy, "Take this new paddy, have it husked and prepared for meals during the training session on 'strengthening the team in charge of the storehouse.'" Drawn by Ha Ngoc; published in *Hai Hung*, 3 December 1977, 4.

*Figure 5.* A man turning into a rat as he leaves a cooperative storehouse in the dead of night carrying a sack of stolen grain. The lock hanging from the open door of the storehouse suggests that the man had keys to the building. Alluding to campaigns to transform villagers into good socialists, the caption reads, "A type of 'transformation.'" Drawn by Ha Ngoc; published in *Hai Hung*, 16 June 1979, 4.

A frequent complaint in several provinces in 1979 was that local authorities consumed large quantities of food and drink during parties and feasts (*lien hoan, che chen*) while ordinary cooperative members were hungry.[45] Dishonest officials also stole collective property and sold it. Those minding cooperative stores in several districts of Hai Hung province, for instance, took grain, flour, seed, fuel, and other goods.[46] Villagers in Vinh Phuc province recall occasions in the late 1970s when half the grain supposedly in the cooperative's granary was "missing." Bags of fertilizer and other supplies also vanished. Cooperative officials, including the person in charge of the storehouse, usually moved the grain and other materials in the middle of the night. Occasionally they did so in broad daylight. If someone spotted them, they said they were taking the bags to another part of the cooperative or to the district storehouse. To hide their misdeeds, they falsified record books and faked receipts.[47] Illicit transactions frequently involved district and provincial authorities "in cahoots" (*moc ngoac*) with cooperative leaders. Ill-gotten material was often sold on the free and black markets, where just about anything that was supposedly available only for purchase through government outlets could be found.[48] Some of the most egregious corruption involved land. A local leader in Ha Son Binh province, for example, usurped over two hectares of land, farmed those fields using seedlings and other resources belonging to the cooperative, and even hired people to do the work. Despite complaints from villagers who labeled him a "new landlord," he abused his position for years before higher authorities investigated in 1978.[49]

Bad leadership, particularly corruption, sapped many villagers' regard for officials and whatever hope they retained for collective farming. For instance, years of leaders' mismanagement, embezzlement, and self-serving behavior caused villagers in a cooperative of Ha Son Binh province to "lose faith in the local party committee and party members" and "not abide by

45. Mai Trong Nguyen, Pho Truong Ban Thanh Tra, BNN, "BC TH Khieu To, CT Xet Giai Quyet, 1979" [Mai Trong Nguyen, deputy head, Investigation Board, MA, "Resolving complaints, first quarter, 1979"], 4 April 1979, 2 (P BNN, hs 290, vv).

46. *Hai Hung*, 19 January 1977, 3, and 17 August 1977, 4. A 1975 investigation in several northern provinces found that government granaries held 12 percent less than had been reported, largely because of poor management and "widespread embezzlement, collusion, and stealing." Ban Thanh Tra Tai Chinh TU, "BCKQ Thanh Tra, LT, Nganh LT" [Central Financial Investigation Board, "Inspection, staple food and foodstuffs industry"], 27 October 1975, 2, 11 (P BTC, hs 3175, vv).

47. Interviews, Tam Canh, 10 and 12 August 2000, and in Dao Duc, 15 August 2000.

48. *Ha Son Binh*, 13 September 1978, 6, and 23 July 1980, 3.

49. The investigation's results are not reported. *Ha Son Binh*, 9 August 1978, 7.

collectivization policies."[50] "Stop leaders' embezzlement, feasting, and oppression of the people," wrote one person to the party's major newspaper in 1980, and cooperative members would be "enthusiastic producers."[51] Otherwise, this and other accounts said, villagers would do collective work poorly and scorn cooperative leaders.[52] A pronounced attitude among villagers, said a study of Nghe Tinh province, was that "the guy hunched over [meaning, the person doing the work] labored so that the guy standing erect [meaning, the local leader giving the order] could eat well."[53] People in numerous villages across the north regarded cooperative leaders as "bullies" (*cuong hao*).[54] Even if leaders in one's own cooperative were respectable, abuses by authorities elsewhere could adversely affect villagers' willingness to do their best and be honest themselves. Imagine, for instance, how villagers felt after learning that 20 to 50 percent of the grain their cooperatives had given to the state for taxes and obligatory sales went "missing" en route to agencies handling food distribution. The main cause was not waste or spoilage, though those were also factors, but collusion among managers of state storehouses and drivers of the transport vehicles.[55]

## Everyday Struggles: "Intense Tug-of-War"

As the drive to reorganize and enlarge the collective cooperatives gathered momentum in 1975–1976, villagers' objections were "widespread and seething," according to one report about Ha Son Binh province.[56] In addition to raising questions and dissenting during meetings and training sessions, people in parts of Ha Bac, Ha Son Binh, Vinh Phu, and other provinces uprooted plants and cut down trees rather than let them become the property of the new, enlarged cooperatives. They sold pigs belonging

50. *Ha Son Binh*, 22 October 1980, 3.

51. *Nhan Dan*, 21 October 1980, 2.

52. Vu Trong Khai, "Ve Van De 'Khoan,'" 26; *Nong Nghiep Ha Bac*, no. 1 (1978): 17–18; Xa Lien Khe, *Lich Su*, 124, 130; interview with a party member who studied cooperatives in the late 1970s–1980s, Hanoi, July 1996.

53. "Thang cong lam cho thang ngay an kha." Hoc Vien KT NN, BNN, "CT K, HTX SX NN" [Agricultural Economics Institute, MA, "Contracts in cooperatives"], 15 October 1980, 7 (P BNN, hs 302, vv).

54. Interview with a party member who taught and did research in a party school, Hanoi, September 1992.

55. *Ha Son Binh*, 16 December 1978, 6; 3 May 1980, 3.

56. Duong Quoc Cam, BQLHTXNNTU, "BC TH, Dieu Khien Hoc, HTX, Ha Tay, Ha Son Binh" [Duong Quoc Cam, CACMC, "Management guidance, cooperatives in Ha Tay / Ha Son Binh"], 5 July 1976, 2 (P UBNNTU, hs 200, vv).

to the smaller cooperatives and divided those proceeds as well as any money, grain, and other assets controlled by the smaller cooperatives.[57] Villagers in Nho described the 1976 enlargement of the cooperative they were in as yet another "rearranging of the mountains and the rivers," one of many they had been through since 1960. Each time, "nearly all property and capital were dispersed."[58] In some places, the assets were widely shared among households in the smaller cooperatives. In others, the property was divided among only a few people, usually the officials, thus aggravating bad relations between them and ordinary cooperative members.

Objections against larger cooperative were so strenuous in some places that collective farming virtually collapsed. Take, for example, Vong Xuyen, a subdistrict in Ha Son Binh province. For one and a half years between 1975 and 1977, many people in the Vong Xuyen's four villages resisted being consolidated into one cooperative. "Left in a small cooperative," many argued, "we'll have enough to eat. Thrown into a big clumsy one, we'll starve."[59] The result of protests during balloting to choose leaders for the enlarged cooperative was that no one received enough votes to win a seat on the new managerial board. A second election chose some nominees, but they then abruptly withdrew, saying they could not serve owing to poor health. Meanwhile only a small minority of households still farmed collectively. Other households took over fields for themselves. A third election in May 1977 finally selected board members, most of them former soldiers who had recently returned from the front and apparently enjoyed villagers' respect. The leaders of this new cooperative then had to contend with numerous families who refused to surrender fields to collective farming.

Official data showing that only 1 or 2 percent of cooperative members requested or were permitted to leave in the second half of the 1970s probably understate the actual proportion who petitioned to leave collective farming.[60] In addition, others wanted to leave but did not even ask because, as people in Vinh Phuc province explained, without some other place to live and work they had no alternative but to stay.[61]

57. *Nong Nghiep Ha Bac,* no. 8 (1977): 7; Duong Quoc Cam, "TB TH" [Enlarged cooperatives], 19 July 1976, 4–5; interviews, Dao Duc and Tien Thang, Vinh Phuc, 15, 16, and 25 August 2000.

58. Hoang Huu Cac, "Dem Trang," 143. Village Nho's location is unspecified; probably it is in a Red River delta province.

59. "De hop tac xa nho con no, gop vao hop tac xa to khong kheo lai doi." Xa Vong Xuyen, *Lich Su,* 116. The rest of my account draws on 115–21.

60. BQLHTXNN, "BC, Mot So Net" [Major features], 10 February 1976, 2; *Vinh Phu,* 23 August 1977, 4; 15 June 1979, 3. Also see appendix 1, table 4.

61. Interviews, four subdistricts, Vinh Phuc, August 2000.

Stuck in the collective cooperatives, some members tried to make them function as well as possible. More prevalent, however, were those who undermined collective farming. The situation in the countryside, according to a 1977 study from the Ministry of Agriculture, was like "an intense tug-of-war" (*dau tranh giang co gay gat*) between "cadres and cooperative members and the cooperative and higher authorities" over grain distribution, food, land, labor, and other resources.[62] I would add that cooperative leaders were themselves often divided and some sided with ordinary villagers. People were not necessarily deliberately seeking to destroy the system. Some were milking the cooperatives for their own gain. Many villagers had low regard for particular leaders of the new cooperatives. People were mostly trying to deal with a system that was seriously constricting their ability to support their families and make a living. In the course of doing that, they indirectly and directly undermined collective production.

People's ways of dealing with the enlarged cooperatives can be grouped into four clusters. First, there was public criticism. Angry and frustrated villagers shouted at and even hit leaders, wrote complaining letters to newspapers, and petitioned higher authorities to investigate wrongdoing. Often what upset them were brigade and cooperative leaders stealing grain and money, fudging records, and being arrogant and authoritarian. For instance, villagers in Chi Dao, Ha Son Binh province, wrote that by manipulating work points and records, the cooperative's accountant and other officials received three to four times as much income as a typical member.[63] In some places, such as Tu Minh cooperative, Hai Hung province, villagers' petitions and letters to district and provincial authorities resulted in investigations, court cases, and even prison terms for cooperative and subdistrict officials.[64] Frequently, however, those higher authorities were unresponsive. Some villagers then sent complaints to offices in Hanoi. The Ministry of Agriculture, for example, received hundreds in 1979. Between 40 and 75 percent of them alleged embezzlement, kickbacks, and other forms of corruption by local officials.[65]

62. BNN, "BC, Kien Nghi" [Purchase prices], 15 February 1977, 8.

63. *Ha Son Binh*, 30 August 1978, 7. Also see *Nhan Dan*, 31 October 1980, 2; Xa Thuong Lam, *Thuong Lam*, 162–63.

64. *Hai Hung*, 18 June 1980, 4. Also see *Hai Hung*, October 1983, 4; 27 August 1986, 3; and *Ha Son Binh*, 9 August 1978, 7.

65. Three quarterly reports by Mai Trong Nguyen, Pho Truong Ban Thanh Tra, BNN [Mai Trong Nguyen, deputy head, Investigation Board, MA]: "BC TH" [Resolving complaints], 4 April 1979, 1–4; "BC Thuc Hien CT 6 Thang, Nhiem Vu CT 6, 1979" [Activities first half, tasks second half of 1979], 3 July 1979, 3; "BCSK CT Quy 3, Nhiem Vu Quy 4, 1979" [Activities third quarter and tasks in the fourth], 19 October 1979, 3 (all in P BNN, hs 290, vv). I found no additional reports from this board for 1979 or other years.

Second, villagers took grain and other collective property. Some people were desperate because their families were hungry. Many took because others did. They believed that, as one man explained, "people in other villages [within the cooperative] are taking, so we'd better, too."[66] They also knew that authorities were dishonest. Taking increased in the 1960s and early 1970s as cooperatives became larger, as members grew more alienated from the organization and distrustful of one another, and as leaders grew more despised. Because these conditions worsened as cooperatives became even larger, taking spread much further in the second half of the 1970s. "People who before had never taken," recalled a man in Dao Duc in Vinh Phuc province, "now during this period also took." Officials, he explained, "couldn't punish members because nearly all of them were taking paddy."[67] One sizable paddy production expense in the Dao Duc cooperative was guarding fields against theft. Nevertheless, villagers still snitched thirty to forty tons of the paddy each season, about 4 percent of the crop. In some places 20, even 50 percent of newly harvested grain vanished.[68] When cooperatives were smaller or members felt more committed, villagers were usually discreet about taking grain. In 1975–1980, their methods were often brazen.[69] Frequently, for every person harvesting, another trailed close behind to glean what the harvester had "missed." Bicycles and carts carrying sheaves of grain from the fields frequently arrived at threshing and drying sites with only two-thirds of the load they had begun with. Between the fields and the sites, individuals pushing the vehicles had taken sheaves for themselves, sometimes even while villagers assigned to guard the grain watched. In broad daylight, people removed bricks from the walls of collective pigpens, dumped fertilizer on their household plots that was supposed to be used in collective fields, and chopped down collectively owned trees for their own use or to sell see figures 6 and 7).

Third, people expressed their sentiments toward collectivization by the way they worked. Some did their best, setting examples that leaders implored others to emulate. At the other extreme were people who did little or no collective work, concentrating almost entirely on their own economic activities. Most villagers put in the required time but exerted modest effort, suspecting that fellow cooperative members were doing the

66. Interview, Tien Thang, Vinh Phuc, 26 August 2000.
67. Interview, Dao Duc, Vinh Phuc, 16 August 2000.
68. Duong Quoc Cam, "BC TH" [Management guidance], 5 July 1976, 3; *Nhan Dan*, 13 October 1980, 2.
69. The following examples come from interviews, Tam Canh, 8 and 12 August 2000, Dao Duc, 15, 16, and 18 August 2000, and Tien Thang, 24 August 2000, all in Vinh Phuc; *Ha Son Binh*, 12 November 1980, 2; *Hai Hung*, 27 July 1977, 4, and 28 September 1977, 3; *Nhan Dan*, 13 October 1980, 2; *Vinh Phu*, 16 December 1980, 2; and Xa Hoa Thach, *Lich Su*, 188.

Figure 6. Looking on as her son steals fish from the cooperative's pond, a mother says, "Looks like our little boy is not so useless after all!" Drawn by Ha Ngoc; published in *Hai Hung*, 11 April 1974, 4.

Figure 7. Watching his son stealing collectively owned bricks, a man says, "Like father, like son!" Drawn by Ha Ngoc; published in *Hai Hung*, lunar new year issue, 1980, 4.

same. Specialized brigades and teams aggravated the problem of alienation, whereby individuals rarely saw a close relationship between what they did and what they received.[70] Villagers who only plowed or grew paddy seedlings or transplanted the seedlings were even further removed from other farm tasks and the actual outcome. When several phases were left to "specialists," people in production brigades were in nearly the same position. Because they did little besides weed or repair bunds, they had little or no involvement in most aspects of farming. Under these circumstances, villagers typically reasoned, the sensible approach to collective work was to concentrate not on production but on accumulating an optimal number of work points. That was more likely than diligent work to bring the maximum return allowed to each cooperative worker. A popular saying in the late 1970s captured this logic: "Work well, eat gruel; work deceitfully, eat rice" (lam tot an chao, lam lao an com).[71] Consequently, people often went through the motions without much regard for outcomes. They transplanted paddy seedlings in a "slipshod manner" (lam au); planted fields "straight," meaning without manure or other fertilizer (cay chay); weeded as though "strolling through the fields" (xep hang di dao qua ruong); and by other sloppy farming practices "tortured the land for whatever it was worth" (khao dat lay cua).[72] They also neglected equipment and draft animals. Ministry of Agriculture studies found that many plows and harrows, which should have lasted several seasons, were useless after only two or three and that four out of ten draft animals were too weak to plow and harrow adequately while many others were overworked.[73]

Fourth, villagers tried as much as possible to earn a living outside the collective cooperative. By the late 1970s, over 70 percent of an average cooperative household's income came from noncollective economic activities.[74] That was even higher than earlier in the decade (see appendix 1, table 7). Most of a typical cooperative family's private income came from raising paddy, potatoes, pigs, poultry, vegetables, and fruits in household plots, home gardens, and possibly land belonging to the cooperative. Yields on these tiny plots of land were two, three, even five and ten times higher

70. Hong Hai, "Ban ve Hieu Qua," 32–33; Nguyen Sinh Cuc, Thuc Trang, 20.

71. Ha Son Binh, 17 December 1980, 2. The optimal number of work points was not necessarily the maximum. See appendix 2.

72. Ha Noi Moi, 9 April 1981, 3; Ha Son Binh, 24 April 1982, 2; Hai Hung, 8 January 1977, 1; 8 May 1980, 3; 13 May 1981, 3; Nhan Dan, 13 October 1980, 2.

73. Nhan Dan, 10 September 1980, 2. See also the report about Ha Son Binh province in Ha Son Binh, 6 September 1978, 3; Vinh Phu, 9 January 1981, 2.

74. Even in "relatively good" cooperatives, 40–50 percent of an average member's income in 1980 came from noncollective work. Le Huu Dao, Cac Moi Quan He, 99.

than what collective farming attained.[75] The main reasons, as before, were diligent farming and more fertilizer. People assiduously gathered manure from their own animals or those they minded for the cooperative. Although required to give or sell manure to their cooperatives, they held back as much as possible for their own fields. They often failed to make their quotas and cheated the cooperative by mixing straw, paddy husks, and debris into what manure they did hand over. This was one reason collective fields were often underfertilized.[76]

Some villagers sold things, usually in unauthorized petty trading (*chay cho*) on the free and black markets (often labeled the "unorganized market" in official reports). Villagers "abandoned cooperative work," occasionally for months at a time, traveling by foot and bicycle to crossroads, bus stations, and towns to sell their goods.[77] In Ha Son Binh province alone, about two hundred people in each district were doing this in 1978; two years later, the average per district was more than four hundred (about 1 percent of the working-age population). In several cooperatives there, three hundred or more members spent much of their time selling. Most traders, cooperative leaders claimed, should have been home doing collective work. Only a few had registered with authorities. Often even they were still illegal because they were selling contraband goods. In addition to legal commodities such as vegetables, chickens, ducks, fish, and firewood, many traders sold commodities that only government markets were supposed to sell: cement, gasoline, machine oil, manure, chemical fertilizers, insecticides, rice, corn, and other staple foods. Fortune-tellers, gamblers, and moneylenders—all practicing outlawed occupations—also operated where traders and buyers congregated. The police's periodic crackdowns failed to stop them. People often had protection from local authorities, for a price.

In many cooperatives, officials had difficulty getting people to do collective tasks. Several families in Da Ton, for example, did little collective work; instead they concentrated on raising and selling chickens and veg-

75. Interviews in Vinh Phuc province, August 2000, and various newspaper articles, for example, *Ha Noi Moi,* 21 August 1979, 3; *Ha Son Binh,* 11 November 1978, 3; 27 August 1980, 2; *Hai Hung,* 14 September 1977, 2; 28 September 1977, 3; 30 August 1980, 3.

76. Also, because only about 5 percent of all pigs were raised collectively, cooperative managers had direct access to only small amounts of pig manure; and the amount of chemical fertilizer dropped 30–50 percent in 1976–1980 compared to the early 1970s. BQLHTXNN, "BC, Mot So Net" [Major features], 10 February 1976, 8; Trinh Dat, "May Y Kien," 44.

77. This paragraph draws on interviews in Vinh Phuc, August 2000, and newspaper articles, among them *Ha Son Binh,* 24 May 1978, 6; 13 September 1978, 6; 23 July 1980, 3; 27 August 1980, 3; 26 May 1982, 2; *Vinh Phu,* 26 August 1977, 2; 29 February 1980, 1.

etables.[78] In seaside villages, such as those in Dong Xa subdistrict, Thai Binh province, people evaded collective paddy farming to fish instead, then sold their catch on the free market.[79] People in several of Hai Hung province's cooperatives refused to do collective work in order to focus on their own economic activities.[80] Officials in Thuong Tin district, Ha Son Binh province, estimated that during the late 1970s and in 1980 6 or 7 percent of members did no collective work. The situation was apparently worse elsewhere in Ha Son Binh; in 1977–1978 30 percent of the province's cooperative members did no collective work.[81] Cooperative leaders in the Red River delta frequently went house to house, pleading and shouting for people to do what they had been assigned. Sometimes officials resorted to sterner measures such as confiscating bicycles that villagers used to transport goods to market until urgent collective work had been completed, and guarding people until they had finished their tasks.[82]

The struggles of ordinary people dealing with the revamped cooperatives involved no organization among villagers across subdistricts. At most, to judge from available information, the only organized activity occurred in small groups, usually of neighbors and relatives within a village, who collaborated and coordinated with one another to hide grain from local officials and other members in their cooperatives, to minimize their collective work, evade authorities' efforts to prevent selling and trading, and so forth.[83] Occasionally, they also made deals with brigade or cooperative officials.

The tug-of-war over work, grain, and whether collective farming would even continue was probably mildest in the 10–15 percent of cooperatives in the north that were "advanced" (tien tien). Examples included Dinh Cong (in Thanh Hoa province), Giao An (Ha Nam Ninh), Vu Ninh (Ha Bac), Vu Thang (Thai Binh), and Tu Trung (Vinh Phu). While some reports exaggerated their accomplishments, they probably were successful compared to other collective cooperatives. During the late 1970s, their members' food consumption reportedly averaged 18–22 kilograms per month of paddy and other staple foods, about double the average for all cooperatives in the

78. Interview, Da Ton, 25 January 1996.

79. Interviews done by Andrew Hardy in Dong Xa, Thai Binh, 1996.

80. Hai Hung, 30 April 1977, 4; 8 May 1980, 3; 13 June 1981, 3.

81. Ha Son Binh, 19 April 1978, 5; 8 April 1981, 2.

82. Ha Noi Moi, 29 November 1979, 3; Vinh Phu, 26 August 1977, 2; interviews, Dao Duc, 15 August 2000, and Tien Thang, 26 August 2000, Vinh Phuc.

83. In addition to the material I collected, I am also thinking here of accounts in Truong Huyen Chi, "Changing Processes," 61–62, 101–7; and DiGregorio, "Iron Works," 260–63.

north.[84] Some of that food came from members' earnings outside the co-operative. Most apparently came from their collective work, the value of which was usually higher than in other cooperatives because yields of paddy and other staple foods were two to four times better.[85] Advanced cooperatives were among the approximately 25 percent of all cooperatives in the north during the mid-1970s that produced five tons or more of paddy per hectare per year, a level the central government wanted all others to reach.[86] Another reason members in several advanced cooperatives had more food was that production was more diversified. In addition to paddy, advanced ones frequently collectively produced vegetables, raised livestock, and manufactured bricks, tiles, and other commodities. In Vu Thang, for instance, 97 percent of the collective production was agricultural in 1968 but only 60 percent was in 1977. The other 40 percent was devoted to livestock and fish.[87] Tu Trung cooperative expanded to handicraft making, carpet weaving, and brick making.[88] More diverse and better production, higher value for work points, and greater earnings were mutually rein-forcing and made villagers more enthusiastic and committed than they were in typical cooperatives.

Why did this favorable combination occur in some collective coopera-tives but not in most? One main reason, according to reports done from the late 1970s onward, was size.[89] They claimed that because large cooper-atives exceeded the management capabilities of local officials, production worsened along with villagers' living conditions and work habits. But advanced cooperatives, according to a study that focused on them, came in all sizes and on average were larger than the norm. If size played any role, said the study, it was that brigades, not the cooperatives themselves, were generally smaller and more efficient in the advanced ones.[90] A condition

84. *Nhan Dan*, 25 August 1980, 2; 29 August 1980, 2; Le Trong, *Mot So Kinh Nghiem*, 49, 91; and Fforde, *Agrarian Question*, 142.

85. *Nhan Dan*, 20 August 1980, 2; Dinh Thu Cuc, "Qua Trinh," 375; Le Huu Dao, *Cac Moi Quan He*, 99.

86. TCTK, *Nien Giam Thong Ke 1975*, 233; BNN, "BC, TCL SX, QL, Phat Trien NN, SX Lon Xa Hoi Chu Nghia" [MA, "Reorganizing production for large-scale socialist production"], November 1976, 4 (P BNN, hs 57, vv).

87. Dinh Thu Cuc, "Qua Trinh," 373–74; Nguyen Manh Huan, "Hop Tac Xa . . . Vu Thang."

88. *Vinh Phu*, 20 April 1979, 2.

89. Nguyen Duy Con, DB Ha Bac, "TL Ha Bac, Cung Co HTX SX NN, KH, 1980, LT" [Nguyen Duy Con, delegate, Ha Bac province, NA, "Strengthening agricultural cooperatives"], December 1979, 2–3 (P QH, hs 1315, vv); Vu Trong Khai, "Ve Van De 'Khoan,'" 25–26; TCTK, *Bao Cao Phan Tich*, 36–37, 139.

90. Le Trong, *Mot So Kinh Nghiem*, 95, 98, 106–7, 165–91, 216. In addition to being too large, Le Trong says, brigades in weak and average cooperatives were often overly specialized.

common to many advanced cooperatives was continuity. Vu Thang, for instance, was established in 1965. Tu Trung and Dinh Cong had been single, subdistrict-sized cooperatives since 1969.[91] Such stability meant that money, draft animals, and other assets were not squandered, as often happened each time a cooperative's composition changed. Cooperatives that became advanced invested their accumulated assets to improve infrastructure and increase production. Those cooperatives also usually had good leadership. Although there were whiffs of corruption in some of them, their leaders usually organized resources relatively effectively and enjoyed members' respect. Leaders typically assigned work and awarded points impartially and treated villagers fairly. They were also reportedly better trained and backed up by party branches composed of better-disciplined and more committed members than in most other places.[92]

A final similarity among many, possibly all, advanced cooperatives was extraordinary government assistance. According to a secretary of the Communist Party in 1982, they "were provided with whatever they needed."[93] Between 1958 and 1967, cooperatives that became advanced had received on average 24 percent more government loans than was the norm among all cooperatives. They also had been able to purchase from the government 35 percent more agricultural inputs. For the 1964–1965 period in particular, the cooperatives that were then or later became advanced usually received 51 percent more loans and 79 percent more inputs from the government than the average cooperative. This helps explain why advanced cooperatives' assets per capita were higher—sometimes nearly five times higher—and why they usually had better irrigation systems.[94] Using these advantages in the 1960s, they became more successful than most other cooperatives, which in turn attracted additional favorable government attention. In the second half of the 1970s, Vu Thang and Dinh Cong, for instance, could borrow considerably more money per capita from state financial institutions, receive higher prices for their products, and obtain more chemical fertilizers and fuel than ordinary cooperatives.[95] Some rel-

91. "Nhung Bai Hoc, HTX Vu Thang va Dinh Cong" [no author; probably from the MA, "Vu Thang and Dinh Cong cooperatives"], n.d. [circa 1978], 1 (P BNN, hs 176, vv); Vinh Phu, 20 April 1979, 2; Le Trong, Mot So Kinh Nghiem, 19, 92.

92. BNN, "BC, K, HTX NN, Dong Bang Trung Du va Khu 4 cu" [MA, "Cooperative contracts in the delta, midlands, and zone 4"], n.d. [circa August 1980], 4 (P BNN, hs 302, vv); Le Trong, Mot So Kinh Nghiem, 198–227.

93. Le Duc Tho, "On the Question," C6.

94. Le Trong, Mot So Kinh Nghiem, 16, 19, 20, 25, 92.

95. "BC, Net Chinh, HTX Da Khao Sat" [unknown author, probably within the MA, "Recent investigations of cooperatives"], n.d. [circa 1979], 6 (P BNN, hs 302, vv); Nguyen Manh Huan, "Hop Tac Xa . . . Dinh Cong," 46–47.

atively good cooperatives, though not among the advanced ones, were also blessed with extraordinary assistance. One substantial reason production in Da Ton significantly improved during the late 1970s was the rapid introduction of newly available high-yielding varieties of paddy. Facilitating that advantage were the expansion of irrigation, which allowed 80 percent of the cooperative's land to be double-cropped in paddy, and considerable assistance from the agricultural college located only a few kilometers away.[96]

Meanwhile, the deterioration of most other cooperatives accelerated during the late 1970s, largely because of everyday politics. In Dao Duc, villagers recall, cooperative officials could not keep abreast of what people were doing or get them to work properly. Fields were poorly prepared, planting was done badly and often late, crops were not well looked after, and people regularly snitched grain from collective fields. Collective farming, summarized one elderly man, was "almost dead."[97] The situation was similar in Dong La, a subdistrict-sized cooperative in Ha Son Binh. Production stagnated and work points became greatly inflated in number and deflated in value. Collective property vanished from fields and storehouses. Brigades hid land from the cooperative's managers while the managers squandered the organization's money and produce. Villagers, "not really interested in the cooperative and collective land, focused instead on their household plots and on doing other things outside." Several people farmed as their own some of the cooperative's fields.[98] In 1977–1978, between 5 and 6 percent of the agricultural land nominally being farmed collectively in Hai Hung and Ha Son Binh provinces was actually not. Usually individual households farmed it.[99] By 1978 families in some cooperatives of Vinh Phu province had usurped as much as one-fourth of the land.[100]

In many cooperatives, people substantially modified the national collective farming model. In 1976–1978, many places in Ha Son Binh, Vinh Phu, and probably other provinces dismantled specialized brigades and divided the enlarged production brigades to reestablish smaller ones with forty to sixty workers each.[101] By 1980, the average size for brigades in the Red

96. Interviews, Da Ton, February and March 1996; Tran Quoc Vuong et al., *Da Ton*, 106–7.

97. Interviews, Dao Duc, 15, 16, and 17 August 2000.

98. Xa Dong La, *Lich Su*, 125. Also, Kleinen, *Facing*, 118–20, 138–39.

99. Calculated from figures in provincial reports published in *Hai Hung*, 14 December 1983, 2, and *Ha Son Binh*, 21 October 1978, 3.

100. *Nhan Dan*, 31 October 1980, 2.

101. Interviews, four Vinh Phuc subdistricts, August 2000; *Ha Son Binh*, 20 September 1978, 3; Hoang Ham, "Buoc Phat Trien," 37; Hoang Quy, "May Van De," 57.

River delta had dropped nearly 30 percent compared to 1979.[102] Leaders in many cooperatives also allowed or turned a blind eye to arrangements that gave more responsibility and latitude to individual households. Initially these arrangements applied to the farming of secondary crops. Soon, however, they also included paddy farming.

Growing secondary crops in the winter had become increasingly possible during the 1970s in the Red River delta because "spring" paddy (*lua xuan*) replaced "fifth month" paddy (*lua chiem*). The latter was planted in October or November and harvested in April or May. The spring variety, which required less time to mature, could be planted in February and harvested in May or June, leaving time to plant a second paddy crop, which was harvested in October. That cycle created a "winter season" (*mua dong*), roughly November–January, during which secondary crops (*hoa mau*) such as corn, cassava, potatoes, beans, and kohlrabi, among other crops, could grow in fields that could be watered.

Beginning in the mid-1960s, national regulations had stipulated that winter crops be raised collectively, just like paddy. Only in rare situations did national rules authorize cooperative leaders to allow individual households to use collective fields to grow secondary crops. In those cases, it was only to be done briefly and primarily to raise cassava.[103] In the second half of the 1970s, central and provincial officials repeatedly stressed that secondary crops were to be produced collectively and condemned violations.[104]

At the same time, authorities urged collective cooperatives to grow more secondary crops. But usually only advanced and relatively well-organized cooperatives were able to mobilize members to grow secondary crops collectively. In many others, leaders made concessions to household farming in order to expand secondary crops. For instance, villagers in a Ha Son Binh cooperative agreed to farm collectively half the winter cropland provided they could grow their own crops on the other half.[105] In a cooperative of Hai Hung province, secondary crop production began to expand in 1976 only after officials allocated all fields to households, who in return gave a certain portion of their winter harvest to the cooperative.[106] So

102. From 126 working-age members in 1979 to 91 in 1980. BNN, "Bao Cao ve Cung Co," 9.

103. BBT, TU Dang, "TT 224, BBT TU Dang, 3 K, QL HTX" [Secretariat, VNWP, "Circular 224, 3 contracts"], 18 November 1969, in *Cam Nang Quan Ly*, 113.

104. See, for example, *Hai Hung*, 17 September 1975, 2; 17 September 1977, 1, 2; *Ha Noi Moi*, 20 April 1978, 2.

105. *Ha Son Binh*, 1 November 1978, 5.

106. *Hai Hung*, 15 October 1980, 3.

numerous were similar arrangements elsewhere in the province that Hai Hung's chief agricultural officer, though pleased with the greatly increased volume of potatoes and other produce, criticized cooperative officials for dividing winter crop fields among villagers to farm individually.[107] Indeed, throughout the north, a Ministry of Agriculture report said in early 1979, the most common arrangements for winter season crops involved individual households farming fields allocated to them.[108]

Some of those arrangements, according to the study, were marginally within the bounds of collective farming. In those cases, the land was divided among households only after the fields had been collectively prepared for planting. Individual households then planted and raised the winter crops on the land allocated to them. Part of what each household harvested was shared collectively. But the vast majority of these arrangements, the report warned, were well outside the parameters of collective farming.[109] Typically in those cases, winter cropland within each brigade was allocated, usually equally, among interested members. Then each household did all the farming on its assigned fields. After harvesting, each paid the cooperative (usually through brigade leaders) the quota that had been determined at the outset of the season. Each household kept whatever it had produced above that quota. Some cooperatives initially paid for seed and other inputs, which households reimbursed to the cooperative at the end of the season. Some let families use draft animals belonging to the cooperative. In some places, households were required to pay nothing or only small amounts of what they grew. Often the amount villagers had to surrender to the cooperatives was contested. Leaders in some places increased the quota each winter season. Villagers apparently did not object if the initial amount had been very low. In other places, however, villagers who opposed the higher amounts refused to plant or paid less than what the cooperative leaders had expected. Frequently, households paid the cooperative not in kind, as required, but in cash. They first sold at a high price on the free market the produce they were supposed give to the cooperative. Then they paid the

107. *Hai Hung*, 17 September 1977, 1.

108. Tran Ngoc Canh, pho truong ban, BQL HTX, Xi Nghiep NN, BNN, "BC TH, QL Cay Vu Dong 1979" [Tran Ngoc Canh, deputy head, Agricultural Enterprise and Cooperative Management Committee, MA, ["Winter crops"], 12 February 1979, 2–3 (P BNN, hs 176, vv).

109. Tran Ngoc Canh, "BC TH" [Winter crops], 12 February 1979, 2–7. The rest of this paragraph draws on this report and the following: *Ha Noi Moi*, 15 July 1980, 2; *Ha Son Binh*, 3 May 1980, 2; 25 October 1980, 3; 6 December 1980, 2; *Hai Hung*, 17 September 1977, 3; *Vinh Phu*, 26 September 1980, 1; 24 March 1981, 2; and Hoc Vien KT NN, "CT K" [Contracts], 15 October 1980, 2, 5, 7.

cooperative an amount of money equal to what that produce was worth at the much lower official prices.

Overall, a later government study acknowledged, these local contractual arrangements worked.[110] Most families exceeded the quotas paid to the cooperative; thus their incomes increased, they were less hungry, and they were eager to plant winter crops again. From the quotas households paid, cooperatives had more produce than before to deliver to state agencies. Finally, the area planted in corn, cassava, and other secondary staple food crops in the north rose from 478,100 hectares in 1974 to 889,000 in 1980. That increase accounted for 92 percent of all the additional area for staple crops (including paddy) in the north between 1974 and 1980.[111]

Similar arrangements, called "sneaky contracts" (*khoan chui*) and "doing things on the sly" (*lam vung*), developed for other products, especially paddy. Reportedly, the first sneaky contracts for paddy in Ha Son Binh province were in Son Cong, a subdistrict-sized cooperative that leaders and district officials had tried for years to improve. Members, however, continued to show up late for collective work, farm fields lackadaisically, and harvest sloppily, while their children gleaned paddy that had been "overlooked." Several cooperative officials also embezzled collective property. In early 1978, one production brigade, apparently with the tacit approval of some members of the cooperative's managerial board, tried a different approach to improving production. After collectively plowing, harrowing, and fertilizing its land, each member—in effect, each household—took charge of separate fields and did all subsequent work, from planting through harvesting. Afterward, each paid a specified amount of paddy per field to the brigade so that it could fill the quota established by the managerial board. Seeing that this household contract system greatly increased production, Son Cong officials in early 1979 let it spread to other brigades but said nothing to higher authorities.[112]

Another example arose in Tam Da, a subdistrict-sized collective cooperative in Hai Hung that was scarcely functioning by early 1977. For lack of care and water control, many fields were idle. Other fields were so badly neglected that harvests were pitifully small. Work points were practically worthless. Consequently, villagers spent most of their time farming their household plots and working outside the cooperative. Several families had

110. BQLHTXNNTU, *Khoan San Pham*, 20–21.

111. Calculated from data in a *Nhan Dan* editorial, 15 September 1980, 1; TCTK, *Nien Giam Thong Ke 1975*, 234; Vu Nong Nghiep, *So Lieu*, 218.

112. *Ha Son Binh*, 5 November 1980, 1; 12 November 1980, 2; 4 December 1982, 2.

taken over some collective fields. Between 1972 and 1976, subdistrict and district party leaders had punished and removed from office numerous cooperative officials and party members for embezzlement and other misdeeds. The cooperative's chairperson changed five times; the subdistrict's party secretary changed four times. In late 1977, district and provincial officials concluded that conditions had deteriorated further, not because of corruption or lower production, but because cooperative leaders had divided among interested households (including those of some party members) about 15 percent of the total area planted in the spring and fall paddy seasons. They also let these households use fertilizer from the cooperative's storehouse. After harvesting, each participating household gave a quota to the cooperative and kept the remainder for themselves. The arrangement, higher authorities declared, violated collective principles and national policies. Some party members in Tam Da agreed. More local party members and cooperative leaders, however, defended their actions as a way to put land back into production. "With land idle and people hungry," they said, "dividing it up [among villagers] is sensible."[113]

By 1976–1978, numerous cooperatives in Red River delta provinces and other parts of the north had "sneaky contracts" to produce secondary crops, paddy, or both.[114] By 1979–1980, the Ministry of Agriculture reported, "every district in every province" in the north had some cooperatives or at least brigades using contracts with households to farm paddy fields.[115] A few cooperatives in Hai Phong reportedly had been quietly operating this way since 1962.[116] Most sneaky contracts apparently developed in 1976–1979. Some were revivals of arrangements that had emerged during the late 1960s before central authorities quashed them. Typically they involved only a small fraction of a cooperative's land at first. Over time the area spread. Frequently changes in one cooperative inspired people in a neighboring one to follow their lead. Near Tam Da was Le Xa cooperative, where people had been avoiding, even refusing, collective work. To resolve the standoff, Le Xa leaders in early 1977 allowed families to grow their own paddy on some collective land.[117] Newspaper stories chastising such initiatives also probably gave people ideas. The particulars of arrangements varied. Some cooperatives permitted households to keep only 80

113. *Hai Hung*, 24 December 1977, 2. Also, *Hai Hung*, 23 July 1977, 3.

114. For an example in an upland part of the north, see Sikor, "Political Economy," 95–98.

115. BNN, "BC, K" [Cooperative contracts], circa August 1980, 8.

116. Dang Phong, "Lo Trinh," 9. See also above, chapter 3.

117. *Hai Hung*, 30 April 1977, 4. Sources do not indicate whether Tam Da influenced Le Xa or vice versa.

percent of what was left of their produce after paying the contracted amount. Others allowed them to keep 100 percent of that difference. Some cooperatives provided seedlings for paddy; others did not. Most provided some fertilizers; others did not. A practice common to nearly all was for villagers to plow and harrow the land collectively (perhaps because they did not individually own draft animals); then each household planted, weeded, tended, and harvested the fields allocated to it. Households and brigade leaders jointly attended to irrigation.

Dismantling specialized brigades, downsizing production brigades, and distributing fields among households usually involved collaboration between ordinary villagers and some local officials, who also tried to hide the modifications from unsympathetic authorities. They falsified reports, for instance, and obfuscated the boundaries of fields assigned to households so as to give the appearance of collective farming.[118] In effect, changes to national collectivization policy were occurring within brigades and cooperatives, the result of explicit and implicit negotiations and understandings between ordinary villagers and local officials. The arrangements, in short, resulted from local officials' responsiveness to villagers' everyday politics.

Officials in many places were caught in a double bind. Their superiors pressured them to make cooperatives function better and produce more. Yet every day they faced a large proportion of cooperative members who were apathetic about, disenchanted with, if not hostile to collective farming. Frequently, to motivate people to farm they had to strike deals with them. The upside was that cooperatives could then better meet production targets and appear to be fulfilling upper authorities' expectations. Also, as a national party leader later acknowledged, the local arrangements were "a way out for the sake of [people's] livelihood" to get crops planted, harvested, and distributed.[119] The downside was that reducing collective production while increasing household farming directly contradicted national policy.

Brigade or cooperative officials did not make deals with villagers everywhere. People in Lang To, Ha Son Binh province, after learning in 1978–1979 that households in nearby La Phu were farming their own fields, asked their cooperative's leaders to allow them to do likewise. The officials refused.[120] In other cooperatives, such as several in Tho Xuan and Thieu Yen districts of Thanh Hoa province, local and even district officials even-

118. See, for instance, the account about Tan Tien cooperative, *Vinh Phu*, 16 December 1980, 2.

119. Le Duc Tho, "On the Question," C7.

120. Kleinen, *Facing*, 139.

tually agreed, but provincial authorities, after hearing about the arrangements, ordered them stopped in 1979.[121]

## National Politics

A year later, Thanh Hoa provincial authorities reportedly "saw their mistakes" and "criticized themselves."[122] They had not anticipated that what they had stopped in 1979 would become the Communist Party's new policy. Those local, sneaky arrangements suddenly earned high-level leaders' approval.

Food shortages during the late 1970s, especially in the north, greatly worried national leaders. Paddy and other staple food, the national government stressed in April 1980, "constitute the number one strategic material, the most fundamental requirement for life, and for a long time the foremost problem facing the party, army, and entire population." Yet, "yields, production, and staple food per capita have been declining for years."[123] Across the Red River delta and the north generally, paddy yields fell 20–21 percent between 1974 and 1980. Paddy production fell 23 percent in the delta and 20 percent for the entire north. Total staple food production dropped less, primarily because of the local arrangements for winter farming described earlier. Nevertheless, staple food production, as officially recorded, reached only 72 percent of what the 1976–1980 five-year plan projected. Paddy production reached only 67 percent.[124] Staple food production per capita, a key indicator for authorities, had recovered to 276 kilograms in 1974, the year when revamping and enlarging the cooperatives began. Although higher than a few years earlier, it was lower than in the late 1950s–early 1960s; and by 1980, all that recovery had vanished when staple food production per capita fell to 223 kilograms in the delta (an 18 percent decline from 1974) and 215 for the entire north (a 22 percent drop), reaching the lowest level among all years for which there were data from 1955 on (see appendix 1, table 1, and graph). Meanwhile, farming costs averaged 45 percent of annual production in the north's agricultural coop-

121. Huu Hanh, "Khoan Lua," 42.

122. Ibid., 43.

123. HDCP, "NQ 09-CP, CS LT" [Council of Ministers, "Resolution 9, staple food policy"], in Ha Noi Moi, 23 April 1980, 3.

124. The target for 1980 was 8.3 million tons of staple food (in paddy equivalent weight), of which 6.5 million was to be paddy. BNN, "BC, TCL" [Reorganizing], November 1976, 1.

eratives in 1976–1980, higher than in the 1970s and higher still than the 25–30 percent range in 1960–1964.[125]

Low production also meant that collective cooperatives often could not meet tax and other obligations to state agencies. Cooperatives, often "advanced ones," that contributed more than 20 percent of their production were models for others to follow. Few apparently did so because in 1976–1980 the state acquired only about 13 percent of total staple food production.[126] Cooperatives in Ha Son Binh province, for instance, typically turned over 9–16 percent of their produce for taxes, obligatory sales, and other requirements, meeting only about 60 percent of their quotas.[127] Hai Phong province regularly failed during the 1970s to meet its obligations.[128] Only 16 to 33 percent of the cooperatives in Vinh Phu province fulfilled theirs in 1977 and 1979.[129] For the north as a whole, said a 1977 Ministry of Agriculture report, "there had yet to be a year when all or even nearly all cooperatives satisfied their obligations to the state or the state obtained the amount of agricultural produce it had planned."[130] Because production continued to drop, so did payments and sales to the state. Consequently, in the late 1970s and early 1980s, state agencies collected only half of what they had expected.[131]

Previously, during the war against the United States, a deputy prime minister said in late 1976, the government could "depend on foreign assistance" to make up for shortfalls in rice and other staple foods. After the war's end, however, foreign aid was "severely limited."[132] That situation continued through the decade.[133] Shortages in the north also could not be compensated with grain from the south because production declined there

125. TCTK, *12 Nam Phat Trien*, 580; BQLHTXNN, "BC, Mot So Net" [Major features of cooperatives], 10 February 1976, 14; Nguyen Sinh Cuc, *Thuc Trang*, 25.

126. Calculations based on TCTK, *Bao Cao Phan Tich*, 45, and Vu Nong Nghiep, *So Lieu*, 119.

127. *Ha Son Binh*, 13 May 1978, 5; 5 November 1980, 1; 10 March 1982, 2; Xa Hoa Thach, *Lich Su*, 187–88; calculations using figures in Chi Cuc Thong Ke, *Nien Giap*, 96, 212.

128. Bui Quang Tao, Bi Thu, Hai Phong, "Mot So Kinh Nghiem KSP, NN, Hai Phong" [Bui Quang Tao, Hai Phong party secretary, "Product contracts in Hai Phong"], in *Khoan San Pham*, 7.

129. Calculated from figures in *Vinh Phu*, 15 April 1980, 4, and Vu Nong Nghiep, *So Lieu*, 61.

130. BNN, "BC, Kien Nghi" [Purchase prices], 15 February 1977, 8.

131. White, "Agricultural Planning," 101.

132. Nguyen Duy Trinh, pho Thu Tuong, Phu Thu Tuong, "Chi Thi, CT LT, mua 1976" [Nguyen Duy Trinh, deputy PM, PMO, "Directive on staple foods, autumn 1976"], 15 November 1976, 1 (P UBNNTU, hs 201, vv).

133. Fforde and de Vylder, *From Plan*, 128–29; Beresford and Dang Phong, *Economic Transition*, 23, 28.

as well, though not as much, between 1976 and 1979. Despite improving in 1980, staple food production in the south still reached only two-thirds of the national government's target.[134]

Contributing to falling production were state agencies that could not fulfill their obligations to the centrally planned economy. Throughout the 1970s, but particularly in 1976–1979, the Ministry of Agriculture and the government's Agricultural Supply Company (*Cong Ty Vat Tu Nong Nghiep*) had too little money and too few vehicles and other resources to acquire and distribute the agricultural supplies specified in the nation's annual and five-year plans.[135] "From 1977 to 1980," said a report on Ha Son Binh, "state investment in and supplies for agriculture" in the province, "especially electricity, fuel, oil, and chemical fertilizers," were substantially below expectations, and consequently aggravated adversity due to floods, "made life harder," and provoked additional "negativism and lethargy in the countryside."[136] Shortages in the state supply system contributed to a 30–50 percent drop in the use of chemical fertilizer between 1976 and 1980. In tractor stations, which some districts had, a third or more of the equipment was inoperable owing to shortages of fuel and spare parts. Insufficient funding and supplies also crippled flood control and irrigation projects.[137]

Additional grave problems confronted Vietnam's leaders. Other aspects of the economy were in bad straits. By 1980, the volume of production in most major industries was below 1976 levels; productivity per worker had declined significantly; and state enterprises generally operated at only 30–50 percent of capacity. Few targets set in the five-year plan for 1976–1980 were reached. Food shortages, especially in the state markets and shops, were common. By most measures, living conditions for both urban and rural people were alarmingly bad.[138] Meanwhile, Vietnam was again at war, this

134. The target was 12.70 million tons of staple food crops (of which 10.5–11.0 million tons was to be paddy); actual production, officials reported, was 8.34 million tons (7.21 in paddy). BNN, "BC, TCL" [Reorganizing], November 1976, 1; and Vu Nong Nghiep, *So Lieu*, 120, 148.

135. Nguyen Xuan Lam, Thu Truong, BNN [Nguyen Xuan Lam, deputy minister, MA] to Ong Bo Truong, Bo Tai Chinh, Ong Tong Giam Doc, Ngan Hang Nha Nuoc TU [finance minister and Central State Bank director], 28 April 1978, 1–3 (P BNN, hs 160, tt); and Nguyen Ngoc Triu, Thu Truong, BNN [Nguyen Ngoc Triu, deputy minister, MA], to So, Ty NN, cac Tinh, Thanh phia Bac [provincial and city offices in the north], 13 January 1979, 1–2 (P BNN, hs 251, tt).

136. *Ha Son Binh*, 5 August 1981, 2.

137. Trinh Dat, "May Y Kien," 44; Yvon-Tran, "Une résistible," 170–72. Also, S. Smith, "Water First," chap. 9.

138. Vo Nhan Tri, *Vietnam's Economic Policy*, 95–96, 106–7; Fforde and de Vylder, *From Plan*, 128–29.

time in Cambodia, where conflict, which had begun in late December 1978, dragged on, putting more stress on the country's economic resources. Relations with China were also dangerously unsettled following a brief clash between the two nations' armies in February 1979.

To address acute economic problems it was vital to boost agricultural production. The reorganization and enlargement of the cooperatives were supposed to have achieved that. Instead, concluded the Communist Party's Agriculture Committee in early October 1980, "agricultural and livestock production is stagnant; results from land, labor, materials, and investment are low; the masses are worried, anxious, and full of misgivings; collectivized labor cannot be mobilized and negativism is pronounced (except in the few advanced and relatively good cooperatives); and the large majority of cooperatives remain weak and average."[139] In Hai Phong, the province's party secretary said, 80 percent of cooperatives were still "weak" or "average" in 1978–1980.[140] Other provinces had similar figures. In the north as a whole, said reports in 1980, only 10–15 percent of cooperatives were "advanced," far short of the goal set in 1974 to turn all cooperatives into advanced ones. About 15 percent were "relatively good" and 70–75 percent were weak and average.[141] In short, the figures had not changed since 1974.

Meanwhile, collectivization in the south also disappointed national authorities. For every successful cooperative—most were in the central coast and highland areas—there were several failures, particularly in and around the Mekong delta, where about 75 percent of the south's farming population lived. Some people openly resisted collectivization. They prepared protest petitions and denounced teams sent to organize cooperatives. Many uprooted fruit trees, slaughtered and sold their livestock, and destroyed crops rather than let cooperatives take them. Some villagers lay down in front of tractors plowing collectivized fields.[142] More commonly, people resisted privately and indirectly. Those methods, said a government researcher who was seeing reports from southern provinces and visiting villages there, amounted to "going in but not going out" (*vao khong ra*). That

139. Ban NN, BCHTU, DCSVN, "De Cuong, Hinh Thuc K, HTX NN, Su Dung LD, Vat Tu, Ky Thuat, Thuc Hien Tot, Tra Cong Cho LD, KH SX" [Agriculture Committee, CEC, VCP, "Guidelines for researching contracts"], 4 October 1980, 1–2 (P BNN, hs 302, vv).

140. Bui Quang Tao, "Mot So Kinh Nghiem," in *Khoan San Pham*, 7.

141. Ban NN, BCHTU, DCSVN, "TB, Nghien Cuu, K HTX NN" [Agriculture Committee, CEC, VCP, "Research on contracts"], n.d. [circa late 1980], 1 (P BNN, hs 548, vv); Nhu Dinh Luyen, "May Van De," 42.

142. Hy Van Luong, "Marxist State," 16–17; Quang Truong, *Agricultural Collectivization*, 265–70; Ngo Vinh Long, "View," 5.

is, "people entered cooperatives but did not go out to the fields" to work as they were supposed to. They ignored instructions or worked in slipshod ways.[143] Consequently, most production teams and collective cooperatives soon dissolved. In Hau Giang province, for instance, only 15 percent of the 2,600 cooperatives formed in the late 1970s still functioned in 1980.[144] The entire Mekong delta and vicinity had about 13,300 production teams and a few hundred cooperatives in 1979, but only 30 percent remained a year later.[145] By 1980–1981, less than 5 percent of the rural households there were in cooperatives.[146]

Also alarming to many provincial and national authorities in the late 1970s was the rapid spread of local arrangements in the north. Those activities, said a national party secretary and member of the party's Political Bureau in July 1980, often amounted to "turning land over to members who pay some rent" (khoan trang thu to). Similar arrangements, he recalled, had sprung up in Vinh Phuc during the 1960s, which the Political Bureau had had to stamp out. If such arrangements continued to proliferate, he warned, the cooperatives would "only be facades" (chi con hinh thuc ben ngoai).[147]

But how, authorities wondered, could the deterioration be stopped? Was clamping down, as in the late 1960s, a viable option? At that time, the deterioration was only in a few places. Now it was widespread. Would another campaign to reinforce collective farming help? Many had already been tried and another would entail insisting on structures and procedures that had been unsuccessful for production and availability of food and unsupported by the peasants.

For some time, muffled debates had occurred within official circles over how to address shortcomings in the centrally planned economy. Debates became more apparent in the late 1970s–early 1980s. Regarding collective cooperatives, many officials in Hanoi had concluded by 1976–1977 that bigger was not better and that managerial and organizational reshuffling

143. Interview, Hanoi, September 2000. Also, Quang Truong, Agricultural Collectivization, 267–68.

144. Ngo Vinh Long, "View," 5.

145. Lam Quang Huyen, Cach Mang, 191–92.

146. The proportions increased by the mid-1980s, when about 20 percent of agricultural households in the Mekong area and 30 percent in the entire south had joined. About half the cooperatives in the Mekong area, however, existed in name only. Vu Nong Nghiep, So Lieu, 37, 39; Nguyen Van Nhat, "Cai Tao," 15–16; Vo Nhan Tri, Vietnam's Economic Policy, 130.

147. Le Thanh Nghi, in Nhan Dan, 7 July 1980, 2. Several other institutions in the centrally planned economy were also being undermined by arrangements that people in state factories, urban neighborhoods, and elsewhere devised with and without the consent of local authorities. See Fforde and de Vylder, From Plan, 130–31, and Dang Phong, "Lo Trinh," 8–10.

was making the organizations worse and villagers more disgusted.[148] Several of these critics worked in research arms of the government's Ministry of Agriculture and the party's Agriculture Committee. From discussions with villagers and cooperative leaders and from numerous local reports, they concluded that peasants needed more material incentives and more opportunity to farm as families on their own fields. As economic conditions continued to deteriorate during the late 1970s, there was support for this position from some high-ranking party and government officials.

Support emerged during discussions about pricing policy. Contending views on the matter had initially surfaced in the early 1960s but disappeared during the war, when fixed prices and obligatory sales of agricultural products to state agencies were justified on national defense grounds. Debate reappeared in 1976–1977 in studies that disagreed with the State Price Commission and other advocates of low agricultural prices. Ministry of Agriculture reports, for example, argued that political education and the reorganization of cooperatives could not make villagers work well collectively. Instead, prices for what they produced would have to be raised. Low prices meant low remuneration to villagers. No wonder, the reports said, people work much harder on their household plots and go outside the cooperative to earn a living. And no wonder they sell any surplus on the free market, where prices are much higher than on the state markets. That is reasonable and understandable behavior, said one report, and "should cause us to seriously reconsider policies about prices and many other matters."[149]

Similar views arose during discussions about why villagers still did collective work lethargically. Weak management and bad cooperative leadership were certainly cited. What was given more emphasis than in the past, however, was that collective production stifled an individual's desire to farm. One researcher's conclusions from studies in Hai Hung province summarize what others had said in the late 1970s. Peasants, he wrote, have a "collective side" to their outlook. But they also have an "individual side." For years, leaders had emphasized the collective side. Now, he said, they needed to "emphasize more and tilt more toward the peasant's individual side. This

---

148. This passage relies on various documents and conversations with four individuals who worked in the 1970s–1980s on agricultural matters in government and party offices, Hanoi, October 1995, June and July 1996, and September 2000. Divisions within central offices are noted in Chu Van Lam et al., *Hop Tac Hoa*, 52–53.

149. Ban Nghien Cuu, "BC, Gia Mua" [Purchase prices], 10 December 1976, 7. See also BNN, "BC, Kien Nghi" [Purchase prices], 15 February 1977, 6–8; and White, "Agricultural Planning."

is one key to encouraging paddy growers to work enthusiastically."[150] Another key, said many, including the minister for agriculture, was to close the gap between what people did and the outcome of their work.

> A transplanter knows only that after planting paddy in a certain field she will get 15 or 20 points. Whether that field will have a high or low yield, the transplanter never knows. Consequently, whether the seedlings are planted deeply or not, properly spaced or not, stepped on and broken or not . . . , she still gets those points. The same for two people sent to scoop water into the field. They know only that after finishing, they will receive eight or ten points. If after one day the field is dry, it's not their problem. [Similarly] . . . the outcome and quality of work done is not closely connected to one's own interests. Whether a field produces well or not, the crop belongs to everyone in general. Just a tiny bit goes to each individual.

The main problem, the minister concluded, was that "the people doing the work bear no responsibility for what the land produces, whether that outcome be high or low."[151]

The high yields on household plots and fields farmed individually through local arrangements influenced officials' thinking in the late 1970s. For more than twenty years, said an August 1980 report, cooperative members had been working their household plots more diligently and getting much better yields than in collective fields. Similarly, in recent years household farming fields belonging to the cooperative achieved yields "at least 20–30 percent, on average 40–60 percent, and often nearly 100 percent" greater than was collectively achieved on the same land the season before.[152]

To better understand household farming, many national officials in 1980 studied locally evolving farming arrangements rather than simply dismissing them. As the party's Secretariat said, those activities were to be looked at "objectively and scientifically" in order to "discover and summarize the good aspects."[153] National offices also tracked the consequences of two small shifts in regulations that allowed cooperative members more opportunity to farm individually. National guidelines in October and November 1978 permitted cooperative leaders in the north, "in the event that all the

150. Article by Duc Uy, *Nhan Dan*, 25 June 1980, 2.

151. Nguyen Ngoc Triu, "Luoc Ghi Y Kien, Nguyen Ngoc Triu, Bo Truong NN, K Lua Hien Nay" [Nguyen Ngoc Triu, "Agriculture minister's views on contract system for paddy"], 5 July 1980, 2 (P BNN, hs 302, vv).

152. BNN, "BC, K" [Cooperative contracts], circa August 1980, 14–15.

153. BBT, "TB 22," 5, also 13. See also BQLHTXNN, "Tai Lieu," 13.

land could not be farmed collectively," to "lend fields to members" during the winter, provided those members would also "work the required number of days on collectively grown winter crops" and return the borrowed land in time for the cooperative to plant paddy or other primary crops in the spring.[154] Then in autumn 1979, the party's Central Executive Committee and the government's Council of Ministers went further, permitting villagers to farm for up to five years small amounts of a cooperative's poorest land. To encourage villagers to sell to the state whatever they raised on these borrowed fields, the new rules stipulated that the prices be negotiated, not imposed by state agencies.[155]

At the time, these concessions to individual farming were stopgap measures to make use of land that cooperative leaders could not mobilize members to farm collectively. In many places, the new regulations legitimated existing practices. For national party and government officials who favored more scope for family production, these modest steps were rewarding victories.[156] In hindsight, these small measures were also among the earliest of several graduated steps that eventually returned agricultural land to individual households.

Another source of information for national authorities on private farming were experiments that national authorities either assented to or in some cases undertook. I mentioned that since the early 1960s leaders in a few cooperatives in Hai Phong had been allowing members to farm individually some land that was supposed to be used collectively. These places served as an inspiration to villagers in other parts of the province, among them Doan Xa, a weak cooperative in which people had lived miserably for years. By spring 1978, possibly earlier, its leaders were allowing households to farm paddy and other crops on some of the cooperative's land in exchange for a specified amount of produce paid by villagers. Production and living conditions immediately improved. In 1979 or early 1980, sensing that higher officials were searching for new ways to stop the fall in production, the people in Doan Xa told authorities in Do Son district what they had been doing. Positive results there influenced the province's leaders

154. BNN, "Chi Thi 34 NN/CT, Muon Dat de SX Vu Dong" [MA, "Directive 34, lending land for winter crops"], 4 November 1978, in Vu Quan Ly Ruong Dat, *Nhung Quy Dinh*, 159.

155. BCHTU, DCSVN, "NQ Hoi Nghi 6," 10–12; and HDCP, "Quyet Dinh (so 318/CP), Tan Dung Ruong Dat NN" [Council of Ministers, "Decision, fully using agricultural land"], 10 September 1979, in BNN, *He Thong Hoa*, 1:105–10. For more on the significance of the CEC's 1979 resolution, see Fforde, *Agrarian Question*, 194–99.

156. Interviews and conversations in Hanoi with four individuals who worked in the 1970s–1980s on agricultural matters in different government and party offices, October 1995, June and July 1996, and September 2000.

to authorize experiments with this contract system in other cooperatives. Those results were also favorable. Provincial authorities wanted to expand the system but decided first to seek higher approval. Hai Phong's party secretary, Doan Duy Thanh, reported the experiments' results to Le Duan, the party's top leader. Le Duan rather quickly approved the expansion. Thanh also sought the approval of Truong Chinh, the national leader who had vigorously objected to similar arrangements in Vinh Phu during the late 1960s. After five meetings, he persuaded Truong Chinh. In July 1980, Hai Phong's party leaders authorized all cooperatives in the province to make contracts with individuals or groups of individuals, including households, to farm all fields in exchange for a portion of the harvests.[157]

In Vinh Phu province, authorized experiments also occurred but at the instigation of national, not provincial, authorities. Indeed, when representatives from the Central Agricultural Cooperative Management Committee instructed the province's party secretary and the people's committee president in mid-1980 to select places for experimental farming by individuals, the provincial officials demurred. When Vinh Phu had done something similar in the 1960s, they reminded their visitors from Hanoi, national authorities publicly chastised the province's leaders. Assured that no recriminations would occur, the provincial leaders chose Tho Tang and Dong Van, two cooperatives in Vinh Lac district long troubled by low production, poor leadership, and complaining members. Some brigades in the cooperatives lent paddy fields to individual members on a product contract basis; other brigades did not, thus serving as a control group in the experiment. The harvests were strikingly better in the experimental brigades.[158]

In the second half of 1980, national agencies—particularly the party's Agriculture Committee, its Secretariat, and the government's Ministry of Agriculture and Central Agricultural Cooperative Management Committee—compiled numerous reports on authorized and unauthorized farming arrangements across the north.[159] They also convened many conferences where study results were presented and representatives from local government and party branches spoke. Meanwhile, the party's national newspaper, *Nhan Dan*, solicited articles on the question of "how to solve society's

157. Dang Phong, "Lo Trinh," 6–7, 9–10; Huu Hanh, "Khoan Lua," 42; Doan Duy Thanh, *Hai Phong*, 102–4; and interview, Doan Duy Thanh, Hanoi, 17 September 1992. The provincial authorization is Thanh Uy Hai Phong, "NQ 24."

158. BNN, "Bao Cao ve Cung Co," 12; *Vinh Phu*, 27 November 1979, 2–3; 16 September 1980, 1; *Nhan Dan*, 31 October 1980, 2; BQLHTXNN, "Tai Lieu," 14–15.

159. The most illuminating are BNN, "BC, K" [Cooperative contracts], circa August 1980; Doan Truong DHNN I, "BC, Khao Sat" [Investigating contracts], circa October 1980; and Hoc Vien KT NN, "CT K" [Contracts], 15 October 1980.

food problem."[160] Submissions came from social scientists, agronomists, engineers, officials at many levels of the government and party, and cooperative leaders.

From these and other sources, many top leaders became convinced between October 1980 and early January 1981 that contractual arrangements with individual members and households resulted in higher yields, lower production costs, and more conscientious farming. They worried, however, that cooperatives were rapidly deteriorating. Product contracts were spreading, often with no authorization, and the diversity was bewildering. Fields were allocated to individuals and families in many ways; the phases of farming done by individual households and those done by the whole brigade varied; the use of draft animals and other collective property was haphazard; the amounts households paid to the cooperative appeared to be arbitrary. Often cooperative members paid nothing. Not only product contracts to individual families were proliferating, the party's Secretariat announced in late October, so were arrangements that gave villagers "blank contracts" (*khoan trang*) to farm whatever and however they wanted, further "enfeebling the cooperative and the battle for socialism in the countryside."[161] Contracting individuals to do some of the farming had definite advantages, central authorities concluded, but "unified guidance from the top down" was required to create uniformity and preserve the cooperatives.[162]

The first evidence of efforts to develop such guidance was an October 1980 pronouncement from the Secretariat authorizing cooperative leaders to contract individual workers or groups of workers to complete certain phases of the farming if properly monitored and done as part of a collective production system. The Secretariat also acknowledged that the reorganization and enlargement drive begun in 1974 had made many cooperatives and brigades unmanageable. They were now to become smaller.[163] By late November party and government agencies were drafting other versions, one of which was discussed and modified by the Central Executive Com-

160. Between 11 June and 20 October, the newspaper published about half of the more than one hundred replies. A synthesis appears in the 20 and 21 October issues. One of the newspaper's editors later wrote about the episode and a conference on the question that *Nhan Dan* organized: Huu Tho, "Nho Hoi Thao."

161. BBT, "TB 22," 3.

162. BNN, "Bao Cao ve Cung Co," 13. Among other documents with similar statements are BNN, "BC, K" [Cooperative contracts], circa August 1980, 15; and a letter from Vo Thuc Dong, Truong Ban, Ban NN, CHTU, DCSVN [head, Agriculture Committee, CEC, VCP], to the BBT TU Dang [Party Secretariat], 10 December 1980 (P BNN, hs 302, vv).

163. BBT, "TB 22," 1–2, 4.

mittee's ninth plenum (fourth party congress) in early December. After further deliberations, including a large conference in Hai Phong that included national and provincial leaders, the party's Secretariat issued guidelines on 13 January 1981.[164] Frequently known as "directive 100" (*chi thi 100*), its documentation number, the guidelines clearly marked the incremental turn that national agencies had been making during the previous year or two toward accommodating local modifications of the cooperatives.

The significant change indicated in directive 100 concerned "contracts." Indeed, in the countryside the change was called "contract 100" (*khoan 100*). Official sources often called the new system the "product contract" (*khoan san*, or *khoan san pham*) or "end product contract" (*khoan san pham cuoi cung*). Collective farming had long involved contracts but, as a report from the party's Agriculture Committee indicated in late 1980, except in the advanced cooperatives the "forms of contracts we had previously required were inappropriate."[165] The new contract system had four principal features. First, cooperatives could allocate farmland to individual working-age members or groups of members. Previously, distribution of collective land to members was prohibited except, beginning in late 1978, for certain hard-to-farm plots or for winter farming. Second, cooperatives could contract an individual worker or group to complete certain phases of the farming on the allocated fields. Previously, cooperatives and brigades were allowed to make contracts with an individual or group only to do discreet tasks, not to complete an entire phase, let alone several phases, of the farming cycle. Third, each person or group promised to give the cooperative part of the produce from each assigned field. Fourth, each person or group could keep all produce beyond that quota. These last two departed sharply from previous procedures, in which members' earnings from collective work were based only on work points. The underlying logic of the new system was that if people saw a close relationship between how they farmed and what they produced, they would work harder, production would increase, and the interests of the individual cooperative member, the cooperative as an organization, and the state would be better served.

In China at about the same time, an analogous logic influenced changes in the collectivization policy. Chinese leaders amended the work point system in the late 1970s. Then, in 1979–1980, they authorized product contracts similar to those in Vietnam but more extensive. In China's villages,

164. BBT, BCHTU, DCSVN, "Chi Thi 100" ["Directive 100: Expanding product contracts"], 13 January 1981, 5–14, in BNNTU, *Cac Van Ban*. An English version appears in the Vietnam Report series of the JPRS, 2 February 1981, 17–23.

165. Ban NN, "TB, Nghien Cuu" [Research on contracts], circa late 1980, 1.

contracts could be, and usually were, made with each household, not individual members and groups. The contracts authorized each household to do all the farming, not just some phases. And fields were allocated on a per capita basis, not just to working-age people.[166] Similar changes would occur rapidly in Vietnam, but they lacked national authorities' approval until the late 1980s.

National leaders in China and Vietnam probably knew what was happening to the other's national programs. Vietnam's leaders also probably knew that the Communist Party government in neighboring Laos had abandoned its efforts to collectivize agriculture in mid-1979, after little more than a year of trying. Vietnam's leaders would also have known that years earlier Communist Party governments in other countries had made concessions to family-based production in order to persist with collective farming. Whether leaders in Hanoi looked again at those countries' experiences for some guidance and whether 1979–1980 events in other socialist countries affected their decisions to modify collectivization are questions beyond the scope of my research. Such considerations, however, do not appear in materials I found.[167]

What is clear is that falling agricultural production and pressures from the countryside were both significant reasons for the shift in Vietnam's national policy. Le Duc Tho, a Political Bureau member, said in 1982, "The Party Secretariat's directive number 100 was not born in the minds of the Party Central Committee but was the recapitulation of the masses' suggestions to set forth a new contract system in agriculture." This new official system, he acknowledged, had been "unofficially applied" and "applied spontaneously" years before.[168] A few years later a party analyst said, "We all know [this policy change] was a creation of the masses (the sneaky contracts they made) and experimentation arising from the grassroots."[169] As early as 1980, national offices credited villagers' unilateral actions. In October, the party's Agriculture Committee, after summarizing the poor state of collective farming, asked why, despite all efforts, did this situation exist? National agencies had asked similar questions in the early 1970s when

166. Parish, "Introduction," 15–18; Wiens, "Poverty and Progress," 84–85; Chan et al., *Chen Village*, 270–72.

167. Because relations between China and Vietnam had deteriorated so badly by the late 1970s, Dang Phong and Melanie Beresford suggest in *Authority Relations*, 65, that reforms in China had little impact on Vietnamese leaders.

168. Le Duc Tho, "On the Question," C7.

169. *Nhan Dan*, 3 July 1985, 2. The parenthetical comment about sneaky contracts is in the original. A similar acknowledgment is in BNN, "BCTK NN, 1983, 1981–1983, Nhiem Vu 1984" [MA, "Agriculture in 1981–1983, 1983, 1984"], February 1984, 14 (P BNN, hs 548, vv).

deliberating on how to boost flagging production and turn weak cooperatives into strong ones. Their answers led to a reorganization and enlargement of cooperatives and a revamping of the brigades. By 1980, however,
many official studies had linked that response to increasingly unwieldy, inefficient, and alienating cooperatives and brigades—conditions that villagers
had criticized directly and indirectly for years. Meanwhile, villagers had
devised alternative arrangements that apparently were better than the official system. The time had come, national agencies said in effect, to listen
to what has happening on the ground. Indeed, the Agriculture Committee said so rather explicitly. Answering its own question, it said the first
reason was that "the state's management systems, economic policies (regarding planning, accounting, extraction of produce, prices, etc.) and other top-
down instructions had deprived cooperatives of their right to take initiatives
in production and economic activities."[170]

The national decision to endorse, while at the same time trying to
control, local initiatives emerged from debates without any notable changes
in leadership. In China the shift away from collective farming occurred
after leadership upheavals within the Communist Party. Nothing like that
occurred in Vietnam. Basically, the same national leaders—including the
party Secretary General Le Duan, Prime Minister Pham Van Dong, and
Political Bureau heavyweight Truong Chinh—who had opposed similar
modifications in the 1960s and had launched the campaign to enlarge collective cooperatives in the 1970s were also the ones who supported the
new product contract system in 1980–1981.[171]

Available material is insufficient to detail who or what agencies in
Vietnam's national policy-making circles were advocating which positions.
The party's national newspaper did detect a tendency among cooperatives
and district officials to support the new contract system, while higher
authorities were more divided.[172] Views apparently did vary among provincial leaders. As of August–September 1980, the party secretaries in Hai
Hung, Ha Nam Ninh, and Ha Bac provinces, for instance, opposed assigning fields to villagers, whereas party secretaries in Hai Phong, Nghe
Tinh, and Vinh Phu provinces favored the move.[173] At the national level,

170. Ban NN, "De Cuong" [Guidelines], 4 October 1980, 2. Comments in parentheses are
in the original. The other cited reasons were many internal weaknesses in most cooperatives,
misuse of land and other resources, and poorly trained leaders who made villagers indignant
and distrustful.

171. Note that the title for the party's first secretary changed to secretary general in 1976.

172. Nhan Dan, 21 October 1980, 2.

173. Ban NN, "TB, Nghien Cuu" [Research on contracts], circa late 1980, 2; BQLHTXNN,
"Tai Lieu," 17; Chu Van Lam et al., Hop Tac Hoa, 52.

according to some sources, the government's Ministry of Agriculture was an early advocate of what became the new position, while the party's Agriculture Committee objected. Others have said, however, that within each of those two key agencies and others in Hanoi, assessments varied about what the studies showed and what was to be done. The party's Central Executive Committee and the Political Bureau, either of which could normally make major policy pronouncements, were both too badly divided to decide. Consequently, the decision, in the form of directive 100, came from the party's Secretariat, the small peak party committee.[174]

Officials skeptical of the product contract system raised numerous objections. Many predicted that farming phases completed individually could not be combined effectively with other phases that would continue to be completed collectively. Skeptics also warned that local officials would not know how much villagers were producing. Consequently, the quotas individuals paid would be too low and the state would receive insufficient quantities of grain and other products. The new system would also make it more difficult to mobilize people to maintain and enlarge irrigation and other infrastructure projects. The main concern of opponents and doubters was that collective farming and socialism itself would be "eroded" (*xoi mon*). Villagers, they predicted, would not be satisfied just to do the planting, tend the crops, and harvest. "Arguing that yields depend greatly on the quality of seedlings, cooperative members will demand to prepare their own seedlings, and to do that they will want their own fields for raising the seedlings. Then they will say that the land preparation [done collectively] is inadequate." They would want to do that themselves too, which would then lead them "to demand that the cooperative's water buffaloes and oxen be divided among them." And so on, until the cooperative had no resources and no power.[175] As everything became individualized, warned these opponents, inequalities would increase and the institutions for looking after disadvantaged families would vanish.[176]

174. Ban NN, "TB, Nghien Cuu" [Research on contracts], circa late 1980, 2; interviews with informed observers and officials, Hanoi: September 1992; May 1993; October 1995; May, June, and August 1996.

175. This synopsis of such views appears in a study done for central authorities: Doan Truong DHNN I, "BC, Khao Sat" [Investigating contracts], circa October 1980, 15.

176. Among additional sources referring to views summarized in this paragraph are BNN, "Bao Cao So Ket," 6; Truong Van Kien, Bi Thu, Nghe Tinh, "KSP, NN, Nghe Tinh, Phat Trien SX, Cung Co, Tang Cuong HTX" [Truong Van Kien, party secretary, Nghe Tinh province, "Product contracts in Nghe Tinh, reinforcing cooperatives"], in *Khoan San Pham*, 27; and Chu Van Lam et al., *Hop Tac Hoa*, 52.

Many proponents of the changes also worried that collective farming would not survive but countered opponents by arguing that cooperatives were already disintegrating. Doing nothing or continuing existing policies was not an option. To save the agricultural cooperatives, authorities needed to embrace and then regulate the local arrangements. Many in this group were convinced that the product contract system was the "principal way" to strengthen cooperatives and improve production. Other proponents, however, saw it not as a long-term modification but as a stopgap measure to boost production until such time as a "systematic solution" to managing collective cooperatives could be developed.[177] A small number of proponents supported directive 100 not as a means for preserving collective farming but as step toward ending it. They had concluded that although collectivization had once been appropriate, especially during the war against the United States, it no longer was.[178]

Although directive 100 was a remarkable shift, the changes it endorsed were modest, as were the subsequent regulations that elaborated them. Improving collective farming remained the overall objective. As before, national authorities still emphasized better management as the way to fix collective farming problems. Indeed, some called the directive the cornerstone of a "new management system."[179] The managerial innovation, they said, was to let individual members do some of the farming on fields assigned to them. The directive stipulated that fields would be assigned only for two to three years, then reallocated among members. Contracts, including the quota each member paid to the cooperative, would be adjusted annually. The directive also insisted that contracts could be made only with individual workers or groups of workers in the cooperative. It studiously avoided the word "family" or "household" as the unit to which land could be assigned.[180] It insisted that brigades and teams do such phases of farming as plowing, harrowing, preparing seeds and seedlings, applying fertilizer, and irrigating fields. Individuals, the directive said, should not "take charge of the whole process of production from preparing the land to harvesting it."[181]

177. Ban NN, "De Cuong" [Guidelines], 4 October 1980, 4; Ban NN, "TB, Nghien Cuu" [Research on contracts], circa late 1980, 2.

178. Conversation in Hanoi with a party official who was well placed to know the various positions, September 2000.

179. Le Duc Tho, "On the Question," C7.

180. So did other official reports leading up to directive 100. See, for instance, BNN, "Bao Cao ve Cung Co," 15.

181. BBT, "Chi Thi 100" [Directive 100], 13 January 1981, 10. Other passages in the directive referred to in this paragraph are on pages 9 and 11.

*Summary*

By the late 1970s, the national campaign to reorganize, enlarge, and thereby improve collective cooperatives and brigades had failed. One reason is that the changes made most cooperatives and their brigades even more unmanageable and unproductive than before. In addition, they made even more improbable the development of conditions favorable for durable collective farming. Moreover, the everyday politics of land, labor, and harvests undermined cooperatives from within. With little confidence in collective farming, in one another, or in their local officials, villagers across the Red River delta and elsewhere frequently did the minimum for the cooperative and the maximum for themselves. They also encroached on collective fields and harvests and devised arrangements, often with tacit or explicit assistance from some local authorities, that reduced collective farming and increased family farming.

Those arrangements and other consequences of villagers' everyday practices influenced the deliberations of authorities who were trying to understand why their remedies had failed and how to reverse the decline in agricultural production. This time, national leaders could not resort to another drive to reinforce collective production. Past attempts had not succeeded. Those experiences, worsening economic conditions, and widespread yet unorganized rural discontent strengthened arguments in national offices that concessions to household farming were the sensible course to take.

# CHAPTER 6

# Dismantling Collective Farming, Expanding the Family Farm, 1981–1990

Critics of the product contract system turned out to be correct. The arrangement did not rescue collective production. Instead, collective farming was dismantled. The critics also accurately predicted how the change would take place: from within the cooperatives themselves, as villagers took over more and more of the farming tasks. Local officials were often powerless to stop this. Some aided it. Meanwhile, higher echelons in the Communist Party and in the government deliberated and debated how to deal with not only this situation but many other structural problems in the country's political economy.

The 1980s proved to be watershed years. The entire state-centered planned economy was transformed into a "market economy with socialist characteristics." The main features of this transformation in the countryside were family farms, public markets, and the more or less free trade of goods and services. This transition "from plan to market," as others have summarized it, was multifaceted and occurred not in one or two years but over more than a decade.[1] The conversion of collective farms into family farms began during the late 1970s. Between 1981 and 1990, the process accelerated and was largely completed.

---

1. Fforde and de Vylder, *From Plan to Market*.

*Spurt, then Sputter*

Because so many places had been using arrangements similar to the product contract system before the policy change, implementation was rapid. Over 90 percent of paddy-producing cooperatives in several Red River delta provinces used product contracts by April 1981, only five months after the party Secretariat's announcement in October 1980 and three months after its "directive 100."[2] Some provinces bordering the delta also exceeded 90 percent levels. It took a little longer for product contracts to be adopted in other provinces. In Vinh Phu, for instance, 65 percent of the cooperatives had the product contract system by April 1981; in Thai Binh, only 34 percent had it. Local party and cooperative officials sometimes held up implementation. In four of the thirty-nine cooperatives in Me Linh district, for example, officials insisted in early 1981 that villagers continue to farm under the old system. After a miserable harvest that season due to the refusal by an unusually large number of villagers to work collectively, authorities allowed product contracts.[3] By the end of 1981, according to official reports, 94 percent or more of the cooperatives in all delta and midland provinces in the north were using product contracts. Most collective cooperatives applied the new system to all fields at once. Between 10 and 20 percent, among them Da Ton, the cooperative in rural Hanoi, phased in product contracts over two or three seasons.

Villagers welcomed the product contract arrangement. Living conditions had become so bad by the late 1970s, recalled an elderly couple in Dao Duc subdistrict, Vinh Phuc province, that "if the fields hadn't been allocated to us, we would have starved to death." With product contracts, said a man in Tien Thang subdistrict, life "became a bit easier."[4] For many villagers the product contract arrangement resulted, at least initially, in more food and some extra money for house repairs, furniture, clothing, and sometimes a bicycle.[5] Pointing to a wooden cabinet with glass doors and

2. Unless otherwise noted, this paragraph is based on Nguyen Ngoc Triu, Bo Truong, BNN, "BC TH, Thi Hanh Chi Thi 100, BBT TU Dang" [Nguyen Ngoc Triu, minister, MA, "Initial steps to implement directive 100"], 4 May 1981, 2 (P BNN, hs 548, vv); interviews, Da Ton, April 1993 and January–April 1996; and BNN, "Bao Cao Viec Thuc Hien," 1.

3. *Ha Noi Moi*, 28 July 1981, 3. At that time, Me Linh was in Hanoi province, not Vinh Phuc, as it is now. Other references to local authorities' opposition to product contracts include *Ha Son Binh*, 29 December 1982, 4; and *Dai Doan Ket*, 12 September 1984, 6.

4. Interviews, Dao Duc, 15, 17, and 18 August 2000, and Tien Thang, 25 August 2000, Vinh Phuc.

5. In Ung Hoa district, Ha Tay province, the number of bicycles owned by cooperative members increased 221 percent during the first years of product contracts, compared to the previous five years. Tran Quang Ngan, "Phan Tich Qua Trinh," 24.

carved trim, a man in Nghiem Xuyen subdistrict, Ha Tay province, said, "I bought this with savings," which were accumulated from surplus paddy he and his family had produced during the first few years of product contracts. Prior to that, he added, "we earned barely enough to eat."[6] Nghiem Xuyen, said a 1981 newspaper account, had long been a weak cooperative in which members typically gave minimal time and effort to the collective fields. Under the new arrangement, however, people farmed energetically, investing nine- and ten-hour days to tend their crops on fields assigned to them.[7] Similar enthusiasm burst out across the Red River delta, according to many reports. One said that villagers, particularly women, worked longer hours and more efficiently. For instance, fields that had previously taken two to three weeks to plant were now completed in seven to ten days.[8] People went to great lengths to use additional fertilizer, pull weeds, and monitor irrigation.[9] Consequently, whereas before crops on collective land had frequently looked forsaken and crops in household plots lush, "now it's hard to tell the difference" between the two, noted a 1982 report from the Ministry of Agriculture.[10] In early 1983 that ministry had to acknowledge that "the many previous campaigns to inspire people to produce well were never able to make villagers as energetic, animated, and efficient as the product contract system has during the past couple of years."[11]

For national authorities, the purpose of the product contract policy was to give individual cooperative members more responsibility and control over land and crops while still farming within a collective system. Implementation involved three main steps. First, the collective land was divided among individual workers. (According to rules and regulations, the land could instead be divided among groups of workers, but only 3 percent of cooperatives chose that option.)[12] Usually each "primary worker" (*lao dong*

6. Interview, Nghiem Xuyen, Ha Tay, 12 May 1993.

7. *Ha Son Binh*, 8 April 1981, 2. Note, at this time, Ha Tay—and hence Nghiem Xuyen—was part of Ha Son Binh province.

8. Ban Tuyen Huan Phu Nu TU, Hoi Lien Hiep Phu Nu VN, "BC TH Giao Duc, Phu Nu Thuc Hien Chi Thi 100, BBT TU Dang" [Central propaganda and training committee, Women's Federation of Vietnam, "Educating members about directive 100"], 20 May 1981, 2–3 (P BNN, hs 548, vv).

9. Various accounts in *Ha Son Binh* and *Hai Hung* during 1981; BQLHTXNNTU, *Khoan San Pham*, 68–69, 72; TCTK, *Bao Cao Phan Tich*, 48–49.

10. BNN, "Bao Cao Viec Thuc Hien," 2.

11. Bo Truong, BNN, "BC TH, Ket Qua SX NN 1982; Nhiem Vu Chu Yeu, SX NN, 1984" [minister, MA, "Agricultural production result, 1982; production tasks, 1983"], 1 March 1983, 6 (P BNN, hs 445, vv).

12. BQLHTXNNTU, *Khoan San Pham*, 66.

*chinh*) in a cooperative was entitled to an equal share and each "secondary worker" (*lao dong phu*) was allocated a fraction of that share. For instance, in Mo Dao village of Dao Duc subdistrict, Vinh Phuc province, Ngo Van Dung and his wife each received one share; their adolescent son and Dung's mother, considered secondary workers because of their ages, each received a half-share. Thus their household had three shares. Their smaller children and others in the household were too young, sick, or frail to be considered "workers" of any kind and thus received no land.[13] The amount of land for each share varied from cooperative to cooperative because the land area and number of workers differed in each. The amount could even vary from one brigade to another within the same cooperative, though cooperative leaders typically tried to minimize those differences by first reallocating land among brigades. Rarely was each person's share of land a single field. Instead, the share was spread across various gradations of land based on soil quality, proximity to irrigation canals, and other factors. In the case of Ngo Van Dung, the three shares in his household equaled 16.8 *sao* (5.6 *sao* per share; 6,048 square meters total). The fields were distributed first across the four gradations of land in the cooperative and then across two or three subgradations. Consequently, his household had some two dozen fields. While the extent of fragmentation may have been unusual in this case, cooperative members often had several small fields.[14]

Second, the quantity to be produced to fulfill the contract (*muc khoan*) was established. According to regulations, that amount, which I call a quota, was to be determined in each cooperative through discussions between managers and members guided by a formula: 10–15 percent more than the average production during the previous three to five years.[15] A quota was typically set for each gradation and subgradation of land. In Mo Dao village, for instance, quotas on paddy land in 1981–1982 ranged from 61 to 106 kilograms per *sao*. In Da Ton, the range was about 90 to 120.

Third, the farmwork was divided. Out of the eight major phases of agricultural work, national guidelines permitted individuals to complete three: planting, tending (weeding, irrigating, fertilizing, and so on), and harvesting fields allocated to them.[16] The other five phases—preparing the land

13. Interview, Dao Duc, 17 August 2000. "Primary workers" were generally females between sixteen and fifty-five years old and males between sixteen and sixty.

14. Interviews, Dao Duc and other subdistricts, Vinh Phuc, August 2000; several newspaper accounts, for instance, *Ha Noi Moi*, 19 March 1981, 3.

15. BNN, "Bao Cao Viec Thuc Hien," 5; BQLHTXNNTU, *Khoan San Pham*, 42.

16. BBT, BCHTU, DCSVN, "Chi Thi 100" ["Directive 100: Expanding product contracts"], 13 January 1981, 9, in BNNTU, *Cac Van Ban*; BQLHTXNNTU, *Khoan San Pham*, 50–59.

(plowing and harrowing), maintaining and operating the irrigation system, preparing seeds and seedlings, managing and distributing fertilizer (overseeing the collection of manure, acquiring and then allocating urea and other chemical fertilizers to members), and preventing and controlling diseases (spraying insecticides, preventing rats, and so on)—were supposed to be done collectively by teams of workers within each brigade or by specialized units within the cooperative. The cooperative's chairperson and other managerial board members were responsible for planning, overseeing, and coordinating all phases of farming and other production.

Product contracts immediately boosted output. According to official figures, staple food production across northern Vietnam in 1981 and 1982 averaged a 24 percent increase over 1980; in the Red River delta, it jumped 27 percent.[17] Production per capita in the north averaged a 19 percent increase in 1981–1982 compared to 1980, the first significant growth in nearly a decade. Most of the increase was paddy, not tubers, corn, and other secondary food crops that had increased in the late 1970s when villagers were allowed to grow their own. Compared to 1980, paddy production was 23 percent higher in 1981 and 41 percent higher in 1982; for the delta, the increases were 27 and 47 percent, respectively. One reason is that somewhat more land was planted in paddy. The main reason, however, was that yields jumped 14 and then 30 percent. That increase was due not to new technologies or seeds, which remained essentially the same, but primarily to better farming.

From about 1983–1984 on, however, improvements slowed, even stopped. By 1986–1987 yields in paddy and staple foods generally, though still higher than in the 1970s, were lower than or about the same as in 1982 (appendix 1, table 1). The area for paddy in 1986–1987 was greater than in 1980, but smaller than in 1981–1982; in the Red River delta, it was smaller than during the late 1970s. Because villagers preferred paddy over secondary crops, the area for the latter dropped more rapidly. Hence, by 1984 the amount of land used for all staple crops was smaller than in the late 1970s. It remained so through 1987. Consequently, by 1986–1987 the amount of paddy and other staple food produced in the delta was about 7 percent lower than in 1982. Meanwhile, the population had increased. Hence staple food production per capita by 1987 had dropped 13 percent in the delta and 10 percent across the north compared to the 1982 high point. It had almost reverted to 1978–1979 levels.

These figures suggest three possible trends. The first is an actual decline in output under the product contract system. The second is a decline in

17. Calculated from figures in appendix 1, table 1.

output even by people who, though nominally in cooperatives, were really farming primarily by themselves. The third is an increase or leveling off in production by individual households without local officials knowing or recording what was produced and who got it. In other words, official records could not capture what people were producing. All three trends probably existed, perhaps often in the same cooperative. To what degree, the available evidence does not allow me to say. In any event, all three scenarios suggest that cooperatives became considerably weaker, even nearly irrelevant for many villagers, except that they imposed lingering burdens. The evidence for this is compelling.

## Persistent Political Shortcomings

Product contracts did little to address enduring political shortcomings in the collective cooperatives. Two shortcomings were low levels of trust and inadequate monitoring. Villagers were still supposed to do considerable work together. In some cooperatives, that collective work continued to be poorly done. Specialized teams in several rural Hanoi cooperatives, for instance, delivered seedlings late or spoiled. Consequently, villagers somehow had to get their own seedlings or leave fields unplanted. Villagers also complained that teams responsible for plowing and harrowing had turned up late or done a terrible job. Many people resorted to hoeing and raking their fields by hand.[18] Similar deficiencies were reported in many places across the north.[19] Through improved monitoring and other measures, members in some troubled cooperatives, such as several in Gia Lam district, rural Hanoi, learned to do their collective work conscientiously. Elsewhere in the same district, however, households abandoned the pretense of doing tasks together and embarked on doing virtually all farmwork individually.[20]

Many cooperatives experienced a burst of good intentions when product contracts were first implemented. One cooperative in Ha Son Binh province, for example, reportedly had failed in the late 1970s to plant 15 percent of its land largely because members were "negligent" (*tre nai*). During the initial seasons with product contracts, however, villagers collectively prepared well all the land and provided seedlings and fertilizers for all the individually allocated fields. Harvests, consequently, were the highest in years. But by 1982–1983, it was one of several cooperatives in

18. *Ha Noi Moi*, 9 April 1981, 3.
19. Ban Tuyen Huan Phu Nu TU, "BC TH Giao Duc" [Educating members], 20 May 1981, 4.
20. *Ha Noi Moi*, 1 October 1981, 3; Hoang Thi Binh, "Tinh Hinh Giao Ruong Dat," 40.

its district noted for work teams that neglected seedlings, people who lacked initiative in their collective work, and collective tasks that were not coordinated.[21] In one of the first cooperatives in Vinh Phu province authorized to implement product contracts, villagers initially were enthusiastic and harvests improved. But by 1983, fields were "daubed and swabbed" (*cay quet bua chui*) rather than properly plowed and harrowed; and draft animals, seedlings, and water for irrigation were hogged by a few people, apparently with impunity. To plow their fields, some villagers hired others who had purchased their own oxen.[22] The pattern was repeated in many other places: People who had previously just gone through the motions of farming together decided to do their best to make the product contract system work for their benefit and that of everyone else in their cooperative. Soon, however, lackadaisical attitudes and the rush to accumulate work points rather than properly complete tasks resurfaced.

Attempting to boost trust and accountability among members, many large cooperatives divided into smaller ones. Authorities were more amenable to this measure in the 1980s than they had been earlier, when the prevailing official mood was "bigger is better." Villagers in Dao Duc and Tien Thang, Vinh Phuc province, said that petitions, which local leaders endorsed, for downsizing their cooperatives were sent in 1980–1981 to district authorities. Several months later, approval came. Dao Duc divided into three cooperatives, one for each of the subdistrict's villages. Tien Thang divided into two: one in Bach Tru village and one, named Kim Thai, composed of the other three villages in the subdistrict.[23] By 1985, northern Vietnam had 33 percent more cooperatives than in 1979 (when the amalgamation of cooperatives had peaked). By 1989 it had 51 percent more. Comparable figures for the Red River delta were 35 and 66 percent.[24] Subdistrict-sized cooperatives in particular broke up. Whereas in early 1978 nearly all cooperatives in the delta and midlands of the north encompassed a subdistrict, by 1986 fewer than half did and by 1989, only 35 percent.[25]

Trust and monitoring depended on governance—a third political issue. If it improved during the product contract system, villagers responded well to leaders who urged conscientious collective work. For example, Binh

21. *Ha Son Binh*, 1 May 1982, 2; and 2 March 1983, 2.
22. *Vinh Phu*, 17 June 1983, 2, 3; *Nhan Dan*, 29 June 1983, 2.
23. Interviews in the two subdistricts, August 2000.
24. Calculated from data in Vu Nong Nghiep, *So Lieu*, 61, 63, 65.
25. "So Lieu Hop Tac Xa," 1–2, and "Hien Trang ve Quan He San Xuat," 8. Both documents probably were prepared for the party's central Agriculture Committee (Ban NN, BCHTU).

Minh, a large cooperative in Ha Son Binh province, was debilitated in the late 1970s by low morale, poor production, and incompetent and often corrupt leaders; but when product contracts were implemented, district authorities helped reform-minded party members sweep out the old leadership. The cooperative rebounded to become exemplary.[26] If governance remained bad, effective collective work was hard to sustain. In one subdistrict in Ha Son Binh province, for example, villagers essentially stopped trying to farm collectively in 1982 after the outgoing chairperson of the cooperative conspired with another individual to purchase five oxen, apparently with money "borrowed" from the cooperative, kept one of the animals, sold the other four, and pocketed the proceeds.[27] People in Yen Phu, Hai Hung province, became disgusted when local officials, who were also party members, used for themselves the land reserved for raising animals belonging to the cooperative. Even after they were found guilty, these individuals continued to use the land with impunity.[28] Local officials in Co Thanh, also in Hai Hung, "lost the trust of the cooperative members" (*mat long tin cua xa vien*) in 1985 after taking more than seven tons of the cooperative's paddy for themselves. To make matter worse, even after district officials confirmed that the embezzlement had occurred, two years passed without much of the paddy being recovered or the culprits punished.[29]

Newspaper accounts suggest that officials in many collective cooperatives across the north abused their authority. Early in the 1980s, newspapers occasionally reported corruption and the like in cooperatives and various government agencies, especially those transporting, storing, and selling commodities that were supposed to be confined to the state marketing system. By 1987–1988, the newspapers were peppered with stories about "new tyrants" (*cuong hao moi*) in the countryside.[30] Stimulating this flurry were imperatives from national authorities, especially the party's new secretary general, Nguyen Van Linh, to "speak directly and truthfully" (*noi*

---

26. *Nhan Dan*, 23 June 1980, 2; *Ha Son Binh*, 13 November 1982, 2; 24 November 1982, 2; 21 September 1985, 1; and Nguyen Ngoc Khoa, Chu Nhiem, HTX Binh Minh, "BC Ket Qua 3 Nam, KSP, LD" [Nguyen Ngoc Khoa, chair, Binh Minh cooperative, "Three years of product contracts"], 20 February 1984, 1–9 (P BNN, hs 548, vv). One account hints, however, that the Binh Minh cooperative's chairperson later built a large house with illicit funds and was scorned by villagers. *Dai Doan Ket*, 17 and 24 September 1988, 5.

27. *Ha Son Binh*, 14 July 1982, 2.

28. *Hai Hung*, 30 May and 11 July 1987, both 4.

29. Ibid., 8 April 1987, 4.

30. For instance, the national paper *Dai Doan Ket* printed many accounts, including a serialized one in 1988: 17 September, 5; 24 September, 5; and 1 October 1988, 5.

*thang, noi that*) and "look truth in the eye" (*nhin thang vao su that*), accompanied by policies officially launched during the party's sixth national congress in December 1986 to "open up" (*mo cua*) and "renovate" (*doi moi*) Vietnam's political economy. Many of those accounts told of grave violations that had begun years before.

For instance, a mid-1987 story about Nguyen Giap cooperative, Hai Hung province, described how the chairperson and other officials, including the party secretary, had been embezzling since 1983, possibly earlier. Within just two years, they had falsified work points, faked receipts and other documents, and used other deceit to steal more than forty tons of paddy and twenty thousand dong.[31] In Vinh Phu province, the cooperative chairperson in Dinh Chu, who was also in charge of the subdistrict's store, had for years used his position to steal money and property from the cooperative. He was finally punished in 1987.[32] In a cooperative in Thai Binh province, the chief accountant and several other officials, most of them Communist Party members, recorded phony expenditures, underreported paddy and other payments members had made, and in other ways stole tons of grain between 1981 and mid-1987, when they were caught. The corruption had continued despite provincial investigations prompted by complaints from some party members and ordinary villagers and despite two cleanups of the local party organization, the first of which, in 1981–1982, had removed forty-four individuals, 25 percent of its membership.[33] Several newspaper stories described badly run cooperatives in Hai Phong province, one of them Dong Phuong, where the chairperson had for years falsified production reports so as to take grain for himself and confidants, had kept the profits from collectively raised fish for his family, and had rigged elections to retain his positions in the cooperative and local party branch. Many villagers had complained to higher authorities and petitioned to divide the subdistrict-sized cooperative into village-sized ones, which the chairperson and other incumbent officials opposed. Not until 1988 did villagers get some satisfaction when district officials authorized Dong Phuong to split into two cooperatives, one for each village in the subdistrict.[34]

Several official reports also refer to considerable corruption and other misconduct among local leaders. Some reports concluded that the product contract arrangement reduced "embezzlement and taking advantage of

31. *Hai Hung*, 3 June 1987, 2.
32. *Vinh Phu*, 11 September 1987, 3.
33. *Dai Doan Ket*, 19 March 1988, 3.
34. Ibid., 26 March 1988, 5; 10 September 1988, 5.

one's position" (*tham o, loi dung*).[35] Others, however, said such behavior continued to debilitate cooperatives. A Ha Son Binh provincial inspection group found in mid-1982 that while most Communist Party members fulfilled their responsibilities well, others embezzled public property, claimed work points they did not deserve, encroached on cooperatives' land, failed to pay what they owed the cooperatives, made illegal booze, and in other ways discredited the party. In several cooperatives and subdistricts, 30–50 percent of the party members had to be disciplined and punished.[36] In Hai Hung, a campaign during 1987 to improve leadership found that in the first fifteen subdistricts inspected "a rather large number" of party members, most of them with responsibilities in cooperatives, were taking bribes, were in cahoots with other people engaged in illegal activities, were trading contraband goods, "had gotten rich on the backs of the state and workers," or had committed other reprehensible acts.[37] For many cooperative officials in Hai Hung and other provinces, one lucrative way to make money, usually in league with some higher authorities, was to steal chemical fertilizers and insecticides from state warehouses, barges, and trucks, then sell these agricultural inputs at several times the official price. In this way, one study estimated, 30 percent of those agricultural inputs as well as seeds and fuel were not delivered to cooperative members (see figure 8).[38]

Another study claimed that "everyone knew" that 40–50 percent of the materials in state warehouses "slipped out into the free market" (*tuon ra thi truong tu do*).[39] Consequently, a June 1987 report from a national party office concluded, a main reason why agricultural development was "slow and from time to time practically standing still" was that "agricultural cadres had yet to meet their required new responsibilities and not a small portion of them were revolutionarily weak, lacked the will to improve, were corrupt," and violated the people's right to rule.[40]

The product contract arrangement per se was not directed at improving how cooperatives were governed. It did, however, require major

35. BNN, "BC TH KSP, LD, HTX, Tap Doan SX NN" [MA, "Implementing product contracts"], 10 February 1984, 43, in BNN, *Hoan Chinh*.

36. The report is published in *Ha Son Binh*, 21 August 1982, 3.

37. See articles and a speech by the province's party secretary in *Hai Hung*, 29 July 1987, 1, 2, 4.

38. Le Ngoc in *Tap Chi Thong Ke* [Journal of statistics], no. 6 (1987): 23, cited in Nguyen Duc Nhuan, "Le district," 361. The study said that 9 percent of the inputs were skimmed off at the provincial level, 14 percent at the district level, and 7 percent at the subdistrict level. For accounts about the illegal trade, see *Hai Hung*, 11 October 1986, 2, and 25 October 1986, 4.

39. Xuan Kieu, "Ve Chinh Sach," 53.

40. Ban NN, "De An Xay Dung," 2–3.

**Đường đi của vật tư nông nghiệp.**

*Figure 8.* The caption under the drawing reads, "The route for agricultural inputs." As fertilizer for the winter and spring crop passes down a pipe, it gets diverted to the province, the district, state enterprises, and other places. The biggest share ends up in a sack labeled "private commerce." The smallest goes into a tiny container labeled "the cooperative." As the chairman of the cooperative stands pointing a finger at the large amount taken for private trading, a lady says, "If the cooperative is short, I can sell you some!" Drawn by Tran Quyet Thang; published in *Nhan Dan*, 12 January 1986, 1.

decisions about allocating land and setting quotas that affected relations between cooperative leaders and ordinary members. Those decisions were supposed to be transparent and impartial and to involve discussions between leaders and members. In many places that was the case. Cooperative members and leaders together classified land according to productivity and other attributes, calculated the total area in each category, divided each by the number of eligible members, then distributed the fields by drawing lots.[41] In many other cooperatives, however, officials gave themselves and close friends the best land and allocated the rest unilaterally, saying to other villagers: "take what's given to you" (*chi dau lay day*).[42]

Outside authorities frequently undermined local decisions about quotas and land distribution and pressed cooperative leaders to follow their instructions rather than heed the cooperative's membership. The reason, according to official studies, was that 40 to 50 percent of cooperatives in the delta had improperly implemented the product contract arrangement.[43] A few cooperatives set quotas too high, authorities said. Many more set them too low. In 1982, half the surveyed cooperatives in Ha Son Binh province had quotas lower than guidelines required. Consequently, villagers too easily exceeded their quota and kept an excessive amount of the harvest for themselves, leaving too little for the cooperative to meet its expenses, pay members for the work done collectively, and fulfill obligations to the state. Errant cooperatives often allocated fields not just to workers but to everyone. This was more fair, contended many villagers, especially those with family members too old, young, or infirm to be counted as workers. It was wrong, objected many villagers in Kim Thai cooperative, "for there to be mouths to feed without fields."[44] Authorities insisted, however, that assigning land according to household size violated regulations. Another mistake in numerous cooperatives, officials said, was that the principle of equitable distribution was taken to an extreme. The result was "excessive scattering" (*manh mun qua*) of fields and inefficient farming.

The fourth political shortcoming was too little commitment or incentive to farm collectively. The reasons were much the same as in the 1970s. Initially, product contract arrangements reduced this problem. Once vil-

41. Interviews, Da Ton, 8 February and 23 March 1996; *Ha Son Binh*, 4 April 1981, 2; Xa Thuong Trung, *Lich Su*, 161; interview, Dao Duc, 17 August 2000.

42. *Ha Son Binh*, 28 December 1985, 2; *Dai Doan Ket*, 16 April 1988, 4; *Ha Noi Moi*, 9 April 1981, 2.

43. *Ha Son Binh*, 6 November 1982, 2; BNN, "BC TH, KSP, LD, HTX, Tap Doan SX NN" [MA, "Report on product contracts"], 15 September 1983, 1–3 (P BNN, hs 509, vv).

44. "Co mom an ma khong co ruong." Interview, Tien Thang, Vinh Phu, 26 August 2000.

lagers were assigned fields, they saw a closer connection between their work and the product, and, knowing that production beyond the quota was theirs to keep, they became somewhat less negative about collective cooperatives. The key to their becoming more committed was that they were able to keep a significant portion of their harvest. That turned out to be extremely hard for most villagers. Meanwhile, living conditions, though often better than in the late 1970s, remained precarious for most of them, another reason for little or no commitment to the cooperative.

Several factors affected the chances of exceeding the quota. One was its size. Villagers understandably wanted as small a quota as possible. Directive 100 indicated that the level was to be reconsidered each year.[45] If production improved, the quota was to increase; if it declined, the quota would decrease. Consequently, determining yields became a major bone of contention. Cooperatives that increased quotas aroused peasants' ire and undermined their incentives to produce more. A second factor was whether investing additional energy and other resources would sufficiently counterbalance a higher quota. Such calculations depended on whether villagers could retain the same fields. Directive 100 and other regulations said that land allocations should be stable for "two or three years so as to give cooperative members peace of mind."[46] Many cooperatives made no or only minor adjustments to the initial allocation. Other cooperatives, like Da Ton, frequently reallocated fields, sometimes every year. That deterred villagers from improving the soil and doing other things to boost productivity in the long run.[47] A third factor was how well fields were farmed. People knew what work they did in their own fields. But they often had little confidence in or control over the collective work in their fields. Badly done collective plowing and harrowing, for instance, undermined work done individually and reduced the field holder's chances of exceeding the quota.

A fourth factor was whether cooperatives and state agencies could supply the inputs promised in the product contract arrangement. Would there be draft animals from the cooperative (or, in some places, tractors from the district machinery station) for plowing and harrowing? Would the chemical fertilizers, insecticides, and seed required for the fast-maturing varieties of paddy arrive on time and in sufficient quantity? Would there be oil, gasoline, and electricity for the irrigation pumps? Too often neither cooperative members nor leaders could confidently answer yes to such ques-

45. BBT, "Chi Thi 100" [Directive 100], 13 January 1981, 11.
46. Ibid., 10–11.
47. Interviews, Da Ton, 8 February and 2 April 1996.

tions. Members themselves were partly to blame. By not conscientiously caring for their cooperatives' draft animals and irrigation facilities, they contributed to a vicious cycle of weaknesses. More important were breakdowns in the state economic system. Already common, they became worse during the 1980s. Agricultural supplies from state warehouses and companies declined. The amount of chemical fertilizer promised to Hai Hung, for instance, was lower in 1985 than in 1984 and 30 percent lower in 1986 than in 1985, well below what the province needed.[48] Moreover, the promised amount rarely arrived or arrived late, delaying planting and causing other setbacks. For the product contract arrangement to function well, said cooperative leaders in Ha Bac province, they needed half the necessary inputs at the beginning of each season. Often state agencies could not provide that much.[49] Dong Ich cooperative, Vinh Phu province, was not unique when it received for its spring 1987 paddy crop only 20 percent of the promised nitrogen fertilizer and even less of other inputs. The province as a whole received only 40 percent of what state agencies had pledged to deliver by October for winter crops.[50] The shortfall was partly due to state factories' inability to produce enough fertilizer and other inputs and to government ministries lack of funds for importing more. Another reason was the theft that occurred as materials moved through the official distribution system. Consequently, by the mid-1980s, if fields received half the needed agricultural inputs from state agencies, that was considered "a lot." Most had less.[51] Some cooperatives managed to buy what they needed on the black or free market. Otherwise, farming proceeded with fewer inputs than required.

During the initial years of product contracts, most villagers were able to exceed the quotas on land assigned to them. Some occasionally surpassed their quotas by up to 85 percent.[52] More commonly, villagers told me, there was little excess.[53] Across the north, according to 1984–1985 surveys, about 80 percent of producers met or exceeded quotas. Sources do not say how many exceeded their quotas. They do say that the excess typically ranged between 5 and 20 percent.[54]

48. *Hai Hung*, 5 April 1986, 3.

49. *Nhan Dan*, 5 September 1986, 2.

50. *Vinh Phu*, 31 March and 6 October 1987, both on 2.

51. Article in *Nhan Dan*, 13 November 1986, 3, summarizing thousands of essays and letters received from peasants, workers, scientists, and others who wrote about agricultural matters in response to the newspaper's request for opinions prior to the sixth party congress.

52. Xa Dong La, *Lich Su Xa*, 195; *Vinh Phu*, 14 May 1985, 2; 16 May 1986, 2.

53. Interviews, four subdistricts, Vinh Phuc, August 2000.

54. TCTK, *Bao Cao Phan Tich*, 50; and Nguyen Sinh Cuc, *Nong Nghiep*, 31.

Sources do not report an average or typical paddy quota, but it can be estimated. One way is to calculate what it would have been had it equaled or exceeded the average yield for paddy. The second method uses the government regulation that quotas should be about 10–15 percent more than the average paddy yields during the previous three to five years. Averaging the paddy yields in the Red River delta during 1978–1980 and assuming that the quota did not change (the situation in some cooperatives but not others), I calculated quotas equal to 10 and 15 percent higher than that average (see appendix 1, table 8).

Table 8 has estimates of how much a typical villager was able to keep of the harvest on a *sao* of land assigned to him or her, assuming the quota was filled and turned over to cooperative officials. These estimates combine the portion of the harvest exceeding the quota and the grain a person received from work points for collective work. The latter was usually between 15 and 20 percent of the quota in the mid-1980s.[55] Take, for instance, a quota of ninety-five kilograms of paddy per *sao* per harvest given to cooperative officials by the villager. The cooperative paid the villager approximately fourteen to nineteen kilograms for collective work she or he had done. If the villager had met but not exceeded the quota, those fourteen to nineteen kilograms would be the full entitlement. The villager who failed to meet the quota would contract a debt, which might be deducted from collective work earnings. If the yield had been one hundred kilograms—5 percent more than the quota—the villager would have about five additional kilograms.

Scenarios in table 8 suggest that reaching or even exceeding the quota by less than 12.5 percent (the midpoint between 5 and 20) meant that an average paddy producer received the same as or less than before product contracts. Even exceeding the quota by 12.5 percent did not leave a villager much better off. In other words, a villager probably needed to produce consistently more than 12.5 percent beyond the quota in order to have noticeably more grain than before. As time went on, the proportion of cooperative members able to do that became smaller.

Why, many villagers grumbled, were payments for collectively completed farming phases only 20 percent or less of the quota? One reason is that the value of a day of collective work was typically not much higher than it had been before product contracts, despite greater output. Population

55. *Ha Son Binh*, 1 January 1988, 2; 2 April 1988, 2; *Nhan Dan*, 11 March 1986, 2; 21 May 1986, 3; 20 August 1987, 2; 16 November 1987, 2; Tinh Hoa Binh, *Lich Su Phong Trao*, 254; TCTK, *Bao Cao Phan Tich*, 51–52; *Nhan Dan*, 4 December 1987, 3.

growth and little nonagricultural production by cooperatives meant that claimants to paddy and other produce increased more rapidly than output. Claimants included children, elderly residents, war invalids, and others who did not work or worked little yet were entitled to grain through the cooperative's distribution system.[56] Another sizable number of claimants were people whose work was not directly involved in farming. They had "indirect work points" (ngay cong gian tiep), sometimes earned from tasks related to farming such as repairing irrigation canals but often from unrelated activities such as guarding offices, organizing children's outings, participating in drama groups, and preparing meals for officials attending meetings. Points for these tasks contributed to the devaluation of all work points.[57] So did the work points paid to officials, not only in the cooperative but in local branches of the Communist Party, Youth League, Women's Association, and other Fatherland Front organizations. The number of officials drawing on cooperative earnings, rather than decreasing as was supposed to happen under the product contract arrangement, typically increased. Consequently, said a study using Ministry of Agriculture reports, officials received not 4 percent or less of all payments to cooperative members as regulations stipulated, but "commonly 6–8 percent and sometimes 10 percent."[58]

Perhaps more significant is that distributable production paid to direct or indirect workers dropped from an average of about 73 percent in 1976–1980 to 67 percent in the early 1980s and 64 percent in 1987.[59] For staple food production alone, 61 percent of the average distributable amount went to cooperative members in 1976–1980, but only 52 percent in 1981–1986 and 50 percent in 1987.[60] The decline came about primarily because two entities—the state and the cooperative itself—were consuming larger shares of what cooperatives produced, leaving less for members.

Although the proportion of all distributable production going to the state did not increase, its share of staple food grew significantly. This was par-

56. Bo Truong, BNN, "Thong Tu: Phan Phoi va Thu Nhap, HTX, TDSX NN" [Circular: income and distribution, cooperatives and production teams], February 1984, 7 (P BNN, hs 548, vv).

57. "Khan Truong Xoa Bo, Bao Cap, HTX NN" [Eliminate subsidy system], 1 November 1986, 100–101, in Khoa Hoc va Ky Thuat Nong Nghiep; and Nhan Dan, 23 June 1986, 2.

58. "Khan Truong Xoa Bo," 1 November 1986, 101.

59. TCTK, Bao Cao Phan Tich, 107; Nguyen Sinh Cuc, Thuc Trang, 25. Distributable production is total production minus production costs (excluding labor, taxes, and other obligations to the state). Higher production costs may have been another reason why producers did not receive more, but I have little evidence about such costs.

60. TCTK, Bao Cao Phan Tich, 108.

ticularly discouraging to villagers because staple food, especially paddy, was the most important as they endeavored to grow enough food for their families and crawl out of poverty. In 1966–1975, state agencies extracted about 19 percent of the distributable staple food production from cooperatives; in 1976–1980, the figure was 21 percent. In 1981–1986, it jumped to 26 percent and in 1987 it reached 29 percent.[61] The main methods were taxes and compulsory sales to state agencies of specified amounts, usually at prices lower than the products fetched on the free market. True enough, paddy production also increased initially during the new contract system. The portion going to the state, however, climbed 16 percent faster than production in 1981 and 42 percent faster in 1983–1984.[62] In the Red River delta and midlands of northern Vietnam, "many cooperatives" that had given the state 20–23 percent of their distributable staple food in 1980 were giving 35–40 percent in 1985.[63] Consequently, by 1986, although "the volume of [farming] inputs from the state that reached the peasantry was much lower than before, the amount of staple food the state extracted (through various means) was higher."[64]

Also increasing was the amount going to a cooperative as an organization. In the late 1960s–late 1970s, a collective cooperative took on average 13–15 percent of distributable production. The proportion increased during the 1980s, reaching 21 percent by 1987.[65] Of distributable staple food production, the average cooperative took 11–13 percent in the mid-1960s–mid-1970s, slightly more in the late 1970s, then 21–22 percent in 1981–1987.[66] Some of this amount funded children's day care facilities, health centers, and other community programs that, according to scattered evidence, were expanding and which villagers appreciated. But some of the proceeds disappeared without a trace of benefit for the membership at large. Another portion went to food, drink, and other expenditures when officials entertained guests, attended meetings, and traveled. A 1984 study of thirty cooperatives in Vinh Phu province estimated that on average they each spent three hundred thousand dong on such things. The report does not say whether this was atypically high; but that much money could represent

61. Ibid.

62. Calculated from figures in BNN, "Bao Cao Tinh Hinh Bao Cap," 4. It is unclear in the report whether the statistics refer to the north or to the entire country.

63. BNN, "Bao Cao Tinh Hinh Bao Cap," 4.

64. Xuan Kieu, "Ve Chinh Sach," 53.

65. TCTK, 12 Nam Phat Trien, 580; BQLHTXNN, UBNNTU, "BC, Mot So Net, HTXSXNN, 1975" [ACMC, CAC, "Major features of cooperatives"], 10 February 1976, 14 (P UBNNTU, hs 160, vv); TCTK, Bao Cao Phan Tich, 107.

66. TCTK, Bao Cao Phan Tich, 108.

about one-fifth of an average cooperative's paddy production.[67] Even if it was only a tenth or a twentieth, it was a great deal to most villagers, who resented officials who squandered resources supposedly belonging to everyone.[68]

Meanwhile, living conditions, after initially improving with product contracts, stagnated or slid backward—or would have if people had conformed to what was expected. For villagers and officials alike, the most telling indicator was food consumption. The Ministry of Agriculture claimed that by late 1982, the average villager in nearly 80 percent of cooperatives ate twenty kilograms per month of staple food (paddy and paddy equivalents). Prior to product contracts, it said, only 10 percent of cooperatives had achieved that level.[69] In some places, this improvement was sustained. One was Vong Xuyen, a cooperative in Ha Son Binh province that had long teetered on the brink of collapse. Its residents in the late 1970s averaged only six or seven kilograms of paddy and other staple food each month. With product contracts, however, the average person by 1986 ate twenty kilograms each month.[70]

More typical, however, were Bach Tru and Kim Thai cooperatives, Vinh Phu province. Villagers there in mid-1986 averaged between thirteen and fourteen kilograms per month. While greater than before product contracts were implemented and before the subdistrict-sized cooperative of Tien Thang was divided into these two smaller ones, many people still went hungry.[71] In several cooperatives in Vinh Phu, 30–70 percent of villagers were usually hungry in 1986–1988.[72] The situation was similar elsewhere in northern Vietnam. In some places villagers were so impoverished that they had only one bowl of watery gruel (*chao loang*) each day.[73] Even in

67. "Khan Truong Xoa Bo," 1 November 1986, 100. To calculate what 300,000 dong represented, I divided Vinh Phu province's 1984 paddy production (271,500,000 kilograms) by the number of cooperatives that year (566) (Vu Nong Nghiep, *So Lieu*, 63, 149). That equals 479,682 kilograms. This sum, times the price state agencies paid in 1984 when purchasing paddy from the province's cooperatives (3 dong per kilogram) yields 1,439,046 dong, which is nearly five times the 300,000 dong figure. (The paddy price is from TCTK, *Bao Cao Phan Tich*, 53.)

68. Interviews, four subdistricts, Vinh Phuc, August 2000; *Vinh Phu*, 29 March 1988, 2; *Dai Doan Ket*, 10 September 1988, 5.

69. BNN, "BC TH" [Report on product contracts], 15 September 1983, 5. Also, *Ha Son Binh*, 26 May 1982, 2.

70. Xa Vong Xuyen, *Lich Su Dang Bo*, 127, 132; *Ha Noi Moi*, 3 April 1986, 3.

71. Interviews, Tien Thang, Vinh Phuc, 22 and 23 August 2000; and entry for 14 June 1986, 85–86, vol. 1 of a notebook belonging to a Bach Tru resident who had been a cooperative official in the 1980s.

72. *Tong Ket Khoa Hoc*, 72; TCTK, *Bao Cao Phan Tich*, 148.

73. *Dai Doan Ket*, 16 April 1988, 4.

Da Ton, a cooperative better off than most, the greatest concern among more than 85 percent of surveyed residents in 1985 was "getting enough to eat."[74] In late 1987, 60 percent of peasants in Ha Son Binh were short of food (*thieu an*); in some of the province's mountainous districts, the figure was 80 percent.[75] Across the north, 40 percent of agricultural people did not have enough to eat and more than a third of those were "intensely hungry" (*doi gay gat*).[76] If villagers in most cooperatives had ever averaged twenty kilograms of staple food per month in the early years of product contracts, they no longer did so by 1985–1987.

## Resistance and Collapse

After a few years of the product contract arrangement, many villagers in the delta were frustrated. They had their own fields, which they had long sought, but did not *really* have them. They wanted to farm those fields as their own, but could not *really* do so. They and their fields were in an organization that they should have run but did not, an organization that was meant to help them farm but usually did not or could not. That organization, the collective cooperative, was not only often useless but cost them a significant proportion of what they produced. To some extent this quandary was their own making. Few did their collective work well, thereby contributing to the organization's problems and thwarting leaders who tried to make the product contract arrangement effective. But, people wondered, how could they work diligently when they could not rely on everyone else—including their own leaders—to do the same, when they received but a small fraction of the increases they produced, and when the cooperative and state agencies took sizable amounts but gave them little in return?

There is only sketchy evidence of people openly expressing their frustrations. One source says that peasants in 1986, driven by hunger and local grievances, stormed warehouses and granaries. While most incidents were in the south, some were in the north. For example, protests in Van Thai, Ha Nam Ninh province, against corrupt local officials culminated in hundreds of villagers taking over the subdistrict's granary to prevent paddy stored there from being transported to the district.[77] More often, villagers

74. Vien Xa Hoi Hoc, "Nghien Cuu su Bien Doi," question 12.
75. Tinh Hoa Binh, *Lich Su Phong Trao*, 267.
76. Nguyen Sinh Cuc, *Nong Nghiep*, 32.
77. Nguyen Duc Nhuan, "Le district," 368.

petitioned to leave the cooperative. Eighty people, including some officials, in Thai Son cooperative, Ha Bac province, did so in 1983 after a particularly poor harvest, which they blamed on collective phases of farming being carried out poorly.[78] Villagers in many cooperatives sent petitions and letters to government offices and newspapers objecting to high quotas, pointing out other farming problems, and especially condemning local officials and corruption.[79] Persistent complaints from villagers in Van Tao, Ha Son Binh province, for instance, led to an investigation, which verified that the cooperative's accountant, storehouse keeper, and other officials had been embezzling for years and hiding their ill-gotten wealth in secret funds.[80] Sometimes the result of complaints was that the complainants, not the officials, were punished. In Tien Tien and Tien Thanh subdistricts, Hai Phong province, officials undermined investigations in 1986 into their misdeeds and then broke into the houses of petitioners, some of them party members, to beat them and take their bicycles, pigs, paddy, and other possessions.[81] Fearing such retribution, villagers often kept quiet, at least until the political atmosphere changed to encourage public objections. Then, as happened in 1987–1989, people were more inclined to speak out and journalists were more apt to write about what had been happening in places such as Tien Lang district. Some villagers even traveled to Hanoi to protest.[82]

Most contestation over the use and distribution of resources in the cooperatives continued to be low-key. Two frequent sites, as in earlier periods, were land and harvests. But the most significant were the farming phases that were supposed to be completed collectively. Consequently the cooperative itself, as a unit of production and distribution, became a primary site of struggle.

As in previous periods, struggles over land included efforts by villagers to expand the area for household plots and to hide fields from authorities. Two new contentious nodes also emerged. First, people refused to let go of fields when cooperative leaders tried to adjust allocations. Second, they

78. *Nong Nghiep Ha Bac*, no.1 (1988): 33. Not stated is whether the petitioners were permitted to leave.

79. In 1987–1988, more such letters appeared in provincial papers than had earlier. One paper received nearly three hundred in July–August 1987, some of which it published, about embezzlement, land encroachment, officials who favored relatives, and police who abused and even beat citizens, among other accusations. *Vinh Phu*, 15 September (possibly August) 1987, 4.

80. *Ha Son Binh*, 15 June 1983, 2; and 20 August 1988, 3.

81. *Dai Doan Ket*, 12 November 1988, 4, 5.

82. Ibid. Also, *Dai Doan Ket*, 19 November 1988, 4; 26 November 1988, 3, 4; *Ha Son Binh*, 4 April 1989, 4.

— Tổ kỹ thuật các cậu chỉ có " trách nhiệm »-phun
thuốc, còn thuốc trừ sâu xã viên phải tự túc nhá...!
Phạm Quang Huynh
(Xí nghiệp khảo sát giao thông tỉnh)

*Figure 9.* A couple of cooperative leaders, sitting around drinking tea and smoking a water pipe, say to the woman with a sprayer strapped to her back and a mask over her face, "The technical team [of the cooperative] is responsible for spraying, but people have to provide their own insecticide, you know!" Drawn by Pham Quang Huynh; published in *Hai Hung*, 11 June 1986, 4.

did the reverse, abandoned fields allocated to them. The latter occurred in the mid-1980s because quotas increased beyond what people calculated they could meet or exceed. Also, cooperatives were not doing what they were supposed to do and villagers on their own were able to farm only some of the fields assigned to them. "If the cooperative can assure that the tasks it is responsible for will be done," said villagers in Tu Tan, Thai Binh province, "then we'll farm all the land." But officials in Tu Tan and many other cooperatives could not supply enough seed, insecticide, and other inputs or see to it that cooperative teams prepared fields and did other required work (see figure 9).

By 1985–1986 many people were so "fed up" (*chan nan*) that they abandoned nearly 6 percent of the Tu Tan's fields.[83] In some places the situa-

83. *Nhan Dan,* 16 November 1987, 2; 3 December 1987, 2. Many other newspaper accounts refer to people who were surrendering fields because they could not farm them or because quotas were too high. These factors and adverse weather probably explain why the area of

tion was worse. "There were seasons," recalled an elderly man in Tien Huong cooperative of Tam Canh subdistrict, Vinh Phuc province, "when hundreds of *mau* were deserted."[84] He explained that because "people had to farm so hard to get so little, they split" (*choai ra*). They concentrated instead on their household gardens, raised pigs and ducks, did petty trade, and made roofing tiles from clay dug illicitly along the edges of the co-operative's ponds. Members of some families went looking for gold in distant places, a long shot that desperate villagers elsewhere also pursued.[85]

Harvests were another site of struggle. The contentious points, however, were different than before. Snitching grain was no longer significant because harvesting was no longer done collectively and the amounts owed to the cooperative had already been determined. Now people could harvest their own fields and thereafter deliver their quotas to cooperative authorities. The new contentious points were quota payments and harvest size. Officials were supposed to collect quotas as quickly as possible. Villagers, however, were inclined to delay and avoid paying the full amount. Officials also wanted to know how much each field produced in order to determine future quotas. Cooperative members, guessing that bigger harvests could mean higher quotas the next year, were inclined to underreport their yields.

Cooperative managers tried various measures to calculate what each field produced and to collect quotas. This was easier, said the Communist Party secretary and other leaders of Vinh Phu province, if cooperative members threshed and dried their grain together in a few locations, as 40 percent of the province's cooperatives did in 1982. In the remainder, people threshed and dried their paddy at home, meaning that usually data for each field were "interfered with" (*bi nhieu*) and cooperative officials "could not learn the true result of production." That also made quota collection more difficult.[86] Officials frequently went house to house, sampling grain to estimate yields and collecting quotas.[87] Leaders in some cooperatives tried to extract quotas before the harvest.[88] Many devised incentives and punish-

---

paddy and other staple food crops farmed in 1984–1986 was about 6 percent smaller than in 1981. See appendix 1, table 1.

84. Interview, Tam Canh, 10 August 2000. I estimate that "hundreds of *mau*" was 10–30 percent of the cooperative's land.

85. Interviews, Tam Canh, 10 and 11 August 2000, and Dao Duc, 18 August 2000, Vinh Phuc; *Ha Son Binh*, 12 March 1983, 2; Xa Hoa Thach, *Lich Su Cach Mang*, 196–97.

86. Hoang Quy, Bi Thu, Vinh Phu, "Phan Dau Khoan San Pham Dong Bo de Phat Huy Tiem Nang Toan Dien, Da Dang cua Nong Nghiep Vinh Phu" [Synchronize production contracts, bring into play agricultural potential], 39–40, in *Khoan San Pham*; and report from the party's provincial Executive Committee, *Vinh Phu*, 10 June 1983, 2.

87. *Ha Son Binh*, 16 June 1982, 2; 27 October 1982, 2; *Vinh Phu*, 26 June 1987, 3.

88. *Ha Son Binh*, 8 May 1982, 2.

ments. For instance, some officials allowed villagers who owed nothing from previous seasons to thresh and dry their grain at home but required those with arrears to do that work at a monitored location. Another incentive was to give a discount to members who delivered their quotas on time.[89] Low quotas were another way to get villagers to pay, but then co-operative officials had difficulties fulfilling obligations to state agencies. Perhaps the most effective method to get villagers to deliver their quotas was for leaders to set good examples by paying what they owed.[90] The most distressing collection methods involved coercion. Officials were authorized to search people's homes for hidden grain. How often searches occurred and how frequently authorities forced their way into houses are unknown, but such things happened. During house-to-house searches in a Thanh Hoa cooperative, some villagers were so apprehensive and frightened that they contemplated suicide.[91] Not finding the grain they were looking for, officials sometimes confiscated bicycles and other possessions, which they sold to recuperate the losses. Another way to reprimand delinquent members was to take their fields.[92]

Available information suggests that quota payments were rarely problematic initially. Later, however, disputation over the size and payment of quotas became a major aspect of cooperative life. The two provinces for which I have adequate information, Ha Son Binh and Thai Binh, reported that by 1985 unpaid quotas were common in more than 80 percent of the cooperatives and 60–70 percent of households had not paid all that officials claimed they owed. The situation was similar elsewhere in the Red River delta.[93] But people apparently managed to withhold only small amounts. In Ha Son Binh and Thai Binh, unpaid grain by early 1985 equaled 6 to 13 percent of paddy or all staple food produced in 1984.[94] This represents not the arrears for that year, but the cumulative amount since 1981 (or earlier in some places). Thus, in any one year, the amount unpaid was not large. What alarmed authorities was that the total was increasing annually as more people withheld grain. In 1984 arrears in Thai

89. Ibid., 30 May 1981, 2; 29 May 1982, 2.

90. Ibid., 17 and 27 March 1982, both 2; 3 July 1982, 2.

91. Phung Gia Loc, "Cai Dem," 9–10. Also, Ha Noi Moi, 21 May 1981, 3; and Nhan Dan, 20 August 1987, 2.

92. Ha Son Binh, 27 March 1982, 2; Hai Hung, 18 October 1986, 4.

93. For Ha Son Binh, see Ha Son Binh, 20 July 1985, 2; for Thai Binh, see Nhan Dan, 18 November 1985, 2. Examples of cooperatives elsewhere appear in Vinh Phu, 11 July 1986, 2; Ha Noi Moi, 2 July 1987, 3; Le Hai Nguyen, "Bien Doi," 21; and interviews, four subdistricts, Vinh Phuc province, August 2000.

94. Calculated using figures in Ha Son Binh, 20 July 1985, 2; Nhan Dan, 18 November 1985, 2; and Vu Nong Nghiep, So Lieu, 63, 121, 135, 149.

Binh were seven times what they had been the first year of product contracts. The rise was similar elsewhere in the mid-1980s.

One reason people held back grain was to express indignation and to
protest against officials. For instance, several people in one village declared:
"No more produce will be delivered to the cooperative until officials have
returned what they have embezzled."[95] They had long believed that officials stole and squandered the cooperative's money and paddy. "These
parasites" (nhung con sau mot), even after being removed from office, one
villager wrote, still "rule over us" through their positions in the local branch
of the Communist Party. Even if corruption was not their concern, villagers often objected because officials themselves had not paid their quotas.
As one person said, referring to particular local officials, "so long as the
families of those men have not paid, we're not paying."[96] A second reason
was that villagers believed they were entitled to more grain. They were
hungry and the quotas were excessive. In one cooperative, for instance, villagers strenuously objected when officials tried to raise quotas for the third
time in three years. Officials claimed that higher levels were warranted
because yields had increased. Members countered, however, that crops were
better not because of what the cooperative had done but because of "additional work and fertilizer we have invested."[97] Indeed, a 1986 investigation
in several Red River delta villages found that people were often "indignant [ham huc] because the cooperative was not doing what it was supposed to," yet authorities insisted that quotas be fully paid.[98]

Disputes over quotas were often related to struggles over the remaining
phases of collective farming. Propelling that behavior were two pervasive
problems: state agencies could not provide what they were supposed to yet
pressed cooperatives to deliver or sell sizable proportions of what was
grown; and most cooperatives could not do or did poorly the work that
the product contract arrangement expected them to handle. "In the face
of such adversities and injustices," wrote a government analyst a few years
later, "peasants didn't just sit around helpless."[99] Often, according to a 1984
Ministry of Agriculture study of 756 cooperatives, "members struggled
to get the organization to fulfill its responsibilities." Failing that, they

95. Ha Noi Moi, 18 June 1987, 3.
96. Ha Son Binh, 17 March 1982, 2.
97. Vinh Phu, 26 July 1983, 2. Villagers often bore the costs when trying to make up for
insecticide, fertilizer, and other materials that cooperatives and state agencies were supposed to
provide. Xuan Kieu, "Ve Chinh Sach," 53–55.
98. Nhan Dan, 1 October 1986, 2.
99. Nguyen Huu Tien, "Phong Trao," 18.

"demanded that the cooperative lower the quota."[100] An increasingly common course of action was for villagers to do as much of the farming as possible and keep as much of what they produced as they could. Despite difficulties, especially in obtaining sufficient inputs, most villagers preferred farming on their own to propping up product contracts or returning to the time when they were not allocated fields to farm.

What happened in Huong Ngoc cooperative is illustrative.[101] The co-operative was formed in 1980–1981 when the subdistrict-sized cooperative in Tam Canh, Vinh Phu province, split into two. (The other cooperative was Tien Huong.) At first, product contracts were implemented according to national instructions. By 1983, however, Huong Ngoc officials could no longer insist that people plow and harrow collectively. The main reason was that the cooperative's draft animals were overworked and sickly. Conse-quently, some people, like Le Quang Nam, then in his late fifties and farming about one-third of a hectare with his wife and grown children, joined with relatives to buy their own water buffalo or ox. Meanwhile, the cooperative's leaders had other problems mobilizing people to farm together. People from the two villages in the cooperative, recalled Le Van Bich, who at the time headed one brigade, "couldn't get along." Many vil-lagers, said another man, "had no confidence" in the cooperative's leaders, hence paid them little mind. Some believed the cooperative's managers were stealing grain and fertilizer. Several faulted officials for not obtaining necessary farm supplies from state agencies. Some villagers said the co-operative did provide chemical fertilizer and insecticide until the late 1980s. Others, however, said those supplies had nearly, if not completely, stopped much sooner. "After one or two years" of product contracts, said Le Van Bich, "cooperative members had to arrange for their own inputs—buy insecticide, for instance, on the free market." (Sometimes, he added, "the stuff sold there was fake.") People also "plowed and harrowed their own fields and looked for their own fertilizers." The one task done collectively was to maintain and supply irrigation as well as possible.

Huong Ngoc villagers liked being on their own. They farmed more dili-gently, their harvests were bigger, and most managed to cope with rising prices on the free market so long as they could retain enough of what they produced. From the outside, district and provincial authorities were unable to see what was really happening. To keep them content, officials inside

100. BNN, "BC TH" [Implementing product contracts], 10 February 1984, 47.
101. Based on interviews, Tam Canh, Vinh Phuc, 10, 11, 12 August 2000, and one villager's two small notebooks with information about 1981–1984.

needed to meet or nearly meet the cooperative's obligations to state granaries and purchasing agencies. Consequently, Huong Ngoc officials had to
extract grain and other produce from villagers. Residents who recall getting
inputs from the cooperative said they paid most of their quotas. Others villagers, however, said that they and their neighbors paid only for irrigation
and a little more to satisfy officials. When dissatisfied, the officials called in
district police (*cong an*) to collect. Once, Le Quang Nam said, officials put
up for sale the bicycles confiscated from families who had not delivered
enough to the cooperative's storehouse. Defiantly, however, "nobody bought
them." Occasionally officials retrieved fields from delinquent villagers.
Usually, however, authorities avoided going to such extremes lest "they
make things worse."[102]

Meanwhile, provincial officials in Vinh Phu campaigned against the deterioration of collective farming and held up as models those places that had
wrested land preparation and other phases from individual households and
had resumed doing them collectively.[103] For every cooperative like that,
however, more continued to disintegrate into family farms. In Kim Thai
cooperative of Tien Thang subdistrict, the rapid deterioration also began
with draft animals. After two product contract seasons, the animals were so
badly cared for collectively that cooperative managers started selling them
to members. Consequently, individual households increasingly prepared
their own fields. At one point officials even hired those with draft animals
to prepare the fields of those without. Soon people without water buffaloes or oxen dealt directly with those who had them, paying for their
fields to be plowed and harrowed or working for the draft animal owner
in exchange for their land being prepared. By 1985–1986, only two brigades
maintained a semblance of collective farming for a few phases of work. In
the others, the cooperative provided little or nothing beyond irrigation, to
which villagers contributed time and some payment for upkeep. When
managers insisted, villagers also paid to meet the cooperative's obligations
to state agencies. In short, a new arrangement had evolved, which villagers
laughingly called the "you're-on-your-own contract" (*khoan mac ke*).[104]
Without authorization from higher authorities, similar informal understandings between cooperative officials and villagers evolved elsewhere in

---

102. The expression, *mo meo lay ca*, literally means "cut open the cat to get the fish." Le
Quang Nam's point was that confiscated fields could end up idle, thus producing nothing for
either the household concerned or the officials.

103. *Vinh Phu*, 15 February 1985, 1; 24 May 1985, 2; 7 June 1985, 2; 10 September 1985, 2;
18 October 1985, 3.

104. Interviews, Tien Thang, 24, 25, 26 August 2000.

Vinh Phu and other provinces. For instance, by 1985 villagers in nearly all three dozen cooperatives in Doan Hung district of Vinh Phu farmed primarily on their own. They reportedly did so "enthusiastically" because they paid the cooperative only half of what the product contract specified, met other farming expenses, and had more for their own consumption than they otherwise would have had.[105]

When taking over more farming, villagers first secured control over seeds and draft animals. Seed they could buy or get from previous harvests. Many people reverted to older varieties of paddy, which took longer to mature but were cheaper to grow.[106] Obtaining draft animals was more difficult. When the product contract system began, draft animals were still collectively owned. Soon many of them were worked to death or nearly so as villagers tried to get their assigned fields thoroughly plowed and harrowed. Cooperative managers attempted various solutions to this problem without much success.[107] To acquire their own draft animals, families, individually or in small groups, bought oxen and water buffaloes on the free market. Others bought the cooperatives' sickly and aging animals, which through proper care were frequently rejuvenated to work for several more years.[108] Scattered newspaper accounts suggest that perhaps a quarter of draft animals in northern Vietnam were privately owned by 1985–1986.[109]

105. *Vinh Phu*, 7 June 1985, 2, 4. For other provinces, see *Hai Hung*, 21 June 1986, 3; 4 April 1987, 3; 22 February 1989, 2; *Nhan Dan*, 12 March 1986, 2; 4 September 1986, 2; 15 March 1987, 2.

106. This meant a shorter winter season, which is one reason why secondary crop production in some provinces declined during the mid-1980s. Another reason is that villagers with insufficient resources to raise both paddy and secondary crops concentrated on paddy. *Ha Son Binh*, 22 September 1982, 2; and *Vinh Phu*, 7 October 1983, 2.

107. See, for instance, *Ha Son Binh*, 14 November 1981, 2; 25 August 1982, 2; 15 June 1985, 2; *Hai Hung*, 5 October 1983, 1; *Vinh Phu*, 26 July 1985, 2. Preparing land with tractors was an option for only a few cooperatives and was not necessarily more reliable or efficient. See *Ha Son Binh*, 16 July 1983, 2; 11 February 1987, 2; *Hai Hung*, 16 July 1983, 3; 19 September 1987, 4.

108. The first report I have of families buying their own animals is in *Ha Noi Moi*, 18 July 1981, 3. Examples of subsequent accounts are Le Duc Tho, "On the Question," C15; BQL-HTXNNTU, *Khoan San Pham*, 52, 97; *Hai Hung*, 25 May 1983, 3; *Vinh Phu*, 28 November 1986, 2.

109. The only available summary figure is for Hai Hung province, where 86 percent of the oxen and 11 percent of the water buffaloes were privately owned in early 1988. *Hai Hung*, 4 June 1988, 1. Private ownership probably accounts for most of the 15 percent increase in the Red River delta's draft animal population and the 30 percent increase across the north between 1980 and 1987, in contrast to declining populations during much of the 1970s. TCTK, *12 Nam Phat Trien*, 427, 429, 433, 463, 465, 469; TCTK, *Nien Giam Thong Ke 1975*, 271, 273, 275; Vu Nong Nghiep, *So Lieu*, 463–69, 484–90.

The process of undermining the collective phases of farming had began soon after the product contract system was implemented. As early as May 1981, national agencies celebrating the rapid implementation of product contracts and improved production also complained that 30–40 percent of cooperatives failed to complete all required phases of production while villagers did more farming on their own than guidelines permitted.[110] By late 1982, the proportion had increased to 40–50 percent.[111] Villagers in 30–50 percent of Ha Son Binh and Vinh Phu provinces' cooperatives in 1982–1983 were preparing land and seedlings themselves; in 12 to 18 percent, cooperatives "essentially leased fields" to villagers, who farmed on their own, "then collected rent."[112] An early 1984 assessment by the Ministry of Agriculture concluded in dismay that, although product contracts were properly carried out in some places, elsewhere peasants often did little work collectively, farmed primarily by themselves with little oversight by cooperative leaders, and "squabbled among themselves over water and draft animals."[113] A June 1985 editorial in Vinh Phu's newspaper complained that "nearly all cooperatives" in the province had "loose management" and "blank contracts" (*khoan trang*), an expression referring to informal arrangements in which villagers did most or all of the farming and gave to cooperative authorities a fraction of the supposed product contract quotas.[114] By then Ha Son Binh and probably other provinces also had a large proportion of cooperatives in which households did far more farmwork than national policy had authorized.[115]

In summary, the situation in the Red River delta by 1983–1985 was that, for most villagers, sticking to the product contract arrangement was not only undesirable but impossible. Many cooperatives could not provide the inputs or complete the collective farming phases that the arrangement required. Meanwhile, cooperative officials, under pressure from higher authorities to supply grain and other produce to state agencies, struggled

110. Nguyen Ngoc Triu, "BC TH" [Initial steps], 4 May 1981, 7; Ban Tuyen Huan Phu Nu TU, "BC TH Giao Duc" [Educating members], 20 May 1981, 4.

111. BQLHTXNNTU, *Khoan San Pham*, 97.

112. *Ha Son Binh*, 22 May 1982, 1; 2 June 1982, 2; 6 November 1982, 2; *Vinh Phu*, 8 March 1983, 2; 24 June 1983, 1, 4.

113. BNN, "BC TH" [Implementing product contracts], 10 February 1984, 46–47.

114. *Vinh Phu*, 7 June 1985, p1, 4. In addition to *khoan trang* and *khoan mac ke*, other terms for arrangements in which villagers did more work individually and less work collectively than product contracts required were *khoan trang tinh* (pure white, entirely blank contract), *khoan nua voi* (contract by halves), *khoan khong dong bo* (unsynchronized contract), and *khoan gon* (package contract). Official accounts typically referred derisively to all of these except the last, which gradually acquired respectability among authorities.

115. *Ha Son Binh*, 20 July 1985, 2.

to get villagers to pay the quotas stipulated in the product contracts. Villagers tried to keep as much of their harvests as they could, though they were willing to pay for irrigation and other services and realized that authorities could coerce them to pay more. Individually and in small groups, they did more and more of the farming in their assigned fields. Some managed this reasonably well and cultivated all the land allocated to them. Others had to give up some fields or leave them fallow. Some put more energy into nonfarming activities. In any case, people were shifting more decisively than before to family farming and away from collective farming.

## Policy Debates and Changes

As collective farming was increasingly replaced with family farming, many Communist Party government leaders became alarmed and intense discussions began in policy-making circles. Authorities debated not only the future of collective agriculture but other aspects of the centrally planned economy.[116] They agreed that the economy was in distress, even though some indicators were more positive in the mid-1980s than they had been at the beginning of the decade. Industrial production, in particular, had increased for many products and overall economic growth had exceeded the government's expectations. Yet per capita output remained very low, most importantly for paddy and other staple food crops. Staple food production was dropping to the low levels of the late 1970s. In many provinces people were hungry. Meanwhile retail prices in state and free markets were rising. In 1985 they were twice what they had been the year before; in 1986–1988, inflation soared to more than 300 percent annually. The change in the nation's currency and other government monetary measures in 1984–1985 only made matters worse.

The nation's leaders disagreed about what to do. Broadly speaking, they debated how the state should or even could control the economy. Some argued that by improving management and planning, the state could control the economy, advance socialism, and avoid capitalism. Others, though also socialists, had concluded that state control of markets, production, and prices was impossible. Trying to exert control, they argued, was

116. This and the next three paragraphs draw on Beresford and Dang Phong, *Economic Transition*, 21–65; Dang T. Tran, *Vietnam*, 32–80; Fforde and de Vylder, *From Plan*, 6–20, 29–42, 125–226; Fforde, "From Plan"; Kolko, *Vietnam*, 24–43; Porter, *Vietnam*, 140–51; Vo Nhan Tri, *Vietnam's Economic Policy*, 125–240; and White, "Debates."

indeed a significant cause of economic problems. These views did not necessarily fall into firm camps. They formed a spectrum along which leaders moved over time and from one issue to another.

Leaders in other Communist Party–governed countries were engaged in similar debates in the mid-1980s. Their discussions and the resulting policy shifts, such as the Soviet Union's perestroika or China's market socialism, probably affected Vietnam. But how they influenced Vietnamese leaders— or vice versa—is not yet known.[117] Meanwhile, discussions Vietnamese leaders had with officials at the International Monetary Fund, the World Bank, United Nations agencies, and various governments in the capitalist world may have altered the course and content of deliberations in Communist Party government offices in Hanoi. Such international influences do show up in higher education policy changes, though not until the early 1990s.[118] They do not appear in materials I have on agrarian policy shifts in the 1980s. I can imagine, however, that widening debates in Communist countries about such pillars of socialism as state markets, central planning, and state industries emboldened Vietnamese policy advisers and national officials to convey more directly to peers and superiors their doubts that collective farming would ever succeed.

While debate in Vietnam continued, policy modifications began. Consequently, during the 1980s the centrally planned economy was not only under discussion but in flux. In hindsight we know that this was the transition process to the market economy Vietnam has today. The changes did not just move slowly, however, they zigzagged. There was no blueprint. And the pace and pattern of transition tended to differ from one sector to another and one region to another. Several shifts, such as the elimination of state subsidies and free negotiation of prices between buyers and sellers, were articulated in general party pronouncements long before they were acted on.

As for the collective cooperatives, authorities distressed that individual families were taking over more aspects of farming in the early 1980s tried to reverse the trend. Land and seedling preparation, in particular, had to be done collectively, they insisted, not left "floating" (*tha noi*) for villagers to do on their own. Allowing individuals "blank contracts" to do what was supposed to be done collectively, warned a June 1982 editorial in the party's provincial newspaper in Ha Son Binh, provided "the germs from which

117. The strongest external influence on deliberations in Vietnam may have come from the Soviet Union and Eastern Europe in the second half of the 1980s. Dang Phong and Beresford, *Authority Relations*, 87.

118. St. George, "Government Policy," 138–65.

differentiation between rich and poor develops" and would "give birth to capitalism."[119] This assessment echoed statements during the party's fifth national congress the previous March stressing that collective farming was vital for socialism. Party leaders then renewed the drive to collectivize agriculture in the south and intensified efforts to stop the deterioration of collective cooperatives in the north. For instance, a December 1983 resolution of the government's Council of Ministers strictly forbade the allocation "of land and draft animals to cooperative members so that they do the work from beginning to end and then give a bit to the cooperative" as though it were "leasing land and receiving rent" (*phat canh thu to*).[120] Reaffirming this view in February 1984, a Ministry of Agriculture report sharply criticized "the rather widespread situation" of cooperative leaders who paid little mind to their duties and "gave a free rein" (*buong long*) to villagers to fend for themselves.[121] The ministry issued more instructions and implored cooperative managers and members to properly implement the product contract system.[122] Provincial officials frequently condemned "blank contracts," unpaid quotas, and stagnant and falling production. They also reprimanded and sometimes removed cooperative officials who let villagers do more farming individually.[123]

Meanwhile, some national leaders seemed to be leaning further toward more family farming. Indications initially appeared in the official stance on the "family economy" (*kinh te gia dinh*). In the 1960s–1970s, the party's leadership did not consider the family economy a part of socialism. It only recognized the "subsidiary family economy," which it regarded as a temporary adjunct to collective farming until socialism could develop fully. In March 1982, a brief passage from the fifth national congress indicated that party members favoring more attention to household-based production had won some concessions during internal debates. The congress endorsed the Central Executive Committee's report, which expunged the modifier "subsidiary" (*phu*) and said: "We must encourage, guide, and help the family

119. *Ha Son Binh*, 2 June 1982, 1.

120. Hoi Dong Bo Truong, "NQ (so 154/HDBT), Hoan Chinh CT KSP Cuoi Cung, LD, HTX, TDSX NN" [Council of Ministers, "Resolution 154, completing end-product contracts"], 14 December 1983, 8, in BNN, *Hoan Chinh*.

121. BNN, "BC TH" [Implementing product contracts], 10 February 1984, 46.

122. For examples, see the four circulars in July 1984, published in BNN, *Hoan Chinh*, 56–76, on calculating quotas, planning production, allocating and assigning farming tasks, and organizing teams to prepare paddy seeds and seedlings.

123. See, for instance, *Ha Son Binh*, 2 July 1983, 2; 20 July 1985, 2; *Hai Hung*, 10 September 1983, 1; *Nong Nghiep Ha Bac*, no.1 (1985): 10; *Vinh Phu*, 21 January 1983, 3; 7 June 1985, 1 and 4; and Dinh Van Ton, "Thanh Tra, Kiem Tra," 11.

economy, and assure that it be an integral part of the socialist economy."[124] This statement stimulated further debate about families as producers and was elaborated in subsequent party instructions. A January 1984 directive went further than the September 1979 policy allowing families to farm unused cooperative land for up to five years. The 1984 directive said families could use such lands for an unspecified "prolonged period" (*lau dai*).[125] This and subsequent government pronouncements also authorized additional land for household plots so that every family could raise vegetables and other crops for their own use.[126] Previously, national authorities had forbidden cooperatives from allocating more land for this purpose.

In 1983–1985, national and provincial reports and conferences publicly praised the family as producer. One striking example was a meeting in December 1984 organized by the party's Agriculture Committee. Its purpose was to assess "the development of the rural family economy." Speakers included Central Committee members, the vice president of the Council of Ministers, and party secretaries of several provinces and districts. They said little about collective cooperatives and a great deal about families who industriously farmed fields assigned to them, used more fertilizer than production brigades had used, and on their own made up for inputs that cooperative managers and state agencies could not provide. Another theme was that families produced most of the nation's eggs, meat, fish, vegetables, fruit, and several other products. Speakers also applauded families that, in addition to farming well the assigned fields, had turned many hillsides, riverbanks, swamps, and other previously unused areas into productive land. Some presenters seemed to think that family-based production was the main way to diversify the rural economy.[127]

124. DCSVN, *Van Kien*, 1:57–58, and 2:29–30. See also Vo Nhan Tri, *Vietnam's Economic Policy*, 131; and Nguyen Huy, "Ve moi Lien He," 17. The resolution from the party's sixth plenum (fourth congress) in 1979 mentioned "family economy" (without the modifier "subsidiary") in a positive way but said nothing about encouraging it or seeing it as part of socialism. BCHTU, DCSVN, "NQ Hoi Nghi 6," 12.

125. BCHTU, DCSVN, "Chi Thi (so 35 CT/TW), Khuyen Khich KT Gia Dinh, Huong Dan Phat Trien KT Gia Dinh" [CEC, VCP, "Directive 37, encouraging the family economy"], 18 January 1984, 5–6, in BNNTU, *Khuyen Khich*. For a sample of continuing debate about the family economy, see Thuy Lan, "Hoi Nghi Khoa Hoc."

126. Hoi Dong Bo Truong, "NQ 146-HDBT, Phat Trien KT Gia Dinh" [Council of Ministers, "Resolution 146, family economy"], 26 November 1986, in *Ha Son Binh*, 7 January 1987, 1, 3. Neither this resolution nor the January 1984 party directive specified how much additional land could be used for household plots. I have been told that by about 1986 national authorities allowed 10 percent of cooperative land for household plots. That would be twice the percentage previously specified.

127. BNNTU, *Khuyen Khich*, 13, 23–26, 39, 42–43, 53, 65–67.

In mid-1985, largely secret debates produced two pronouncements that made concessions to those who favored replacing the planned economy and collective production with a market economy and family production. The first was a resolution of the party's eighth plenum (fifth congress) in June 1985 that said that "bureaucratic centralism and state subsidies" (*tap trung quan lieu-bao cap*) for commodities and salaries contributed significantly to the country's economic ills. Recovery, it said, required a shift from "commanding the economy mainly with administrative orders" to "economic accounting and socialist business practices" that linked the real costs of property, capital, and labor to real output and benefit for the economy.[128] Its implication for agriculture was that low state prices for farm products would be eliminated, and rural producers would thus get more income from their crops. These market changes, however, did not happen immediately. Implementation of the resolution encountered many problems, including opposition within the party bureaucracy and government ministries, and occurred in fits and starts during the next four years.[129]

The second significant pronouncement, also in June 1985, was a directive from the party's Central Executive Committee.[130] Characteristic of product contracts in many cooperatives, particularly those producing paddy, it said, were bad management, unpaid quotas, and collective phases of production "drifting" to individuals. To fix these problems, it itemized several measures. The most specific ones, in a section about "improving the product contract," concerned two highly contentious matters in the countryside: quotas and collective farming. To encourage villagers to invest more in farming, the directive instructed, quotas should not be reconsidered every year. Also unlike previous regulations, which allowed cooperative managers to increase quotas as production rose, the instruction said that quotas could be altered only if "factors of production" changed. While not elaborated, those factors seem to have pertained to a second specific change. Alluding to many places that were not doing the collective farming phases previous regulations had required, it said that, while every cooperative should be involved "directly or indirectly" in all aspects of production, the balance

128. These are excerpts from and paraphrases of the resolution in "Xa Luan," 5, and "Thoroughly Understanding," 79. I never found the resolution itself. A translated announcement about it appears in *Summary of World Broadcasts*, 22 June 1985, FE/7984/B/6–7. Other publications at the time discussing the resolution include *Nhan Dan*, 18 June 1985, 1; 21 June 1985, 1; 18 September 1985, 2; and an article *Nhan Dan* published in twenty-three installments during July and August, the first of which appeared 8 July 1985, 2.

129. For an informative analysis of what ensued, see Porter, *Vietnam*, 142–51.

130. BCHTU, DCSVN, "Chi Thi (67 CT-TW)." Quoted passages in this paragraph are on pages 4–5. Another version appears in *Nhan Dan*, 1 July 1985, 2.

between collectively and individually done work could be adjusted according to circumstances. Regarding paddy farming, "there is no need to be inflexible about five phases being done collectively and three phases by individuals." If a cooperative "is not in a position" to do certain things, for example, if it "has no more seedlings" or "lacks enough draft animals to prepare the land," then "the cooperative member's initiative should be brought into play and the cooperative should solve the problem." The member, it said, should be compensated accordingly. It was not clear how this was to come about but a reduction in the quota was implied.

In effect, this directive from the party's national leadership authorized villagers to do what many were already doing: use their initiative to farm as much of the fields assigned to them as possible, which included doing more work individually rather than collectively and negotiating quotas and other conditions with local officials.[131] Previously, national authorities had criticized villagers for doing such things. The authorities were by and large the same. No leadership shake-up had occurred. What was changing was leaders' assessments of what could and could not be done in light of the countless villagers who were eroding collective farming and demonstrating the superiority of family farming.[132]

That directive and previous pronouncements favoring more family farming accelerated the trend in official circles away from collective agriculture. Debates, however, continued. Collectivization remained the overall policy. Many national leaders and party analysts still wanted most phases of farming done collectively. Newspapers still chastised cooperatives in which farming had devolved to individual households and applauded those that had resumed farming collectively. Many provincial and district officials were of the same mind. Provincial authorities in Hai Hung, for instance, insisted that five out of the eight main phases of paddy farming be done collectively and rebuked cooperatives that did otherwise. Only in April 1987 did

131. The only similar official statement that came from a national office earlier than this directive is an oblique passage in a July 1984 circular from the MA saying that if a cooperative cannot "provide a level of investment in keeping with the contract plan, it can mobilize members to find alternative ways" and reduce accordingly each member's quota. Referring only to a failure to meet investment obligations, the circular avoids talking about how to handle a cooperative's failure to complete certain phases of production. BNN, "Thong Tu (02 TT-NN), San Luong K va Giao Ruong KSP, LD, HTX, TDSX NN" [MA, "Circular 02, defining quotas and allocating product contract fields"], 6 July 1984, 57–56, in BNN, *Hoan Chinh*.

132. Not until December 1986 did top personnel of the Communist Party change significantly, following the death in July of the long-serving secretary general Le Duan. His replacement, Nguyen Van Linh, encouraged reforms. But strong pressures against collective farming meant that decollectivization had begun well before the leadership change.

they modify their stance, authorizing households to grow their own seedlings if that task could not be done collectively.[133]

Yet other district and provincial authorities endorsed, even encouraged, modifications of the product contract arrangement. The earliest evidence I have concerns Xuan Khanh cooperative in Yen Lap, a mountainous district in Vinh Phu. In early 1986, the district authorized the cooperative's leaders to give "paddy contracts to workers" (*hop dong cay lua den nguoi lao dong*).[134] In this arrangement, "the cooperative could do whatever [farming] tasks it could and individuals could do whatever they could." Everyone knew in advance the amount of paddy to be paid for taxes and the cost for whatever the cooperative provided. Each field holder was entitled to the entire harvest minus taxes and fee-for-service payments to the cooperative. Although this was not explicitly stated, the report implied that work points had been abolished.

Vinh Phu's Communist Party secretary later said Xuan Khanh was the first of several cooperatives in the province with approved "experiments in a new contract system" between 1986 and 1988.[135] Possibly authorities were simply approving alterations that already existed within the cooperatives. That seems to have been the case in Ha Son Binh province. For some years several cooperatives there had been "bravely trying out new ways" of getting the farmwork done, said an official account written years later.[136] In May 1986, after monitoring two places—Binh Minh and Lien Son— that had replaced the product contract with different arrangements, the party's provincial standing committee endorsed these "new types of co-operatives." In October 1987, after monitoring other places using new arrangements, Ha Son Binh authorities approved them for all parts of the province.[137]

By September 1987, farming arrangements other than product contracts prevailed in 70 percent or more of all cooperatives in Vietnam.[138] By then many had approval from district and provincial offices, though most had begun informally, hidden as much as possible from those higher authorities. Authorized "experimentation" in cooperatives accelerated, especially after the party's sixth national congress in December 1986. That congress

133. *Hai Hung*, 4 April 1987, 3.
134. *Vinh Phu*, 18 December 1987, 2.
135. Ibid., 20 May 1988, 1.
136. Tinh Hoa Binh, *Lich Su Phong Trao*, 255–56.
137. Ibid., 267–68.
138. Seventy percent, according to Luu Van Sung, "Nhung Van De," 38; 80 percent, according to Le Trong, "Thuc Chat," 66, and Ban Bien Tap, "Ve Khoan," 55. The authors of all three publications had information from high levels of the Communist Party.

solidly endorsed the trend away from the centrally planned economy and toward free markets and officially launched the party's "renovation" (*doi moi*) program, which continues today. Although not specifically approving changes in the cooperatives, pronouncements from that congress "greatly spurred on" (*khuyen khich manh me*) the alterations.[139] Another stimulus from the center was an August 1987 national conference, organized by the party's Agriculture Committee, that apparently endorsed "suggestions for renovating agricultural management" that gave households more control over farming.[140]

As the variations gained legitimacy among authorities, they acquired more respectable names. The term "blank contract" was used less, except by critics. Increasingly, official accounts, newspapers, and journals used "product contract in line with unit price and a complete settlement of accounts" (*khoan san pham theo don gia-thanh toan gon*). This was a mouthful and was often abbreviated to "package contract" (*khoan gon*). Replacing that term by late 1987–early 1988 was "household contract" (*khoan den ho* or *khoan ho*), which stuck and remains widely used today. It is the same term—and refers to much the same practice—that authorities had earlier denounced, most poignantly in 1967–1968 when national party leaders chastised cooperatives in Vinh Phuc (Vinh Phu) province for letting families farm individually.

The many forms of "package contracts" or "household contracts" across the country shared several main features.[141] First, fields were allocated to everyone in a household, not just to "workers." Within a cooperative, every working-age person usually received the same amount and other members of a family were allocated a fraction of that according to age and other circumstances. In the interest of distributing land equitably, authorities also took the fields' qualities, proximity to roads and irrigation canals, and other factors into consideration. Each household could use the assigned fields for several years—three to five was the range in 1987. Second, a household did

139. Interviews, Hanoi, September 1992 and April 1993, with officials who had worked during the 1980s in the party's central Agriculture Committee.

140. Interviews, officials in Hanoi, September 1992 and April 1993; and Tieu Ban Tong Ket Hop Tac Hoa Nong Nghiep, "Bao Cao Tong Ket," 16.

141. This paragraph draws on evidence about different provinces. Ha Bac: *Nhan Dan*, 11 December 1987, 2; *Nong Nghiep Ha Bac*, no. 2 (1988): 8–9, 32. Ha Son Binh: interviews, Van Nhan (Phu Xuyen district), 29 October 1992, Dung Tien and Nghiem Xuyen (Thuong Tin district), 21 and 22 October 1992; *Ha Son Binh*, 19 December 1987, 2; 20 April 1988, 2. Thai Binh: *Nhan Dan*, 16 November 1987, 2, and 3 and 11 December 1987, both 2. Vinh Phu: interviews, Dao Duc, Quat Luu, and Tam Canh (Binh Xuyen district) and Tien Thang (Me Linh district), August 2000; *Vinh Phu*, 1 and 18 December 1987, both 2, 1 April 1988, 2, 16 September 1988, 2.

as much of the farming as it wanted or was able to do. Eliminated was the product contract provision that plowing, seed preparation, and certain other phases be completed collectively. For tasks that a family could not do but that the cooperative could, the household paid the cooperative. Irrigation was the most common service that the cooperative continued to provide. Third, work points were abolished. Each household was entitled to whatever it harvested. Fourth, the household also had to bear all farming expenses. Those included payments for irrigation, fertilizer, or other inputs from the cooperative. They also included taxes to the government. If the cooperative continued to run preschools, health centers, or other community programs, each household also paid fees for those services. A household knew at the beginning of each season how much the fees, charges, and taxes would be. Fifth, the number of officials running the cooperative dropped significantly, frequently by more than 40 percent. A larger number could not be justified and in any case could not be supported because payments from villagers were much lower. People who had previously received income from cooperative funds were now farming their own fields and doing other work. Sixth, households usually netted considerably more income from farming than before. A vivid way to see this is to compare the amount a family received of the quota each field was supposed to produce. During the product contract arrangement, a villager received as payment about 15–20 percent of the quota. In the new arrangement, a villager kept, after all expenses and taxes, 38–42 percent of the quota.

The replacement of collective farming with family farming still distressed many party officials and analysts in 1986–1987. Some wanted the product contract arrangement to be implemented properly. To achieve that, they urged smaller and better-managed cooperatives, stronger but smaller production brigades, and timely delivery of agricultural inputs through contracts between suppliers and cooperatives.[142] Other opponents wanted to return to the way cooperatives were supposed to have been operating in the 1960s–1970s. The product contract system, they argued, was impossible to fix because it artificially divided farming phases into three for individual work and five for collective work. "Everyone knows," said one, "that production results from all eight." Consequently, "it was inevitable" that product contracts "would turn into blank contracts" with all eight being done individually, not collectively.[143] Both types of critics denounced "blank contracts," "end product contracts to families," and other variations that

142. Nguyen Anh Bac, "May Suy Nghi"; and Dao Quang Cat, "Can Doi Moi," 70–72.
143. Le Trong, "Thuc Chat," 66.

gave households more control over farming. Those arrangements, they said, were eroding socialist relations of production, creating rich and poor peasants, and reviving class exploitation.[144]

Others party analysts and officials, however, fervently supported the trend. "Apply and expand package contracts," urged the party's Agriculture Committee in June 1987.[145] The changes, proponents predicted, would greatly improve production, create more surplus for the state, and raise peasants' incomes. The scrapping of work points, which poorly compensated members for their labor and discouraged them from producing well, was by itself a major improvement, they said. The package contract arrangement, advocates argued, would not end socialism. On the country, it was an appropriate method at Vietnam's state of development to mobilize the creativity, enthusiasm, and productive capacity of households to build socialism. Problems, of course, remained and others lay ahead. But overall, the new direction was superior to the previous one.[146]

The point of no return for collective farming was the December 1987 land law from the National Assembly, the nation's highest legislative body. The law authorized cooperatives to "entrust to their member households an amount of land" for "family economy purposes."[147] The law did not require cooperatives to do this or instruct them to distribute all land to households. But it certainly allowed them to do both. Provincial authorities could decide how much land would be distributed. Allocations to each household within a cooperative were to be more or less equal. Households would not own the land (all land in the nation still "belonged to the people" and was "managed by the state"). But they could use the area allocated to them for a "prolonged period" and keep or sell whatever they produced on it.

Soon after, in April 1988, the party's Political Bureau issued a resolution for "renovating agricultural economic management."[148] Popularly known now as "resolution 10," it was heralded then and afterward as the begin-

144. Dao Quang Cat, "Can Doi Moi," 69; Le Trong, "Thuc Chat," 67; Ban Bien Tap, "Ve Khoan," 54–55.

145. "Van dung rong rai hinh thuc khoan gon." Ban NN, "De An Xay Dung," 20.

146. Luu Van Sung, "Nhung Van De," 40–41; Nguyen Huy, "Van Dung Quy Luat," 64; Ban NN, "De An Xay Dung," 3–5, 16, 21–22; Ban NN, "Du thao: De An," 7, 14–15, 23, 29, 31; and accounts of conferences assessing new arrangements authorized in Ha Bac and Thai Binh provinces, Nhan Dan, 3 and 11 December 1987, both 2.

147. "Luat Dat Dai," 29 December 1987, article 27.1, in Luat Dat Dai. My discussion here also draws on articles 1, 3, 27.2, and 28 of this law.

148. BCHTU, DCSVN, "NQ (so 10-NQ/TW) Bo Chinh Tri, Doi Moi QL KT NN" [CEC, VCP, "Resolution 10, renovating agricultural economic management"], 5 April 1988, 20–25, in DCSVN, Nghi Quyet Bo Chinh Tri. For an English edition, see Renovation, 9–52.

ning of decollectivization. Actually, however, it was a synthesis of several earlier directives and policy shifts. It also endorsed, albeit indirectly, widespread practices that had already replaced collective farming with family farming. While still speaking in terms of "improving the product contract system," it emphasized contracts to individual households or groups of households. It said little about contracts to workers or groups of workers. It endorsed the "development of the family economy." It also stipulated that each cooperative was to decide which, if any, phases of farming would be done collectively. Each field would still have a production quota. The household farming that field, it said, was to retain "about 40 percent" at least of that quota (as well as keep all produce exceeding the quota). That percentage would probably increase as the household took over more farming phases. A new provision in the resolution was that a household could use the land assigned to it for fifteen to twenty years.

## The End and a New Beginning

The land law and resolution 10 gave villagers and local officials the green light to proceed pell-mell with allocating land to individual families. By late 1988 households in virtually all the cooperatives in the Red River delta, and for that matter elsewhere in the country, had "use rights" (*quyen su dung*) to farmland. The length of time for those rights was less then ten years in most places.[149] In the 1990s, many places redistributed land again, this time for longer periods. A revised land law from the National Assembly in 1993 set a maximum of twenty years for fields growing paddy, corn, potatoes, and most other food crops.

Having use rights rather than land ownership did not bother most villagers in the Red River delta.[150] They saw the arrangement as protection against the accumulation of land by a few people and as an assurance that all farming families would have fields. It also enabled a periodic reallocation among farming families according to the number of people in their households and other factors. Providing equal access to land was popular, as was designating some land for community purposes.

149. Bo Nong Nghiep va Cong Nghiep Thuc Pham, "Bao Cao," 8.
150. This paragraph draws on interviews in six subdistricts in Ha Tay and four in Hanoi, September and October 1992, and four subdistricts in Vinh Phuc, August 2000, as well as on Le Van Sinh, "On Becoming." Sentiments similar to those noted here have been better documented by research among villagers in China following decollectivization. See, in particular, Kung, "Equal Entitlement"; and Kung and Liu, "Farmers' Preferences."

How fields were divided among households varied.[151] The 1987 land law, resolution 10, and subsequent national guidelines basically allowed each subdistrict, with some oversight from district and provincial offices, to decide how to allocate land equitably. Frequently, the actual division of land occurred within each village or even neighborhood (*xom*, sometimes called *doi*, a carryover from collectivization). Broadly speaking, most subdistricts, at least in the Red River delta, established two, three, sometimes four "land funds" (*cac quy dat*). The largest, encompassing about 70–90 percent of the agricultural (and, when relevant, aquacultural) area, was divided equally among all qualified people.[152] To further ensure equality, the fields each household received were of different grades, from the best to worst land. Modest concessions, such as more of the best fields, often went to war invalids and families of soldiers killed in battle. The second "fund" had land (and often fish ponds) for one or two purposes. Some places reserved a portion for allocation later as the population grew. The rest they put out for tender (*dau thau*). Other places tendered all of it. The highest bidders used those areas for a year or two. The amount they paid was supposed to finance remaining cooperative activities and such community services as health care and senior citizen programs. Often a third fund included the household plots families had used during collectivization. Some places also had a fund for orchards or other areas designated for specific purposes.

To villagers, having their own fields was the end of collectivization and a new beginning. "It was a second land reform," said Tran Hung Son of Da Ton subdistrict in rural Hanoi. Many middle-aged and elderly villagers I interviewed said much the same thing. Tran Hung Son had been a teenager in 1954–1955 when the first land reform under the Communist Party government redistributed land equitably. Similar to what he recalls about that time, life for his family greatly improved after households obtained land in the late 1980s. "We don't worry any more about having enough food," he said, stressing the first measure of improvement. Another measure was that by 1993 his household of seven people had four bicycles, a small television, and an electric fan, possessions unimaginable during collectivization.[153] "Since fields were allocated to us," said a sixty-four-year-

151. Interviews in six subdistricts in Ha Tay and four in Hanoi, September and October 1992, and four subdistricts in Vinh Phuc, August 2000; Le Van Sinh, "On Becoming"; provincial newspaper accounts in 1988–1990; and Ban NN, "Du thao: Tong Ket."

152. Basically, any resident who wanted to farm qualified, though the amount of land allocated usually varied by age. Who counted as a resident was sometimes a highly contentious matter.

153. Interview, Da Ton, 23 April 1993.

old peasant in Vinh Phuc province, "our lives have improved severalfold."[154] A 1992–1993 survey found better living conditions during the previous five years in 95 percent of sampled rural communities across Vietnam. The main explanation villagers cited was agricultural policy change.[155] People could farm more efficiently and keep more of what they produced. "It used to take a month and a half to collectively harvest all the fields in the co-operative," said an elderly woman in Vinh Phuc. With family farming, "all fields are harvested in a week."[156] To collectively farm thirty-six hundred square meters of paddy (one *mau*) from start to finish "required two hundred and forty workdays," said Vo Minh Kha of Da Ton. He had worked in collective fields from the time he was a teenager in the mid-1960s. That same land farmed by individual households, he said with a touch of triumph, "now requires only ninety work days and the yields are much higher." The main explanation is "little wasted time or sloppy work today."[157] These calculations broadly correspond to other villagers' assess-ments. After paying farming expenses and taxes, most households end up with much more of what they produce than they did during collective farming. Another improvement has been the opportunity to diversify. Vil-lagers in many places revived wood carving, weaving, pottery, sewing, and other crafts that dwindled during collectivization.[158] They also freely buy farming inputs and other necessities and sell what they make and any grain, vegetables, fruit, and meat that they produce.[159]

This upbeat attitude among villagers is reflected in production figures. In the Red River delta and the north generally, the volume and yields of paddy by 1992–1993 were markedly higher than during the beginning of product contracts ten years earlier, and higher still than in the late 1970s, even though the farming technology remained essentially the same. In the delta, staple food production per capita in 1993 was 27 to 36 percent higher than in any of highest years prior to 1988. For the north as a whole, it was greater than at any time since the mid-1960s.[160]

The demise of collective farming did not end rural families' difficulties. In the late 1980s–early 1990s, the process of redistributing land ignited local

154. Interview, Tien Thang, 26 August 2000.
155. World Bank, *Vietnam*, 9. See also Raymond, "Rational Resistance," 79–95.
156. Interview, Dao Duc, 17 August 2000.
157. Interview, Da Ton, 8 February 1996.
158. For examples, see Nguyen Van Chinh, "Work without Name," and DiGregorio, "Iron Works."
159. By 1989, supply and demand, rather than state agencies, determined the prices for paddy and most other goods and services. Fforde and de Vylder, *From Plan*, 175–78.
160. Compare figures in appendix 1, table 1.

disputes and even violence over boundaries between neighboring villages and subdistricts. Although those problems were resolved, other conflicts periodically erupt in the countryside, typically over land allocations, land use, and corruption.[161] Widening inequalities between the majority of villagers who remain poor and the few who are well-off also create social tensions. In many places, villagers also bitterly complain about abusive officials, low prices for their produce, and scarce employment opportunities for young people.

As for the former cooperatives, they no longer do collective farming. About 13 percent of them had totally dissolved by 1995 and 38 percent existed in name only.[162] An example is Tien Huong in Tam Canh subdistrict, Vinh Phuc province. Its remaining draft animals, farming equipment, and other assets in the late 1980s were sold. The money apparently went to the officials. "Members," said one resident in disgust, "didn't get a cent."[163] Officials sometimes tried to impose levies on villagers even though the cooperatives provided nothing in return. About 35 percent of the cooperatives remained moderately active as of the mid-1990s. Often their principal activity was managing irrigation, for which members paid user fees. Efforts to do much more often foundered. For instance, the chairperson of the cooperative in Quat Luu wanted it to buy fertilizer in bulk and sell it at below retail prices to members. But, he said shaking his head, "we have no money, no savings, no capital." He tried to get members to invest funds for this purpose but "they made excuses for why they can't."[164] Only about 14 percent of the cooperatives remained energetic. They typically sold services to members, such as irrigation, low interest loans, fertilizer and seed at discounted prices, and marketing advice. Some, like the one in Da Ton, have retained a few fields on which to grow seedlings that members may buy, though they are free to grow their own or buy elsewhere.[165]

Meanwhile, villagers in many parts of the country have formed their own associations for mutual assistance. In 1996, the government made a law aimed at regulating such organizations. The Communist Party also instructed local party leaders to organize villagers into various kinds of "new cooperatives" (hop tac xa kieu moi).[166] Although such directives had

161. Kerkvliet, "Rural Society"; Tuong Lai, "Bao Cao So Bo."

162. These and other percentages in this paragraph are based on Vu Nong Nghiep, So Lieu, 65; Nguyen Huu Tien, "HTX Nong Nghiep," 23–24; and "Hien Trang ve Quan He San Xuat," 17–18.

163. Interview, Tam Canh, 12 August 2000.

164. Interview, Quat Luu, Vinh Phuc, 2 August 2000.

165. Interview, Da Ton, 11 October 2000.

166. Luat Hop Tac Xa; Nhan Dan, 27 May 1996, 1, 2.

little impact by 2001, they indicate that national leaders still tried to organize villagers' lives. No longer, however, did authorities insist on one model
of cooperative for the entire country. Nor did they demand that farming
and other production be done collectively.

## Summary

In 1980–1981 the Communist Party leaders in Vietnam tried to save collective farming by authorizing "product contracts," which made concessions to individual farming. By 1987–1988, national leaders had given up.
The December 1987 land law from the National Assembly and the April
1988 resolution from the party's Political Bureau in effect announced that
collective farming was gone. The Communist Party government now supported family farming.

That law and resolution basically approved what had become widespread
practice in the cooperatives. Villagers on their own or in league with local
officials had already nearly dismantled collective production. Their unilateral modifications of the official product contract system became known
as "blank contract" arrangements. Together with worsening economic
conditions across the country, the widespread grassroots replacement of
collective farming with family farming intensified debates within
policy-making circles of the Communist Party. Gradually, particularly from
about mid-1985 on, provincial and national authorities began to accommodate and eventually endorsed the local changes, which acquired the
more respectable names of "package contracts" and "household contracts."

It was not easy for rural people to make themselves heard and influence
high authorities. Hardly ever did they dare organize and protest openly.
When they publicly criticized, they usually did so in official meetings and
in letters and petitions to newspapers and authorities. Sometimes those
efforts brought relief from particularly incompetent or corrupt cooperative
leaders. Sometimes, however, such expressions of discontent provoked local
authorities to persecute those who criticized. For the most part, villagers
looked for ways to make a living and provide their families with at least
the basics in life. In the early 1980s, people in many cooperatives could do
that better than before by conforming to the product contract arrangement. But thereafter, product contracts became burdensome and often
unworkable. To ease the burden, villagers struggled with local authorities
to reduce payments to the cooperative and keep more paddy and other

produce for themselves. To get around the unworkable features, they took over more and more of the farming themselves.

Ultimately the product contracts collapsed because they did not remedy significant shortcomings that had dogged collective farming since the 1960s. In most places, villagers still did not sufficiently trust one another to do collective work well. Meanwhile, monitoring of the quality and quantity of members' work remained lax. People often doubted that cooperative leaders enforced rules fairly. They also knew or suspected that officials stole paddy, draft animals, and money. Finally, the product contract arrangement did not enhance people's commitment to collective farming. Initially it raised villagers' expectations that the cooperatives would improve. After a few seasons, however, their hopes faded especially because of a lack of trust, discontent with governance in the cooperatives, unreliable supplies of agricultural inputs, and persistent poverty.

# CHAPTER 7

# Conclusion

Everyday politics matters. That, in a nutshell, is a central conclusion to draw from this book. It can have a huge impact on national policy. Consider what happened in Vietnam. Collective farming, a major program of the Communist Party government, collapsed without social upheaval, without violence, without a change in government, without even organized opposition. Yet national authorities were pressured into giving up on collective farming and allowing family farming instead. To a significant degree, that pressure came from everyday practices of villagers in the Red River delta and other parts of northern Vietnam. To a considerable extent, those practices were political because they involved the distribution and control of vital resources. Those everyday political practices were often at odds with what collective farming required, what authorities wanted, and what national policy prescribed. Consequently, everyday politics put collective farming, authorities, and policy under enormous strain.

The Vietnam case suggests that everyday politics intersects and feeds into official politics in two or three ways. One is through interaction between citizens and local officials. Local officials in charge of running the cooperative organizations and making collective cooperatives function well had to deal with villagers who were supposed to do the work. While many people did their best for the cooperative, complying with instructions from production brigade and managerial board leaders, more villagers over time farmed collective fields lethargically, diverted fertilizer from those fields to the small plots they still held; concentrated as much of their time and labor as possible on producing things within their own households, encroached on collective land, and so forth. Efforts to stop or prevent these practices were numerous but only periodically effective. Consequently, at various times and in various places, local officials came to terms with these practices by agreeing to modify what national policy prescribed in exchange for sufficient compliance from villagers to allow the cooperative to have something positive to show to local officials' superiors. Villagers and officials hid, or tried to hide, from other authorities what in effect were local modifications of national policy. Locally developed variations and arrangements often ultimately went beyond what consenting officials had expected or had thought they had approved. Given an inch, villagers frequently took a mile.

Local arrangements arising from everyday politics can also feed into higher levels of official politics, becoming policy alternatives for authorities to consider or at least confront. Higher officials may take them, or at least part of them, on board as new policies or variations on existing policies. That is essentially what Vinh Phuc provincial officials did in the mid-1960s when they allowed modifications devised in a few cooperatives to be applied provincewide. Authorities may also reject them, which is what national party leaders did when they compelled those modifications in Vinh Phuc to stop. Years later, however, similar arrangements emerged in many cooperatives across northern Vietnam. Those and other local variations that diminished collective farming became, in effect, models that provincial and national authorities pondered as they debated possible policy changes.

Everyday politics also intersects official politics by affecting outcomes important to authorities. Harvest results, farm production per capita, hectares of farmland in the cooperatives, proportion of villagers' time devoted to collective work, number of pigs and draft animals, the amount of manure used in collective fields—these things mattered to authorities all the way to the top of the party and the government bureaucracy responsible for implementing collective farming. Statistics on these outcomes and countless studies by Communist Party government agencies figured in the deliberations of authorities assessing successes and failures. Favorable figures and reports indicated that the collective cooperatives functioned well; poor results indicated the opposite. Disappointing outcomes in a few places caused concern among national authorities. Poor outcomes in many places across several provinces contributed to national action.

Other factors, of course, influence policy changes and condition the impact of everyday politics. Particularly significant in Vietnam during collective farming was the war against the United States and for national reunification, which lasted until 1975. It stimulated villagers to work harder in the collective cooperatives than they might otherwise have done, thus diminishing and diluting behavior out of line with regulations. Many people believed that the survival of their loved ones in the military and of their nation depended on everyone doing their best to make collective farming successful. Others who doubted this argument nevertheless usually went along with it because to question it or collectivization itself would have appeared disloyal to the cause of national defense and reunification. Meanwhile, the war boosted many leaders' resolve to strengthen collective farming and greatly limited what they were able to learn from numerous indicators of dissatisfaction and weaknesses in the collective cooperatives. Another important condition was the considerable assistance, especially huge quantities of grain and other food, the Communist Party government's foreign allies gave to Vietnam. That aid compensated for a sizable proportion of the collective cooperatives' shortfalls in agricultural production.

Also conditioning the impact of everyday politics at the national level was local officials' behavior. As the war drew to an end, national leaders knew that collective farming in most cooperatives was weak and had only half-hearted support among villagers. A major cause, they concluded, was mismanagement and poor leadership within the collective cooperatives themselves. For that they had considerable evidence. Some came from official studies and investigations. Some came directly from villagers through letters and petitions occasionally sent to newspapers and to provincial and national offices. Much evidence came from villagers indirectly, through their everyday political practices. Haphazard care for collective crops, draft animals, and equipment, and other behavior contrary to collective farming often expressed villagers' disgust with cooperative leaders and local party officials who embezzled grain and money belonging to the cooperative, favored close relatives and friends at the expense of other cooperative members, and abused their positions in other ways. National leaders, by and large, were confident that managerial and leadership solutions could fix these and other problems. With peace near at hand, they launched a major drive to reorganize and strengthen collective farming.

Consequently, during the first fifteen years of collective farming in the north, between the early 1960s and the mid-1970s, everyday politics, combined with villagers' rare public criticisms, affected collective farming but not national policy, at least not in a spectacular way. It contributed to the fact that most cooperatives fell well short of authorities' expectations. It affected debates and deliberations within party and government circles about how to improve collective production. It influenced authorities' decisions to launch various campaigns aimed at correcting shortcomings and bolstering collectivization. It also shaped collective cooperatives to some extent, making them different from what national leaders had originally intended. When collective farming began, authorities insisted that villagers not grow paddy in their household plots. Paddy, they said, should only be produced collectively. Little by little, however, more and more people grew it in their household plots. Within a few years authorities gave up trying to stop them. Authorities wanted draft animals to be raised collectively and looked after by specialized teams and brigades in the cooperatives. That method, however, resulted in a sharp decline in the number of animals. To reverse the trend, local officials allowed individual households to care for water buffaloes and oxen on behalf of the cooperatives, arrangements that higher authorities criticized but came to accept. National leaders expected collective cooperatives to raise pigs. But only a small proportion of pigs were ever raised collectively. Individual households raised nearly all of them.

In the late 1970s and 1980s, everyday politics greatly affected national policy, partly because the context had changed. The war had ended, removing one justification authorities had for insisting on collective farming. The war's end also meant that many villagers had considerably less reason to maintain collective cooperatives. Foreign food aid declined substantially, making better agricultural production even more imperative. Yet collective production was falling, and the reorganization of the cooperatives had failed to remedy management and leadership problems. In general, collective cooperatives in the north were in no better shape and in some ways were in worse shape than they had been before. And in southern Vietnam, the government's drive to collectivize farming had stalled. Other major features of Vietnam's planned economy were also faltering, aggravating problems in the cooperatives. Debate over the future of cooperatives and other aspects of the socialist system increased in Vietnam's Communist Party government. Meanwhile, village households in the north were doing more and more farming on their own, further undermining collective production from within the cooperatives themselves. Local officials either were helpless to stop the trend, turned a blind eye, or countenanced the new arrangements in an effort to capture some of what households produced so that cooperatives could meet some of their obligations to the state. National leaders, increasingly desperate to improve production and stop collective farming from disappearing entirely, endorsed modifications in 1980–1981 that allowed individuals to complete some farming phases. This compromise halted the deterioration only briefly. By 1985, national authorities made further concessions and in 1987–1988 they capitulated, allowing family farming to replace all collective farming.

The power of everyday politics to undermine collective farming in Vietnam is not an isolated case. The phenomenon in Vietnam has parallels in other Communist party–governed countries. In Vietnam itself, other research suggests, significant policy changes regarding housing, markets, and state enterprises also resulted in part from the Communist Party government's decision to alter its rules and regulations so as to conform with what people wanted and needed as expressed through their everyday practices.[1] I would hazard to guess that everyday politics may be the first place to look for signs of pressure for altering policy, especially in national political systems with little room for advocacy politics that questions and criticizes officials and policies.

Even if everyday politics does not affect leaders and their policies, it still matters for another reason. It conveys people's views, values, and appraisals of authorities and how resources are used and distributed. While not the only medium for such ideas, everyday political behavior is significant, particularly if advocacy politics is severely constrained. In Vietnam, much everyday activity at odds with collective farming or aspects of it revolved around how land, labor, draft animals, work points, and harvests were to be used and distributed. Individually and in small groups that rarely included more than close relatives and neighbors within a single village, people skimped on labor and manure owed to the cooperative, optimized their work points from collective work, encroached on collective land, and gave priority to their own family-based production.

For this behavior, villagers usually had several reasons and justifications, which were often intertwined. First, they needed to provide the basics in life for their families. Hungry villagers often devised ways to get some grain from collective fields for their families first, before the harvest was available for general distribution. That distribution, they knew or strongly suspected, would not meet their needs. Family considerations also figured into how people worked in collective fields. Because produce was distributed to cooperative members according to formulas using work points, people emphasized the points rather than doing well the tasks assigned to them. Given how cooperatives usually operated, diligent work was unlikely to result in more income for one's family and hence people tended not to do it.

Second, other cooperative members violated the rules and avoided doing what they were supposed to do. People snitched and hid grain from col-

1. Koh, "Wards of Hanoi," 205–56; Fforde and de Vylder, *From Plan*, 136–37; Thrift and Forbes, *Price of War*, 165–67 and passim.

lective fields because they knew, or strongly suspected, that other members of the cooperative were doing likewise. Consequently, many villagers reasoned, they had to take grain and other produce from collective fields in an effort to get what they deserved. Sloppy work was also common in many cooperatives. People in a group that had properly completed an assigned task were frequently discouraged from doing so again because other groups doing subsequent tasks performed poorly, thus spoiling what they had done well. Animosities and rivalries, often among people from different hamlets and villages in the same collective cooperative, also figured into some people's claims to grain and how they labored. They took grain because they thought they deserved more than others. Or they saw no point in working hard when others whom they regarded as lazy or whom they disliked or distrusted would benefit.

Third, villagers were disgusted and angered by local officials and other authorities. Why not snitch paddy from fields, many reasoned, considering that cooperative leaders or district officials were taking not just a few sheaves of grain here or a couple of kilograms there but cartloads, even truckloads, from cooperative storehouses and government granaries. Why work diligently, many wondered, when officials were more likely to benefit than the people actually doing the work? In several places, villagers looked on collective cooperatives as organizations run largely by and for the managerial board and other officials. Also infuriating to many villagers were authorities who implored everyone to be good cooperative citizens while they secretly ripped off collective assets and gave favors to selected relatives and friends. Consequently, for many villagers, their lackadaisical work and other transgressions were forms of everyday resistance, a specific type of everyday politics. Their behavior may also have been a surreptitious slap in the face to collectivization policy and the authorities who imposed it.

Meanwhile, families assiduously tended crops in their own gardens and household plots. Such activity also had political content. A major dynamic in collective cooperatives revolved around contending ideas about how to farm: collectively, as the Communist Party government insisted, or as family units, which most villagers generally favored. This view, though rarely expressed openly, was conveyed through villagers' persistent efforts to invest labor, fertilizer, and other resources in farming their household plots and the land they had usurped from the cooperative. They also ventured where they could into household handicrafts, buying and selling, and other family-centered economic activities, often at the expense of resources that were supposed to go to collective production. By regularly getting higher yields from what they grew individually than from what they produced together, villagers knew long before authorities publicly acknowledged it that family farming was more productive and a better use of resources than collective farming.

Worth noting is that the everyday politics of collective farming did not convey widespread discontent with the Communist Party government, which had insisted on collectivization in the first place. In the early stages of collectivization, many villagers went along with collectivization, some of them enthusiastically, in part because they had considerable trust in and goodwill toward the party and its government. To judge from available evidence, even when collective cooperative organizers resorted to coercion, it did not create long-lasting animosity among rural people toward the Communist Party government. Perhaps anger at the time diminished during the war against the United States and for reunification, then faded further in the late 1970s and 1980s, when authorities increasingly made concessions to family farming, until they finally endorsed it at the expense of collective farming.

The final importance of everyday politics is that it can feed into advocacy politics, which is organized and deliberately aimed at authorities and policies. Advocacy politics might support officials and their programs and policies; or it might criticize, even rebel against them. In northern Vietnam the only significant activity of this kind regarding collectivization were organizations that periodically helped mobilize villagers to form and revamp cooperatives. Those organizations were entwined with, if not the creations of, the Communist Party. No protest movement against collectivization developed. Indeed, rarely did outbursts of rural discontent occur in the north. They were probably more numerous and widespread in the south between about 1978 and 1985. The only advocacy politics in the north that was critical of collective farming or aspects of it consisted of individuals and small groups articulating, in public and sometimes in writing, complaints and criticism that normally were expressed only through everyday political practices.

The fact that unorganized, quotidian activities could significantly influence the course of collectivization and contribute to the Communist Party government's decision to redistribute land to households and embrace family farming is significant for understanding Vietnam's political system. Two common models developed by scholars—the dominating state and the mobilizational corporatist state—can account for how collectivization policy emerged and for aspects of how the authorities attempted to implement it through the Communist Party, government agencies, and authorized organizations of peasants and other sectors of society. Those models are inadequate, however, for understanding the ebb and flow of implementation, the problems encountered, and the policy shift to family farming. They do not credit ongoing discourses outside official avenues about cooperatives and collective farming. Yet, as I have argued, what happened in those areas is a major part of the story about the rise and decline of collectivization. The findings here support a dialogical interpretation of political life in Vietnam, which draws attention to the behavior and voices of people outside formal organizations and to their influence on authorities and policies.

This feature of the political system has aroused conflicting views within national policy-making circles. During the 1980s, some officials bemoaned the party's inability to stop villagers from undermining collective farming. For instance, one party analyst, disgusted with the spread of "blank contracts" and other signs of family farming, wrote in September 1987 that national and local leaders had "discovered that blocking them was extremely difficult." " 'Blank contracts' to households," he continued, were the "symbol of [leaders'] helplessness as the collectivization movement degenerated."[2] Others in the party, however, celebrated the fact that ordinary people were influencing a significant policy change. At a conference in Thai Binh province in November 1987, Le Phuoc Tho, a member of the party's Secretariat who also chaired its central Agriculture Committee, praised the locally developed "package contract" for overcoming the negative aspects of the product contract that national policy had prescribed. "Once again," he said, "we see that the working masses at the grass roots were the first to create concrete economic forms, which the party must know how to summarize, elevate into policy, and then disseminate."[3]

Authorities in Vietnam who try to rule in a top-down manner and rely only on what comes through official channels are probably in for trouble. Nguyen Thanh Binh, speaking on behalf of the party's central Secretariat, alluded to this in October 1985 while summarizing the dynamics of the shift in policy toward family farming. Leaders, he observed, thought they had been serving "the masses' vital interests." Large numbers of villagers, however, disagreed. They "objected and did not heed" what they were told. For the well-being of peasants and the party, he suggested, authorities need to pay attention to why "people do not eat or swallow what leaders bring

2. Le Trong, "Thuc Chat," 68.
3. Le Phuoc Tho's speech appears in *Nhan Dan*, 4 December 1987, 2, 3. The quoted passage is on 3. Other ranking party members have said much the same. One told me: "It was the people who rejected collective farming and finally, when conditions became so bad, the party's leaders had to admit the mistake and start to correct it." Interview, Hanoi, May 1993.

to their mouths."[4] Because the political system today still includes little or no avenues for organized criticism, let alone opposition, to authorities and their policies, this advice is as relevant now as it was in the 1980s. Nearly 75 percent of Vietnamese still live in rural areas. The Communist Party government's base of support remains the peasantry. Were it to lose that backing, its days would be numbered. To retain that support, it and rural people must engage in dialogue. In particular, party and government authorities must not do all the talking; they must listen to what villagers say. Not to do so could result in peasants rejecting what authorities say, perhaps not openly and immediately but surreptitiously and gradually. Listening to and interacting with villagers can occur through formal government and party channels. But ordinary people's concerns, preferences, and objections may also be expressed through how they work and live and through local initiatives at odds with what has been authorized. Those practices may be the harbingers of better policies and programs. Policy may, in other words, follow practice. The example of how family farming replaced collective farming suggests that in order for the Communist Party government to lead, it sometimes must follow.

A reader might be tempted to conclude that peasants in Vietnam, and possibly elsewhere, are inherently opposed to collective or even simpler forms of cooperation. That conclusion would be unwarranted. Villages in Vietnam and other countries have rich histories of people working together, exchanging labor, helping one another to achieve common objectives ranging from maintaining irrigation systems to resisting oppressive governments and fighting foreign invaders. Active today in the Red River delta and elsewhere in Vietnam are many agrarian associations.

What can be concluded is that collective farming cannot be sustained unless certain political conditions are met. The same conclusion can probably be made about other common-use organizations, such as cooperatives in which people farm on their own but share water, equipment, or other resources. Vietnam's experience with collective cooperatives supports other studies' findings that if common-use agrarian organizations fail to meet conditions regarding trust, commitment, monitoring, and governance, they will not be durable. It takes time and nurturing to achieve these requirements. Knowing this, Vietnamese authorities started out to develop collective farming gradually. But they did not continue that approach. Nor did they allow people to leave cooperatives or develop their own forms of cooperation. Had the collective cooperatives in Vietnam remained small—

4. *Dai Doan Ket*, 9 October 1985, 7.

each corresponding to a neighborhood or a hamlet or at most to a village—their chances for durability would probably have increased. But even many small collective cooperatives had problems, as evidence for the early 1960s shows. And in 1980–1981, many large cooperatives divided into smaller ones yet still were not sustainable. The requirements for durable common-use organizations are entwined, and it is difficult to isolate one from the rest. If pressed, however, to identify which of the ones examined in this study was most deficient in Vietnam's collective cooperatives, I would say governance. Intervention from higher authorities frequently pushed villagers in directions counterproductive to viable cooperation, and in many places dishonest and corrupt local officials violated people's trust and sapped whatever commitment villagers had made to collective farming.

# *Appendix 1*

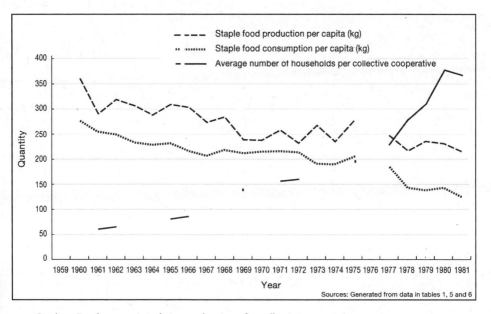

*Graph 1.* Food per capita relative to the size of a collective cooperative.

Table 1. Food production in the Red River delta and all of northern Vietnam, 1939, 1954–1994

| | Staple foods (incl. paddy) | | | | | | | | Paddy only | | | | | | | |
|---|---|---|---|---|---|---|---|---|---|---|---|---|---|---|---|---|
| | Area planted (1,000 ha.) | | Production (1,000 metric tons, paddy equivalent) | | Yield (metric tons, paddy equivalent per ha.) | | Production per capita (kg paddy equivalent) | | Area planted (1,000 ha.) | | Production (1,000 metric tons) | | Yield (1,000 metric tons) | | Production per capita (kg) | |
| Year | North | RRD | North | RRD | North | RRD | North | RRD | North | RRD | North | RRD | North | RRD | North | RRD |
| 1939 | 2,240 | | 2,713 | | 1.21 | | 211 | | | | 2,472 | | | | | |
| 1955 | 2,402 | | 3,759 | | 1.56 | | 277 | | 2,066 | 937 | 3,304 | 1,500 | 1.60 | 1.60 | 243 | |
| 1956 | 2,607 | | 4,738 | | 1.82 | | 337 | | 2,214 | | 4,128 | | 1.86 | | 294 | |
| 1957 | 2,433 | | 4,293 | | 1.76 | | 296 | | 2,136 | | 3,859 | | 1.81 | | 266 | |
| 1958 | 2,474 | | 4,839 | | 1.96 | | 322 | | 2,189 | | 4,454 | | 2.03 | | 296 | |
| 1959 | 2,547 | | 5,596 | | 2.20 | | 360 | | 2,230 | | 5,056 | | 2.27 | | 325 | |
| 1960 | 2,625 | 1,064 | 4,698 | 1,971 | 1.79 | 1.85 | 292 | 259 | 2,268 | 990 | 4,177 | 1,854 | 1.84 | 1.87 | 259 | |
| 1961 | 2,882 | | 5,201 | | 1.80 | | 318 | 289 | 2,390 | 1,030 | 4,393 | 2,062 | 1.84 | 2.00 | 269 | |
| 1962 | 2,921 | | 5,173 | | 1.77 | | 307 | 273 | 2,406 | 1,021 | 4,388 | 2,042 | 1.82 | 2.00 | 260 | |
| 1963 | 2,949 | | 5,013 | | 1.70 | | 288 | 262 | 2,360 | 995 | 4,112 | 1,921 | 1.74 | 1.93 | 236 | |
| 1964 | 3,075 | | 5,515 | | 1.79 | | 308 | 280 | 2,434 | 1,027 | 4,424 | 2,049 | 1.82 | 2.00 | 247 | |
| 1965 | 3,012 | 1,132 | 5,562 | 2,340 | 2.18 | 2.07 | 304 | 288 | 2,398 | 1,007 | 4,547 | 2,093 | 1.90 | 2.08 | 249 | |
| 1966 | 3,011 | | 5,100 | | 1.69 | | 274 | 271 | 2,386 | | 4,126 | | 1.73 | | 222 | |
| 1967 | 2,846 | | 5,398 | | 1.90 | | 284 | 292 | 2,190 | 946 | 4,291 | 2,222 | 1.96 | 2.35 | 226 | |
| 1968 | 2,661 | 974 | 4,629 | 1,934 | 1.74 | 1.98 | 239 | | 2,080 | 851 | 3,706 | 1,691 | 1.78 | 1.99 | 192 | |
| 1969 | 2,674 | | 4,709 | | 1.76 | | 237 | | 2,151 | 913 | 3,907 | 1,883 | 1.82 | 2.06 | 197 | |
| 1970 | 2,722 | 1,028 | 5,279 | 2,384 | 1.94 | 2.32 | 257 | 251 | 2,213 | 935 | 4,453 | 2,190 | 2.01 | 2.34 | 217 | |
| 1971 | 2,580 | 908 | 4,921 | 2,106 | 1.91 | 2.32 | 233 | | 2,066 | 826 | 4,123 | 1,936 | 2.00 | 2.35 | 195 | |
| 1972 | 2,698 | 998 | 5,742 | 2,541 | 2.13 | 2.54 | 267 | | 2,195 | 921 | 4,921 | 2,377 | 2.24 | 2.58 | 229 | |
| 1973 | 2,558 | 956 | 5,190 | 2,276 | 2.03 | 2.38 | 236 | | 2,088 | 878 | 4,468 | 2,135 | 2.14 | 2.43 | 204 | |
| 1974 | 2,747 | 1,018 | 6,277 | 2,920 | 2.29 | 2.87 | 276 | | 2,268 | 951 | 5,460 | 2,772 | 2.41 | 2.91 | 242 | |
| 1975 | | | | | | | | | | | | | | | | |

| | | | | | | | | | | | | | | | |
|---|---|---|---|---|---|---|---|---|---|---|---|---|---|---|---|
| 1976 | 2,932 | 1,163 | 6,392 | 3,131 | 2.18 | 2.69 | 247 | 273 | 2,384 | 1,060 | 5,458 | 2,903 | 2.29 | 2.78 | | |
| 1977 | 3,008 | 1,179 | 5,748 | 2,602 | 1.91 | 2.21 | 218 | 231 | 2,327 | 1,055 | 4,646 | 2,356 | 2.00 | 2.23 | | |
| 1978 | 3,236 | 1,218 | 6,209 | 2,766 | 1.92. | 2.27 | 235 | 241 | 2,426 | 1,054 | 4,750 | 2,390 | 1.96 | 2.27 | | |
| 1979 | 3,237 | 1,264 | 6,258 | 2,897 | 1.93 | 2.29 | 231 | 246 | 2,440 | 1,053 | 4,879 | 2,461 | 2.02 | 2.34 | | |
| 1980 | 3,196 | 1,174 | 5,964 | 2,692 | 1.87 | 2.29 | 215 | 223 | 2,306 | 937 | 4,371 | 2,145 | 1.90 | 2.29 | | |
| 1981 | 3,358 | 1,286 | 7,038 | 3,243 | 2.10 | 2.52 | 246 | 263 | 2,481 | 1,053 | 5,401 | 2,727 | 2.18 | 2.59 | | |
| 1982 | 3,301 | 1,245 | 7,714 | 3,602 | 2.34 | 2.89 | 264 | 286 | 2,495 | 1,055 | 6,170 | 3,158 | 2.47 | 2.99 | | |
| 1983 | 3,202 | 1,207 | 7,450 | 3,440 | 2.33 | 2.85 | 252 | 269 | 2,476 | 1,054 | 6,174 | 3,128 | 2.49 | 2.96 | | |
| 1984 | 3,162 | 1,187 | 7,474 | 3,271 | 2.36 | 2.76 | 247 | 252 | 2,471 | 1,048 | 6,200 | 3,003 | 2.51 | 2.86 | | |
| 1985 | 3,188 | 1,185 | 7,593 | 3,387 | 2.38 | 2.86 | 247 | 255 | 2,502 | 1,052 | 6,292 | 3,092 | 2.51 | 2.94 | | |
| 1986 | 3,146 | 1,196 | 7,688 | 3,290 | 2.44 | 2.75 | 246 | 244 | 2,442 | 1,037 | 6,263 | 2,929 | 2.56 | 2.82 | | |
| 1987 | 3,170 | 1,215 | 7,620 | 3,433 | 2.40 | 2.82 | 239 | 250 | 2,450 | 1,041 | 6,075 | 2,955 | 2.48 | 2.84 | | |
| 1988 | 3,303 | 1,288 | 8,369 | 3,994 | 2.53 | 3.10 | 257 | 288 | 2,465 | 1,050 | 6,709 | 3,455 | 2.72 | 3.29 | | |
| 1989 | 3,312 | 1,289 | 8,955 | 4,289 | 2.70 | 3.32 | 268 | 314 | 2,481 | 1,058 | 7,275 | 3,744 | 2.93 | 3.54 | | |
| 1990 | 3,224 | 1,247 | 8,448 | 4,101 | 2.62 | 3.29 | 255 | 294 | 2,484 | 1,058 | 6,962 | 3,618 | 2.80 | 3.42 | 210 | 290 |
| 1991 | 3,301 | 1,263 | 7,834 | 3,457 | 2.37 | 2.74 | 231 | 256 | 2,510 | 1,014 | 6,258 | 3,038 | 2.49 | 3.00 | 185 | 229 |
| 1992 | 3,398 | 1,236 | 9,701 | 4,693 | 2.85 | 3.80 | 271 | 346 | 2,522 | 1,025 | 7,885 | 4,102 | 3.13 | 4.00 | 227 | 302 |
| 1993 | 3,391 | 1,233 | 10,798 | 5,388 | 3.18 | 4.37 | 286 | 371 | 2,519 | 1,033 | 8,973 | 4,843 | 3.56 | 4.69 | 253 | 351 |
| 1994 | 3,338 | 1,209 | | | | | | | 2,507 | 1,027 | 8,242 | 4,121 | 3.29 | 4.01 | 228 | 293 |

*Note:* Blank cells mean no available data.

*Sources:* Figures are taken or calculated from TCTK, *Bao Cao Phan Tich*, 7; TCTK, "Nhung Chi Tieu, NN, 1955–1967" [GSO, "Agriculture, 1955–1967"], 1968, tables 59 and 169 (P TCTK, hs 760, vv); TCTK, *12 Nam Phat Trien*, 94, 95, 107–11, 122, 123, 125, 133, 136; TCTK, *Nien Giam Thong Ke 1975*, 216–18, 220, 222, 224; Vu Nong Nghiep, *So Lieu*, 87, 117–23, 126–51; TCTK, *Nien Giam Thong Ke 1993*, 29; TCTK, *Nien Giam Thong Ke 1995*, 85, 87, 89.

Table 2. Labor exchange groups in northern Vietnam, 1955–1960

| Year | Number of groups | Average number households per group | Percentage of all agricultural households in the groups | | |
| | | | All groups | "Regular" groups | "Work point" groups |
| --- | --- | --- | --- | --- | --- |
| End 1955 | 153,000 | 7.1 | 40 | | |
| End 1956 | 190,200 | 7.1 | 50 | | |
| Mid-1957 | 72,000 | | 19[a] | | |
| End 1957 | 100,900 | 5.9 | 22 | 2 | |
| End 1958 | 244,400 | 7.3 | 66 | 21 | 8 |
| April 1959 | 249,025 | | 69 | 26 | 11 |
| End 1959 | 97,600 | 10.6 | 38 | | |
| End 1960 | 12,971[b] | 9.8 | 5 | | |

[a] Calculated by extrapolation.
[b] Incomplete count.
Notes: Blank cells mean no information available.
Sources: TCTK, 12 Nam Phat Trien, 59; TCTK, "Nhung Chi Tieu, NN, 1955–1967" [GSO, "Agriculture, 1955–1967"], 1968, table 25 (P TCTK, hs 760, vv); Tran Van Dai, BCTNT TU, "BC TH, HTH, San Xuat 6 thang, 1959" [Tran Van Dai, RAC, "Cooperativization, half of 1959"], 30 July 1959, 1 (P UBKHNN, hs 1258, vv); and Vickerman, Fate, 126–27.

Table 3. Agricultural collective cooperatives in northern Vietnam, 1955–1960

| | Number | Percentage of agricultural households | Percentage of cultivated land | Average size | |
| | | | | Households | Hectares |
| --- | --- | --- | --- | --- | --- |
| By Year | | | | | |
| End 1955 | 10[a] | | | | |
| End 1956 | 42 | | | | |
| Mid 1957 | 33 | | | 13 | 10 |
| Mid 1958 | 134 | | | | |
| End 1958 | 4,720[b] | 5 | 5 | 26 | 17 |
| Mid 1959 | 16,150 | 22 | | 35 | |
| End 1959 | 28,840 | 45 | 41 | 43 | 25 |
| End 1960 | 40,420 | 86 | 68 | 59 | 34 |
| By region | | | | | |
| Mountainous | 8,190 | 66 | | | |
| Midlands | 4,680 | 91 | | | |
| Delta | 16,390 | 89 | 80 | | |
| Zone 4 | 110,160 | 88 | | | |

[a] Includes four that survived the war against the French and six experimental ones that the government established in 1955.
[b] Figures from end of 1958 through 1960 are rounded.
Sources: "BCTK CT Xay Dung Thi Diem HTX SXNN, du thao" ["Experimental cooperatives"], n.d. [circa September 1957], 1–2 (P UBKHNN, hs 616, tt); BCHTU, DLDVN, "NQ, Hoi Nghi Trung Uong, lan thu 16," 1; Cuc Thong Ke TU, "So Lieu Dieu Tra HTHNN 1959 [Central Statistics Office, "Agricultural cooperativization, 1959"], 1959, table 1 (P UBKHNN, hs 1258, vv); Tran Van Dai, BCTNT TU, "BC TH, HTH, San Xuat 6 thang, 1959" [Tran Van Dai, RAC, "Cooperativization, half of 1959"], 30 July 1959, 1 (P UBKHNN, hs 1258, vv); TCTK, "Nhung Chi Tieu, NN, 1955–1967" [GSO, "Agriculture, 1955–1967"], 1968, tables 27, 29, and 30 (P TCTK, hs 760, vv); TCTK, Bao Cao Phan Tich, 9; and Vu Nong Nghiep, So Lieu, 60.

Table 4. Proportion of northern Vietnam agrarian households in collective cooperatives, 1960–1981 (rounded to nearest whole percentage)

| Region or province | 1960 | 1961 | 1962 | 1963 | 1964 | 1965 | 1968 | 1970 | 1971 | 1976 | 1977 | 1978 | 1979 | 1980 | 1981 |
|---|---|---|---|---|---|---|---|---|---|---|---|---|---|---|---|
| Entire north | 86 | 89 | 86 | 85 | 85 | 90 | 95 | 96 | 96 | 93 | 93 | 95 | 97 | 97 | 96 |
| Red River delta | 89 | 91 | 87 | 86 | 85 | 89 | 95 | 96 | 97 | 99 | 99 | 99 | 99 | 99 | 99 |
| Hanoi | 87 | 94 | 81 | 89 | 89 | 94 | 97 | 98 | 98 | 100 | 99 | 98 | 98 | 99 | 99 |
| Ha Nam Ninh | | | | | | | | | | 98 | 99 | 99 | 99 | 99 | 99 |
| Nam Ha | 88 | 91 | 89 | 92 | 88 | 83 | 94 | 96 | 97 | | | | | | |
| Ninh Binh | 89 | 93 | 90 | 79 | 89 | 94 | 97 | 99 | 99 | | | | | | |
| Ha Son Binh | | | | | | | | | | 100 | 100 | 99 | 99 | 99 | 100 |
| Ha Tay | 91 | 91 | 88 | 83 | 81 | 86 | 95 | 97 | 97 | | | | | | |
| Hai Duong | 91 | 94 | 94 | 94 | 91 | 93 | | | | | | | | | |
| Hai Hung | | | | | | | 97 | 98 | 98 | 99 | 100 | 100 | 100 | 100 | 100 |
| Hung Yen | 92 | 92 | 87 | 88 | 86 | 90 | 93 | 93 | 94 | 97 | 98 | 98 | 98 | 99 | 99 |
| Hai Phong | 84 | 87 | 88 | 82 | 84 | 90 | 93 | 94 | 94 | 99 | 99 | 100 | 100 | 100 | 100 |
| Thai Binh | 85 | 87 | 77 | 77 | 78 | 86 | 96 | 97 | 97 | 99 | 99 | 99 | 99 | 99 | 98 |
| Midlands[a] | 91 | 92 | 89 | 88 | 93 | 94 | | | | | | | | | |
| Phu Tho | 89 | 94 | 95 | 96 | 93 | 96 | | | | | | | | | |
| Vinh Phu | | | | | | | 99 | 99 | 99 | 100 | 100 | 100 | 99 | 99 | 98 |
| Vinh Phuc | 96 | 96 | 95 | 95 | 96 | 97 | | | | | | | | | |
| Zone 4 | 88 | 91 | 90 | 90 | 90 | 92 | 96 | 97 | 98 | 86 | 85 | 89 | 96 | 96 | 97 |
| Mountain areas | 66 | 75 | 72 | 70 | 73 | 79 | 91 | 89 | 89 | 82 | 83 | 85 | 86 | 87 | 85 |

*Note:* No data available for missing years.

[a] Incomplete list of provinces in midlands.

*Sources:* TCTK, "So Lieu 5 Nam HTX 1960–1965" [GSO, "Cooperatives, 1960–1965"], February 1966, table 3 (P TCTK, hs 661, vv); TCTK, *12 Nam Phat Trien,* 561; Vu Nong Nghiep, *So Lieu,* 36–38.

Table 5. Consumption of staple and other food by collective cooperative peasants in northern Vietnam, 1959–1974, 1976–1980 (average per person, per month)

| Year | Staple food [luong thuc] (paddy equivalent, kg) | Paddy (kg) | % of all staple food | Meat (kg) | Fish, shrimp (kg) | Eggs (no.) | Vegetables (kg) | Fish sauce, soy sauce (liter) |
|------|------|------|------|------|------|------|------|------|
| 1959 | 23.0 | 20.7 | 90 | 0.48 | 0.48 | | | 0.13 |
| 1960 | 21.3 | 20.5 | 96 | 0.44 | 0.38 | 0.41 | 2.4 | 0.15 |
| 1961 | 20.9 | 18.3 | 87 | 0.46 | 0.42 | 0.46 | 2.6 | 0.22 |
| 1962 | 19.5 | 17.5 | 90 | 0.51 | 0.47 | 0.42 | 3.0 | 0.16 |
| 1963 | 19.1 | 16.5 | 86 | 0.52 | 0.42 | 0.43 | 3.2 | 0.22 |
| 1964 | 19.4 | 16.0 | 82 | 0.44 | 0.34 | 0.42 | 3.4 | 0.18 |
| 1965 | 18.1 | 15.9 | 88 | 0.46 | 0.40 | 0.40 | 3.3 | 0.16 |
| 1966 | 17.2 | 15.0 | 87 | 0.40 | 0.34 | 0.34 | 2.9 | 0.19 |
| 1967 | 18.2 | 14.8 | 81 | 0.40 | 0.29 | 0.39 | 3.4 | 0.30 |
| 1968 | 17.6 | 14.9 | 85 | 0.42 | 0.38 | 0.54 | 3.9 | 0.33 |
| 1969 | 17.9 | 14.5 | 81 | 0.46 | 0.33 | 0.51 | 3.5 | 0.30 |
| 1970 | 18.1 | 15.6 | 86 | 0.56 | 0.32 | 0.52 | 3.9 | 0.34 |
| 1971 | 17.8 | 15.8 | 89 | 0.46 | 0.36 | 0.47 | 3.9 | 0.31 |
| 1972 | 15.9 | 14.3 | 90 | | | | | |
| 1973 | 15.9 | 14.3 | 90 | | | | | |
| 1974 | 17.2 | 16.1 | 94 | | | | | |
| 1976 | 15.4 | | | | | | | |
| 1977 | 12.0 | | | | | | | |
| 1978 | 11.6 | | | | | | | |
| 1979 | 11.9 | | | | | | | |
| 1980 | 10.4 | | | | | | | |

Note: Blank cells mean no available data; and no data for 1975.

Sources: TCTK, "Nhung Chi Tieu, NN, 1955–1967" [GSO, "Agriculture, 1955–1967"], 1968, table 290 (P TCTK, hs 760, vv); TCTK, 12 Nam Phat Trien, 590; BQLHTXNN, UBNNTU, "BC, Mot So Net, HTX SXNN, 1975" [ACMC, CAC, "Major features of cooperatives"], 10 February 1976, 14 (P UBNNTU, hs 160, vv); "Sau 30 Nam," 36.

Table 6. Households per agricultural collective cooperative and annual production per capita in northern Vietnam, 1959–1980

| Year | Entire North | | | Red River delta | | | Vinh Phu (Vinh Phuc and Phu Tho) | | |
|---|---|---|---|---|---|---|---|---|---|
| | Av. number of households per collective cooperative | Staple food production per capita (kg) | Staple food consumption per capita (kg) | Av. number of households per collective cooperative | Staple food production per capita (kg) | Staple food consumption per capita (kg) | Av. number of households per collective cooperative | Staple food production per capita (kg) | Staple food consumption per capita (kg) |
| 1959 | 60 | 360 | 276 | 77 | 259 | | 80 | 336 | |
| 1960 | 65 | 292 | 255 | 89 | 289 | 264 | 89 | | 288 |
| 1961 | | 318 | 250 | | 273 | | | | |
| 1962 | | 307 | 234 | | 262 | | | | |
| 1963 | | 288 | 229 | | | | | | |
| 1964 | 80 | 308 | 232 | 123 | 280 | 228 | 115 | | 264 |
| 1965 | 85 | 304 | 217 | 139 | 288 | | 124 | 362 | |
| 1966 | | 274 | 207 | | 271 | 216 | | | 204 |
| 1967 | | 284 | 219 | | 292 | 220 | 207 | | 228 |
| 1968 | 138 | 239 | 211 | 299 | | | | | |
| 1969 | | 237 | 215 | | | | | | |
| 1970 | 156 | 257 | 217 | 321 | 251 | | 216 | | |
| 1971 | 160 | 233 | 214 | 328 | | | 218 | | |
| 1972 | | 267 | 191 | | | | | | |
| 1973 | | 236 | 191 | | | | | | |
| 1974 | | 276 | 206 | | | | | | |
| 1975 | 199 | | | | | | | | |
| 1976 | 229 | 247 | 185 | 528 | 273 | | 340 | 253 | |
| 1977 | 278 | 218 | 144 | 732 | 231 | | 557 | 214 | |
| 1978 | 310 | 235 | 139 | 830 | 241 | | 609 | 225 | |
| 1979 | 378 | 231 | 143 | 918 | 246 | | 583 | 208 | |
| 1980 | 368 | 215 | 125 | 898 | 223 | | 589 | 189 | |

*Note:* Blank cells mean no available data.

*Sources:* TCTK, "Nhung Chi Tieu, NN, 1955–1967" [GSO, "Agriculture, 1955–1967"], 1968, tables 59 and 290 (P TCTK, hs 760, vv); TCTK, "So Lieu, TH SX, Phan Phoi, LT, Mien Bac," [GSO, "Staple foods, production, distribution], 30 March 1969, table 45 (P TCTK, hs 761, vv); TCTK, 12 *Nam Phat Trien*, 557, 559, 590; Vu Nong Nghiep, So *Lieu*, 73, 87, 125–26; TCTK, *Tinh Hinh Phat Trien*, 110–11; BQLHTXNN, UBNNTU, "BC, Mot So Net, HTX SXNN, 1975" [ACMC, CAC, "Major features of cooperatives"], 10 February 1976, 14 (P UBNNTU, hs 160, vv); "Sau 30 Nam," 36.

Table 7. Income sources of an average collective cooperative member

| Year | Collective cooperative[a] | Private | | Total |
| --- | --- | --- | --- | --- |
| | | Family[b] | Other[c] | |
| 1961 | 39% | 50% | 11% | 61% |
| 1962 | 38 | 55 | 6 | 61 |
| 1963 | 38 | 54 | 8 | 62 |
| 1964 | 40 | 52 | 9 | 61 |
| 1965 | 39 | 52 | 9 | 61 |
| 1966 | 36 | 53 | 10 | 63 |
| 1967 | 36 | 54 | 10 | 64 |
| 1968 | 33 | 56 | 11 | 67 |
| 1970 | 35 | 54 | 12 | 66 |
| 1971 | 30 | 52 | 19 | 71 |
| 1973 | 34 | 53 | 13 | 66 |
| 1974 | 36 | 53 | 11 | 64 |
| 1975 | 35 | 54 | 11 | 65 |
| 1976 | 35 | 54 | 11 | 65 |
| 1977 | 29 | 61 | 10 | 71 |
| 1978 | 29 | 61 | 10 | 71 |
| 1979 | 24 | 67 | 9 | 76 |
| 1980 | 28 | 61 | 10 | 71 |
| 1981 | 24 | 65 | 11 | 76 |

Note: All 1961–1975 data are for northern Vietnam only; 1976–1981 data probably are as well, although the sources do not make this explicit. Percentages are calculated from figures for net yearly or monthly income of an average collective member according to surveys done by officials in northern Vietnam. Due to rounding, the sum of figures for collective and private sources may not equal 100. No data are available for missing years.

[a] Collective cooperative income is the monetary value of all grain, fruits, vegetables, and other commodities, as well as cash earned from collective work.

[b] Family income includes the monetary value of what a family produces for itself and money earned by selling what it produced minus production costs.

[c] Other income includes payment for work done for someone else, interest earnings, proceeds from selling personal possessions, and benefits received from elsewhere (such as relatives and the state).

Sources: TCTK, "Nhung Chi Tieu, NN, 1955–1967" [GSO, "Agriculture, 1955–1967"], 1968, table 287 (P TCTK, hs 760, vv); TCTK, 12 Nam Phat Trien, 586; TCTK, "Nhung So Lieu, Doi Song Nong Dan, Mien Bac" [GSO, "Lives of collectivized peasants"], September 1967, 14 (P TCTK, hs 2871, vv); TCTK, Tinh Hinh Phat Trien, 180; Fforde, Agrarian Question, 218.

Table 8. What is left for an average paddy producer in Red River delta collective cooperatives prior to and during the product contract arrangement

| Prior to product contracts, 1978–1980 | (1) Av. yield (kg/*sao*/season)[a] | (2) 55% of (1) for distribution[b] | Producer gets (3) 52% of (2)[c] |
|---|---|---|---|
| | 83 | 46 | 24 |

During product contracts, 1984–1985

Method 1

| | | | Producer gets | | |
| | Scenarios[d] | Quota[e] (kg/*sao*/season) | Amount beyond quota (kg) | From work points (15–20% of quota)[f] | Total (kg) |
|---|---|---|---|---|---|
| A. Meets but does not exceed quota | | 104 | 0 | 16–21 | 16–21 |
| B. Exceeds quota by 5% | | 99 | 5 | 15–20 | 20–25 |
| C. Exceeds quota by 12.5% | | 93 | 12 | 14–18 | 26–30 |
| D. Exceeds quota by 20% | | 87 | 17 | 13–17 | 30–34 |

Method 2

| | | | Producer gets | | |
| | Scenarios[d] | Quota[g] (kg/*sao*/season) | Amount beyond quota (kg) | From work points (15–20% of quota)[f] | Total (kg) |
|---|---|---|---|---|---|
| A. Meets but does not exceed quota | | 91 | 0 | 14–18 | 14–18 |
| | | 95 | 0 | 14–19 | 14–19 |
| B. Exceeds quota by 5% | | 91 | 4 | 14–18 | 18–22 |
| | | 95 | 5 | 14–19 | 19–24 |
| C. Exceeds quota by 12.5% | | 91 | 11 | 14–18 | 25–29 |
| | | 95 | 12 | 14–19 | 26–31 |
| D. Exceeds quota by 20% | | 91 | 18 | 14–18 | 32–36 |
| | | 95 | 19 | 14–19 | 33–38 |

[a] Calculated from data in appendix 1, table 1, rounded to nearest whole number.
[b] The other 45 percent went to production costs. Nguyen Sinh Cuc, *Thuc Trang*, 25.
[c] Based on survey results reported in TCTK, *Bao Cao Phan Tich*, 108.
[d] According to survey data circa mid-1980s, 80 percent of villagers with product contracts (*khoan san pham*) reached or exceeded their contracted production quotas. For villagers exceeding the quota, the typical excess was 5 to 20 percent beyond the contracted yield. TCTK, *Bao Cao Phan Tich*, 50; and Nguyen Sinh Cuc, *Nong Nghiep*, 31.
[e] The amount equals the average paddy yield in the Red River delta for 1984 and 1985 (calculated from data in appendix 1, table 1) divided by the proportion by which the quota was exceeded in each of the scenarios and rounded to nearest whole number.
[f] The 15–20 percent range is based on several reports about particular villages and provinces in the Red River delta and the situation generally in northern Vietnam. Examples of those reports are Tinh Hoa Binh, *Lich Su Phong Trao*, 254; TCTK, *Bao Cao Phan Tich*, 51–52; and a statement from the head of the Communist Party's central office for agriculture published in *Nhan Dan*, 4 December 1987, 3.
[g] A quota is calculated by the formula specified in official regulations issued to cooperative managerial boards: add approximately 10 to 15 percent to the average yield during the previous three to five years. Used for these scenarios is the average paddy yield in the Red River delta in 1978–1980 (83 kilograms per *sao* per season). For the regulations, see BQLHTXNNTU, *Khoan San Pham*, 42; and BNN, "Bao Cao Viec Thuc Hien," 5.

# Appendix 2
## Distribution to Collective Cooperative Members

Each collective cooperative's produce was divided among the state, the cooperative organization, and the members.

The cooperative organization needed some of what cooperative members produced to pay for fertilizers, equipment, irrigation, and so forth, and to compensate the chairperson, other officials, mechanics, storehouse managers, and brigade leaders. Cooperatives were also supposed to run primary schools, day care centers, and health clinics, as well as to keep funds available for future investments (*quy tich luy*) and social welfare (*quy cong ich*). Government agencies tried to regulate these expenditures and funds. Actual amounts, however, for welfare and investment were usually lower than guidelines .required, while production expenses were often higher. Government and party offices repeatedly implored cooperative leaders to reduce production costs by eliminating waste (*lang phi*).

Distribution to members was supposed to reward efficient work and penalize poor work, minimize inequalities, and provide for young, elderly, sickly, and other disadvantaged members.[1] The distribution typically started with each member's production brigade. From the early 1960s, national authorities pressed cooperative leaders to implement the "three contracts"

1. The following discussion is based on interviews with villagers and former cooperative officials and on written materials. Some of the latter are Pham Cong, *De Quan Ly Tot*, 38–54; Tran Ngoc Canh, *Cai Tien*, 39–59; Cuong Pham, "Management"; Thu Tuong Chinh Phu, "Chi Thi, 275-TTg, CT LT, Triet De QD so 75-CP" [prime minister, "Instruction 275, regarding staple crops, implementing decision 75"], 1 November 1974, in *Cong Bao*, 15 November 1974, 266–68; Vo Thuc Dong, Chu Nhiem UBNNTU, "Thong Tu, Phan Phoi LT, HTXSXNN" [Vo Thuc Dong, chairperson, Central Agriculture Commission, "Distributing staple foods in cooperatives"], 30 April 1975, 1–6 (P UBNNTU, hs 161, vv).

system (*ba khoan*). The three contracts comprised: the amount to be produced; the amount of inputs (seed, fertilizer, draft animals, plows, irrigation, and so on); and the number of workdays. The managerial board and brigade leaders drew up these contracts each season. A brigade that fulfilled the contracts or produced more with fewer inputs and workdays would be rewarded. If a brigade failed to fulfill the contracts—for example, if it produced too little or exceeded the contracted amount of inputs and workdays—it would be penalized. The rewards and penalties were passed on to members in the value set for each of their workdays.

The value of a workday in any particular season could vary from one brigade to another within the same collective cooperative. Usually, however, such differences within a cooperative were slight. A brigade that produced more for a lower cost and fewer workdays than was contracted received 5–85 percent of the difference, depending on the size of that difference and on what the managerial board allowed. The board often took some of the difference to augment the cooperative's funds, pay other expenses, and meet its obligations to government agencies. Brigades frequently failed to fulfill their contracts. Brigades that did not come within 10 percent of a contract were supposed to pay a fine in workdays, paddy (or other produce), or a combination of both. The fine was not supposed to exceed 50 percent of the shortfall.

Leaders in a cooperative could—and frequently did—change a brigade's composition (number of households, amount of land, and so on). The main reason was to maintain relative equality among the brigades and prevent one brigade and its members from becoming significantly better or worse off than the others. Otherwise, a brigade that consistently did better than its contracts required would accumulate surpluses, which was against the rules, and/or its members would become much better off than others in the cooperative, which went against the Communist Party government's effort to minimize inequalities.

The amount of paddy or other collectively produced goods that a member received was based on three components.[2] The calculation of that amount was a complicated affair. The first component was the number of work points (*cong diem*) a member had earned. A certain number of points, usually ten, equaled one workday (*ngay cong*). The value of each workday within a brigade equaled the amount of produce available for distribution to its members divided by the total workdays that had been expended. The

2. The system is similar to what Jean Oi reports in *State and Peasant*, 36–41, about distribution in China's collective farms in the 1960s–1970s.

second component was the amount to which a person was entitled (*ty le dinh suat giu nguyen*). This varied over time and from place to place. Cooperative and brigade leaders set it by using national guidelines (which also prescribed upper and lower limits) and dividing the amount of produce available for distribution by the number of people. Each person was entitled to something. How much depended on age, type of worker, number of workdays, and other criteria.[3] A youngster in school, for instance, was typically entitled to one ration (*dinh suat*) but one not yet in school was entitled to less, for example, 60 percent of a ration. A "primary worker" (*lao dong chinh*) was entitled to more than a single ration, for example, 160 percent; a "secondary worker" (*lao dong phu*) received less but still more than one ration, for example, 120 percent. A primary worker who had, say, 200 workdays was entitled to more than a primary worker who, for instance, had only 160 or 170 work days.[4] The third component was an adjustment to "harmonize" (*dieu hoa*) what everyone received. The purpose of this and the second component was to take into account how well a member had worked while also paying attention to equality and assuring that everyone received something. An additional rationale behind the third component was the government's effort to control the marketing of paddy and other staple foods.

To illustrate the use of these three components, let us consider accounts of the process in Da Ton, a subdistrict in rural Hanoi, in the late 1960s–early 1970s. Take, for instance, one villager who was a primary worker. (1) At the end of one paddy season, she had 80 workdays to her credit. Within her brigade that season, a workday equaled 0.80 kilograms. Hence, she had earned 64 kilograms of paddy. (2) The ration at that time was 50 kilograms of paddy (10 kg per month for 5 months). As a primary worker, she was entitled to 150 percent of a ration, or 75 kilograms. But the value of her workdays amounted to only 64 kilograms, leaving a difference of 11 kilograms. (3) A primary worker with 110 workdays was permitted 90 percent of that difference. The woman, having only 80 workdays, was permitted, according to local regulations at the time, 70 percent of that difference, or 7.70 kilograms. This amount she was entitled to purchase from the cooperative's warehouse at the official price. After selling a pig her family had

3. In the early 1960s, men were typically entitled to more than women who did the same or similar work. This may have persisted in some areas but by the late 1960s, gender was not supposed to be a factor.

4. The required number of workdays for female primary workers was usually less than for males. The required number varied over time and, to a lesser extent, from one cooperative to the next.

raised, she was able to make that purchase. Thus, in the end, she ended up with 71.70 kilograms.

Take the case of another female primary worker. (1) She had 110 work-days. In her brigade, each workday was worth 0.82 kilograms of paddy. Hence, she earned 90.20 kilograms. (2) The ration in this case was 53 kilo-grams of paddy. She was entitled to 150 percent of a ration, or 79.50 kilo-grams. Consequently, she had earned 10.70 kilograms *more* than she was entitled to. (3) Harmonization regulations allowed her to keep 20 percent of that excess, or 2.14 kilograms of paddy. She had to sell the remaining 8.56 kilograms to the cooperative warehouse at the official price.

Permission to keep about 20 percent of what had been earned beyond the amount to which an individual was entitled was supposed to encour-age cooperative members to work harder. Regulations did not permit a cooperative member to keep more. Authorities' reasoning seems to have been twofold. First, instead of going to an individual, "excess" paddy earn-ings was to be distributed through cooperatives and markets that sold paddy at official prices (which were low) to people who had too little paddy. This was in line with the Communist Party government's effort to minimize inequality and make grain and other essential foods available at low prices to people in need. Second, by requiring "excess" paddy to be sold to autho-rized buyers, authorities hoped to prevent cooperative members from selling that grain on the "unorganized, free market" (*thi truong khong to chuc, thi truong tu do*), where prices were much higher than official ones. This provision was one of many efforts to control the market for essential commodities.

In a household, people totaled what each member received to see what the whole family would get from collective work. Households with few primary workers often earned less paddy than they were entitled to. For instance, a household in the early 1970s with one primary worker, two sec-ondary workers (including a disabled war veteran), and three young chil-dren had earned 129 kilograms of paddy during a particular season but was entitled to 325 kilograms. After taking into account "harmonization," the household was permitted to acquire an additional 145 kilograms. Using benefits the war veteran received and cash the family earned by other means, the household had enough to purchase on the official market about 110 of those kilograms. At about the same time, another family in Da Ton with three primary and two secondary workers had earned about 60 kilograms more than all household members together were entitled to. The family was permitted to keep 12. It had to sell the rest at the official price.

This was how distribution within collective cooperatives was supposed to take place. Deviations, however, were common over time and from one cooperative to another. As one might imagine, struggles during the distribution process were pervasive.

# *Vietnamese Glossary*

This glossary has the full spelling of Vietnamese names and terms used in the text and notes (but not the source listings themselves). Not included are the few names for which diacritics are unknown (because the sources in which they appeared did not have diacritics).

An Đồng

ăn cắp

ăn cắp công điểm

ăn đong

ăn quả nhớ kẻ trồng cây

ăn trộm

âm ỷ

ba khoán

Ba Vì

Bạch Trữ

ban bí thư

Ban Bí Thư Trung Ương

Ban Công Tác Nông Thôn Trung Ương

ban quản trị

ban vận động

bảo thủ rụt rè

Bát Tràng

Bắc Cạn

Bắc Giang

Bắc Ninh

băn khoăn

bậc công việc

bần cố nông

bần nông

bí thư

bị hút vào

bị nhiễu

bình công chấm điểm

Bình Minh

bình thường

Bình Xuyên

Bộ Chính Trị

Bộ Lương Thực và Thực Phẩm

Bộ Nông Nghiệp

Bộ Văn Hoá

Bùi Phụng

buông lỏng

các quỹ đất

cải tiến quản lý

Cam Thượng

261

cám

Cao Bằng

Cao Bình

cào cỏ khua đục nước

cày gãi bừa chùi

cày quẹt bừa chùi

Cẩm La

Cẩm Phúc

cấy chay

cha chung không ai khóc

chán nản

cháo

cháo loãng

chạy chợ

Châu Giang

chè chén

chi bộ

Chí Đạo

chỉ có xác mà không có hồn

chỉ còn hình thức bên ngoài

chỉ đâu lấy đấy

Chỉ mấy anh em một nhà mà không làm chung được với nhau thì làm thế nào mà có thể giải quyết số đông gia đình làm chung với nhau được?

chỉ thị

Chiêm Hóa

cho gọn chuyện

Chò

choãi ra

chỗ dựa

Chỗ nào làm đông là hợp tác xã mà chỗ nào to tiếng cũng là hợp tác xã.

chống

chống Mỹ cứu Nước

chợ đen

Chu Hữu Quý

chủ nhiệm

chủ tịch

chủ tịch xã

Chử Văn Lâm

Chương Mỹ

Có mồm ăn mà không có ruộng

còng lưng ăn cháo, làm láo ăn cơm

cố gắng

cố nông

Cổ Thanh

công an

công điểm

công khai

Công Ty Vật Tư Nông Nghiệp

cuộc đấu tranh

cường hào

cường hào gian ác

cường hào mới

cứu sống

dân chủ

do phong trào lôi cuốn và thúc đẩy mà tham gia

dỗi

Dũng Tiến

Dương Quốc Cẩm

Đa Tốn

đã đến lúc hết

Đại đa số làm theo vì đảng chúng tôi là đảng cầm quyền, độc quyền lãnh đạo.

Đại Đoàn Kết

Đại Đồng

Đại Hội Đại Biểu Xã Viên

Đại Hội Xã Viên

Đại Kim

Đảng Lao Động Việt Nam

Đảng viên lấy một cây đóm, xã viên sẽ vác cả bó củi.

Đanh Minh

Đào Thế Tuấn

Đào Xuyên

Đạo Đức

Đặng Phong

Đặng Xuân Kháng

đất năm phần trăm
đấu thầu
đấu tranh
đấu tranh giằng co gay gắt
Để hợp tác xã nhỏ còn no, gộp vào hợp
    tác xã to không khéo lại đói.
địa chủ
địa chủ kháng chiến
địa chủ mới
Điện Biên Phủ
điều hoà
điều lệ
Đinh Trung Kiên
Đình Chu
Định Công
định mức lao động
định suất
Đoan Hùng
Đoàn Duy Thành
Đoàn Thiện Thuật
Đoàn Xá
đói
đói gay gắt
Đô Lương
Đồ Sơn
đổi mới
đội
đội chuyên
đội sản xuất
đội trưởng
Đội trưởng yêu nên tốt, ghét nên xấu.
độn
Đông La
Đông Phương
Đông Xá
đồng
đồng chí
Đồng Ích
Đồng Quế
Đồng Văn

Đồng Xuân
đột
Đức Thông
ganh tỵ
gậm, nhấm
Gia Lâm
Gia Lộc
Gia Tân
Giao An
giáp hạt
gò ép
gò ép không được tự do thoải mái
Hà
Hà Bắc
Hà Đông
Hà Nam
Hà Nam Ninh
Hà Nội
Hà Sơn Bình
Hà Tây
Hà Tĩnh
Hải Dương
Hải Hưng
Hải Ninh
Hải Phòng
hậm hực
hầu hết cán bộ, đảng viên cũng đồng tình
    với xã viên, chạy theo lợi nhuận gia
    đình
hầu như tan rã
Hậu Giang
hệ thống hộ khẩu
Hiệp Hoà
hình thức
hoa lợi cho ruộng đất
hoa mầu
Hoà Bình
Hoà Nghĩa
Hoà Thạch
Hoàng Anh

Học Viện Nguyễn Ái Quốc
hợp đồng cây lúa đến người lao động
hợp tác hóa
hợp tác hóa nông nghiệp
hợp tác xã kiểu mới
Hợp tác xã là nhà, xã viên là chủ.
hợp tác xã sản xuất nông nghiệp bậc cao
hợp tác xã sản xuất nông nghiệp bậc thấp
Hồ Chí Minh
hộ khẩu
hội nghị
Hồng Quảng
hống hách
Hùng Tiến
hủy diệt
huyện
Hưng Yên
Hường Ngọc
kèn cựa
khá
khá phổ biến
khá phổ biến và kéo dài
Kháng chiến gắn với hợp tác xã. Không có hợp tác xã sẽ không làm được việc hậu phương và mặt trận.
khảo đất lấy của
Khoan Tế
khoán
khoán chui
khoán đến hộ
khoán gọn
khoán hộ
khoán không đồng bộ
khoán mặc kệ
khoán nửa vời
khoán sản
khoán sản lượng cho hộ
khoán sản phẩm
khoán sản phẩm cho từng hộ
khoán sản phẩm cuối cùng

khoán sản phẩm theo đơn giá-thanh toán gọn
khoán thẳng
khoán trắng
khoán trắng thu tô
khoán trắng tinh
không bắt ép mà hơi bắt ép
không công bằng
không được tự do
không suy nghĩ hơn thiệt
không thực sự phấn khởi
Khu 4
Khu 4 cũ
Khu Lao-Hà-Yên
Khu Tả Ngạn
Khu Thái Mèo
khuyến khích
khuyến khích mạnh mẽ
Kiến An
Kiến Thụy
Kim Bôi
Kim Lan
Kim Ngọc
Kim Ninh
Kim Thái
kinh tế gia đình
kinh tế phụ gia đình
La Phù
làm ẩu
làm thế nào được ăn no mặc ấm
làm tốt ăn cháo, làm láo ăn cơm
làm vụng
lãn công
làng
lãng phí
lao động
lao động chính
lao động phụ
Lao Hà Yên
lạt

lấn chiếm

Lập Thạch

lâu dài

lấy

Lê Duẩn

Lê Đức Thọ

Lê Nhật Quang

Lê Quang Nam

Lê Phước Thọ

Lê Thanh

Lê Thanh Nghị

Lê Thị Ngân

Lê Trọng

Lê Văn

Lê Văn Bích

Lê Văn Bùi

Lê Văn Sinh

Lệ Xá

Liên Bạt

liên hoan

Liên Khu

Liên Sơn

liên thôn

lòng tin

lỏng lẻo

lợi dụng

lúa chiêm

lúa xuân

lười

lương thực

manh mún quá

mặc kệ

mất lòng tin của xã viên

mẫu

Mê Linh

mệnh lệnh

móc ngoặc

mổ mèo lấy cá

Mộ Đạo

Mộc Châu

Mỗi người làm việc bằng hai,
  để cho chủ nhiệm mua đài mua xe.

Mỗi người làm việc bằng ba,
  để cho cán bộ xây nhà xây sân.

mở cửa

mùa đông

mức khoán

Mỹ Đức

Nam Định

Nam Đồng

Nam Hà

Nam Sách

năm đói

năm thước rau xanh bằng vài sào đất của
  hợp tác xã

nâng cao không ngừng

ngày công

ngày công gián tiếp

Ngày làm ít giờ, giờ làm ít việc

nghèo ngang nhau

Nghệ An

Nghệ Tĩnh

nghi ngờ

nghĩa vụ

Nghiêm Xuyên

Ngọc Động

Ngô Đình Diệm

Ngô Văn Dũng

Ngô Văn Khoa

Ngô Văn Tịnh

Ngô Vĩnh Long

Nguyên Giáp

nguyên tắc tự nguyện

Nguyễn Anh Quế

Nguyễn Chí Thanh

Nguyễn Đình Lê

Nguyễn Hữu Tiến

Nguyễn Kim Thư

Nguyễn Nghĩa Biên

Nguyễn Quang Ngọc

Nguyễn Thanh Bình

Nguyễn Thị Mận

Nguyễn Thị Minh Hiền

Nguyễn Thị Thuận

Nguyễn Thị Tuyết

Nguyễn Văn Chính

Nguyễn Văn Linh

Nguyễn Văn Phòng

Người làm kỹ sẽ bị đói vì người làm dối
  sẽ được nhiều điểm

Nhân Dân

Nhân Văn Giai Phẩm

nhìn thẳng vào sự thật

Nho

những con sâu mọt

Ninh Bình

nói thẳng, nói thật

nóng vội

nông dân

Nông Hội

Phạm Thu Lan

Phạm Thu Thủy

Phạm Văn Đồng

Phạm Văn Học

Phan Đại Doãn

Phan Đình Thay

Phan Đình Thế

Phan Huy Lê

Phan Phương Thảo

Phan Văn Hùng

phát canh thu tô

phẩm chất đạo đức

phấn đấu

Phí Văn Ba

phong trào hợp tác hoá nông nghiệp

phổ biến và khá nghiêm trọng

phông

phú nông

Phú Thọ

Phú Xuyên

phụ

Phúc Yên

Phùng Hữu Phú

quản lý dân chủ

Quảng Bình

Quất Lưu

Quốc Hội

quy mô liên xã

quy thóc

quý lắm

quỹ công ích

quỹ đen

quỹ tích lũy

quyền sử dụng

Quỳnh Phụ

rau muống

rầm rộ

rong công phóng điểm

sào

Sơn Công

Sơn Tây

suy bì tị nạnh

sự lãnh đạo

Tả Ngạn

tạ

Tam Canh

Tam Đa

Tam Hưng

tâm lý

Tân Tiến

tấn

tập đoàn sản xuất

tập trung quan liêu-bao cấp

thả nổi

thả trùng quần

Thái Bình

Thái Nguyên

Thái Sơn

tham nhũng

tham ô

tháng làm đủ ngày, ngày làm đủ giờ, giờ
  làm nhiều việc tốt
Thanh Ba
Thanh Hà
Thanh Hoá
Thanh Liệt
Thanh Oai
thành kiến sâu sắc
thắc mắc sôi nổi
Thằng còng làm cho thằng ngay ăn khá
thị trường không tổ chức
thị trường tự do
thiếu
thiếu ăn
thiếu công khai
thiếu dân chủ
thiếu thốn
Thiệu Yên
Thịnh Liệt
Thọ Xuân
thóc
thôn
Thôn Thượng
thông cảm
thông tri
thống nhất nhận định
Thuận Tốn
thuế
Thuyên Quang
thước
Thường Tín
Thượng Lâm
Thượng Trưng
Tích cực công tác có gì hơn những kẻ
  tham ô lười biếng?
tích cực lãnh đạo, tiến bước vững chắc
Tiên Hường
Tiên Lãng
Tiên Thanh
Tiên Tiến

tiên tiến
tiên tiến và khá
Tiến Thắng
tin tưởng
tình cảm
tính tích cực
tỉnh
Tỉnh tấn huyện, huyện tấn xã, xã tấn hợp
  tác xã, hợp tác xã tấn đội, đội tấn xã
  viên
Tổ chức lại sản xuất và cải tiến quản lý
  nông nghiệp
tổ đổi công bình công chấm điểm
tổ đổi công thường xuyên
tổ đổi công từng vụ, từng việc
tổ phó
tổ trưởng
Tôn Thất Quỳnh Du
Tổng Cục Thống Kê
Trại
Trấn Đức
Trần Hùng Sơn
Trần Hữu Dục
trễ nải
Tri Trỉ
trung du
Trung Hà
Trung Lập
trung nông
trung nông dưới
trung nông trên
Trung Tâm Lưu Trữ Quốc Gia
Trung Tâm Nghiên Cứu và Giao Lưu Văn
  Hóa
Trung Yên
Trương Bửu Lâm
Trường Chinh
Tuân Chính
tuồn ra thị trường tự do
Tuyên Quang

tư tưởng riêng lẻ tư hữu
Tứ Lộc
Tứ Trưng
Tử Minh
tự do
Tự Tân
Tương Lai
tỷ lệ định suất giữ nguyên
uất ức
Ủy Ban Hành Chính Khu Tả Ngạn
Ủy Ban Kế Hoạch Nhà Nước
Ủy Ban Kháng Chiến Hành Chính Liên
  Khu
Ủy Ban Nông Nghiệp Trung Ương
Vạn Thái
vào không ra
Văn Nhân
Văn Hoàng
Vân Tảo
Vận dụng rộng rãi hình thức khoán gọn
vận động
vật lộn
Viện Kinh Tế Học
Việt Nam
Việt Trì
Vĩnh Bảo

Vĩnh Lạc
Vĩnh Phú
Vĩnh Phúc
Vĩnh Tường
Võ Minh Giang
Vô Minh Kha
Võ Nguyên Giáp
Võng Xuyên
Vũ Ninh
Vũ Thắng
Vũ Thư
Vụ Trưởng
vườn chè
xã
xếp hàng đi dạo qua ruộng
xói mòn
xóm
Xuân Hoà
Xuân Khánh
Xuân Thủy
Yên Lập
Yên Lỗ
Yên Phú
Yên Sở
Yến
yếu kém

# Selected Places and Terms

Ban:   Committee

Da Ton:   A subdistrict in the district of Gia Lam, rural Hanoi, in which I did interviews with several families and officials in each of its five villages in October 1992, April 1993, January–April 1996, and October 2000. Located about ten kilometers downstream and on the other side of the Red River from Hanoi city, it remains primarily an agricultural community. Other economic activities include pottery making, which a few residents have learned by working for potters in nearby Bat Trang, a famous site for ceramics production.

Dao Duc:   A subdistrict of Binh Xuyen district, Vinh Phuc province, where I interviewed residents in August 2000. It has three villages. The primary occupation of most people is paddy farming.

dong:   Vietnamese currency

Ha Bac:   Province on the northern edge of the Red River delta

Ha Dong:   *See* Red River delta

Ha Nam:   *See* Red River delta

Ha Nam Ninh:   *See* Red River delta

Ha Son Binh:   *See* Red River delta

Ha Tay:   *See* Red River delta

Hai Duong:   *See* Red River delta

Hai Hung:   *See* Red River delta

Hai Phong:   *See* Red River delta

Hoa Binh:   *See* Red River delta

Hung Yen:   *See* Red River delta

Kien An:   *See* Red River delta

Lien Khu 3:   Interzone 3, one of the northern administrative regions of the Democratic Republic of Vietnam's government as it fought the French in the late 1940s. The provinces included Ha Dong, Ha Nam, Hai Duong, Hung Yen, Nam Dinh, Ninh Binh, Thai Binh, and, according to some records, Son Tay and/or Kien An.

*mau*:   Thirty-six hundred square meters of land in northern Vietnam

Nam Dinh:   *See* Red River delta

Nam Ha:   *See* Red River delta

Nghe Tinh:   A province in the southern part of northern Vietnam; it includes Ha Tinh and Nghe An, which have been provinces in their own right at various times.

Nghiem Xuyen:   A subdistrict in Thuong Tin district, Ha Tay province, that I visited in October 1992, May 1993, and May 1996. Located about twenty kilometers south of Hanoi city, it has three villages. Residents' primary economic activity is paddy farming.

Ninh Binh:   *See* Red River delta

paddy:   Unhusked rice (*thoc* in Vietnamese)

Phu Tho:   A midlands province. *See also* Vinh Phu

Quat Luu:   A subdistrict of Binh Xuyen district, Vinh Phuc province, where I interviewed villagers in August 2000. During the collectivization period, it had three villages. In 1999, two of them were separated to form a new subdistrict; hence today Quat Luu is but one village consisting of seven rather scattered hamlets (*xom*). Agriculture is the main occupation of most residents.

Red River delta:   By administrative convention, the region extends from greater Hanoi (the rural areas as well as the city) southeast to the mouth of the river. During the period covered in this book, the configurations and names of delta provinces changed two or three times. Listed here are the provinces as of 1990. In parentheses are names of other provinces that also appear in this book before or after they were included in the larger province. Ha Nam Ninh (includes Ha Nam, Nam Dinh, Nam Ha, and Ninh Binh), Ha Noi (written as Hanoi in this book), Ha Son Binh (includes Ha Dong, Ha Tay, Hoa Binh, and Son Tay), Hai Hung (includes Hai Duong and Hung Yen), Hai Phong (includes Kien An), and Thai Binh.

*sao*:   Three hundred and sixty square meters of land

Son Tay:   *See* Red River delta

staple foods:   *Luong thuc* in Vietnamese; includes paddy and other basic foods such as corn, cassava, and various kinds of potatoes. Its weight is expressed in "paddy equivalents" (*quy thoc*).

subdistrict (*xa*):   Smallest administrative unit, under the district (*huyen*); it usually has two or more villages (*thon*, also *lang*, among other terms). See chap. 1, n. 3 for my translation of *xa*.

Ta Ngan zone (*Khu Ta Ngan*):   An administrative unit in the early 1950s, it included Hai Duong, Hung Yen, Kien An, and Thai Binh provinces

Tam Canh:   A subdistrict in Binh Xuyen district, Vinh Phuc province, where I interviewed villagers in August 2000. In three of its villages, people are primarily farmers. In a fourth, they make clay tiles and bricks.

Thai Binh:   *See* Red River delta

Thanh Hoa:   A province on the southern edge of the Red River delta

*thuoc*:   A measure for area. One *thuoc* of land in northern Vietnam equals twenty-four square meters.

Tien Thang:   A subdistrict of Me Linh district, Vinh Phuc province, where I interviewed villagers in August 2000. Residents in all four of its villages are primarily paddy and vegetable farmers.

ton:   Metric ton, one thousand kilograms

Vietnam Workers' Party:   Name of the Vietnam Communist Party from 1951 until late 1976

Vinh Phu:   A province composed of Vinh Phuc and Phu Tho, which were separate before 1967 and became so again when Vinh Phu was eliminated in 1996

Vinh Phuc:   A province that borders Hanoi to the northwest. Although most of it has physical features similar to provinces in the Red River delta, official reports usually place it in the midlands (*trung du*). *See also* Vinh Phu.

# Abbreviations

| | |
|---|---|
| ACMC | Agricultural Cooperative Management Committee |
| BBT | *Ban Bi Thu*, secretariat |
| BC | *bao cao*, report |
| BCCT | *bao cao cong tac*, assignment or work report |
| BCH | *Ban chap hanh*, Executive Committee |
| BCHTU | *Ban Chap Hanh Trung Uong*, Central Executive Committee |
| BCKQ | *bao cao ket qua*, report on results |
| BCSK | *bao cao so ket*, preliminary report |
| BCTK | *bao cao tong ket*, summary report, review |
| BCTNT | *Ban Cong Tac Nong Thon*, Rural Affairs Committee |
| BLTTP | *Bo Luong Thuc va Thuc Pham*, Ministry of Staple Foods and Food Stuffs |
| BNN | *Bo Nong Nghiep*, Ministry of Agriculture |
| BNNTU | *Ban Nong Nghiep Trung Uong*, Agriculture Committee |
| BQL | *ban quan ly*, management committee |
| BQLHTXNN | *Ban Quan Ly Hop Tac Xa Nong Nghiep*, Agricultural Cooperative Management Committee |
| BQLHTXNNTU | *Ban Quan Ly Hop Tac Xa Nong Nghiep Trung Uong*, Central Agricultural Cooperative Management Committee |
| BTC | *Bo Tai Chinh*, Ministry of Finance |
| BVH | *Bo Van Hoa*, Ministry of Culture |
| CAC | Central Agriculture Commission |
| CACMC | Central Agricultural Cooperative Management Committee |
| CC | Central Committee |
| CCTK | *chi cuc thong ke*, statistics office |
| CEC | Central Executive Committee |

| | |
|---|---|
| CNXH | *chu nghia xa hoi*, socialism |
| CS | *chinh sach*, policy |
| CT | *cong tac*, assignment, mission, official work |
| CTTW | *chi thi trung uong*, central directive |
| DB | *dai bieu*, delegate |
| DCSVN | *Dang Cong San Viet Nam*, Vietnam Communist Party |
| DHNN | *Dai Hoc Nong Nghiep*, Agriculture University |
| DHQGH | *Dai Hoc Quoc Gia Ha Noi*, Hanoi National University |
| DLDVN | *Dang Lao Dong Viet Nam*, Vietnam Workers' Party |
| DRV | Democratic Republic of Vietnam |
| EC | Executive Committee |
| GSO | General Statistics Office |
| ha. | hectare(s) |
| HDCP | *Hoi Dong Chinh Phu*, Council of Ministers |
| HN | *hoi nghi*, conference, plenum |
| hs | *ho so*, folder or file in a record group, National Archives, Hanoi |
| HTH | *hop tac hoa*, cooperativization |
| HTHNN | *hop tac hoa nong nghiep*, agricultural cooperativization |
| HTX | *hop tac xa*, cooperative |
| HTXNN | *hop tac xa nong nghiep*, agricultural cooperative |
| HTXSXNN | *hop tac xa san xuat nong nghiep*, agricultural production cooperative |
| JPRS | Joint Publications Research Service of the U.S. government |
| K | *khoan*, contract |
| KH | *ke hoach*, plan |
| KHNN | *Ke Hoach Nha Nuoc*, state plan |
| KHXHNV | *Khoa Hoc Xa Hoi va Nhan Van*, Social Sciences and the Humanities |
| KSP | *khoan san pham*, product contract |
| KT | *kinh te*, economy, economics |
| LD | *lao dong*, work, labor, worker, laborer |
| LK | *Lien Khu*, interzone |
| LT | *luong thuc*, staple foods |
| MA | Ministry of Agriculture |
| MC | Ministry of Culture |
| NA | National Assembly |
| n.d. | no date |
| NN | *nong nghiep*, agriculture |
| n.p. | no place of publication provided |
| NQ | *Nghi Quyet*, resolution |
| NT | *nong thon*, rural area, countryside |
| Nxb | *nha xuat ban*, publishing house |

| | |
|---|---|
| P | *phong*, a record group in the National Archives, Hanoi |
| PHNV | *phuong huong nhiem vu*, guidelines and tasks |
| PM | prime minister |
| PMO | Prime Minister's Office |
| QD | *Quyet Dinh*, decision |
| QH | *Quoc Hoi*, National Assembly |
| QL | *quan ly*, manage, management |
| RAC | Rural Affairs Committee |
| RRD | Red River delta |
| SX | *san xuat*, production |
| SXNN | *san xuat nong nghiep*, agricultural production |
| TB | *thong bao*, announcement, bulletin, communiqué |
| TCL | *to chuc lai*, reorganize |
| TCT | *to cong tac*, group with an assignment or mission |
| TCTK | *Tong Cuc Thong Ke*, General Statistics Office |
| TDH | *Truong Dai Hoc*, college |
| TDSX | *tap doan san xuat*, production team |
| TH | *tinh hinh*, situation, condition |
| TK | *tong ket*, summary, summarize, review |
| TL | *tham luan*, speech, address |
| tt | *tam thoi*, temporary number for a folder (*ho so*) in a record group in the National Archives, Hanoi |
| TT | *Thong Tri*, circular |
| TU | *trung uong*, center, central |
| UBHC | *Uy Ban Hanh Chinh*, Administrative Committee |
| UBHCKTN | *Uy Ban Hanh Chinh Khu Ta Ngan*, Administrative Committee for the Left Bank Zone |
| UBKCHC | *Uy Ban Khang Chien Hanh Chinh*, Committee for Resistance Administration |
| UBKH | *Uy Ban Ke Hoach*, Planning Committee |
| UBKHNN | *Uy Ban Ke Hoach Nha Nuoc*, State Planning Committee |
| UBNNTU | *Uy Ban Nong Nghiep Trung Uong*, Central Agriculture Commission |
| VCP | Vietnam Communist Party |
| VH | *van hoa*, culture, cultural |
| VN | *Viet Nam*, Vietnam |
| VWP | Vietnam Workers' Party |
| vv | *vinh vien*, permanent number for a folder (*ho so*) in a record group in the National Archives, Hanoi |

# Bibliography

ARCHIVAL DOCUMENTS

At Vietnam's National Archives Number 3 in Hanoi (*Trung Tam Luu Tru Quoc Gia, so 3*), I examined the record groups (*phong*) listed below. Documents are footnoted in a condensed fashion (sufficiently, however, to locate them in the archives), followed by a brief English translation and a parenthetical notation for record group and folder. The condensed citation is shortened further after a document is first used in a chapter. Details for archival documents are cited only in footnotes.

*Bo Luong Thuc va Thuc Pham* [Ministry of Staple Foods and Food Processing]
*Bo Nong Nghiep* [Ministry of Agriculture]
*Bo Van Hoa* [Ministry of Culture]
*Quoc Hoi* [National Parliament]
*Tong Cuc Thong Ke* [General Statistics Office]
*Uy Ban Hanh Chinh Khu Ta Ngan* [Administrative Committee for the Left Bank zone]
*Uy Ban Ke Hoach Nha Nuoc* [State Planning Committee]
*Uy Ban Khang Chien Hanh Chinh Lien Khu 3* [Committee for Resistance Administration in Interzone 3]
*Uy Ban Nong Nghiep Trung Uong* [Central Agricultural Commission]

INTERVIEWS

Between 1992 and 2000, I interviewed villagers, provincial and district officials, and people in urban Hanoi knowledgeable about agrarian policy matters. Chapter one elaborates; the glossary on places provides information about the locations.

OTHER SOURCES

For Vietnamese titles, I provide only an abbreviated English translation. Vietnamese authors are alphabetized by their family names. Documents in published books, journals, and newspapers are cited in footnotes, not here.

Abrami, Regina Marie. "Self-making, Class Struggle, and Labor Autarky: The Political Origins of Private Entrepreneurship in Vietnam and China." Ph.D. diss., University of California, Berkeley, 2002.

Adams, Arthur E., and Jan S. Adams. *Men versus Systems: Agriculture in the USSR, Poland, and Czechoslovakia.* New York: Free Press, 1971.

Anderson, Leslie. "Between Quiescence and Rebellion among the Peasantry." *Journal of Theoretical Politics* 9, 4 (1997): 503–32.

*Asian Survey* 36 (March 1996): 227–337.

Axelrod, Robert. *The Evolution of Cooperation.* New York: Basic Books, 1984.

Baland, Jean-Marie, and Jean-Philippe Platteau. *Halting Degradation of Natural Resources: Is There a Role for Rural Communities?* Oxford: Clarendon Press, 1996.

Ball, Alan R. *Modern Politics and Government.* 5th edition. London: Macmillan, 1993.

Ban Bien Tap. "Ve Khoan San Pham trong Nong Nghiep" [Agricultural product contracts]. *Tap Chi Cong San* no. 12 (1987): 53–58.

Ban NN, BCHTU, DCSVN. "De An Xay Dung va Cung Co Quan He San Xuat Xa Hoi Chu Nghia, Su Dung va Cai Tao cac Thanh Phan Kinh Te tren Mat Tran Nong Nghiep" [Strengthening socialist relations of production], June 1987.

———. "Du thao: De An Xay Dung Cung Co Quan He San Xuat XHCN, Su Dung, Cai Tao cac Thanh Phan Kinh Te tren Mat Tran Nong Nghiep" [Draft proposal, strengthening socialist relations of production], 13 August 1987.

———. "Du thao: Tong Ket 3 nam Thuc Hien Nghi Quyet 10 cua Bo Chinh Tri ve Doi Moi Quan Ly Kinh Te Nong Nghiep" [Draft, three years implementing resolution 10], 10 December 1990.

Banfield, Edward C. *The Moral Basis of a Backward Society.* New York: Free Press, 1958.

Baring, Arnulf. *Uprising in East Germany: June 17, 1953.* Translated by Gerald Onn. Ithaca, N.Y.: Cornell University Press, 1972.

BBT, BCHTU, DCSVN. "TB 22 Ket Luan cua Ban Bi Thu ve Mot So Cong Tac Truoc Mat trong Viec Cung Co Hop Tac Xa Nong Nghiep" [Secretariat's conclusions regarding strengthening agricultural cooperatives], 21 October 1980.

BCH, Vinh Phuc, DLDVN. "Nghi Quyet cua Ban Thuong Vu Tinh Uy ve mot so Van De Quan Ly Lao Dong Nong Nghiep trong Hop Tac Xa Hien Nay," so 68NQ/TU [Managing agricultural labor, resolution 68NQ/TU], 10 September 1966.

BCHTU, DCSVN. "Chi Thi (67 CT-TW) ve viec Cai Tien Quan Ly Kinh Te, Hoan Thien Co Che Khoan San Pham Cuoi Cung den Nhom va Nguoi Lao Dong trong cac Hop Tac Xa va Tap Doan San Xuat Nong Nghiep" [Directive 67, improving economic management and the final product contract], 22 June 1985.

———. "NQ Hoi Nghi 6 (khoa IV) ve Tinh Hinh va Nhiem Vu Cap Bach" [Resolution, sixth plenum, pressing conditions and tasks], September 1979.

BCHTU, DLDVN. "NQ, Hoi Nghi Trung Uong, lan thu 14" [Party resolution, fourteenth plenum], November 1958.

———. "NQ, Hoi Nghi Trung Uong, lan thu 16 ve van de Hop Tac Hoa Nong Nghiep" [Party resolution on agricultural cooperativization], April 1959.

———. "NQ, Hoi Nghi Trung Uong, lan thu Nam (Thang 7 1961) ve Van De Phat Trien Nong Nghiep trong Ke Hoach 5 Nam Lan thu Nhat 1961–1965" [Resolution, agricultural development, 1961–1965 five-year plan], July 1961.

———. "TT ve Viec Chan Chinh Cong Tac Ba Khoan va Quan Ly Ruong Dat cua Hop Tac Xa San Xuat Nong Nghiep o mot so Dia Phuong," so 224-TT/TW [Circular regulating three contracts, land management, agricultural production cooperatives], 12 December 1968.

BCHTU, Hoi Nong Dan Viet Nam [Vietnam Peasants' Association]. "Bao Cao cua BCHTU Hoi Nong Dan Viet Nam (Khoa 1) tai Dai Hoi Dai Bieu Toan Quoc Lan Thu 2" [CEC's report to the association's national plenum], 15–19 November 1993.

BCHTU, Hoi Nong Dan Viet Nam, va Vien Lich Su Dang [Vietnam Peasants' Association and the History Institute of the Party]. "De Cuong Chi Tiet Lich Su Phong Trao Nong Dan va Hoi Nong Dan Viet Nam, 1930–1992" [Outline history of Vietnam peasants' association], 1992.

BCTNT, TU, DLDVN. *Cai Tien Cong Tac Quan Ly Hop Tac Xa Nong Nghiep* [Improving management, agricultural cooperatives]. Hanoi: Nxb Su That, 1963. Second printing; first issued December 1961.

Bennett, John W. *Hutterian Brethren: The Agricultural Economy and Social Organization of a Communal People.* Stanford, Calif.: Stanford University Press, 1967.

Beresford, Melanie. "Household and Collective in Vietnamese Agriculture." *Journal of Contemporary Asia* 15, 1 (1985): 5–36.

——. *National Unification and Economic Development in Vietnam.* London: Macmillan, 1989.

——. *Vietnam: Politics, Economics, and Society.* London: Pinter, 1988.

Beresford, Melanie, and Adam Fforde. "A Methodology for Analysing the Process of Economic Reform in Vietnam: The Case of Domestic Trade." *Journal of Communist Studies and Transition Politics* 13 (December 1997): 99–128.

Beresford, Melanie, and Dang Phong. *Economic Transition in Vietnam: Trade and Aid in the Demise of a Centrally Planned Economy.* Cheltenham: Edward Elgar, 2000.

BNN. "Bao Cao So Ket Viec Thuc Hien 'Khoan San Pham' den Nhom Lao Dong va Nguoi Lao Dong trong Hop Tac Xa San Xuat Nong Nghiep vu San Xuat Dong Xuan nam 1980–1981" [Product contracts in agricultural cooperatives, winter–spring 1980–1981], March 1981.

——. "Bao Cao Tinh Hinh Bao Cap trong Hop Tac Xa Nong Nghiep va Nhung Bien Phap Khac Phuc" [Overcoming subsidies in agricultural cooperatives], n.d. [circa 1986].

——. "Bao Cao ve Cung Co Hop Tac Xa San Xuat Nong Nghiep theo Tinh Than TB 22-TB/TW cua Ban Bi Thu tai Hoi Nghi Hop o Hai Phong tu 3–7/1/1981" [Reinforcing cooperatives as per party central secretariat bulletin], January 1981.

——. "Bao Cao Viec Thuc Hien Khoan San Pham den Nhom Lao Dong va Nguoi Lao Dong trong cac HTX Nong nghiep 1981" [Product contracts in agricultural cooperatives, 1981], 12 February 1982.

——. *He Thong Hoa Luat Le ve Nong Nghiep* [Agricultural laws, regulations]. 3 vols. Hanoi: Nxb Nong Nghiep, 1984.

——. *Hoan Chinh Khoan San Pham Cuoi Cung den Nhom va Nguoi Lao Dong trong HTX va Tap Doan San Xuat Nong Nghiep* [Product contracts to groups and individual workers]. Hanoi: Nxb Nong Nghiep, 1984.

BNNTU. *Cac Van Ban Quan Trong cua Dang ve Nong Nghiep* [Important party texts regarding agriculture]. Hanoi: Nxb Nong Nghiep, 1985.

——. *Khuyen Khich Kinh Te Gia Dinh Phat Trien Manh Me va Dung Huong* [Encouraging family economy]. Hanoi, February 1985.

Bo Noi Vu [Interior Ministry]. *Van Kien Dang* [Party documents]. Vol. 6. Hanoi: Vien Nghien Cuu Khoa Hoc Cong An, 1978.

Bo Nong Nghiep va Cong Nghiep Thuc Pham [Ministry of Agriculture and Food Indus-
try]. "Bao Cao cua Bo Nong nghiep va Cong Nghiep Thuc Pham ve Tinh Hinh Nong
Nghiep tu sau khi Thuc Hien Nghi Quyet 10 cua Bo Chinh Tri va nhung Bien Phap
Phat Trien Nong Nghiep trong Thoi Gian Toi" [Agricultural situation since resolution
10], 19 May 1992.

Bokovoy, Melissa K. "Peasants and Partisans: Politics of a Yugoslav Countryside, 1945–1953."
In *State-Society Relations in Yugoslavia, 1945–1992*, edited by Melissa K. Bokovoy, Jull A.
Irvine, and Carol S. Lilly, 115–36. New York: St. Martin's, 1997.

BQLHTXNN, BNN. "Tai Lieu Nghien Cuu Xung Quanh Chi Thi 100" [Research materials surrounding directive 100], n.d. [circa 1993].

BQLHTXNNTU. "Bao Cao ve Van De Khoan trong Hop Tac Xa Nong Nghiep" [Con-
tracts in cooperatives], December 1980.

———. *Huong Dan Phan Phoi Thu Nhap trong Hop Tac Xa va Tap Doan San Xuat Nong Nghiep*
[Guidelines, distributing income in cooperatives]. Hanoi: Nxb Nong Nghiep,
1980.

———. *Khoan San Pham trong cac Hop Tac Xa va Tap Doan San Xuat Nong Nghiep: Nhung
Cau Hoi va Tra Loi* [Product contracts: questions and answers]. Hanoi: Nxb Su That,
1982.

Bui Cong Trung and Luu Quang Hoa. *Hop Tac Hoa Nong Nghiep o Mien Bac Viet Nam*
[Agricultural cooperativization, northern Vietnam]. Hanoi: Nxb Su That, 1960.

Bui Phung. *Tu Dien Viet Anh—Vietnamese-English Dictionary*. Hanoi: Nxb The Gioi, 1996.

Burns, John P. *Political Participation in Rural China*. Berkeley: University of California Press,
1988.

*Cam Nang Quan Ly Ruong Dat* [Handbook on managing land]. Hai Duong: Uy Ban Hanh
Chinh, Hai Hung, 1974.

Cao Van Bien. "Ve Nan Doi Nam At Dau" [Famine in the year of the rooster]. *Nghien
Cuu Lich Su*, no. 4 (1990): 50–55, 60.

Chaliand, Gerard. *The Peasants of North Vietnam*. Harmondsworth, UK: Penguin,
1969.

Chan, Anita, Richard Madsen, and Jonathan Unger. *Chen Village: Under Mao and Deng*.
Berkeley: University of California Press, 1992.

Chayanov, Alexander. *The Theory of Peasant Co-operatives*. Translated from a 1927 edition
by David Wedgwood Benn. Columbus: Ohio State University Press, 1991.

———. *The Theory of Peasant Economy*. Edited by Daniel Thorner, Basile Kerblay, and R. E.
F. Smith. Madison: University of Wisconsin Press, 1986.

Chi Chuc Thong Ke [Statistical office]. *Nien Giam Thong Ke tinh Ha Son Binh nam 1965,
1970–1976* [Statistical yearbook, Ha Son Binh province]. Ha Son Binh: 1977.

*Chinh Sach, Luat Le ve Hop Tac Xa* [Policy and law regarding cooperatives]. Hanoi: Vien
Kiem Sat Nhan Dan Toi Cao, 1963.

Christiansen-Ruffman, Linda. "Women's Conceptions of the Political: Three Canadian
Women's Organizations." In *Feminist Organizations: Harvest of the New Women's Move-
ment*, edited by Myra Marx Ferree and Patricia Yancy Martin, 372–93. Philadelphia:
Temple University Press, 1995.

Chu Van Lam, Nguyen Thai Nguyen, Phung Huu Phu, Trang Quoc Toan, and Dang Tho
Xuong. *Hop Tac Hoa Nong Nghiep Viet Nam: Lich Su, Van De, Trien Vong* [Agricultural
cooperativization]. Hanoi: Nxb Su That, 1992.

*Cong Bao* [Official Gazette]. Selected issues, 1970–1980.

*Cong Tac Quan Ly Hop Tac Xa San Xuat Nong Nghiep* [Managing agricultural production collectives]. Vol. 1. *Tai Lieu Hoc Tap cho Can Bo, Truong Dang Co So* [Training material for cadres, basic party school]. N.p., 1964.

Conquest, Robert. *Harvest of Sorrow: Soviet Collectivization and the Terror-Famine.* London: Hutchinson, 1986.

Creed, Gerald W. *Domesticating Revolution: From Socialist Reform to Ambivalent Transition in a Bulgarian Village.* University Park: Pennsylvania State University Press, 1998.

Cuong Pham. "Management in Agricultural Co-operatives." *Vietnamese Studies*, no. 2 (1964): 102–19.

*Dai Doan Ket.* National newspaper of the Fatherland Front. Selected years, 1981–1988.

Dam Mai. "Nhung Chuyen Bien Moi trong Huyen Nong Cong" [New developments in Nong Cong district]. *Tap Chi Cong San*, no. 1 (1978): 90–96, 105.

Dang Phong. "Lo Trinh Kinh Te Viet Nam: Nhung Su Kien va Nhan To Dinh Huong" [The course of Vietnam's economy: Orienting factors and events]. 1997.

Dang Phong and Melanie Beresford. *Authority Relations and Economic Decision-Making in Vietnam: An Historical Perspective.* Copenhagen: Nordic Institute of Asian Studies, 1998.

Dang T. Tran. *Vietnam: Socialist Economic Development, 1955–1992.* San Francisco: International Center for Economic Growth, 1994.

Dang Tho Xuong, Nguyen Quang Hong, Nguyen Thi Tao, Vu Thi Phe, and Nguyen Van Quy. "Tong Thuat, Phan Tich He Thong, Quan Diem cua Dang trong cac Van Kien ve Nong Nghiep va Phat Trien Nong Thon" [Views in party documents regarding agriculture and rural development]. Report for Chuong Trinh KX-08–01–03 [Government project concerning agriculture], November 1992.

Dao Quang Cat. "Can Doi Moi cach Khoan San Pham trong Nong Nghiep" [Renovating product contracts]. *Tap Chi Cong San*, no. 7 (1987): 68–72.

DCSVN. *Nghi Quyet Bo Chinh Tri ve Doi Moi Quan Ly Kinh Te Nong Nghiep* [Political bureau resolutions, agricultural economic management]. Hanoi: Nxb Su That, 1988.

——. *Van Kien Dai Hoi Dai Bieu Toan Quoc Lan Thu V,* [Documents, fifth national party congress]. Vols. 1 and 2. Hanoi: Nxb Su That, 1982.

DiGregorio, Michael Robert. "Iron Works: Excavating Alternative Futures in a Northern Vietnamese Craft Village." Ph.D. diss., University of California Los Angeles, 2001.

Dinh Thu Cuc. "Qua Trinh To Chuc Lai San Xuat theo Huong San Xuat Lon Xa Hoi Chu Nghia o mot so Hop Tac Xa Nong Nghiep Tien Tien vung Trong Lua" [Revamping cooperatives in accordance with large-scale socialist production]. In *Nong Dan Viet Nam Tien Len Chu Nghia Xa Hoi*, edited by Vien Su Hoc, 332–89. Hanoi: Nxb Khoa Hoc Xa Hoi, 1979.

Dinh Van Ton. "Thanh Tra, Kiem Tra Phap Luat Ruong Dat tai Ha Nam Ninh" [Agricultural land law inspections, Ha Nam Ninh province]. *Quan Ly Ruong Dat*, no. 2 (1984): 9–12, 14.

Dittmer, Lowell, Haruhiro Fukui, and Peter N. S. Lee, eds. *Informal Politics in East Asia.* Cambridge, UK: Cambridge University Press, 2000.

Doan Duy Thanh. *Hai Phong trong Chang Duong Dau cua Thoi Ky Qua Do* [Hai Phong, initial transition]. Hai Phong: Nxb Hai Phong, 1985.

Dong Chi B [Comrade B]. "Am Muu cua Bon Phan Dong Trung Quoc doi voi Viet Nam" [Chinese reactionaries' conspiracies toward Vietnam]. Excerpts. 1979.

Duong Loi, Chinh Sach Hop Tac Hoa Nong Nghiep: Trich Nhung Nghi Quyet, Chi Thi cua Trung Uong Dang va mot so Thong Tri cua Ban Cong Tac Nong Thon Trung Uong [Agricultural cooperatives, party directives, and decisions]. Hanoi: Nxb Su That, 1962.

Duong Quoc Cam. Kinh Te Tap The Hop Tac Xa va Kinh Te Phu Gia Dinh Xa Vien [Collective economy and the subsidiary family economy]. Hanoi: Nxb Su That, 1963.

——. Mot So Kinh Nghiem qua dot I cuoc Van Dong Cai Tien Quan Ly Hop Tac Xa Cai Tien Ky Thuat nham Phat Trien San Xuat Nong Nghiep Toan Dien, Manh Me va Vung Chac [First wave in campaign to improve cooperatives]. Hanoi: Nxb Nong Thon, 1963.

——. Mot So Kinh Nghiem qua dot III, dot IV cuoc Van Dong Cai Tien Quan Ly Hop Tac Xa Cai Tien Ky Thuat nham Phat Trien San Xuat Nong Nghiep Toan Dien, Manh Me va Vung Chac [Waves 3 and 4 in the campaign to improve cooperatives]. Hanoi: Nxb Nong Thon, 1964.

Elliott, David. "Revolutionary Re-integration: A Comparison of the Foundation of Post-Liberation Political Systems in North Vietnam and China." Ph.D. diss., Cornell University, 1976.

——. Transcript (in Vietnamese) of a late 1960s interview with a Communist Party member who had been a cadre in Thai Binh province during the early 1960s, 117–56.

Elshtain, Jean Bethke. Real Politics: At the Center of Everyday Life. Baltimore: Johns Hopkins University Press, 1997.

Evans, Grant. Lao Peasants under Socialism. New Haven, Conn.: Yale University Press, 1990.

Fall, Bernard B. The Viet-Minh Regime: Government and Administration in the Democratic Republic of Vietnam. Data Paper 14, Southeast Asia Program, Cornell University, 1954.

Fegan, Brian. "Tenants' Non-Violent Resistance to Landowner Claims in a Central Luzon Village." In Everyday Forms of Peasant Resistance in Southeast Asia, edited by James C. Scott and Benedict J. Tria Kerkvliet, 87–106. London: Frank Cass, 1986.

Fewsmith, Joseph. Dilemmas of Reform in China: Political Conflict and Economic Debate. Armonk, N.Y.: M.E. Sharpe, 1994.

Fforde, Adam. The Agrarian Question in North Vietnam, 1974–1979. Armonk, N.Y.: M.E. Sharpe, 1989.

——. "From Plan to Market: The Economic Transition in Vietnam and China Compared." In Transforming Asian Socialism, edited by Anita Chan, Benedict J. Tria Kerkvliet, and Jonathan Unger, 43–72. Boulder, Colo.: Rowman & Littlefield, 1999.

——. "The Historical Background to Agricultural Collectivization in North Vietnam: The Changing Role of 'Corporate' Economic Power." Birkbeck Discussion Paper 148, Department of Economics, Birkbeck College, University of London, 1983.

——. "Law and Socialist Agricultural Development in Vietnam: The Statute for Agricultural Producer Cooperatives." Review of Socialist Law 10 (1984): 315–36.

Fforde, Adam, and Stefan de Vylder. From Plan to Market: The Economic Transition in Vietnam. Boulder, Colo.: Westview, 1996.

Fitzpatrick, Sheila. Stalin's Peasants: Resistance and Survival in the Russian Village after Collectivization. New York: Oxford University Press, 1995.

Francisco, Ronald A. "Agricultural Collectivization in the German Democratic Republic." In The Political Economy of Collectivized Agriculture, edited by Ronald A. Francisco, Betty A. Lair, and Roy D. Laird, 63–85. New York: Pergamon, 1979.

Gamson, William A., Bruce Fireman, and Steven Rytina. Encounters with Unjust Authority. Homewood, Ill.: Dorsey, 1982.

Gordon, Alec. "North Vietnam's Collectivisation Campaigns: Class Struggle, Production, and the 'Middle Peasant' Problem." *Journal of Contemporary Asia* 11, 1 (1981): 19–43.

Gourou, Pierre. *The Peasants of the Tonkin Delta: A Study of Human Geography*. Translated by Richard R. Miller. New Haven, Conn.: Human Relations Area Files, 1955.

Grossheim, Martin. *Nordvietnamesische Dorfgemeinschaften: Kontinuitat und Wandel* [North Vietnam communities: continuity and change]. Hamburg: Mitteilungen des Instituts fur Asienkunde, 1997.

*Ha Noi Moi*. Hanoi daily newspaper. Selected issues, 1970s–1980s.

Hanoi, Ban Tuyen Giao Thanh Uy Hanoi [Hanoi, Board of education and propaganda, Hanoi People's Committee]. *Mot So Kinh Nghiem ve Cong Tac Chinh Tri Tu Tuong o Hop Tac Xa San Xuat Nong nghiep Yen My va Ha Lo* [Political and ideological work, Yen My and Ha Lo cooperatives]. Hanoi: July 1971.

Hanoi, BCH Thanh Pho Hanoi, Dang Lao Dong Viet Nam [Hanoi's EC, Vietnam Workers' Party]. *Bao Cao Ket Qua Dieu Tra tinh hinh Quan Ly o 30 Hop Tac Xa San Xuat Nong Nghiep Ngoai Thanh Hanoi* [Survey in thirty Hanoi agricultural cooperatives]. Hanoi: 12 October 1972.

*Ha Son Binh*. Newspaper published by the Ha Son Binh branch of the VCP. Selected years, 1978–1989.

*Hai Hung*. Newspaper published by the Hai Hung branch of the VCP. Selected years, 1974–1989.

Hardy, Andrew. *Red Hills: Migrants and the State in the Highlands of Vietnam*. Copenhagen: NIAS, 2003.

Havel, Vaclav. "The Power of the Powerless." In *The Power of the Powerless: Citizens Against the State in Central-Eastern Europe*, edited by John Keane, 23–96. Armonk, N.Y.: M.E. Sharpe, 1985.

Hedlund, Stefan. "Private Plots as a System Stabilizer." In *Communist Agriculture: Farming in the Soviet Union and Eastern Europe*, edited by Karl-Eugen Wadekin, 215–29. London: Routledge, 1990.

Heng, Russell Hiang-Khng. "Of the State, for the State, Yet against the State: The Struggle Paradigm in Vietnam's Media Politics." Ph.D. diss., Australian National University, 1999.

"Hien Trang ve Quan He San Xuat trong Nong Thon" [Rural relations of production], 8 August 1990. Probably prepared for the Communist Party's Agriculture Committee.

Hirschman, Albert O. *Exit, Voice, and Loyalty*. Cambridge, Mass.: Harvard University Press, 1970.

Hoang Ham. "Buoc Phat Trien Moi cua Huyen Vinh Lac trong Qua Trinh To Chuc Lai San Xuat" [Reorganizing production in Vinh Lac district]. *Tap Chi Cong San*, no. 10 (1980): 35–39, 59.

Hoang Huu Cac. "Dem Trang" [Sleepless night]. In *Nguoi Dan Ba Quy: Tap Truyen Ky Chon Loc* [Kneeling woman: Selected biographies], 129–44. Hanoi: Nxb Nong Nghiep, 1988.

Hoang Quoc Viet. "Kien Quyet Dau Tranh Chong Quan Lieu, Menh Lenh, Tang Cuong Che Do Lam Chu Tap The cua Quan Chung Xa Vien o Nong Thon" [Struggle against bureaucratic and overbearing management, strengthen collective mastery]. *Hoc Tap*, no. 8 (1970): 29–41.

Hoang Quy. "May Van De trong Nong Nghiep Vinh Phu" [Agricultural issues in Vinh Phu]. *Tap Chi Cong San*, no. 8 (1980): 56–60.

Hoang Thi Binh. "Tinh Hinh Giao Ruong Dat On Dinh Lau Dai cho Ho Nong Dan o Xa Trau Quy, huyen Gia Lam, Hanoi" [Allocating land, Trau Quy subdistrict, Gia Lam district, Hanoi]. Luan van tot nghiep [thesis], TDH NN 1, 2000.

Hobsbawm, Eric. "Peasants and Politics." *Journal of Peasant Studies* 1 (October 1973): 3–22.

Hong Hai. "Ban ve Hieu Qua Kinh Te va Phuong Huong Hoan Thien cac Hinh Thuc To Chuc Lao Dong trong cac Hop Tac Xa" [Economic results, improved guidelines for how cooperatives organize labor]. *Nghien Cuu Kinh Te*, no. 5 (1980): 24–39.

Houtart, François, and Genevieve Lemercinier. *Hai Van: Life in a Vietnamese Commune.* London: Zed, 1984.

HTX Yen So [Yen So cooperative]. "Bao Cao Tong Ket 10 Nam Hop Tac Xa Nong Nghiep Yen So" [Ten-year report], n.d. [circa 1979].

Hughès, James. *Stalinism in a Russian Province: A Study of Collectivization and Dekulakization in Siberia.* London: Macmillan, 1996.

Humphrey, Caroline. *Karl Marx Collective: Economy, Society, and Religion in a Siberian Collective Farm.* Cambridge, UK: Cambridge University Press, 1983.

*Hung Yen.* Newspaper published by the Hung Yen branch of the VCP. 1961–early 1963.

Huntington, Samuel P., and Joan M. Nelson. *No Easy Choice: Political Participation in Developing Countries.* Cambridge, Mass.: Harvard University Press, 1976.

Huu Hanh. "Khoan Lua" [Paddy contracts]. *Tap Chi Cong San*, no. 12 (1980): 35–43.

Huu Tho. "Nho Hoi Thao Con Son" [Remembering the Con Son conference]. In *Nho Mot Thoi Lam Bao Nhan Dan*, 159–68. Hanoi: Nxb Chinh Tri Quoc Gia, 1996.

Huyen Chuong My. BCH Dang Bo [Chuong My district. Party EC]. *Lich Su Dang Bo Huyen Chuong My, 1954–1991* [History, party branch, Chuong My district]. Vol. 2. Chuong My, Ha Tay: 1995.

Huyen Tien Lang. BCH Dang Bo [Tien Lang district, Party EC]. *Lich Su Dang Bo Huyen Tien Lang, 1930–1975* [History, Tien Lang's party branch]. Hai Phong: Nxb Hai Phong, 1988.

Hy Van Luong. "Agrarian Unrest from an Anthropological Perspective: The Case of Vietnam." *Comparative Politics* 17 (January 1985): 153–74.

——. "The Marxist State and Dialogic Re-structuration of Culture in Rural Vietnam." In *Indochina: Social and Cultural Change*, edited by David W. P. Elliott, Ben Kiernan, Hy Van Luong, and Terese M. Mahoney, 79–117. Claremont, Calif.: Keck Center for International and Strategic Studies, Claremont McKenna College, 1994.

——. *Revolution in the Village: Tradition and Transformation in North Vietnam, 1925–1988.* Honolulu: University of Hawaii Press, 1992.

Hyden, Goran. *Beyond Ujamaa in Tanzania: Underdevelopment and an Uncaptured Peasantry.* Berkeley: University of California Press, 1980.

Jean-Klein, Iris. "Nationalism and Resistance: Two Faces of Everyday Activism in Palestine during the Intifada." *Cultural Anthropology* 16 (February 2001): 83–126.

Jeong, Yeonsik. "The Rise of State Corporatism in Vietnam." *Contemporary Southeast Asia* 19 (September 1997): 152–71.

Kanter, Rosabeth Moss. *Commitment and Community: Communes and Utopias in Sociological Perspective.* Cambridge, Mass.: Harvard University Press, 1972.

Kelliher, Daniel. *Peasant Power in China.* New Haven, Conn.: Yale University Press, 1992.

Kerkvliet, Benedict J. Tria. "Claiming the Land: Take-overs by Villagers in the Philippines with Comparisons to Indonesia, Peru, Portugal, and Russia." *Journal of Peasant Studies* 20 (April 1993): 459–93.

———. "Dialogical Law Making and Implementation in Vietnam." In *East Asia—Human Rights, Nation-Building, Trade*, edited by Alice Tay, 372–400. Baden-Baden: Nomos Verlagsgesellschaft, 1999.

———. *Everyday Politics in the Philippines*. Berkeley: University of California Press, 1990; Boulder, Colo.: Rowman and Littlefield, 2002.

———. "Rural Society and State Relations." In *Vietnam's Rural Transformation*, edited by Benedict J. Tria Kerkvliet and Doug J. Porter, 65–96. Boulder and Singapore: Westview and the Institute of Southeast Asian Studies, 1995.

———. "Village-State Relations in Vietnam: The Effect of Everyday Politics on Decollectivization." *Journal of Asian Studies* 54 (May 1995): 396–418.

*Khoa Hoc va Ky Thuat Nong Nghiep* [Agricultural science and technology] (March, 1987).

*Khoan San Pham trong Nong Nghiep: Nhung Van De Co Tinh Tong Ket Thuc Tien* [Implementing agricultural product contracts]. Hanoi: Nxb Su That, 1982.

Kideckel, David A. "The Dialectic of Rural Development: Cooperative Farm Goals and Family Strategies in a Romanian Commune." *Journal of Rural Cooperation* 5, 1 (1977): 43–61.

———. "The Socialist Transformation of Agriculture in a Romanian Commune, 1945–62." *American Ethnologist* 9 (May 1982): 320–40.

Kiernan, Ben. *The Pol Pot Regime: Race, Power, and Genocide in Cambodia under the Khmer Rouge, 1975–79*. New Haven, Conn.: Yale University Press, 1996.

Kim Ngoc. "Quyet Tam Sua Chua Khuyet Diem, Dua Phong Trao Hop Tac Hoa va San Xuat Nong Nghiep cua tinh Vinh Phu Vung Buoc Tien Len" [Correct shortcomings, advance cooperativization, Vinh Phu]. *Hoc Tap*, no. 6 (1969): 36–45.

Kitschelt, Herbert P. "Political Opportunity Structures and Political Protest: Anti-Nuclear Movements in Four Democracies." *British Journal of Political Science* 16 (1986): 57–85.

Kleinen, John. *Facing the Future, Reviving the Past: A Study of Social Change in a Northern Vietnamese Village*. Singapore: Institute for Southeast Asian Studies, 1999.

Koh, David Wee Hock. "Wards of Hanoi and State-Society Relations in the Socialist Republic of Vietnam." Ph.D. diss., Australian National University, 2000.

Kolko, Gabriel. *Vietnam: Anatomy of a Peace*. London: Routledge, 1997.

Korbonski, Andrzej. *Politics of Socialist Agriculture in Poland: 1945–1960*. New York: Columbia University Press, 1965.

Korovkin, Tanya. "Weak Weapons, Strong Weapons? Hidden Resistance and Political Protest in Rural Ecuador." *Journal of Peasant Studies* 27 (April 2000): 1–29.

Kung, James. "Equal Entitlement versus Tenure Security under a Regime of Collective Property Rights: Peasants Preference for Institutions in Post Reform Chinese Agriculture." *Journal of Comparative Economics* 21 (August 1995): 82–111.

Kung, James Kai-sing, and Shouying Liu. "Farmers' Preferences regarding Ownership and Land Tenure in Post-Mao China: Unexpected Evidence from Eight Counties." *China Journal*, no. 38 (July 1997): 33–63.

Lam Quang Huyen. *Cach Mang Ruong Dat o Mien Nam Viet Nam* [Land reform, south Vietnam]. Hanoi: Nxb Khoa Hoc Xa Hoi, 1985.

Lasswell, Harold. *Politics: Who Gets What, When, How*. Cleveland: World Publishing, 1958.

Le Duan. *On the Socialist Revolution in Vietnam*. Vols. 1–2. Hanoi: Foreign Languages Publishing House, 1965.

———. *On the Socialist Revolution in Vietnam*. Vol. 3. Hanoi: Foreign Languages Publishing House, 1967.

——. "Ra Suc Phan Dau Xay Dung Nen Nong nghiep Lon Xa Hoi Chu Nghia" [Struggle for large-scale socialist agriculture] In *Ve To Chuc Lai San Xuat va Cai Tien Quan Ly Nong Nghiep*, edited by Le Duan and Pham Van Dong, 7–62. Hanoi: Nxb Su That, 1975.

Le Duc Tho. "On the Question of Developing New Factors and Perfecting the New Management System in Agricultural Co-operatives." *Summary of World Broadcasts*, 30 September 1982, FE/7144/C1–C20.

Le Hai Nguyen. "Bien Doi Co Cau Kinh Te-Xa Hoi o Xa Luu Hiem, Thuy Nguyen, Hai Phong, 1981–1996" [Structural change, Luu Hiem subdistrict, Thuy Nguyen district, Hai Phong province]. Luan van tot nghiep, Khoa Su [thesis, Faculty of History], TDH KHXHNV, DHQGH, 1998.

Le Huu Dao. *Cac Moi Quan He Chu Yeu trong Ke Hoach Hoa Phan Phoi Thu Nhap o cac Hop Tac Xa Nong Nghiep* [Income distribution planning in cooperatives]. Hanoi: Nxb Nong Nghiep, 1986.

Le Huy Phan. "May Suy Nghi ve Co Che Quan Ly Kinh Te o Nuoc ta tu truoc den nay va ve Phuong Huong Doi Moi Co Che Do" [Economic management and the course for renovating it]. *Nghien Cuu Kinh Te*, no. 4 (1985): 10–22, 30.

Le Luu. *Truyen Ngan* [Short stories]. Hanoi: Nxb Van Hoc, 1996.

Le Thanh Nghi. *Cai Tien Cong Tac Khoan, Mo Rong Khoan San Pham De Thuc Day San Xuat, Cung Co Hop Tac Xa Nong Nghiep* [Improving contracts, strengthening cooperatives]. Hanoi: Nxb Su That, 1981.

Le Trong. *Mot So Kinh Nghiem cua cac Hop Tac Xa Nong Nghiep Tien Tien* [Experiences of advanced cooperatives]. Hanoi: Nxb Nong Nghiep, 1983.

——. "Thuc Chat cua 'Khoan Moi' voi cung co Quan He San Xuat Xa Hoi Chu Nghia trong Nong Nghiep" [New contracts strengthening socialist relations of agricultural production]. *Tap Chi Cong San*, no. 9 (1987): 65–68.

——. *To Chuc Lao Dong trong Hop Tac Xa San Xuat Nong Nghiep* [Organizing work in cooperatives]. Hanoi: Nxb Nong Nghiep, 1980.

——. "Ve Thu Lao Lao Dong trong Hop Tac Xa Nong Nghiep" [Compensating labor cooperatives]. *Nghien Cuu Kinh Te*, no. 3 (1980): 22–31, 44.

Le Trung Viet. *Kinh Te Phu Gia Dinh cua Xa Vien* [Family economy in cooperatives]. Hanoi: Nxb Pho Thong, 1961.

Le Van Sinh. "On Becoming. a More Diversified Countryside: Some Observations on Socio-economic Changes in Two Northern Vietnamese Villagers." Paper for EuroViet Conference, Amsterdam, July 1997. (Part of the paper was published in Vietnamese: "Qua Trinh Da Dang Hoa Kinh Te: Xa Hoi o Nong Thon Viet Nam sau 10 nam Doi Moi." In *Mot Chang Duong Nghien Cuu Lich Su, 1995–2000*, 260–75. Hanoi: Nxb Chinh Tri Quoc Gia, 2000.)

Leftwich, Adrian. "Politics: People, Resources, and Power." In *What is Politics?* edited by Adrian Leftwich, 62–84. Oxford: Basil Blackwell, 1984.

Lichbach, Mark I. "Contentious Maps of Contentious Politics." *Mobilization: An International Journal* 2, 1 (1997): 87–98.

——. *The Cooperator's Dilemma*. Ann Arbor: University of Michigan Press, 1996.

Lu, Aiguo. "Household and Collective in Chinese and Soviet Agriculture." Ph.D. diss., State University of New York, Binghamton, 1992.

*Luat Dat Dai va Huong Dan Thi Hanh* [Land law and implementation guidelines]. Hanoi: Nxb Phap Ly, 1992.

*Luat Hop Tac Xa—Law on Cooperatives*. Hanoi: Nxb Chinh Tri Quoc Gia, 1996.

Luu Van Sung. "Nhung Hinh Thuc Hop Tac trong Nong Nghiep o Huyen Viet Yen tinh Ha Bac" [Forms of agricultural cooperation, Viet Yen district, Ha Bac province]. In "Kinh Te Ho Gia Dinh va cac Hinh Thuc Kinh Te Hop Tac o Co So," edited by Dao The Tuan, 421–80. Report for Chuong Trinh KX-08–5 [Government project concerning agriculture], 1992.

———. "Nhung Van De Dat Ra cua Khoan San Pham trong Nong Nghiep va Phuong Huong Cai Tien Quan Ly HTX Hien Nay" [Problems with product contracts, guidelines for improving management in cooperatives]. Nghien Cuu Kinh Te, no. 5 (1987): 37–42.

Malarney, Shaun Kingsley. Culture, Ritual, and Revolution in Vietnam. London: Routledge-Curzon, 2002.

Management of Cooperatives. Entire issue of Vietnamese Studies, no. 51 (1977).

Marr, David G. Vietnam 1945: The Quest for Power. Berkeley: University of California Press, 1995.

Martin, Marie Alexandrin. Cambodia: A Shattered Society. Translated by Mark W. McLeod. Berkeley: University of California Press, 1994.

McAdam, Doug. "Conceptual Origins, Current Problems, Future Directions." In Comparative Perspectives on Social Movements, edited by Doug McAdam, John McCarthy, and Mayer Zald, 23–40. Cambridge, U.K.: Cambridge University Press, 1996.

McAdam, Doug, John McCarthy, and Mayer Zald. "Introduction: Opportunities, Mobilizing Structures, and Framing Processes—Toward a Synthetic, Comparative Perspective on Social Movements." In Comparative Perspectives on Social Movements, edited by Doug McAdam, John McCarthy, and Mayer Zald, 1–20. Cambridge, UK: Cambridge University Press, 1996.

Melucci, Alberto. "Getting Involved: Identity and Mobilization in Social Movements." International Social Movement Research 1 (1988): 329–48.

Miller, Hugh T. "Everyday Politics in Public Administration." American Review of Public Administration 23 (June 1993): 99–117.

Miller, R. F. "Group Farming Practices in Yugoslavia." In Cooperative and Commune: Group Farming in the Economic Development of Agriculture, edited by Peter Dorner, 163–97. Madison: University of Wisconsin Press, 1975.

Moise, Edwin E. Land Reform in China and North Vietnam. Chapel Hill: University of North Carolina Press, 1983.

Morrow, Christopher E., and Rebecca Watts Hull. "Donor-Initiated Common Pool Resource Institutions: The Case of the Yanesha Forestry Cooperative." World Development 24, 10 (1996): 1641–57.

Myant, Martin. The Czechoslovak Economy, 1948–1988. Cambridge, UK: Cambridge University Press, 1989.

Nam Ha. May Kinh Nghiem ve Cong Tac Phu Nu trong Cai Tien Quan Ly Hop Tac Xa Nong Nghiep [Women during management improvement in cooperatives]. Hanoi: Nxb Phu Nu, 1965.

Nash, June, and Nicholas S. Hopkins. "Anthropological Approaches to the Study of Cooperatives, Collectives, and Self-Management." In Popular Participation in Social Change: Cooperatives, Collectives, and Nationalized Industry, edited by June Nash, Jorge Dandler, and Nicholas S. Hopkins, 3–32. The Hague: Mouton, 1976.

Netting, Robert McC. Smallholders, Householders: Farm Families and the Ecology of Intensive, Sustainable Agriculture. Stanford, Calif.: Stanford University Press, 1993.

Ngo Vinh Long. "Communal Property and Peasant Revolutionary Struggles in Vietnam." *Peasant Studies* 17 (Winter 1990): 121–40.

——. "View from the Village." *Indochina Issues*, no.12 (December 1980): 1, 4–7.

Nguyen Anh Bac. "May Suy Nghi ve Hoan Thien Co Che Khoan San Pham Cuoi Cung den Ho Gia Dinh o cac Hop Tac Xa Nong Nghiep" [Improving product contract system]. *Tap Chi Cong San*, no. 10 (1987): 59–61.

Nguyen Chi Thanh. "May Kinh Nghiem Lon ve Hop Tac Hoa Nong nghiep cua Chung Ta" [Experiences of our agricultural cooperativization]. *Hoc Tap*, no. 11 (1964): 1–20.

——. *Ve San Xuat Nong Nghiep va Hop Tac Hoa Nong Nghiep* [Agricultural production and cooperativization]. Hanoi: Nxb Su That, 1969.

Nguyen Duc Nghinh. "Lang Xa Co Truyen Viet Nam o Bac Bo tren Duong Chuyen Bien" [Traditional northern Vietnam village community]. In *Lang o vung Chau Tho Song Hong: Van De con Bo Ngo*, edited by Philippe Papin and Olivier Tessier, 413–46. Hanoi: Trung Tam Khoa Hoc Xa Hoi va Nhan Van Quoc Gia, 2002.

——. "Le district rural vietnamien ou L'état en campagne." In *Habitations et habitat d'Asie du Sud-Est continentale*, edited by Jacqueline Matras-Guin and Christian Taillard, 343–76. Paris: Editions L'Harmattan, 1992.

Nguyen Huu Khieu. "Phat Trien Kinh Te Tap The cua Hop Tac Xa Nong Nghiep" [Developing collectivized economy]. *Hoc Tap*, no. 9 (1964): 32–38.

Nguyen Huu Tien. "HTX Nong Nghiep: Nhung Van De Noi Com" [Problems in cooperatives]. *Tap Chi Kinh Te Nong Nghiep*, no. 10 (1999): 22–24.

——. "Phong Trao Hop Tac Hoa Nong Nghiep 30 Nam: Vung Dong Bang Song Hong va Trung Du Mien Bac" [Thirty years of agricultural cooperativization: Red River Delta and northern Midlands]. 1991.

Nguyen Huy. *Dua Nong Nghiep tu San Xuat Nho len San Xuat Lon Xa Hoi Chu Nghia* [From small-scale to large-scale socialist agricultural production]. Hanoi: Nxb Khoa Hoc Xa Hoi, 1983.

——. "Van Dung Quy Luat Phan Phoi theo Lao Dong trong Dieu Kien Khoan San Pham den Nguoi Lao Dong trong Nong Nghiep Nuoc Ta" [Distribution according to work, product contracts to workers]. *Tap Chi Cong San*, no. 9 (1987): 61–64, 68.

——. "Ve moi Lien He giua Kinh Te Tap The va Kinh Te Gia Dinh Xa Vien" [Relations between collective and family economies]. *Nghien Cuu Kinh Te*, no. 3 (1983): 17–23.

Nguyen Khai and Le Van Bam, Tong Cuc Quan Ly Ruong Dat [National Land Management Office]. "May Y Kien ve Chinh Sach Dat Lam Kinh Te Gia Dinh trong Hop Tac Xa va Tap Doan San Xuat Nong Nghiep" [Land policy for household economy in agricultural cooperatives]. *Quan Ly Ruong Dat*, no. 4 (1986): 30–32.

Nguyen Manh Huan. "Hop Tac Xa Nong Nghiep Dinh Cong" [Dinh Cong cooperative]. *Nghien Cuu Kinh Te*, no. 4 (1980): 42–48, 61.

——. "Hop Tac Xa Nong Nghiep Vu Thang" [Vu Thang cooperative]. *Nghien Cuu Kinh Te*, no. 1 (1979): 35–44, 68.

Nguyen Ngoc Luu. "Peasants, Party, and Revolution: The Politics of Agrarian Transformation in Northern Vietnam, 1930–1975." Ph.D. diss., Institute of Social Studies, The Hague, 1987.

Nguyen Quang Hong. "Tu Tuong Chi Dao cua Dang ve Cuoc Van Dong Hop Tac Hoa Nong nghiep o Mien Bac, thoi ky 1955–1960" [Guiding thoughts, mobilizing agricultural cooperatives, 1955–1960]. Report on collectivization at Hoc Vien Nguyen Ai Quoc, Hanoi, 1989.

Nguyen Sinh Cuc. *Nong Nghiep Viet Nam: 1945–1995* [Agriculture, 1945–1995]. Hanoi: Nxb Tong Cuc Thong Ke, 1995.

——. *Thuc Trang Nong Nghiep, Nong Thon, va Nong Dan Viet Nam, 1976–1990* [The agricultural and rural situation, 1976–1990]. Hanoi: Nxb Thong Ke, 1991.

Nguyen Tien Hung. *Economic Development of Socialist Vietnam, 1955–1980.* New York: Praeger, 1977.

Nguyen Tu Chi. "The Traditional Viet Village in Bac Bo: Its Organizational Structure and Problems." In *The Traditional Village in Vietnam*, 44–142. Hanoi: The Gioi, 1993.

Nguyen Van Chinh. "Work without Name: Changing Patterns of Children's Work in a Northern Vietnamese Village." Ph.D. diss., University of Amsterdam, 2000.

Nguyen Van Khanh and Trang Van Phuc. "Bo May Quyen Luc Cap Xa: Co Cau To Chuc va Phuong Thuc Van Hanh" [Subdistrict's power, organizational structure, operation]. In *Quan Ly Xa Hoi Nong Thon Nuoc Ta Hien Nay: Mot So Van De va Giai Phap*, edited by Phan Dai Doan, 110–46. Hanoi: Nxb Chinh Tri Quoc Gia, 1996.

Nguyen Van Nhat. "Cai Tao Nong Nghiep o Nam Bo: Nhung Chang Duong va Bai Hoc" [Revamping agriculture in the southeast and Mekong delta]. *Nghien Cuu Lich Su*, no. 3 (1990): 11–20.

*Nhan Dan* [The People]. National newspaper of the VCP, 1955–1995.

Nhu Dinh Luyen. "May Van De Co Ban cua Qui Mo va Chi Tieu Xac Dinh Qui Mo Xi Nghiep Nong Nghiep" [Norms for the agricultural enterprises]. *Nghien Cuu Kinh Te*, no. 6 (1979): 41–49.

Nolan, Peter. "Collectivization in China: Some Comparisons with the USSR." *Journal of Peasant Studies* 3 (January 1976): 192–220.

——. *The Political Economy of Collective Farms.* Cambridge, UK: Polity, 1988.

*Nong Dan Moi* [New peasant]. Newspaper of the official peasants' association, 1985–1988.

*Nong Dan Viet Nam* [Vietnam peasant]. Newspaper of the official peasants' association, 1988–1995.

*Nong Nghiep Ha Bac* [Ha Bac agriculture]. Publication of Ha Bac province's agricultural committee, selected years, 1970s–1980s.

*Nong Thon Ngay Nay* [Countryside today]. National newspaper of the official peasants' association, 1995–1998.

Oi, Jean. *State and Peasant in Contemporary China.* Berkeley: University of California Press, 1989.

O'Rourke, Dara. "Community-driven Regulation: Toward an Improved Model of Environmental Regulation in Vietnam." In *Livable Cities? Urban Struggles for Livelihood and Sustainability*, edited by Peter Evans, 95–131. Berkeley: University of California Press, 2002.

Ostrom, Elinor. *Governing the Commons.* Cambridge, UK: Cambridge University Press, 1990.

——. "Reformulating the Commons." Paper for the Workshop in Political Theory and Policy Analysis, Indiana University, Bloomington, 1999.

Parish, William L. "Introduction: Historical Background and Current Issues." In *Chinese Rural Development*, edited by William L. Parish, 3–29. N.Y.: M.E. Sharpe, 1985.

Pelzer, Kristin. "Socio-Cultural Dimensions of Renovation in Vietnam: *Doi Moi* as Dialogue and Transformation in Gender Relations." In *Reinventing Vietnamese Socialism*, edited by William S. Turley and Mark Selden, 309–36. Boulder, Colo.: Westview, 1993.

Peter, Karl A. *The Dynamics of Hutterite Society: An Analytical Approach*. Edmonton: University of Alberta Press, 1987.

Peukert, Detlev J. K. *Inside Nazi Germany: Conformity, Opposition, and Racism in Everyday Life*. Translated by Richard Deveson. London: B.T. Batsford, 1987.

Pham Cong. *De Quan Ly Tot Hop Tac Xa Nong Nghiep* [Good management in cooperatives]. Hanoi: Nxb Pho Thong, 1962.

Pham Cuong and Nguyen Van Ba. *Nam Hong: Revolution in the Village, 1945–1975*. Hanoi: Foreign Languages Publishing House, 1976.

Pham Quang Minh. *Zwischen Theorie und Praxis: Agrarpolitik in Vietnam seit 1945* [Between theory and practice: Agrarian politics in Vietnam]. Berlin: Berliner Südostasien-Studien, 2003.

Pham Toan. "The Ngo Xuyen Co-operative." *Vietnamese Studies*, no. 27 (1971): 209–49.

Phan Dai Doan. "May Suy Nghi ve Xu Ly cac Thiet Che Chinh Tri Xa Hoi Nong Thon Hien Nay" [Today's rural social and political institutions]. In *Kinh Nghiem To Chuc Quan Ly Nong Thon Viet Nam trong Lich Su*, edited by Phan Dai Doan and Nguyen Quang Ngoc, 42–72. Hanoi: Nxb Chinh Tri Quoc Gia, 1994.

Phan Khanh. *So Thao Lich Su Thuy Loi Viet Nam, 1945–1995* [History of irrigation in Vietnam]. Hanoi: Nxb Chinh Tri Quoc Gia, 1997.

Phu Thu Tuong [Prime Minister's Office]. "Chi Thi (68-TTg/TN) ve Viec Thong Nhat Quan Ly Phan Phoi Luong Thuc vao Nha Nuoc va Hop Tac Xa Nong Nghiep, Tich Cuc Thu Hep va Tien Toi Xoa Bo Thi Truong Tu Do ve Luong Thuc" [Directive 68, staple food management and distribution, eliminating free market for staples]. 19 July 1968.

Phung Gia Loc. "Cai Dem Hom Ay Dem Gi" [What night was it that night]. In *Nguoi Dan Ba Quy: Tap Truyen Ky Chon Loc* [Kneeling woman: Selected biographies], 5–15. Hanoi: Nxb Nong Nghiep, 1988.

Piven, Frances Fox, and Richard A. Cloward. *Poor People's Movements: Why They Succeed, How They Fail*. New York: Vintage, 1977.

Porter, Gareth. *Vietnam: The Politics of Bureaucratic Socialism*. Ithaca, N.Y.: Cornell University Press, 1993.

Post, Ken. *Revolution, Socialism, and Nationalism in Vietnam*. Vol. 3. Belmont, Calif.: Wadsworth, 1989.

Potter, Sulamith Heins, and Jack M. Potter. *China's Peasants: The Anthropology of a Revolution*. Cambridge, UK: Cambridge University Press, 1990.

Pryor, Frederic L. *The Red and the Green: The Rise and Fall of Collectivized Agriculture in Marxist Regimes*. Princeton, N.J.: Princeton University Press, 1992.

Putman, Robert D., with Robert Leonardi and Raffaella Y. Nanetti. *Making Democracy Work: Civic Traditions in Modern Italy*. Princeton, N.J.: Princeton University Press, 1993.

Putterman, Louis. "Extrinsic versus Intrinsic Problems of Agricultural Cooperation: Anti-incentivism in Tanzania and China." *Journal of Development Studies* 21 (January 1985): 175–204.

Quang Truong. *Agricultural Collectivization and Rural Development in Vietnam: A North/South Study, 1955–1985*. Amsterdam: Vrije Universiteit te Amsterdam, 1987.

Rambo, A. Terry. *A Comparison of Peasant Social Systems of Northern and Southern Viet-Nam: A Study of Ecological Adaptation, Social Succession, and Cultural Evolution*. Carbondale: Center for Vietnamese Studies, Southern Illinois University, 1973.

Raymond, Chad. "Rational Resistance to a Weak Authoritarian State: The Political Economy of Vietnamese Farmers from Collectivization to Doi Moi." Ph.D. diss., University of Hawaii, 2000.

*The Renovation of Agricultural Economic Management.* Hanoi: Foreign Languages Publishing House, 1990.

Rev, Istvan. "The Advantages of Being Atomized: How Hungarian Peasants Coped with Collectivization." *Dissent* 34 (Summer 1987): 335–50.

Rusinow, Dennison. *The Yugoslav Experiment, 1948–1974.* Berkeley: University of California Pres, 1977.

"Sau 30 Nam Hop Tac Hoa Nong Nghiep: Doi Song Nong Dan va Van De Quan Ly San Xuat Nong Nghiep Hien Nay" [Thirty years of cooperativization]. In *Thuc Trang Kinh Te—Xa Hoi Viet Nam Giai Doan 1986–1990,* 27–60. Hanoi: Tap Chi Thong Ke, 1990.

Scott, James C. "Everyday Forms of Resistance." In *Everyday Forms of Peasant Resistance,* edited by Forrest D. Colburn, 3–33. Armonk, N.Y.: M.E. Sharpe, 1989.

——. *The Moral Economy of the Peasant: Rebellion and Subsistence in Southeast Asia.* New Haven, Conn.: Yale University Press, 1976.

——. "Resistance without Protest and without Organization: Peasant Opposition to the Islamic Zakat and the Christian Tithe." *Comparative Studies in Society and History* 29 (1987): 417–52.

——. *Seeing like a State: How Certain Schemes to Improve the Human Condition Have Failed.* New Haven, Conn.: Yale University Press, 1998.

——. *Weapons of the Weak: Everyday Forms of Peasant Resistance.* New Haven, Conn.: Yale University Press, 1985.

Selden, Mark. *The Political Economy of Chinese Development.* Armonk, N.Y.: M.E. Sharpe, 1993.

Sikor, Thomas. "The Political Economy of Decollectivization: A Study of Differentiation in and among Black Thai Villages of Northern Vietnam." Ph.D. diss., University of California, Berkeley, 1999.

Smith, Gavin. *Livelihood and Resistance: Peasants and the Politics of Land in Peru.* Berkeley: University of California Press, 1989.

Smith, Louis P. F. *The Evolution of Agricultural Co-operation.* Oxford: Basil Blackwell, 1961.

Smith, S. Andrew Enticknap. "Water First: A Political History of Hydraulics in Vietnam's Red River Delta." Ph.D. diss., Australian National University, 2002.

"So Lieu Hop Tac Xa Nong Nghiep Mien Bac 1986 va 1989" [Data, northern agricultural cooperatives], n.d. [circa 1990]. Probably prepared for the Communist Party's central Agriculture Committee.

Sokolovsky, Joan. *Peasants and Power: State Autonomy and the Collectivization of Eastern Europe.* Boulder, Colo.: Westview, 1990.

Spoor, Max. "Finance in a Socialist Transition: The Case of the Democratic Republic of Vietnam, 1955–1964." *Journal of Contemporary Asia* 17, 3 (1987): 339–65.

St. George, Elizabeth. "Government Policy and Changes to Higher Education in Vietnam, 1986–1998: Education in Transition for Development?" Ph.D. diss., Australian National University, 2003.

Stern, Lewis. *Renovating the Vietnamese Communist Party.* New York: St. Martin's, 1993.

Stoker, Gerry. "Introduction." In *Theory and Methods in Political Science,* edited by David Marsh and Gerry Stoker, 1–18. London: Macmillan, 1995.

Stromseth, Jonathan R. "Reform and Response in Vietnam: State-Society Relations and the Changing Political Economy." Ph.D. diss., Columbia University, 1998.

Stuart-Fox, Martin. *Buddhist Kingdom, Marxist State: The Making of Modern Laos.* Bangkok: White Lotus, 1996.

*Summary of World Broadcasts.* Part 3: *Asia-Pacific/Far East.* Selected issues, 1960s–1980s.

Swain, Nigel. *Collective Farms Which Work?* Cambridge, UK: Cambridge University Press, 1985.

Szymanski, Albert. *Class Struggle in Socialist Poland.* New York: Praeger, 1984.

Tarrow, Sidney. *Power in Movement: Social Movements and Contentious Politics.* 2nd edition. Cambridge, UK: Cambridge University Press, 1998.

TCTK. *12 Nam Phat Trien Nen Nong Nghiep nuoc Viet Nam Dan Chu Cong Hoa, 1960–1971* [12 years of agricultural development]. Hanoi: Tong Cuc Thong Ke, 1973.

——. *Bao Cao Phan Tich Thong Ke: 30 Nam Hop Tac Hoa Nong Nghiep, 1958–1988* [Thirty years of agricultural cooperativization]. Hanoi: Tong Cuc Thong Ke, July 1989.

——. *Kinh Te Van Hoa Viet Nam 1930–1980* [Economics and culture in Vietnam]. Hanoi: 1980.

——. *Nien Giam Thong Ke 1975* [Statistical yearbook 1975]. Hanoi: Tong Cuc Thong Ke, n.d. [circa 1976].

——. *Nien Giam Thong Ke 1990* [Statistical yearbook 1990]. Hanoi: Nxb Tong Cuc Thong Ke, 1992.

——. *Nien Giam Thong Ke 1993* [Statistical yearbook 1993]. Hanoi: Nxb Thong Ke, 1994.

——. *Nien Giam Thong Ke 1995* [Statistical yearbook 1995]. Hanoi: Nxb Thong Ke, 1996.

——. *So Lieu Thong Ke Nong, Lam, Ngu Nghiep Viet Nam 1985–1993* [Statistics on agriculture, forestry, and fisheries]. Hanoi: Nxb Thong Ke, 1994.

——. *Tinh Hinh Phat Trien Kinh Te va Van Hoa Mien Bac Xa Hoi Chu Nghia Viet Nam, 1960–1975* [Development in Vietnam's socialist north]. Hanoi: Tong Cuc Thong Ke, 1978.

Thai Quang Trung. *Collective Leadership and Factionalism.* Singapore: Institute of Southeast Asian Studies, 1985.

Thanh Uy Hai Phong, DCSVN [Hai Phong committee, VCP]. "NQ 24, Ban Thuong Vu Thanh Uy ve Cung Co, To Chuc Hop Tac Xa Nong Nghiep Nham Day Manh San Xuat Luong Thuc, Thuc Pham" [Resolution 24, strengthen, organize agricultural cooperatives to boost food production]. 27 June 1980.

Thayer, Carlyle. "Political Reform in Vietnam: *Doi Moi* and the Emergence of Civil Society." In *The Developments of Civil Society in Communist Systems,* edited by Robert F. Miller, 110–29. Sydney: Allen and Unwin, 1992.

"Thoroughly Understanding the Basic Spirit of Resolution 8." *Giao Duc Ly Luan* (October 1985). In Joint Publications Research Service, JPRS-SEA-86-065, 17 April 1986, 79–88.

Thrift, Nigel, and Dean Forbes. *The Price of War: Urbanization in Vietnam, 1954–1985.* London: Allen and Unwin, 1986.

Thuy Lan. "Hoi Nghi Khoa Hoc ve Nghi Quyet Dai Hoi V va Nghi Quyet Hoi Nghi Trung Uong 3 cua Dang" [Party's fifth national conference and its third plenum]. *Nghien Cuu Kinh Te,* no. 6 (1983): 72–75.

Tianjian Shi. *Political Participation in Beijing.* Cambridge, Mass.: Harvard University Press, 1997.

Tieu Ban Tong Ket Hop Tac Hoa Nong Nghiep, Bo Nong Nghiep va Cong Nghiep Thuc Pham [Subcommittee to review agricultural cooperativization, Ministry of Agriculture and Food Industry]. "Bao Cao Tong Ket Hop Tac Hoa Nong Nghiep,

1958–1990" [Agricultural collectivization and cooperativization, 1958–1990]. Draft 8. June 1991.

Timofeev, Lev. *Soviet Peasants (or: The Peasants' Art of Starving)*. Translated by Jean Alexander and Alexander Zaslavsky. New York: Telos, 1985.

Tinh Hoa Binh [Hoa Binh province]. BCH Hoi Nong Dan Viet Nam. *Lich Su Phong Trao Nong Dan tinh Hoa Binh, 1930–1975* [Peasant movement in Hoa Binh province]. Hanoi: Nxb Chinh Tri Quoc Gia, 1998.

To Lan. "On Communal Land in the Traditional Viet Village." In *The Traditional Village in Vietnam*, 156–94. Hanoi: The Gioi, 1993.

Tomasevich, Jozo. "Collectivization of Agriculture in Yugoslavia." In *Collectivization of Agriculture in Eastern Europe*, edited by Irwin Sanders, 166–92. N.p.: University of Kentucky Press, 1958.

Tong Cuc Luong Thuc [Staple Foods headquarters]. *Chinh Sach Luong Thuc Moi: Tai Lieu Hoc Tap* [New staple foods policies]. N.p., Tong Cuc Luong Thuc, 1969.

*Tong Ket Khoa Hoc Thuc Tien Phat Trien Kinh Te-Xa Hoi Nong Thon* [Rural social and economic development]. Hanoi: Chuong Trinh Khoa Hoc Cap Nha Nuoc ve Phat Trien Toan Dien Kinh Te-Xa Hoi Nong Thon KX-08, August 1994.

Tran Duc. *Hop Tac trong Nong Thon Xua va Nay* [Rural cooperation, past and present]. Hanoi: Nxb Nong Nghiep, 1994.

——. *Hop Tac Xa va Thoi Vang Son cua Kinh Te Gia Dinh* [Cooperatives and the household economy]. Hanoi: Nxb Tu Tuong-Van Hoa, 1991.

Tran Duc Cuong. "Nhin Lai Qua Trinh Chuyen Hop Tac Xa San Xuat nong Nghiep tu Bac Thap len Bac Cao o Mien Bac Nuoc Ta" [How agricultural cooperatives went from low to high levels], *Nghien Cuu Kinh Te*, no. 4 (1979): 14–22.

Tran Ngoc Canh. *Cai Tien Cong Tac Quan Ly Lao Dong trong Hop Tac Xa San Xuat Nong Nghiep* [Improve labor management in cooperatives]. Hanoi: Nxb Nong Thon, 1964.

Tran Nhu Trang. "The Transformation of the Peasantry in North Viet Nam." Ph.D. diss., University of Pittsburgh, 1972.

Tran Quang Ngan. "Phan Tich Qua Trinh Thuc Hien Chinh Sach Ruong Dat Huyen Ung Hoa, Ha Tay, qua cac Giai Doan" [Implementing land policies, Hung Hoa district, Ha Tay]. Luan van tot nghiep [thesis], TDH NN 1, 1993.

Tran Quoc Vuong, Nguyen Dinh Chien, and Tran Kim Dinh. *Da Ton: Truyen Thong va Cach Mang* [Da Ton: Tradition and revolution]. Gia Lam, Hanoi: BCH Dang Bo Da Ton, 1990.

Tran Thi My Huong, "Buoc Dau Tim Hieu Chu Truong Khoan Nong Nghiep Vinh Phuc Nhung Nam 60" [Agricultural contracts, Vinh Phuc]. Luan van tot nghiep, Khoa Su [thesis, Faculty of History], TDH KHXHNV, DHQGH, 2000.

Tran Thi Que. *Vietnam's Agriculture: The Challenges and Achievements*. Singapore: Institute of Southeast Asian Studies, 1998.

Trinh Dat. "May Y Kien ve Phuong Huong Phat Trien San Xuat cua cac Hop Tac Xa Trong Lua o Bac Bo" [Production in northern rice-producing cooperatives]. *Nghien Cuu Kinh Te*, no. 1 (1983): 42–51.

Truong Chinh. *Kien Quyet Sua Chua Khuyet Diem Phat Huy Uu Diem Dua Phong Trao Hop Tac Hoa Nong nghiep Vung Buoc Tien Len* [Correct shortcomings, advance agricultural cooperativization]. Hanoi: Nxb Su That, 1969.

——. *Resolutely Taking the North Viet Nam Countryside to Socialism through Agricultural Cooperation*. Hanoi: Foreign Languages Publishing House, 1959.

Truong Huyen Chi. "Changing Processes of Social Reproduction in the Northern Vietnamese Countryside." Ph.D. diss., University of Toronto, 2001.

Tu Dien Tieng Viet [Vietnamese dictionary]. Hanoi: Nxb Khoa Hoc Xa Hoi, 1988.

Tuong Lai. "Bao Cao So Bo ve cuoc Khao Sat Xa Hoi tai Thai Binh cuoi Thang Sau, dau Thang Bay nam 1997 [Investigation, Thai Binh, June–July 1997]. 8 August 1997. http://members.aol.com/tdxanh/th-binh.htm.

Turley, William S. "Party, State, and People: Political Structure and Economic Prospects." In Reinventing Vietnamese Socialism, edited by William S. Turley and Mark Selden, 257–76. Boulder, Colo.: Westview, 1993.

——. "Political Renovation in Vietnam: Renewal and Adaptation." In The Challenge of Reform in Indochina, edited by Borje Ljunggren, 327–47. Cambridge, Mass.: Harvard Institute for International Development, 1993.

UBHC, Ha Tay [EC, Ha Tay province]. "Thong Tu: Quy Dinh Cu The Giai Quyet Sua Chua Sai Lam ve Quan Ly Ruong Dat va Thu Hoi No Hop Tac Xa San Xuat Nong Nghiep" [Regulations, land management and debts in cooperatives]. 22 January 1970.

Unger, Jonathan. "Collective Incentives in the Chinese Countryside: Lessons from Chen Village." World Development 6 (1978): 583–601.

——. The Transformation of Rural China. Armonk, N.Y.: M.E. Sharpe, 2002.

Van Kien cua Dang va Nha Nuoc ve Cuoc Van Dong Tang Cuong Che Do Lam Chu Tap The o Nong Thon [Party and state documents, the collective mastery regime]. Hanoi: Nxb Su That, 1971.

Van Tao. "Vai Net ve Qua Trinh Xay Dung va Phat Trien cua Nha Nuoc Cach Mang Viet Nam 20 Nam Qua" [20 years of Vietnam's revolutionary state]. Nghien Cuu Lich Su, no. 8 (1965): 12–27.

Vasary, Ildiko. Beyond the Plan: Social Change in a Hungarian Village. Boulder, Colo.: Westview, 1987.

Vasavakul, Thaveeporn. "Vietnam: The Changing Models of Legitimation." In Political Legitimacy in Southeast Asia: The Quest for Moral Authority, edited by Muthiah Alagappa, 257–89. Stanford, Calif.: Stanford University Press, 1986.

Verdery, Katherine. "Theorizing Socialism: A Prologue to the 'Transition.'" American Ethnologist 18 (August 1991): 419–39.

Vickerman, Andrew. The Fate of the Peasantry: Premature "Transition to Socialism" in the Democratic Republic of Vietnam. New Haven, Conn.: Southeast Asia Studies, Yale University, 1986.

Vien Xa Hoi Hoc, Uy Ban Khoa Hoc Xa Hoi, Viet Nam [Sociology institute, Vietnam Social Science Committee]. "Nghien Cuu su Bien Doi Co Cau Kinh Te Xa Hoi, xa Da Ton, Gia Lam, Hanoi" [Social and economic changes, Da Ton subdistrict]. June 1985.

Vietnamese Studies. Selected issues, 1960s–1990s.

Vinh Phu. Hoc Tap va Thi Dua voi Hop Tac Xa Dong Xuan [Learn from Dong Xuan cooperative]. Vinh Phu: BCH tinh Dang Bo, DLDVN, July 1968.

Vinh Phu. Newspaper published by the Vinh Phu branch of the VCP. Selected years, 1968–1990.

Vinh Phuc. Newspaper published by the Vinh Phuc branch of the VCP, 1965–1967

Viola, Lynne. Peasant Rebels under Stalin: Collectivization and the Culture of Peasant Resistance. New York: Oxford University Press, 1996.

Vo Nhan Tri. Vietnam's Economic Policy since 1975. Singapore: Institute of Southeast Asian Studies, 1990.

Volgyes, Ivan. "Dynamic Change: Rural Transformation, 1945–1975." In *The Modernization of Agriculture: Rural Transformation in Hungary, 1848–1975*, edited by Joseph Held, 351–508. Boulder, Colo.: East European Monographs, 1980, distributed by Columbia University Press, New York, 1980.

Vu Nong Nghiep, TCTK, va Vien Quy Hoach va Thiet Ke, Bo Nong Nghiep va Cong Nghiep Thuc Pham [Agriculture Department, GSO; and the Institute for Planning and Design, Ministry of Agriculture and Food Industry]. *So Lieu Nong Nghiep Viet Nam 35 Nam, 1956–1990*. [Agricultural statistics]. Hanoi: Nxb Thong Ke, 1991.

Vu Quan Ly Ruong Dat [Land Management Bureau]. *Nhung Quy Dinh ve Quan Ly va Su Dung Ruong Dat, 1953–1979* [Land regulations]. Hanoi: Nxb Nong Nghiep, 1980.

Vu Quang Viet, Dang Tho Xuong, Nguyen Van Chinh, and Nguyen Sinh Cuc. "Kinh Te Nong Thon Viet Nam sau Doi Moi va Vien Tuong Tuong Lai" [Vietnam's rural economy after renovation and its prospects]. *Thoi Dai*, no. 1 (1997): 85–116.

Vu Trong Khai. "Ve Van De 'Khoan' trong cac Hop Tac Xa Nong Nghiep Hien Nay" [Contracts in agricultural collectives]. *Nghien Cuu Kinh Te*, no. 6 (1980): 24–35.

Vu Tuan Anh and Tran Thi Van Anh. *Kinh Te Ho: Lich Su va Trien Vong Phat Trien* [Household economy]. Hanoi: Nxb Khoa Hoc Xa Hoi, 1997.

Vu Van Nam. "Mot So Bien Doi ve Tinh Hinh Kinh Te Xa Hoi cua Xa An Tho, Huyen An Lao, Hai Phong, 1981–1998" [Social and economic changes, An Tho subdistrict, An Lao district, Hai Phong]. Luan van tot nghiep, Khoa Su [thesis, Faculty of History], TDH KHXHNV, DHQGH, 1999.

Wade, Robert. *Village Republics: Economic Conditions for Collective Action in South India.* Cambridge, UK: Cambridge University Press, 1988.

Wadekin, K. E. *The Private Sector in Soviet Agriculture.* Edited and translated by Keith Bush. Berkeley: University of California Press, 1973.

Walker, Jack L. *Mobilizing Interest Groups in America: Patrons, Professions, and Social Movements.* Ann Arbor: University of Michigan Press, 1991.

Weintraub, D., M. Lissak, and Y. Azmon. *Moshava, Kibbutz, and Moshav.* Ithaca, N.Y.: Cornell University Press, 1969.

Werner, Jayne. "Cooperativization, the Family Economy, and the New Family in Wartime Vietnam, 1960–1975." In *The American War in Vietnam*, edited by Jayne Werner and David Hunt, 77–92. Ithaca, N.Y.: Southeast Asia Program, Cornell University, 1993.

Wesson, Robert. *Soviet Communes.* New Brunswick, N.J.: Rutgers University Press, 1963.

White, Christine. "Agrarian Reform and National Liberation in the Vietnamese Revolution, 1920–1957." Ph.D. diss., Cornell University, 1981.

———. "Agricultural Planning, Pricing Policy, and Co-operatives in Vietnam." *World Development* 13 (January 1985): 97–114.

———. "Alternative Approaches to the Socialist Transformation of Agriculture in Postwar Vietnam." In *Postwar Vietnam: Dilemmas in Socialist Development*, edited by David G. Marr and Christine White, 143–46. Ithaca, N.Y.: Southeast Asia Program, Cornell University, 1988.

———. "Debates in Vietnamese Development Policy." Discussion paper 171, Institute for Development Studies, Sussex, UK, March 1982.

———. "Everyday Resistance, Socialist Revolution, and Rural Development: The Vietnamese Case." In *Everyday Forms of Peasant Resistance in Southeast Asia*, edited by James C. Scott and Benedict J. Tria Kerkvliet, 49–63. London: Frank Cass, 1986.

——. "Interview with Nguyen Huu Tho, Agricultural Editor of *Nhan Dan.*" *Journal of Contemporary Asia* 11, 1 (1981): 127–31.

Wiegersma, Nan. "Peasant Patriarchy and the Subversion of the Collective in Vietnam." *Review of Radical Political Economics* 23, 3 and 4 (1991): 175–91.

Wiens, Thomas B. "Poverty and Progress in the Huang and Huai River Basins." In *Chinese Rural Development: The Great Transformation*, edited by William L. Parish, 57–94. Armonk, N.Y.: M.E. Sharpe, 1985.

Wolf, Eric R. "Closed Corporate Peasant Communities in Mesoamerica and Central Java." *Southwestern Journal of Anthropology* 13, 1 (1957): 1–18.

——. "Types of Latin American Peasantry: A Preliminary Discussion." *American Anthropologist* 57, 3 (1955): 452–71.

Womack, Brantly. "The Party and the People: Revolutionary and Postrevolutionary Politics in China and Vietnam." *World Politics* 39 (July 1987): 479–507.

——. "Reform in Vietnam: Backwards Toward the Future." *Government and Opposition* 27 (Spring 1992): 177–89.

Woodside, Alexander. *Community and Revolution in Modern Vietnam.* Boston: Houghton Mifflin, 1976.

——. "Decolonization and Agricultural Reform in Northern Vietnam." *Asian Survey* 10 (August 1970): 705–23.

——. "Nationalism and Poverty in the Breakdown of Sino-Vietnamese Relations." *Pacific Affairs* 52 (Fall 1979): 381–401.

——. "Peasants and the State in the Aftermath of the Vietnamese Revolution." *Peasant Studies* 16 (Summer 1989): 283–97.

World Bank. Country Operations Division. *Vietnam: Poverty Assessment and Strategy.* January 1995.

Xa Dong La. Dang Bo Xa Dong La, huyen Hoai Duc, tinh Ha Tay [Xa Dong subdistrict, party branch]. *Lich Su Xa Dong La* [Dong La history]. Hanoi: Nxb Lao Dong, 1995.

Xa Hoa Thach. BCH Dang Bo Xa Hoa Thach [Hoa Thach subdistrict, party EC]. *Lich Su Cach Mang Xa Hoa Thach, 1945–1995* [History of revolution in Hoa Thach]. Hanoi: Nxb The Gioi, 1997.

Xa Lien Khe. BCH Dang Bo Xa Lien Khe [Lien Khe subdistrict, party EC]. *Lich Su Dang Bo Xa Lien Khe, 1945–1985* [History of the party branch in Lien Khe]. Hai Phong: Nxb Hai Phong, 1988.

"Xa Luan: Xoa Bo Co Che Quan Lieu-Bao Cap Chuyen Han Sang Hach Toan Kinh Te va Kinh Doanh Xa Hoi Chu Nghia" [Editorial: Replace subsidy system with economic accounting]. *Tap Chi Cong San*, no. 7 (1985): 3–10.

Xa Thuong Lam. BCH Dang Bo Dang Cong San Viet Nam Xa Thuong Lam, huyen My Duc [Thuong Lam subdistrict, party EC]. *Thuong Lam Tren Nhung Chang Duong Lich Su* [Historical phases of Thuong Lam]. Ha Son Binh: 1988.

Xa Thuong Trung. BCH Dang Bo [Thuong Trung subdistrict, party EC]. *Lich Su Dang Bo Xa Thuong Trung 1936–1986* [Party history, Thuong Trung subdistrict]. Vinh Phu: Ban Tuyen Giao Tinh Uy, 1987.

Xa Vong Xuyen. BCH Dang Bo [Vong Xuyen subdistrict, party EC]. *Lich Su Dang Bo Xa Vong Xuyen, Huyen Phuc Tho, Tinh Ha Tay, 1945–1986* [Party history, Vong Xuyen subdistrict]. Ha Tay: 1995.

Xuan Kieu. "Ve Chinh Sach Cung Ung Vat Tu cua Nha Nuoc doi voi Nong Nghiep" [State policies for supplying agricultural inputs]. *Tap Chi Cong San*, no. 6 (1987): 53–57.

Yvon-Tran, Florence. "Une résistible collectivisation: L'agriculture au Nord Viet Nam, 1959–1988" [Resistible collectivization in north Vietnam]. Ph.D. diss., Université de Paris VII, 1994.

Zhou, Kate Xiao. *How the Farmers Changed China*. Boulder, Colo.: Westview, 1996.

Zhou, Xueguang. "Unorganized Interests and Collective Action in Communist China." *American Sociological Review* 58 (February 1993): 54–73.

Zweig, David. *Agrarian Radicalism in China, 1968–1981*. Cambridge, Mass.: Harvard University Press, 1989.

# Index